IFIP Advances in Information and Communication Technology

524

Editor-in-Chief

Kai Rannenberg, Goethe University Frankfurt, Germany

Editorial Board Members

TC 1 – Foundations of Computer Science
  Jacques Sakarovitch, Télécom ParisTech, France
TC 2 – Software: Theory and Practice
  Michael Goedicke, University of Duisburg-Essen, Germany
TC 3 – Education
  Arthur Tatnall, Victoria University, Melbourne, Australia
TC 5 – Information Technology Applications
  Erich J. Neuhold, University of Vienna, Austria
TC 6 – Communication Systems
  Aiko Pras, University of Twente, Enschede, The Netherlands
TC 7 – System Modeling and Optimization
  Fredi Tröltzsch, TU Berlin, Germany
TC 8 – Information Systems
  Jan Pries-Heje, Roskilde University, Denmark
TC 9 – ICT and Society
  David Kreps, University of Salford, Greater Manchester, UK
TC 10 – Computer Systems Technology
  Ricardo Reis, Federal University of Rio Grande do Sul, Porto Alegre, Brazil
TC 11 – Security and Privacy Protection in Information Processing Systems
  Steven Furnell, Plymouth University, UK
TC 12 – Artificial Intelligence
  Ulrich Furbach, University of Koblenz-Landau, Germany
TC 13 – Human-Computer Interaction
  Marco Winckler, University of Nice Sophia Antipolis, France
TC 14 – Entertainment Computing
  Rainer Malaka, University of Bremen, Germany

IFIP – The International Federation for Information Processing

IFIP was founded in 1960 under the auspices of UNESCO, following the first World Computer Congress held in Paris the previous year. A federation for societies working in information processing, IFIP's aim is two-fold: to support information processing in the countries of its members and to encourage technology transfer to developing nations. As its mission statement clearly states:

> IFIP is the global non-profit federation of societies of ICT professionals that aims at achieving a worldwide professional and socially responsible development and application of information and communication technologies.

IFIP is a non-profit-making organization, run almost solely by 2500 volunteers. It operates through a number of technical committees and working groups, which organize events and publications. IFIP's events range from large international open conferences to working conferences and local seminars.

The flagship event is the IFIP World Computer Congress, at which both invited and contributed papers are presented. Contributed papers are rigorously refereed and the rejection rate is high.

As with the Congress, participation in the open conferences is open to all and papers may be invited or submitted. Again, submitted papers are stringently refereed.

The working conferences are structured differently. They are usually run by a working group and attendance is generally smaller and occasionally by invitation only. Their purpose is to create an atmosphere conducive to innovation and development. Refereeing is also rigorous and papers are subjected to extensive group discussion.

Publications arising from IFIP events vary. The papers presented at the IFIP World Computer Congress and at open conferences are published as conference proceedings, while the results of the working conferences are often published as collections of selected and edited papers.

IFIP distinguishes three types of institutional membership: Country Representative Members, Members at Large, and Associate Members. The type of organization that can apply for membership is a wide variety and includes national or international societies of individual computer scientists/ICT professionals, associations or federations of such societies, government institutions/government related organizations, national or international research institutes or consortia, universities, academies of sciences, companies, national or international associations or federations of companies.

More information about this series at http://www.springer.com/series/6102

Don Passey · Rosa Bottino ·
Cathy Lewin · Eric Sanchez (Eds.)

Empowering Learners for Life in the Digital Age

IFIP TC 3 Open Conference on Computers in Education, OCCE 2018
Linz, Austria, June 24–28, 2018
Revised Selected Papers

 Springer

Editors
Don Passey
Lancaster University
Lancaster, UK

Cathy Lewin
Manchester Metropolitan University
Manchester, UK

Rosa Bottino
Consiglio Nazionale delle Ricerche
Genova, Italy

Eric Sanchez
University of Fribourg
Fribourg, Switzerland

ISSN 1868-4238   ISSN 1868-422X (electronic)
IFIP Advances in Information and Communication Technology
ISBN 978-3-030-23512-3   ISBN 978-3-030-23513-0 (eBook)
https://doi.org/10.1007/978-3-030-23513-0

© IFIP International Federation for Information Processing 2019
This work is subject to copyright. All rights are reserved by the Publisher, whether the whole or part of the material is concerned, specifically the rights of translation, reprinting, reuse of illustrations, recitation, broadcasting, reproduction on microfilms or in any other physical way, and transmission or information storage and retrieval, electronic adaptation, computer software, or by similar or dissimilar methodology now known or hereafter developed.
The use of general descriptive names, registered names, trademarks, service marks, etc. in this publication does not imply, even in the absence of a specific statement, that such names are exempt from the relevant protective laws and regulations and therefore free for general use.
The publisher, the authors and the editors are safe to assume that the advice and information in this book are believed to be true and accurate at the date of publication. Neither the publisher nor the authors or the editors give a warranty, expressed or implied, with respect to the material contained herein or for any errors or omissions that may have been made. The publisher remains neutral with regard to jurisdictional claims in published maps and institutional affiliations.

This Springer imprint is published by the registered company Springer Nature Switzerland AG
The registered company address is: Gewerbestrasse 11, 6330 Cham, Switzerland

Preface

The IFIP TC3 Open Conference on Computers in Education (OCCE) 2018 was held in Linz, Austria, from June 25–28, 2018, with a doctoral consortium event held on June 24, 2018. Participation was truly international, with contributions from authors ranging from Armenia to the United Kingdom, from Botswana to Taiwan, from Colombia to South Africa, and from Kyrgyzstan to New Zealand. In total, lead authors came from 31 countries, across five continents.

In total, 63 papers were submitted to the conference (all subjected to double-blind review by two independent reviewers), 35 were submitted for consideration for this post-conference book (with 18 subjected to a second round of double-blind review by two independent reviewers), and, following these later reviews, 27 were selected and accepted. On average, with 162 reviews undertaken in total (independent of reviews by the editors), each of the 63 papers were subjected to 2.6 reviews, and each of the 27 selected papers were subjected to 6 reviews. We are delighted to present the outcomes of the research undertaken by these 27 authors and their collaborators in this volume.

The conference theme "Empowering Learners for Life in the Digital Age" drives our attention to the increasingly urgent need to allow each citizen to be able to face a society dramatically changed by technological evolution. Such a broad topic can be addressed in different ways and with different perspectives, which means that not only new skills and abilities are to be identified and addressed, but that the learning environment as a whole is to be reconsidered and questioned. In essence, the relationship among learners, digital tools, and knowledge is not simple and direct, and must be approached in a critical way with due consideration for the complexity of the underlying processes. The contributions that have been selected for this book discuss a number of key emerging topics and evolving practices in this area that have been divided into seven sections. These sections focus on: computational thinking; programming and computer science education; teachers' education and professional development; games-based learning and gamification; learning in specific and disciplinary contexts; learning in social networking environments; and self-assessment, e-assessment, and e-examinations.

Section 1 - Computational Thinking. As a background to this topic, and from a thorough literature review, Bollin and Micheuz offer a debate on computational thinking from two complementary perspectives—that of an Austrian teacher and that of software engineer—each reflecting on their personal expertise. They conclude that computational thinking can be considered as a cultural technique, which leads to a refined working definition. Considering the relationship of computational thinking and problem-solving skills, Eickelmann, Labusch, and Vennemann describe how a large-scale study compares students' competences in computational thinking (CT) with the underlying conditions of acquisition at an international level. The data are provided by the International Computer and Information Literacy Study 2018 (ICILS 2018), and they discuss how these competences will be compared with students' problem-solving skills through a German national extension to ICILS 2018. Considering another related skill area, Kadijevich, in a theoretical paper, examines how data modeling using interactive displays may cultivate CT practices across a range of school subjects. The author states that, while working with data is not explicitly mentioned in some CT definitions, such practices might enable a range of CT needs, such as abstraction, decomposition, and pattern recognition. In terms of students using computational thinking skills, Fluck, Chin, and Ranmuthugala report a study of students aged 12 years, who mastered computational thinking in mathematics (integral calculus) through use of multi-media learning materials and specialist mathematics software, demonstrating ability commensurate with university engineering students.

Section 2 - Programming and Computer Science Education. Programming and computer science education continue to be integrated into compulsory education in many countries. Kelter, Kramer, and Brinda have investigated teachers' perspectives about some popular learning and programming environments used in secondary computer science education in Germany. Contrary to outcomes reported in prior studies, they have showed that teachers do not see the editor as a key identifier of difference, while student-friendly debugging messages as well as a step-by-step execution of programs were identified as important features, with a clear favorite being BlueJ. Considering different ways that students might be assessed in terms of their computational thinking skills and practice, Matsuzawa, Murata, and Tani compared three testing methods (programming testing, traditional paper testing, and Bebras Challenges), finding that there was a clear correlation between outcomes assessed using the Bebras Challenge and actual programming. The development of programming and computer science across age ranges is also leading to the development of innovative methodological approaches. Djelil, Muller, and Sanchez investigated programmer behaviors when beginners interact with a programming microworld. They developed and used an innovative methodology that considered an analysis of learners' attitudes, rather than collecting learners' points of views or observing their score progression by means of knowledge tests or questionnaires. Also from a methodological perspective, Pasterk, Kesselbacher, and Bollin present a description of a semi-automated approach to categorize learning outcomes of computer science-related curricula into the two categories of computer science (CS) and digital literacy. Using this system, they showed high levels of match between learning outcomes classified by this approach and those classified by experts in the field.

Section 3 - Teachers' Education and Professional Development. The integration of computer science and computational thinking into wide age ranges across education will clearly depend upon the development of skills and practices in the teaching workforce. McLeod and Carabott's study of pre-service teachers in an Australian university explored whether the information and communications technologies (ICT) content was appropriate in preparing them to implement the national curriculum. They found that it did not meet all their needs, challenging assumptions being made about digital competence, and recommended that universities review their expectations of digital competence and how to address these in teaching ICT in teaching degrees. In another country context, Tosato and Banzato's exploratory study investigated self-efficacy beliefs, intrinsic motivation and perceived efforts of a group of teachers from Italian schools who, on a voluntary basis, engaged in a 20-hour workshop on CS teaching. They showed that there was a significant improvement in self-efficacy, despite the teachers' perceptions of needing to commit high levels of effort to master the subject content. Considering how teachers can develop and integrate ICT-based resources into their teaching, Yiannoutsou, Otero, Müller, Neofytou, Miltiadous, and Hadzilacos report their development of a decision-making system to support teachers in appropriating innovative scenarios that employ uses of ICT for teaching and learning. The system enables them to select, decompose, combine, enact, and revise different resources, and the authors' study investigated how teaching objectives can make use, or not, of the potential of digital technologies. In terms of teachers developing online courses, Haugsbakken and Langseth describe and conceptualize the outline features and processes of an infrastructure for organizing their production in continuous and further education. This consists of a network of employees with complementary competences (technical, pedagogical, and multimedia) to coach, mentor, and support educators through the entire online course production process, working in designated teams. Considering teaching, its development and its quality, Reçi and Bollin report how their study is considering teaching as a process, and how they are looking at existing approaches to assess teacher maturity. They introduce the idea of a teaching maturity model (TeaM) for school and university teachers, and offer the results of a pilot study testing its usability and acceptability with informatics lecturers in one university.

Section 4 - Games-Based Learning and Gamification. Games-based learning and games-based resources are both aspects that continue to emerge in the field, and they are being explored through a range of research perspectives. Holvikivi, Juurola, and Nuorteva describe an innovation platform development for the co-creation of serious games, offering modes of collaboration for schools, universities, citizens, and companies, based in three universities and two science centers in Finland. From their findings, they offer recommendations for best practices in universities to find efficient ways of implementation when developing serious games. In terms of using games within educational contexts, Sanchez, Paukovics, Müller, Kramar, and Widmer report an empirical study carried out during a museum school visit, aiming to understand the influence of a game on students' conduct in the museum. Their findings have led to the identification of different conducts and situations performed by students, depending on their gameplay. In terms of teachers using games, Bonvin, Sanchez, Champin, Casado, Guin, and Lefevre report a study of how a digital role-playing game allowed teachers to create teams. They assessed to what extent the game fostered students' engagement and showed that social engagement varied across time and gender, which seemed to be linked to specific features of the game and how it was played. Concerned with similar student interaction intentions, Ehlenz, Leonhardt, and Schroeder present a multi-touch learning game (MTLG) framework, designed to support cooperative, collaborative, and competitive interactions, and they show how a user-centered learning analytics data model could gather results, which led to the identification of challenges and lessons learned.

Section 5 - Learning in Specific and Disciplinary Contexts. Researchers continue to explore the ways in which existing and emerging technologies can be used to support learning in different contexts. In the context of English language learning in the United Arab Emirates, AlOkaily reports a case study exploring uses of a specific learning environment, integrating a dubbing project designed and implemented in an English language listening and speaking course. Utilizing students' mobile devices for anywhere, anytime learning, students produced videos, which were entered in an internally organized competition; as a result, they demonstrated high levels of motivation, increased learning, confidence and sense of achievement, and pride in their resulting work. In the context of second language learning in Norway, De Caro-Barek studied the making of massive open online courses (MooCs) in a second language. Findings highlighted the need for course developers to critically look at how to build more innovative and interactive language MooCs within the framework of self-instructed courses using new convergent technologies such as Web real-time communication (WebRTC). In the context of school students aged 12–13 years learning biology in the UK, Webb, Tracey, Harwin, Tokatli, Hwang, Barrett, Jones, and Johnson report a study investigating whether the addition of haptics (virtual touch) to a three-dimensional (3D) virtual reality (VR) simulation would promote learning of key concepts. They concluded that there were significant knowledge gains, but no significant differences between the haptic and non-haptic condition. In the context of university students in Austria and Slovakia, Mujkanovic and Bollin report a study evaluating the extent to which it is possible to enhance student group outcomes by systematically reconstructing the groups of students. They found statistically significant improvements of outcomes for those groups that were systematically constructed.

Section 6 - Learning in Social Networking Environments. Learning using social networking environments continues to be an area of research study. Considering different social networks that might be used, Katz reports a study where three similar groups of students were enrolled in an 'Introduction to Ethics' course, exposed to either Facebook-based, WhatsApp-based, or Twitter-based delivery of ethical concepts on their smartphones. The author found that the WhatsApp, and to a lesser extent, Facebook students, were associated with higher enhanced achievement and positive feelings toward their delivery platforms compared with Twitter students. In terms of knowledge sharing using a social networking environment, Haugsbakken reports a case study of how a county authority in a Nordic country implemented an enterprise social media platform. The author found that when a group of employees tried to make sense of the practice of sharing by reflection-on-action, they interpreted sharing as an informing practice, resulting in information-overload and disengaged users.

Section 7 - Self-Assessment, e-Assessment, and e-Examinations. An emerging area of practice development and research study concerns uses of technologies for self-assessment, e-assessment, and e-examinations. In the context of developing an ICT-based method for the self-assessment of ICT skills, Voňková, Černochová, Selcuk, Hrabák, and Králová report a pilot study exploring uses of anchoring vignettes in the analysis of Czech upper secondary school students' self-assessment of ICT skills. They conclude that the enhanced research method they used, based on anchoring vignettes, could be used for further studies, as they found high variability of the use of scale by respondents in their self-assessments. In terms of using technologies for e-examination, Hillier and Lyon report a study investigating students' perceptions of a bring-your-own (BYO) laptop-based e-examination system trialed in an Australian pre-university college in geography and globalization. They found that many of the typists were taking a computerized supervised test for the first time and concluded that there is a need to ensure adequate support for students who might not be all equally prepared for the computerization of high-stakes examinations. In a follow-up paper, they report students' expressed strategies, habits, and preferences with respect to responding to supervised text-based assessments. They conclude that there was significant alignment between preferred writing strategies and choice of text production method, but that grades achieved between typists and hand-writers did not differ significantly. In terms of student perceptions of e-assessment, Küppers and Schroeder report findings from a survey, with evidence gathered from several higher education institutes. They found that students seemed to be open-minded regarding e-assessment, but that there was a need to completely convince the students of opportunities offered by e-assessment that would go beyond those offered through uses of more traditional media.

The varied mix of papers presented in this book shows some of the many perspectives and addressed topics that characterize educational computing research. These trends can give an idea of the opportunities offered by ICT to improve teaching and learning processes but also highlight how the integration of ICT in education is neither straightforward nor simple, as it leads to increasing organizational and management complexity. This raises the question of how innovative experiences and studies can be transferred on a wide scale and which systemic changes not only in educational practices but also in educational policies can support effective innovation.

Last but not least, we would like to thank the organizers and Program Committee members of this conference for enabling this range of important contributions to become accessible to us, and the reviewers for their thorough and insightful comments that have enhanced the quality of the papers. Primarily, of course, we thank the authors for their commitment and dedication, in providing us with a wide range of complementary perspectives that brings knowledge in this field to our attention, and highlights the contributions that researchers are making in this field.

May 2019

Don Passey
Rosa Bottino

Organization

Program Committee Chairs

Cathy Lewin	Manchester Metropolitan University, UK
Eric Sanchez	University of Fribourg, Switzerland

Program Committee

Rosa Bottino (Editor)	National Research Council, Italy
Jaana Holvikivi	Metropolia University of Applied Sciences, Finland
Anton J. Knierzinger (Organizing Committee Chair)	University College of Education Linz, Austria
Astrid Leeb	Education Group Linz, Austria
Zdena Lustigova	Charles University, Czech Republic
Don Passey (Editor, Doctoral Consortium Chair)	Lancaster University, UK
Sindre Røsvik (IFIP TC3 Chair)	Giske Kommune, Norway

Organizing Committee

Andrea Bock	Federal Ministry of Education, Austria
Gerald Futschek	Vienna University of Technology, Austria
Josef Grabner	Competence Center eEducation Linz, Austria
Christine Haas	Austrian Computer Society, Austria
Astrid Leeb	Education Group Linz, Austria
Susanna Macher	Linz Tourismus, Austria
Peter Micheuz	Alpen-Adria-Universität Klagenfurt, Austria
Christine Wahlmüller	Austrian Computer Society, Austria
Anton J. Knierzinger (Chair)	University College of Education Linz, Austria
Harald De Zottis	BildungOnline, Austria

Additional Reviewers

Ben Akoh
Monica Banzato
Christine Bescherer
Torsten Brinda
Ana Carvalho
Miroslava Cernochova
Sue Cranmer
Eva Dakich

Andrew Fluck
Gerald Futschek
Robert Gajewski
Julia Gerick
Monique Grandbastien
Andreas Grillenberger
Donna Gronn
John Hannon
David Hauger
Annariina Koivu
Volkan Kukul
Denise Leahy
Angela Lee

Nicholas Mavengere
Robert Munro
Kleopatra Nikolopoulou
Paul T. Nleya
Mikko Ruohonen
Nalin Sharda
Alan Strickley
Maciej Syslo
Paul Thabano
Keith Turvey
John van Niekerk
Maina WaGioko
Lawrence Williams

Contents

Computational Thinking

Computational Thinking on the Way to a Cultural Technique: A Debate on Lords and Servants.................................... 3
  Andreas Bollin and Peter Micheuz

Computational Thinking and Problem-Solving in the Context of IEA-ICILS 2018... 14
  Birgit Eickelmann, Amelie Labusch, and Mario Vennemann

Cultivating Computational Thinking Through Data Practice.............. 24
  Djordje M. Kadijevich

Transformative Computational Thinking in Mathematics: A Comparison by Student Age.. 34
  Andrew E. Fluck, C. K. H. Chin, and Dev Ranmuthugala

Programming and Computer Science Education

Teachers' Perspectives on Learning and Programming Environments for Secondary Education 47
  Riko Kelter, Matthias Kramer, and Torsten Brinda

Multivocal Challenge Toward Measuring Computational Thinking: Bebras Challenge Versus Computer Programming........................ 56
  Yoshiaki Matsuzawa, Kazuyoshi Murata, and Seiichi Tani

Investigating Learners' Behaviours When Interacting with a Programming Microworld: An Empirical Study Based on Playing Analytics............ 67
  Fahima Djelil, Pierre-Alain Muller, and Eric Sanchez

A Semi-automated Approach to Categorise Learning Outcomes into Digital Literacy or Computer Science..................................... 77
  Stefan Pasterk, Max Kesselbacher, and Andreas Bollin

Teachers' Education and Professional Development

Who's Teaching the Teachers? Viewing the ICT Content of a Teaching Degree Through the Eyes of Pre-service Teachers........... 91
  Amber McLeod and Kelly Carabott

Exploratory Study on the Effort Perceived by In-service K-12 Teachers from Subject Areas not Specialising in Computer Science Who Are Complete CS Novices.. 101
    Paolo Tosato and Monica Banzato

Hanging Pictures or Searching the Web: Informing the Design of a Decision-Making System that Empowers Teachers to Appropriate Educational Resources to Their School's Infrastructure 112
    N. Yiannoutsou, N. Otero, W. Müller, C. Neofytou, M. Miltiadous, and T. Hadzilacos

Designing an Educational Action Task Force for MOOCs and Online Course Production... 122
    Halvdan Haugsbakken and Inger Langseth

A Teaching Process Oriented Model for Quality Assurance in Education - Usability and Acceptability... 128
    Elisa Reçi and Andreas Bollin

Games-Based Learning and Gamification

Collaboration Platform for Public and Private Actors in Educational Games Development 141
    Jaana Holvikivi, Leenu Juurola, and Maija Nuorteva

Students' Conducts During a Digital Game-Based Museum School Visit 151
    Eric Sanchez, Elsa Paukovics, Sylvia Müller, Nicolas Kramar, and Antoine Widmer

Assessing Social Engagement in a Digital Role-Playing Game: Changes over Time and Gender Differences 161
    Guillaume Bonvin, Eric Sanchez, Pierre-Antoine Champin, Rémi Casado, Nathalie Guin, and Marie Lefevre

A Learning Analytics Approach in Web-Based Multi-user Learning Games.... 167
    Matthias Ehlenz, Thiemo Leonhardt, and Ulrik Schroeder

Learning in Specific and Disciplinary Contexts

The Role of Audiovisual Translation in Mediating Foreign Language Learning: Activity Theory Perspective 175
    Rasha AlOkaily

Innovation in Language Teaching and Learning: What Do We Need to Make a Massive Open Online Course (MooC) for Language Learning Genuinely Innovative?... 187
    Veruska De Caro-Barek

An Investigation of the Impact of Haptics for Promoting Understanding
of Difficult Concepts in Cell Biology 197
   Mary Webb, Megan Tracey, William Harwin, Ozan Tokatli,
   Faustina Hwang, Natasha Barrett, Chris Jones, and Ros Johnson

Personality-Based Group Formation: A Large-Scale Study on the Role
of Skills and Personality in Software Engineering Education 207
   Amir Mujkanovic and Andreas Bollin

Learning in Social Networking Environments

Social Networks as Learning Delivery Platforms: Academic Achievement
and Attitudes of Students...................................... 221
   Yaacov J. Katz

Learning to Share by Reflection-on-Action on an Enterprise
Social Media Platform... 231
   Halvdan Haugsbakken

Self-Assessment, e-Assessment and e-Examinations

The Application of Anchoring Vignettes in the Analysis of Self-assessment
of ICT Skills: A Pilot Study Among Czech Secondary School Students..... 243
   Hana Voňková, Miroslava Černochová, Hasan Selcuk, Jan Hrabák,
   and Kateřina Králová

Student Experiences with a Bring Your Own Laptop e-Exam System
in Pre-university College 253
   Mathew Hillier and Nathaniel Lyon

Writing e-Exams in Pre-University College 264
   Mathew Hillier and Nathaniel Lyon

Students' Perceptions of e-Assessment: A Case Study from Germany 275
   Bastian Küppers and Ulrik Schroeder

Author Index 285

Computational Thinking

Computational Thinking on the Way to a Cultural Technique

A Debate on Lords and Servants

Andreas Bollin[✉] and Peter Micheuz

Universität Klagenfurt, Klagenfurt, Austria
{Andreas.Bollin, Peter.Micheuz}@aau.at

Abstract. Based on a thorough literature review and on personal expertise in different areas of computer science (education) fields, we reflect and debate on computational thinking from different perspectives. One is that of an Austrian teacher who is confronted with a curriculum for a new subject called 'Basic Digital Education', with computational thinking as an explicit part of it. The other view is that from a reflective software engineer with a holistic perspective on computational thinking and concrete ideas about its limitations. The debate concludes with an agreement on computational thinking as a cultural technique and a mutual approach to a refined working definition.

Keywords: Computational thinking · Computer science · Life-long-learning · Engineering · Curriculum development

1 Introduction

In an interview with the German "Süddeutsche Zeitung" at the end of January 2018, Armin Grunwald, head of the Office of Technology Assessment at the German Bundestag, said that if *"we just have to work to run after the technology, then something is wrong. Hegel has already put this in a nutshell, with the relationship of master and servant... The more the Lord relies on his servant, the more dependent he becomes on him"* [1]. Indeed, for decades, educators (and politicians) have had to deal with the question of what to teach and how to be able to produce (or perhaps guarantee) politically mature and technologically up-to-date people. But, what does this mean in the context of current developments: robots, drones, artificial intelligence, smart devices and, not to forget, the Internet of things and smart homes? Is digital education following a scattergun approach?

With the publication of a CACM viewpoint article about computational thinking (CT) in 2006, Jeanette Wing popularised the idea of a new fundamental skill used by everyone in the world by the middle of the 21st century [2]. She defined computational thinking as *"the thought processes involved in formulating a problem and expressing its solution(s) in such a way that a computer – human or machine – can effectively carry out"*. In the Gödel Lecture at Vienna University of Technology on June 9 2016, she also shared many examples of where to find computational thinking aspects in different disciplines, be it economics, law, healthcare or geosciences. So, together with introducing computer science to our classes, do we have a silver-bullet for dealing with today's challenges?

In her 2006 seminal paper, Wing did not primarily think of computational thinking in primary and secondary education [2]. It was not foreseeable which worldwide avalanche has been set off by her, especially among educationalists and teachers. Maybe it goes too far to refer to it as a hype. But if not, it could be a worthwhile endeavour to show that Gartner's Hype Cycle can even be applied to this phenomenon, with the peak of inflated expectations being apparently behind us. Currently, we find ourselves at the slope of enlightenment, in the form of reasonable and viable definitions of that all-in-all still fuzzy term. Reviews on existing literature strengthen some core concepts of CT: logical and algorithmic thinking, decomposition, generalisation and pattern recognition, modelling and abstraction [13].

CT is seen as a fundamental set of mental skills used by everybody, as fundamental as reading, writing and arithmetic [12]. Martin describes CT simply in a few words: "It is about connecting computing to the world" [9]. Moreover, it seems to be widely accepted that coding is an indispensable part of CT [10]. It is seen as an aid to learning software development [11], and is thus coupled with software engineering [20, 21].

The list of publications in the context of CT is amazing. But, even more surprising is the fact that the debate about "How much of computer science and computational thinking should be taught?" is camouflaged by the support from technology enthusiasts, industry, and politicians. So, though there are numerous different curricula and definitions of computational thinking around [3–7], there still is no common understanding about how far we need to go. This paper, therefore, tries to answer the question of what computational thinking (also at primary and secondary schools) is, and elaborating on it closer, what it *is not*. We try to approach the border between computational thinking (as a set of skills that is needed due to contemporary demands, addressing the characteristics of a new cultural technique) and the skills of an engineering education that are needed by professionals.

The idea behind this paper was born during a trip of the two authors from Klagenfurt to Vienna, where we were trying to define computational thinking in the Austrian context. Both authors have years of teaching experience in computer science, but the first author has a strong engineering background, whereas the second author is involved in political discussions, adapting the school system in Austria for many years. It seems natural to us to approach this topic in the form of a debate, where statements are presented and redefined along the discussion, finally coming up with a reliable definition of the border between CT and not-CT.

2 A Debate on CT in the (Austrian) Educational System

"Basic Digital Education" is the name for a new subject which will be introduced in all Austrian lower secondary schools beginning in the school year 2018–2019. There is one curriculum covering four years of lower secondary education (age groups from 10–14 years) and encompassing eight main topics:

- Social aspects of media change and digitisation
- Information, data and media competence
- Operating systems and standard applications
- Media design
- Digital communication and social media
- Security
- Technical problem-solving
- Computational thinking

Obviously, these topics stand for a broad curriculum, which encompasses digital competence, media competence, and political competence as well. Digital competence in particular is expected to empower pupils, based on a comprehensive overview of digital tools (hardware and software), for coping with certain scenarios in educational, vocational and private contexts in a reflective manner.

At first sight, informatics (computer science) does not play a prevalent and visible role. Media pedagogy and digital literacy are apparently better represented than core informatics. At a second glance, computer science is represented explicitly as CT. This term has not been translated into the German synonym "Informatisches Denken" and appears in the curriculum as the (global) driving force for implementing elements of core informatics into a seemingly overcrowded curriculum.

Table 1. CT in the Austrian curriculum for basic digital education [23]

Computational thinking	Basic level (2 h per week)	Advanced level 1 (+1 h)	Advanced level 2 (+1 h)
Working with algorithms	Pupils – name and describe everyday processes – use, build and reflect codes (e.g. secret writing, QR-Code) – reproduce distinct instructions (algorithms) and carry them out – formulate distinct instructions verbally and in written form	Pupils – discover similarities and rules (patterns) within instructions (algorithms) – discover the importance of algorithms in automatic digital processes (e.g. automated proposal of potentially interesting information)	Pupils – can evaluate intuitive user interfaces and its underlying processes
Creative use of programming languages	Pupils – produce simple programs or web applications with appropriate tools to solve a problem or to complete tasks – know different programming languages and production processes	Pupils – master basic programming structures (decision, loops, procedures)	Pupils – reflect the boundaries and options of simulations

All topics of the curriculum are divided into further subtopics and detailed competence descriptions and learning goals. The main topic CT is split into a basic and advanced level (see Table 1 for more details).

For the first time in the history of computing education in Austria, all lower secondary schools – "some" teachers and all pupils – are exposed to a binding curriculum wherein computing, algorithms and programming play a more or less clearly defined and specified role. Digital education in general and CT in particular are no longer optional for a special cohort of pupils, but obligatory for all. It would be too much to go into the details of the challenging organisational issues required to implement the curriculum. All there is to say about it is that within the framework of school autonomy, schools can change the number of hours within a certain range. They have to decide autonomously to introduce the curriculum for 'Basic Education' as an independent subject (2 to 4 h per week, which means an assumed 64 to 128 h of lessons) within 4 years, in a completely integrative way in other subjects (64 to 128 h) or all hybrid forms between these extremes. But independent from the justified question of how to cover all topics, with, all-in-all, over one hundred learning goals in a very limited time, the main questions are: to what extent is the Austrian definition of CT in line with international views among experts including scientists and teachers, and does it already answer the question of what CT is definitely not? The explicit topic CT in the Austrian curriculum could lead to the assumption that it has nothing to do with the other topics, like standard applications, technical problem-solving or security or even media design.

2.1 Proper or Improper

The opening statement of A. Bollin: The article of Bocconi et al. [8] about computational thinking approaches and orientations in K-12 education brings us exactly to the point: there are still different views on what computational thinking is. Some of them include programming; some of them do not. For motivational reasons, curricula sooner or later will introduce coding or programming in their lecture units. According to the new Austrian curriculum, pupils should be able to produce simple programs or web-applications and should know different programming languages. This seems to be in-line with the current trend, but when it is not introduced for good reasons and correctly, this is putting the cart before the horse.

In the vision of Wing, everyone should be able to use well-established techniques that have been applied by engineers for a long time already. It is about formulating problems in such a way that, maybe with the help of others (or even machines), problems can be solved easier. Thus, it is not surprising that the problem-solving activity includes logical reasoning, algorithmic thinking, abstraction, decomposition, generalisation, pattern detection and languages (notations) for communication and representing information. But, this is quite individualistic, and nowadays by far not enough to solve larger (and more complex) problems. Missiroli et al. [14] thus suggest combining computational thinking skills and team-based skills, as needed by software developers, when developing software in an agile manner. Figure 1 summarises their concept, combining problem solving and social skills to a new literacy they call "co-operative thinking".

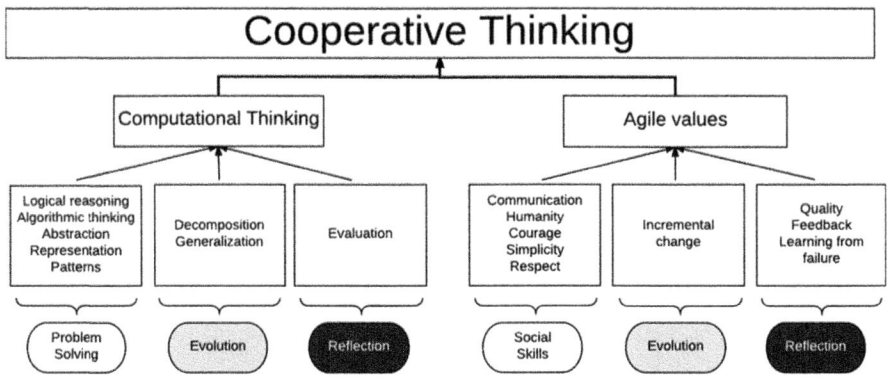

Fig. 1. Cooperative thinking as a combination of CT and agile development breakdown (according to Missiroli et al. [14] and following Computing at School [15] and Beck [16])

So, when introducing programming, it should not be done to just to illustrate how algorithms can be used and executed. We should not be dumb Lords. One should be honest and state that nowadays it is about solving real-world problems. But, this then includes more than just being able to write some lines of (computer-readable) text. It is also about including some software engineering skills.

2.2 Step-by-Step

The follow-up statement of P. Micheuz: "The secret of getting ahead is getting started. The secret of getting started is breaking your complex overwhelming tasks into small manageable tasks and starting on the first one." This little-known quote from poet Mark Twain on problem-solving can be seen as a remarkable historical precursor, long before CT began to rack the brains of thousands of educational experts in the field. Every software engineer working on solving so-called real-world problems in teams, and with the aid of digital tools, has learned "simply to go" by practicing and internalising basic concepts and, to a reasonable extent, also some (especially among many educationalists), disreputable rote learning. There is another quote, "He who wants to build high towers must dwell with the fundament for a long time" from the Austrian composer Anton Bruckner. It supports the truism that CT as a cultural technique needs an early beginning, a coherent and sustainable construction of skills and competences in the form of a spiral curriculum.

Looking at the ambitious and overloaded curriculum, with CT as a comparatively small part, and even under the assumption that motivated and CT-proven teachers follow the intended curriculum, it is rather unlikely that all pupils can meet all goals of the whole curriculum in 64 to 128 h of lessons within four years.

It is self-evident that CT for primary, lower/upper secondary and tertiary level (must) have different characteristic forms. I can live with the fact that advanced aspects of software engineering and bigger projects should play a role, at the earliest, at upper and tertiary level, but for primary and lower secondary level that would go too far. Nonetheless, cooperative thinking, or better, cooperative acting, can be harnessed as a valuable general teaching method, especially in programming and CT-related lessons. I doubt that software engineering in its full definition is an adequate term for lower age groups. That would overstrain teachers who are already struggling with CT, but willing to undergo professional development in that field. But, often things are not as bad as they seem. From this perspective, the fact that CT lacks a precise definition must be considered predominantly an advantage, as it is scalable and adaptable for various age groups and even interdisciplinary implementations.

The explicit learning goal of producing (simple) programs confronts Austrian teachers and pupils with a fait accompli. CT in the new curriculum covers more than mere algorithmic thinking, but less than dealing with (complex) real-world problems.

2.3 Past and Future

The follow-up statement of A. Bollin: Interestingly, history is repeating. The introduction of spreadsheets decades ago led to a situation where every user was using sheets without noticing that he or she was (and is) in fact programming [19] (and not following quality standards a software engineer would naturally follow). Debugging aids for spreadsheets are getting better nowadays, but still a lot of erroneous spreadsheets are around, forming the basis for (private as well as industrial) disastrous decisions. We should not educate pupils in a way where oversimplifications potentially lead to a misuse or misunderstanding of reality.

The "proper or improper" claim does not mean that even more skills are to be packed into the tight schedule in schools under the umbrella of computational thinking, but it is a hint toward a problem that we are running into. In one work, Hermans and Aivaloglou [17] show that using block-oriented languages (which are quite often chosen for novice programmers) dramatically hampers learning programming later at universities. Without taking care of software engineering practices from the beginning (as examined in their paper), a lot of effort, time and resources are needed to produce the engineers that the industry is longing for. Now, not everybody will (and should) strive for a career as a (software) engineer. But, this is not a reason for showing programming in a way nobody ever would and should program. The problem focus and the context are missing, and in our classrooms, we continue having a lot of bored pupils.

This viewpoint is partially also supported by neuro-didactic findings: people have enormous difficulty learning when either parts or wholes are neglected. Hence, the learning brain needs the whole and the details; it requires both a big picture and paying attention to the individual parts [18]. In our case, the real world is needed, and the individual parts could be programming tasks or the meaningful use of technology.

To me, programming already is part of the engineering discipline, and CT covers parts of the skills an engineer needs to successfully solve problems and to create something new. Sure, for didactic reasons, one might start to introduce small programs to show the application of CT techniques in a bigger context. It is also clear that one has to start step-by-step. But, as another comparison with a cultural technique shows, when we start learning to read, we do not stop after recognising the letters. We continue with combining the letters together and with learning to recognise syllables, words, etc., until we reach some level of proficiency.

To summarise, when defining programming as not being part of CT, then we definitely should add computer science (and software techniques) to our curricula in order to show the whole picture. When we say that programming is part of CT, then we should not do it in an inappropriate (context-neglecting) way and need to add more hours to our syllabi. It also means investing more resources and training our teachers (including all the lecturers at universities) accordingly. This is the only way that pupils (and parents and teachers) will responsibly know why to decide either for or against a technical study or technique-related working place later on. It is also the only way to keep technological change being the servant and not allow it to take over.

2.4 In the Right Place at the Right Time with a Sense of Proportion – P. Micheuz

The final statement of P. Micheuz: Digital education in its full complexity will remain a big challenge in traditional formal educational settings. So will the recent decision from an expert group to embed CT explicitly into the Austrian curriculum. It does not solve the problem of age-appropriateness and does not even guarantee dedicated lessons for computing. It transfers the responsibility for its implementation - to what extent and at which age level - to schools and teachers. In contrast to traditional subjects such as language education and mathematics, the drivers of the main cultural techniques of reading, writing and arithmetic, currently CT cannot rely on sequenced and coherent age appropriate lessons. Accordingly, there is legitimate concern that within 4 years of lower secondary education, CT will not be taught properly. It may be assumed that in the initial phase of executing the curriculum of 'Basic Digital Education' in some schools, CT will play little role.

Regarding the introduction of programming with a block-based approach (Scratch or similar development environments), I am quite optimistic. The question remains when to switch to the first steps of textual coding. As for today, the Austrian curriculum for 'Basic Digital Education' has no answer for that.

It cannot be expected that (m)any teachers at this school level see the whole picture of software development. Basic CT education with first steps in problem-solving, algorithmic thinking and first programming experiences on a small scale should be also feasible without having deep experiences in software engineering.

But even these first steps cannot be taken for granted. CT education for pupils needs CT-educated teachers and professional development in that field on a large scale. In the next years, nationwide measures in the form of pre-service and in-service training in various formats will need to be taken.

3 A Working Definition of Computational Thinking

In the previous section, we tried to take two positions, one from the viewpoint of a software engineer, and one from the viewpoint of teachers who need to make the next generations fit for exciting technological changes and current threats. Now, we try to converge and to find a working definition in the context of the Austrian situation and with regard to CT as a cultural technique.

3.1 About Cultural Techniques

When reflecting on cultural techniques, we think primarily of the cognitively most fundamental cultural techniques of reading, writing and arithmetic, and of its lengthy and laborious acquisition in dedicated school subjects. But, in our increasingly digitally penetrated culture, there are demands for extended skills and competences as widely elaborated in the Digital Competence Framework for Citizens [22].

If we accept CT as a new cultural technique, it might be helpful to look closer at what a cultural technique really is. Cultural techniques are a set of skills, concepts and competences that help human beings "function properly" in a given culture. They help in dealing with tasks and solving problems in different situations of life, like making a fire, using a calendar, or being able to communicate in social networks.

As cultural techniques are solution concepts for tasks and problems of human beings, we have to be clear about current human needs (cf. Maslow's hierarchy). In the context of new technological demands and secondary education, this list of needs encompasses being able to:

- Communicate with others using state-of-the-art communication technology.
- Search for, assess and work with available information.
- Solve tasks in a sustainable manner with the help of new state-of-the-art technology.
- Protect him- or herself against fraud.

Apart from these needs, which are well covered also in the new Austrian curriculum for 'Basic Digital Education' (see Sect. 2), one also needs to know about the limits of the solution concepts and being able to protect oneself from a misuse, so the list has to be extended by:

- Knowing what computer science and software engineering is about.
- Being aware of potential limitations and side-effects.

Last, but not least, computational thinking definitely does not include the cultural technique of typewriting or information technology (IT)-literacy such as using office software and digital devices at a cursory level. And, it is rather unthinkable that there are computational thinkers who are not fluent in harnessing computers, but it is quite possible that fluent computer users are not yet educated computational thinkers.

With all these reflections in mind, one can give a quite crisp definition of what computational thinking in secondary education is and what it is not.

3.2 A Working Definition

Computational thinking **is a cultural technique** consisting of a set of skills needed to complete a task in a responsible, sustainable manner including problem-solving, evolutionary and reflection steps. These steps encompass *logical reasoning, algorithmic thinking, abstraction, generalisation, decomposition, design/solution patterns, evaluation techniques*, and as computers might be involved in the solution process, *different representation forms*. It also includes knowing about related disciplines like computer science and software engineering. As such, it should be thought about to its fullest extent, but in an age-appropriate manner, at the secondary level in Austria.

Computational thinking **is not about** being able to work like a *software engineer or computer scientist*. It is not necessarily about *finalising (software) products in a correct, efficient and cost-oriented manner*. It is also not about *proving and searching for algorithmic properties or creating new physical devices*. But, it is knowing about the limits of one's own solution ideas.

Now, as our debate was also about programming and coding, it is up to the educator to what extent to include programming languages (in graphical or textual form) to motivate for a technique or skill. However, it is then his or her responsibility to make the difference to software engineering clear. The implications for a teacher (and for teacher education) are obvious: he or she needs to know more about computer science and software engineering, as at least a portion of teaching CT is about teaching the differences/boundaries to neighbouring disciplines.

4 Summary and Outlook

In this paper, we tried to further the approach to defining computational thinking, reflecting on discussion among scientific and educational experts in the educational field of computing. It stresses the fact that CT is at the border of engineering disciplines, and, when coding is involved, it is also close to the border of software engineering.

More than a decade after the seminal work of Jeanette Wing [2], the wave of its public perception reached Austria. Since computational thinking is an explicit part of the new curriculum 'Basic Digital Education', it will be a starting point of many discussions and debates.

The debate in this paper results in a working definition from the perspective of software engineering and CT as a cultural technique, having in mind the limits and challenges of school education in general and the introduction of a new subject in particular.

We agree that CT in the way we see it must be considered an important cultural technique in the 21st century. But, we are realistic enough to know that CT as imagined in the heads of many educational experts, including our abstract working definition above, still has a long and difficult way to go from the conception stage to its implementation.

There is hope that its future will not be that of the term and subject of informatics in Austrian lower secondary schools where, according to a very broad interpretation of its definition, the subject informatics in Austrian schools created its own reality. Maybe a reality with some CT-related parts were included, but from a vast majority of teachers they were not realised as CT defined above. Only when carefully knowing the borders, were we able to deal with current and future human needs. And thus, it is more likely to keep the role of a Lord not being dependent on his or her (technical) servants.

References

1. Bauchmüller, M., Braun, S.: SZ Online. http://www.sueddeutsche.de/wirtschaft/gefahren-der-digitalisierung-die-leute-merken-nicht-mehr-wie-fragil-das-system-ist-1.3842973-3. Accessed 11 Jan 2019
2. Wing, J.: Computational thinking. CACM Viewpoint **49**, 33–35 (2006)
3. Webb, M., et al.: Computer science in K-12 school curricula of the 2lst century: why, what and when? Educ. Inf. Technol. **22**(2), 445–468 (2017)
4. Gallenbacher, J.: Abenteuer Informatik. Hands-on exhibits for learning about computational thinking. Paper Presented at WiPCSE 2012, Germany (2012)
5. Dierbach, C., et al.: A model for piloting pathways for computational thinking in general education. In: SIGCSE 2011, pp. 257–262. ACM, New York (2011)
6. Seiter, L., Foreman, B., Carroll, J.: Modeling the learning progressions of computational thinking of primary grade students. In: 9th International ACM Conference on International Computing Education Research, pp. 59–66. ACM, New York (2013)
7. Cole, E.: On pre-requisite skills for universal computational thinking education. In: Procceedings of ICER 2015, Omaha, NE, pp. 253–254 (2015)
8. Bocconi, S., Ferrari, A., Kampylis, P.: Developing computational thinking: approaches and orientations in K-12 education. In: EdMedia 2016, Vancouver, BC, pp. 13–18 (2016)
9. Martin, F.: Rethinking Computational Thinking. http://advocate.csteachers.org/2018/02/17/rethinking-computational-thinking. Accessed 11 Jan 2019
10. Prottsman, K., Krauss, J.: Computational Thinking and Coding for Every Student: The Teacher's Getting-Started Guide. SAGE Publications, Thousand Oaks (2017)
11. Beecher, K.: Computational Thinking. A Beginner's Guide to Problem-Solving and Programming. BCS Learning & Development Ltd., Swindon (2017)
12. Wing, J.: Computational Thinking Benefits Society. Social Issues in Society. http://socialissues.cs.toronto.edu. Accessed 11 Jan 2019
13. Selby, C., Woollard, J.: Computational Thinking: the developing definition. University of Southampton (2013). https://eprints.soton.ac.uk/356481. Accessed 11 Jan 2019
14. Missiroli, M., Russo, D., Ciancarini, P.: Cooperative thinking, or: computational thinking meets agile. In: Proceedings of the 30th IEEE Conference on Software Engineering Education and Training. Savannah, GA, pp. 187–191 (2017)
15. Beck, K., Andres, C.: Extreme Programming Explained. Addison-Wesley, Boston (2004)
16. Csizmadia, A., et al.: Computational thinking: a guide for teachers. Computing at Schools E-Book (2015)
17. Hermans, F., Aivaloglou, E.: Do code smells hamper novice programming: a controlled experiment on Scratch Programs. In: Proceedings of the 24th IEEE International Conference on Program Comprehension, Austin, TX, pp. 1–10 (2016)
18. Caine, R.N., Caine, G.: Understanding a brain-based approach to learning and teaching. Educ. Leadersh. **48**(2), 66–70 (1990)
19. Mittermeir, R., Clermont, M., Hodnigg, K.: Protecting spreadsheets against fraud. In: Proceedings of the European Spreadsheet Risks International Group (2005)
20. Bollin, A., Sabitzer, B.: Teaching software engineering in schools – on the right time to introduce software engineering concepts. In: 6th IEEE Global Engineering Education Conference, EDUCON, pp. 511–518 (2015)
21. Bollin, A., Pasterk, S., Antonitsch, P., Sabitzer, B.: Software engineering in primary and secondary schools – informatics education is more than programming. In: IEEE 20th Conference on Software Engineering Education and Training, CSEE&T, pp. 132–136 (2016)

22. Digital Competence Framework for Citizens. htttps://ec.europa.eu/jrc/en/digcomp. Accessed 11 Jan 2019
23. Digital Basic Education. (in German). https://bildung.bmbwf.gv.at/schulen/schule40/dgb/index.html. Accessed 11 Jan 2019

Computational Thinking and Problem-Solving in the Context of IEA-ICILS 2018

Birgit Eickelmann, Amelie Labusch[✉], and Mario Vennemann

Institute for Educational Science, Paderborn University, Paderborn, Germany
{birgit.eickelmann,amelie.labusch,
mario.vennemann}@upb.de

Abstract. Computational thinking has grown in importance in recent years as an important key competence of the 21st century [1]. In order to equip students for life in the digital age, it is necessary to enable them to acquire competences in this area. In this context, there are a number of concepts of computational thinking; and the curricular embedding of these competences in schools has progressed to varying extents in educational systems [2]. What is therefore required is a large-scale study that compares students' competences in computational thinking and the underlying conditions of acquisition at an international level, as provided by the International Computer and Information Literacy Study 2018 (ICILS 2018). In addition, to draw on well-proven problem-solving theories and facilitate access for non-computer scientists, it is important to compare these competences with students' problem-solving skills [3]. This will be accomplished through a German national extension to ICILS 2018 which, on a representative basis at the national level, will enable comprehensive analysis of this relationship. The purpose of the present paper is to introduce computational thinking and problem-solving in the context of ICILS 2018. This study should then provide a starting point for empowering students for life in the digital age.

Keywords: Computational thinking · Problem-solving · ICILS 2018

1 Introduction

In today's knowledge and information society, competent handling of information and communication technologies is indispensable in order to meet the diverse requirements of the various areas of life. In this context, it is important that students develop the necessary skills to use these technologies in their daily lives to allow them an active and full participation in today's digital age [4–7]. Based on research studies and on recent developments, changes in the digital technologies themselves and changes in the notions of the importance of digital skills, an understanding of the required skills and competences has been expanded to include computational thinking [8, 9]. Since publication of Wing's [10] influential article, in which she states her grand vision that everyone should have skills in this field and be able to use them, computational thinking has been the subject of research and scientific discourse. However, it also assigns an important role to the school systems and thus to the school as a mediating authority for corresponding competences [2, 11]. As a result, many initiatives have been launched in K-12 schools [12].

In this context, there are differences between educational systems in the integration of computational thinking into compulsory education. This leads to the need to study the results of the implementation of computational thinking and related teaching and evaluation methods [13], also with a view to enabling comparability of computational thinking outcomes within and between educational systems.

However, the broad spectrum of perspectives on computational thinking also means that various elements of definition have emerged, resulting in a lack of clarity as to what computational thinking should be [14].

When it comes to the question of how computational thinking can be conceptualised, it becomes apparent that the construct of computational thinking is known to be poorly defined [15], that there is no universally accepted definition [16] and that there is thus the challenge to assess computational thinking [17]. These circumstances complicate the widespread integration of computational thinking in the learning and teaching context, as educational systems place different emphases on how to learn and teach computational thinking. This is also reflected in teacher education, as there is a great need to prepare well-trained teachers to integrate computational thinking into their daily teaching activities [18]. Yet, there is still only marginal understanding of how non-computer science teachers can be engaged in computational thinking [19, 20].

What is taught, however, are problem-solving skills. Students are expected to work in new environments, overcome problems they are unfamiliar with, and apply multi-disciplinary reasoning skills that are not tied to specific content [21]. The majority of existing computational thinking definitions and a few existing studies suggest that there is a high correlation between student competences in computational thinking and problem-solving skills [9, 22–24].

If it can be shown that this high correlation between computational thinking and problem-solving does in fact exist, then this finding can be used to structure computational thinking lessons accordingly, which necessitates investigation of the relationship between computational thinking and problem-solving [25].

Measuring this relationship has several benefits. In addition to the referral to well-proven problem-solving theories to explain computational thinking, it might provide an explanatory approach for variation in students' achievement in computational thinking.

Summarising all these aspects related to the increasing relevance of computational thinking, the inconsistent conceptualisation, the different emphases in learning and teaching computational thinking in different educational systems, and the resulting advantage of measuring the correlation between computational thinking and general problem-solving, leads to three major challenges: conceptualising computational thinking and problem-solving; finding an appropriate research design; and highlighting the benefits and nature of the results. This raises the three research questions, which are addressed in this article:

1. How are computational thinking and general problem-solving to be conceptualised, where do they overlap and how can this be presented on a theoretical level?
2. Which data and which research approach are appropriate for an empirical examination of the theoretical understanding?

3. Which kind of results with respect to the overlap between computational thinking and problem-solving will be obtained in such a research process?

Section 2 is concerned with answering the first question, whereby, firstly, the conceptualisation of computational thinking (Sect. 2.1) and problem-solving (Sect. 2.2) and then their overlapping areas (Sect. 2.3) and, thus, the relationship at the theoretical level, are covered. Section 3 responds to question 2 by introducing the International Computer and Information Literacy Study 2018 and thereby presenting the international option computational thinking (Sect. 3.1) and the German national extension to problem-solving (Sect. 3.2). Finally, Sect. 4 addresses question 3 and outlines the expected results related to the overlap between computational thinking and problem-solving.

2 Computational Thinking and Problem-Solving at a Theoretical Level

2.1 Conceptualisation of Computational Thinking

The identification of the spectrum of computational thinking skills is a balancing act between algorithmic procedural thinking related to computer programming and a wider range of transferable problem-solving skills and dispositions [1, 22, 26].

There are many definitions and conceptualisations of computational thinking, all with different emphases. Wing, for instance, argues that computational thinking should not be limited to programming and that it should be added to the analytical skills of all people [10]. Denning [27] asserts that definitions of computational thinking are "vague and confusing" (p. 33) when they do not originate in the field of computer science. Thus, it makes a difference whether the definition comes from the field of computer science or from the field of education.

In the International Computer and Information Literacy Study 2018 (ICILS 2018), computational thinking is defined as "Computational thinking refers to an individual's ability to recognize aspects of real-world problems which are appropriate for computational formulation and to evaluate and develop algorithmic solutions to those problems so that the solutions could be operationalized with a Computer" [28] (p. 27).

The computational thinking construct in ICILS 2018 consists of two general conceptual categories (strands) and three or respectively two specific content categories within a strand (aspects). Strand 1 focuses on the conceptualisation of problems, assuming that before developing solutions, problems must first be understood and designed in such a way that algorithmic thinking or system thinking can support the process of solution development. This includes, for instance, the aspect of knowing about and understanding computer systems, whereby students should have the ability to recognise and describe the characteristics of systems. On a declarative level, a person should be able to describe rules and boundary conditions. A second aspect describes the formulation and analysis of problems. For this purpose, a problem is broken down into smaller, manageable parts (decomposition) and the properties of the task are systematised in such a way that a computational solution can be developed. The third aspect of the first strand refers to the meaningful collection and representation of relevant data in order to effectively assess the problem solution within a system.

Strand 2 comprises the operationalisation of solutions in the form of planning, implementation, testing and evaluation of algorithmic solutions to real-world problems. On the one hand, the strand focuses on the aspect of planning and evaluating solutions. Typically, there is a wide range of possible computer-based solutions for a particular problem. It is therefore important to be able to plan and evaluate solutions from different perspectives and to understand the advantages, disadvantages and effects of different solutions. On the other hand, the second strand includes the developing of algorithms, programs and interfaces. This does not assume that the students are familiar with the syntax and functions of a particular programming language, but rather with the logical reasoning underlying the development of algorithms for problem-solving [2, 28].

Computational thinking processes emerge from the framework on three levels. On the level of problem conceptualisation (strand 1), problem identification and definition are important, as is decomposition, in which a problem is broken down into sub-steps to make it easier to deal with. On the second level - the operationalisation of solutions (strand 2) - various processes play a role, such as pattern recognition, pattern matching and algorithmic thinking, which contain abstraction. On the third level - the evaluation of solutions - the focus is on the debugging and evaluation of the solution. This level is closely linked to the second level of operationalisation of solutions, which is reflected in the fact that this is included in aspect 2.1 of the framework under the second strand [29].

2.2 Conceptualisation of Problem-Solving

When considering computational thinking as a competence and/or a competence area, it becomes apparent that it requires the development of both domain-specific and general problem-solving skills [9]. Nevertheless, the investigation of general problem-solving is not the approach considered in the above-mentioned computational thinking construct, but rather it focuses on domain-specific problem-solving (although the framework would also apply to general problem-solving).

Problem-solving can be described as a transformation from an undesirable initial state to a desirable final state [30] by overcoming a barrier. Achieving this requires higher order thinking skills [31].

A problem-solving process is frequently described as a seven-stage cycle [32]. On the level of problem conceptualisation, it comprises the recognition or identification of a problem and the definition and mental representation of the problem. On the level of the operationalisation of solutions, the development of a strategy to solve the problem, the organisation of knowledge concerning the problem, as well as the allocation of mental and physical resources needed to solve the problem, all play a role. Monitoring of progress towards the goal, and evaluation of the solution in terms of accuracy are on the third level, which focuses on evaluating solutions.

2.3 Overlapping Areas of Computational Thinking and Problem-Solving

On a theoretical level, there are apparent indications of a strong correlation between computational thinking and problem-solving processes [29]. When comparing the two constructs, there is considerable overlap between them, as illustrated in Fig. 1.

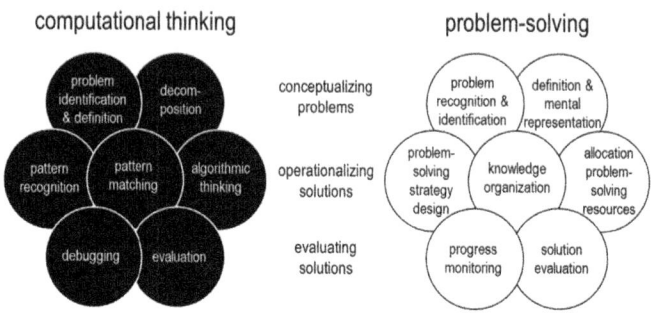

Fig. 1. Overlapping areas of computational thinking and problem-solving

Therefore, introducing students to problem-solving and algorithmic thinking at an early age is useful in enabling them to learn computational thinking step-by-step. This ensures that all students have sufficient skills at the end of their schooling to keep up with technological progress. To further develop these initiatives, it is necessary to know which competences the students already possess and where similarities and differences exist with regard to their general problem-solving skills.

For this purpose, it is necessary to introduce a study in which empirical research can be conducted into the introduced theoretical constructs, also to support students' acquisition of computational thinking in schools and taking school context and learning as well as student characteristics into account.

3 Computational Thinking and Problem-Solving in ICILS 2018

3.1 Computational Thinking as an International Option of ICILS 2018

Based on the described computational thinking construct, the International Computer and Information Literacy Study 2018 (ICILS 2018) meets the challenge of measuring student competences in the field of computational thinking on a representative basis, with an international comparison, by having integrated computational thinking as an international option (as a response to the increasing relevance of this field in research, scientific discourse and school life).

With ICILS 2018, the International Association for the Evaluation of Educational Achievement (IEA) provides for the second time after ICILS 2013, with the help of an internationally developed and elaborated set of tools, the empirically validated assessment of students' computer and information literacy (CIL; comparable to information and communication technologies (ICT) literacy) in the participating countries with an international comparison. For the first time, the IEA also supplied the international option computational thinking [8]. In addition, the relationship of these competences to the school and extracurricular context of learning was examined [2].

Educational systems participating in ICILS 2018 could decide whether they also wanted to participate in this international option. Denmark, Finland, France, Germany, Luxembourg, Portugal, the Republic of Korea, the United States of America (USA), as well as North-Rhine-Westphalia (Germany) as benchmark participant, took the opportunity to do so.

The international option for ICILS 2018 is essentially aimed at clarifying the research questions as to: (1) which computational thinking competences students have and how the conditions for acquiring these competences are related to the competence level of the students; and (2) how students' achievements in computational thinking relate to their computer and information literacy skills. While the first question aims to capture computational thinking as a new area of competence for the first time and to explain the conditions for acquiring competences at student, school and educational system level, the second research question focuses on empirically clarifying the relationship with the area of computer and information literacy.

The sample in ICILS 2018 is 20 students per school in Grade 8 with a minimum age of 13.5 years, 15 teachers per school who teach in Grade 8, and the school principal and ICT coordinator at school level. In all participating countries, a representative random sample of at least 150 schools was drawn and a sample of students and teachers was taken in these schools [28].

The concept of the additional module in computational thinking is that students' achievement in computational thinking is measured in the same student cohort by extending the computer-based student tests by two test modules.

Computer-based testing with authentic tasks in a software-based test environment is essential for measuring the construct to be captured. A major challenge in test design has been that the computer-based student tests must be applicable to eighth graders, whether they have learned a programming language or not, must be applicable in a wide range of countries and curricula, and must have the least possible overlap with other disciplines (e.g. mathematics). In ICILS 2018, this area is made accessible for the first time using an adequately developed test instrument in the form of computer-based measurement with an international comparison, which can be used without knowledge of programming languages, but includes typical features of computer-based problem-solving processes such as the use of algorithms and loops for systematic and repeated problem-solving steps. A visual coding approach is used to consider algorithmic logic. The international computer-based student tests consist of questions and tasks that are embedded in real-life contexts [28].

All students complete two computer and information literacy modules. In the countries participating in the international option computational thinking, students complete two additional 25-min test modules. According to the computational thinking construct in ICILS 2018 with two strands (problem conceptualisation and solution operationalisation), each of the two computational thinking test modules concentrates on one of these strands. The computational thinking test modules contain information-based response tasks and nonlinear competence tasks.

Since competences are always embedded in a context, the research questions featured in ICILS 2018 focus in addition on the measurement of Grade 8 students' computer and information literacy as well as the relationship between Computational thinking literacy and Computer and Information literacy in terms of individual characteristics and the school context. By means of supplemented items in the background questionnaires of ICILS 2018, factors related to specific individual, school and teaching contexts and conditions in the field of computational thinking are also considered. The student and teacher questionnaires collect process-related context factors, including students' reports on the extent of learning about approaches to computational thinking at school, and teachers' emphasis on teaching approaches to computational thinking in class. School ICT coordinators were asked about their perceptions of school emphasis on teaching computational thinking activities to students. The data obtained from the so-called National Context Survey are intended to support the interpretation of the results of the student, teacher and school questionnaires [28].

The results of ICILS 2018 will be published in the international and national report on November 5, 2019.

3.2 Problem-Solving as a German National Extension to ICILS 2018

In addition, the participating educational systems had the possibility to add national extensions, of which several took advantage [3, 33]. In Germany, reading tests and tests on cognitive abilities [2], items aiming to examine the correlation between computational thinking and general problem-solving skills [3], information about students' self-reported proficiency in completing computational thinking tasks, and items focusing on computer science and its practice in schools, were therefore also gathered within the context of computational thinking. This means that the relationship between computational thinking and problem-solving could only be addressed for Germany.

The aim is to design an empirically verifiable theoretical analysis model that investigates this relationship with statistical controls for individual student characteristics such as students' self-reported proficiency in computational thinking and their background characteristics, as well as for the school context such as students' reports on the extent of learning about approaches to computational thinking at school and teachers' emphasis on teaching approaches to computational thinking in class.

4 Expected Outcomes and Discussion on the Overlap of Computational Thinking and Problem-Solving

Studying the relationship between students' computational thinking achievement and their general problem-solving skills, taking into consideration individual student characteristics and the school context, aims to provide a starting point for achieving a deeper understanding from a theoretical and empirical perspective as well as a holistic picture of computational thinking. The benefit of this is that all relationships are examined in the same sample and are calculated in one model on two levels [34].

Focusing on the relationship between computational thinking and general problem-solving and on their links would be of interest for the development of educational systems. As a matter of fact, this would allow in the coming years to work specifically on computational thinking and to use well-proven problem-solving theories, thus making it possible to implement development measures in each considered country (e.g. Germany).

Obviously, the question arises as to whether everyone should be able to learn and apply computational thinking [34] as Wing [3, 10] proposed, but in the spirit of equal opportunities, it would not necessarily be reasonable to deny some students the possibility of acquiring computational thinking skills that are becoming increasingly important for their professional future. When it comes to bringing computational thinking into schools as a cross-curricular competence, there is no alternative to conceptualise computational thinking in such a way that it can also be taught by non-computer science teachers and can also be learned by students who do not attend computer science classes. In doing so, it must also be kept in mind that neither students nor teachers with little knowledge of computer science can be expected to be familiar with a programming language. The logical conditions behind computational thinking can, however, be explained to them and it can then be left up to them to decide whether they want to gain a deeper understanding of the subject matter and acquire knowledge of or skills in a programming language or not.

However, society has the responsibility to offer young people the opportunity to acquire at least basic competences in the field of computational thinking, which they can then upgrade in line with their own particular preferences and needs. Students need a different kind of knowledge that enables them to succeed in a rapidly changing environment. If schools only prepare their students to meet current expectations, the knowledge and skills they may have to use in their private and professional lives can soon become outdated [21].

To ensure students are properly prepared for life in the digital age, it is of great relevance to consider and investigate computational thinking in the context of general problem-solving. This is addressed on a representative basis in the German national extension to ICILS 2018. Germany is currently thus the only educational system, which, with the help of a national extension to ICILS 2018, is able to investigate the relationship between computational thinking and general problem-solving, in an analysis controlling for other individual student characteristics and the school context. Results will be published in November 2019 and in-depth results in 2020.

References

1. Voogt, J., Fisser, P., Good, J., Mishra, P., Yadav, A.: Computational thinking in compulsory education: towards an agenda for research and practice. Educ. Inf. Technol. **20**(4), 715–728 (2015)
2. Eickelmann, B.: Measuring secondary school students' competence in computational thinking in ICILS 2018 – challenges, concepts and potential implications for school systems around the world. In: Kong, S.C., Abelson, H. (eds.) Computational Thinking Education. Springer, Singapore (2019). https://doi.org/10.1007/978-981-13-6528-7_4

3. Labusch, A., Eickelmann, B.: Computational thinking as a key competence - a research concept. In: Kong, S.C., Sheldon, J., Li, K.Y. (eds.) International Conference on Computational Thinking Education 2017. The Education University of Hong Kong, Hong Kong (2017)
4. Fraillon, J., Ainley, J., Schulz, W., Friedman, T., Gebhardt, E.: Preparing for life in a digital age: the IEA international computer and information literacy study. International Report. SpringerOpen, Amsterdam (2014)
5. Wilson, M., Scalise, K., Gochyyev, P.: Rethinking ICT literacy: from computer skills to social network settings. Think. Skills Creat. **18**, 65–80 (2015)
6. OECD: Skills for a Digital World: Policy Brief on the Future of Work. OECD Publishing, Paris (2016)
7. Ainley, J., Schulz, W., Fraillon, J.: A Global Measure of Digital and ICT Literacy Skills. UNESCO Publishing, Paris (2016)
8. IEA: The IEA's International Computer and Information Literacy Study (ICILS) 2018: What's Next for IEA's ICILS in 2018? IEA, Amsterdam (2016)
9. Yadav, A., Good, J., Voogt, J., Fisser, P.: Computational thinking as an emerging competence domain. In: Mulder, M. (ed.) Competence-Based Vocational and Professional Education: Bridging the Worlds of Work and Education. Springer, Cham (2017). https://doi.org/10.1007/978-3-319-41713-4_49
10. Wing, J.M.: Computational thinking. Commun. ACM **49**(3), 33–35 (2006)
11. Lockwood, J., Mooney, A.: Computational thinking in education: where does it fit? A systematic literary review. Maynooth University, Ireland (2017)
12. Czerkawski, B.: Computational thinking and teacher education: are we there yet? In: Chamblee, G., Langub, L. (eds.) Proceedings of Society for Information Technology and Teacher Education International Conference. AACE, Savannah (2016)
13. Bocconi, S., Chioccariello, A., Dettori, G., Ferrari, A., Engelhardt, K.: Developing Computational Thinking in Compulsory Education-Implications for Policy and Practice. Publications Office of the European Union, Luxembourg (2016)
14. Rich, P.J., Langton, M.B.: Computational thinking: toward a unifying definition. In: Spector, J.M., Ifenthaler, D., Sampson, D.G., Isaias, P. (eds.) Competencies in Teaching, Learning and Educational Leadership in the Digital Age. Springer, Cham (2016). https://doi.org/10.1007/978-3-319-30295-9_14
15. Román-González, M., Pérez-González, J.-C., Moreno-León, J., Robles, G.: Extending the nomological network of computational thinking with non-cognitive factors. Comput. Hum. Behav. **80**, 441–459 (2018)
16. Mannila, L., et al.: Computational thinking in K-9 education. In: Clear, A.C., Lister, R. (eds.) Proceedings of the Working Group Reports of the 2014 on Innovation and Technology in Computer Science Education Conference (ITiCSE-WGR 2014). ACM, New York (2014)
17. Brennan, K., Resnick, M.: New frameworks for studying and assessing the development of computational thinking. Paper Presented at the AERA 2012, Vancouver (2012). https://web.media.mit.edu/~kbrennan/files/Brennan_Resnick_AERA2012_CT.pdf
18. Lye, S.Y., Koh, J.H.L.: Review on teaching and learning of computational thinking through programming: what is next for K-12? Comput. Hum. Behav. **41**, 51–61 (2014)
19. Yadav, A., Mayfield, C., Zhou, N., Hambrusch, S., Korb, J.T.: Computational thinking in elementary and secondary teacher education. ACM Trans. Comput. Educ. **14**(1), 1–16 (2014). Article 5
20. Yadav, A., Stephenson, C., Hong, H.: Computational thinking for teacher education. Commun. ACM **60**(4), 55–62 (2017)

21. Csapó, B., Funke, J.: The development and assessment of problem solving in 21st-century schools. In: Csapó, B., Funke, J. (eds.) The Nature of Problem Solving: Using Research to Inspire 21st Century Learning, Educational Research and Innovation, pp. 19–32. OECD Publishing, Paris (2017)
22. Barr, V., Stephenson, C.: Bringing computational thinking to K-12: what is involved and what is the role of the computer science education community? ACM Inroads **2**(1), 48–54 (2011)
23. Román-González, M., Pérez-González, J.-C., Jiménez-Fernandez, C.: Which cognitive abilities underlie computational thinking? Criterion validity of the Computational Thinking Test. Comput. Hum. Behav. **72**, 678–691 (2017)
24. Boom, K.-D., Bower, M., Arguel, A., Siemon, J., Scholkmann, A.: Relationship between computational thinking and a measure of intelligence as a general problem-solving ability. In: Proceedings of the 23rd Annual ACM Conference on Innovation and Technology in Computer Science Education (ITiCSE 2018), pp. 206–211. ACM, New York (2018)
25. Labusch, A., Eickelmann, B.: Computational thinking and problem-solving – a research approach in the context of ICILS 2018. In: Langran, E., Borup, J. (eds.) Proceedings of Society for Information Technology and Teacher Education International Conference, pp. 3724–3729. AACE, Washington, D.C. (2018)
26. Barr, D., Harrison, J., Conery, L.: Computational thinking: a digital age skill for everyone. Learn. Learn. Technol. **38**(6), 20–23 (2011)
27. Denning, P.J.: Remaining trouble spots with computational thinking. Commun. ACM **6**(60), 33–39 (2017)
28. Fraillon, J., Schulz, W., Friedman, T., Duckworth, D.: Assessment Framework of ICILS 2018. IEA, Amsterdam (2019)
29. Labusch, A., Eickelmann, B., Vennemann, M.: Computational thinking processes and their congruence with problem-solving and information-processing. In: Kong, S.C., Abelson, H. (eds.) Computational Thinking Education. Springer, Singapore (2019). https://doi.org/10.1007/978-981-13-6528-7_5
30. Beecher, K.: Computational Thinking: A Beginner's Guide to Problem-Solving and Programming. BCS Learning & Development Limited, Swindon, UK (2017)
31. Spector, J.M., Park, S.W.: Argumentation, critical reasoning, and problem solving. In: Fee, S.B., Belland, B.R. (eds.) The Role of Criticism in Understanding Problem Solving, pp. 13–33. Springer, New York (2012). https://doi.org/10.1007/978-1-4614-3540-2_2
32. Pretz, J.E., Naples, A.J., Sternberg, R.J.: Recognizing, defining and representing problems. In: Davidson, J.E., Sternberg, R.J. (eds.) The Psychology of Problem Solving, pp. 3–30. Cambridge University Press, Cambridge (2003)
33. Caeli, E.N., Bundsgaard, J.: Computational thinking initiatives in Danish Grade 8 classes. A quantitative study of how students are taught to think computationally. Symposium Paper Presented at ECER 2018, Bolzano, Italy (2018). https://eera-ecer.de/ecer-programmes/conference/23/contribution/46129/
34. Grover, S., Pea, R.: Computational thinking in K–12: a review of the state of the field. Educ. Res. **42**(1), 38–43 (2013)

Cultivating Computational Thinking Through Data Practice

Djordje M. Kadijevich(✉)

Institute for Educational Research, Belgrade, Serbia
djkadijevic@ipi.ac.rs

Abstract. After summarising the research context regarding defining, cultivating, and assessing computational thinking (CT), this theoretical paper examines data modelling using interactive displays, a CT practice that may be cultivated across several school subjects. Although working with data is not explicitly mentioned in some CT definitions, this work may activate different CT components, such as abstraction, decomposition, and pattern recognition. Furthermore, interactive displays, which are primarily a means for visualising data, can also be tools for modelling purposes if used within a modelling cycle. Focusing on this modelling in secondary education, we first consider main activities and their underlying skills, and outline what kind of support should be given to modellers, especially novices, in assisting them to complete this as easily as possible. We then consider what computational environment to use, which learning path to follow, and what assessment of learning to apply. Implications for teacher professional development are included.

Keywords: Computational thinking · Data modelling · Interactive charts · K-12 education · Teacher education

1 Introduction

Today, education needs to prepare students to cope successfully with increasingly complex life and work environments, which often rely on technology (i.e. on automated computations). Because of that, following Wing's account of computational thinking (CT) as one of the basic student abilities [1], many studies have dealt with CT in primary and secondary education across a number of school subjects by using various cultivation means. It seems that, in doing so, CT has not been intended to replace other contemporary approaches (e.g. problem-solving, critical thinking, creative thinking), but rather to complement and strengthen them by using concepts, tools, and techniques from computer science (e.g. [2]). As a result, students will be more than just technology-literate [3].

CT was originally used to denote thinking processes applied in problem-solving to formulate solutions in such representations that could be efficiently processed by computers [1]. It was viewed as an important literacy of the 21st century, which would, to some extent, enable everyone (all learners) to: recognise aspects of problems amenable to computation; match those aspects to appropriate computational supports (concepts, tools, techniques, strategies); understand the opportunities and limitations of those supports; apply the supports in adapted or novel ways; and use computational strategies (e.g. a top-down approach) in any domain [4]. On the other hand, regarding scientists, engineers and other professionals, it was supposed that CT would enable them to reformulate problems to be (more) amenable to computation, develop and use new computational methods, ask and answer questions that rely on large data sets or intensive computations, and use computational terms to explain problems and solutions [4]. It can thus be said that CT may, in general, be viewed as a process whereby we recognise aspects of computations in our surroundings and deal, at introductory or advanced levels, with various systems and processes in these surroundings by applying tools and techniques from computer science [5].

Increasing societal reliance on technology and data calls for connecting CT and data practice in the classroom. In the rest of this theoretical contribution, we first summarise the research context regarding defining, cultivating, and assessing CT. We then examine data modelling in secondary education by using interactive displays. Focusing on this, we first consider main activities and their underlying skills, and outline what kind of support should be given to modellers, especially novices, in assisting them to complete the modelling as easily as possible. We then consider what kind of computational environment should be used (one in which CT components may additionally be fostered), what learning paths could be followed in doing that, and how modellers' progression along this path might be assessed. The paper ends with implications for teachers' professional development.

2 Research Context

2.1 Defining CT

Various definitions of CT have been proposed in the literature (e.g. [2, 6, 7]). Although the term has been used broadly, there has been no widely accepted definition so far [8]. For some researchers, from a general perspective, CT is concerned with algorithmic thinking, critical thinking, problem solving, and working cooperatively [9]. For some others, core CT facets are abstraction (data collection and analysis, pattern recognition, modelling), decomposition, algorithms (algorithm design, parallelism, automation), iteration, debugging, and generalisation [7]. Other researchers, looking at K-12 education, assume that CT is a critical component of problem-solving supported by technology [10, 11], and propose concepts, such as data collection, data analysis, data representation, problem decomposition, abstraction, algorithm and procedures, automation, parallelisation, and simulation as core ideas. It seems that the main goal behind the request to cultivate CT in K-12 education is to prepare students to use computational tools in productive and creative ways within different school subjects [6].

Apart from general frameworks, CT has been examined within subject-specific frameworks. For example, in the context of programming with Scratch, Brennan and Resnick [12] applied a CT framework with three dimensions, namely: *CT concepts* (e.g. data, operators, loops), *CT practice* (e.g. abstracting, modularising, debugging), and *CT perspectives* (e.g. questioning, connecting). In the STEM (Science, Technology, Engineering and Mathematics) context, focusing on high school mathematics and science education, a CT definition was given in the form of a taxonomy comprising four main practice categories [13]: *data practices* (e.g. collecting, visualising), *modelling and simulation practices* (e.g. building and using computational models), *computational problem-solving practices* (e.g. programming, troubleshooting), and *system-thinking practices* (e.g. defining systems, managing complexity). Another general CT framework [14], exemplified for mathematics pedagogy, comprises four overlapping activities with various objects (of digital, tangible, or conceptual nature). These activities are: *unplugging* (not using computers), *tinkering* (taking objects apart and changing/modifying their components), *making* (constructing new objects), and *remixing* (appropriating of objects or their components to use them at other places or for other purposes).

Clearly, a standard definition of CT is lacking. However, because of its pedagogical utility, it seems promising to define CT using various CT practices and activities, examined in terms of underlying CT concepts and skills (extrapolated from the NRC [15]). Although working with data is not explicitly mentioned in some CT definitions, one CT practice, namely data practice [13], should be included, since it may activate a number of CT components (e.g. abstraction, decomposition, and pattern recognition). Not only was the relevance of this practice for CT development (in particular, of data collection, representation, and analysis) recognised by the Computer Science Teacher Association (CSTA) and International Society for Technology in Education (ISTE) [11], but work with data has also been included in an international assessment of students' computer and informational literacy, which assumed that, apart from programming, the CT domain deals with structuring and manipulating data sets as well (for more details, see https://www.iea.nl/icils).

2.2 Cultivating and Assessing CT

Despite a relevant educational goal "CT for all" (initiated by Wing [1]), our knowledge of how to integrate CT in K-12 education is still in its infancy, because research on integration is scarce [6]. However, teacher education may, for example, benefit from examining examples of the use of CT in daily life. In other words, CT concepts (e.g. algorithm, abstraction, debugging) may be illustrated with concrete examples from teachers' daily experiences [16]. This approach, basically exemplifying various CT activities, has, for example, been applied by CSTA and ISTE [11]. If teacher education is based on the framework of technological pedagogical content knowledge [8], the main focus should be on developing knowledge of CT-related concepts, tools, and practice (technological knowledge) and combining them with disciplinary content (i.e. content knowledge) and pedagogical strategies (i.e. pedagogical knowledge). Additionally, to promote appropriate CT within specific subject domains, teachers should be encouraged to avoid using just a few tools (e.g. concepts mapping tools, interactive whiteboards) and CT concepts and practices (e.g. automation, problem decomposition).

Research also evidences that, in general, we should cultivate CT within rich computational environments (in different domains such as game design and development, and with various CT instances such as abstraction and automation), and, in doing so, apply a use-modify-create learning path [17]. Of course, having in mind different school subjects or university courses, CT practice should support or empower relevant scientific practice involving disciplinary knowledge and skills. Although CT may be promoted through activities without the use of computers (e.g. CS Unplugged [18]), the use of computing tools is nevertheless indispensable as they help learners test and revise their solutions involving CT concepts and practices (i.e. CT is primarily promoted through problem-solving with computing tools [10]).

Regarding CT assessment, there seems to be a vacuum in measuring and assessing CT achievement, which makes it difficult to judge the effectiveness of CT-based instruction [19]. In particular, because a standard definition of CT is lacking, measurements of this construct are diverse, which, as Shute and colleagues [7] underlined, not only raises questions regarding results obtained, but also makes them difficult to compare. These researchers also stressed that assessing CT in classrooms is challenging and that to support a teacher's instruction, real-time assessments that monitor students' progress may be required.

Having in mind Brennan and Resnick [12], appropriate assessments could be based on the analysis of students' project portfolios (involving artifact-based interviews with them), assuming that novice students progress in developing projects along, in our terms, an understand-debug-extend trajectory (i.e. from understanding a developed project via debugging this project to extending it). With more experienced students, a use-modify-create learning path [17] might be applied and assessed. To assess instruction that promotes CT among students by using computational tools in conjunction with content and pedagogy, we might use a technology integration rubric, whose criteria, as in [8], evaluate choosing and using tools and practices with respect to curriculum goals and instructional strategies, simultaneously aligning content, pedagogy, and technology.

3 Data Practice Using Interactive Displays

Despite the fact that a standard definition of CT is lacking, data practice, data analysis, or work with data can, as already mentioned, be recognised in a number of CT definitions (e.g. [7, 11, 13]). Even when work with data is not mentioned explicitly in a CT definition (e.g. as in Google's main CT elements: decomposition, pattern recognition, abstraction, and algorithm design; https://youtu.be/sxUJKn6TJOI), it is clear that, for example, pattern recognition, dealing with regularities and trends in data, are based on data practice, which may make use of suitable technology, such as interactive displays.

3.1 Interactive Displays and Their Educational Relevance

Interactive charts are digital devices for the visual presentation of data, whose content updates automatically after changes in considered data or variables. Interactive displays are digital artifacts comprising one or more such charts, possibly coupled with other interactive reports, such as tables or summary measures. Interactive displays composed of two or more interactive reports, usually interactive charts, are called dashboards.

Typically built in a drag-and-drop fashion, interactive charts can be, as a descriptive, exploratory tool, (relatively effortlessly) used to visualise regularities and trends in data, if any. Several interesting interactive charts may, for example, be found at https://www.dur.ac.uk/smart.centre/. The application of these charts, especially for dashboards (typically also built in the drag-and-drop fashion), has increased considerably in recent years (e.g. [20]; visit https://www.idashboards.com/dashboard-examples/, to view dashboards concerning various industries and areas). Learning analytics is, for example, one domain in which dashboards are widely used (e.g. [21]).

Because of such widespread and increasing use of dashboards, as well as possible learning and professional benefits, it is not surprising that there has been noticeable demand recently for the introduction of work with data using interactive displays in secondary education (e.g. [22–26]). Although this work has traditionally been associated with data analysis, possibly based upon complex mathematical and statistical models, it is unlikely that most students would be required to perform such analyses in their future jobs. They would rather do some basic data modelling using dashboards, whether produced by others or resulting from their own modelling, to support their professional claims and actions (e.g. "peer feedback has been used by less than one-third of e-learners"; "another drug dose must be administered to that patient"), which may particularly be relevant to the STEM disciplines [27].[1] This modelling just makes use of simple mathematical models (e.g. frequencies, sums, and means) connecting independent and dependent variables; each model is, after the developer's chart selection, automatically applied by the tool used. Although interactive displays are primarily a means for visualising data, they can also be tools for modelling purposes if used within a modelling cycle.

3.2 Considering Data Practice Through Modelling

Knowing that even simple data preparation (e.g. querying datasets, (re)organising data) may be quite challenging for novice modellers [25], data to model (with just a few variables) should be given to them. In that case, data modelling may only require them to complete three main activities, namely: asking questions; visualising data; and answering questions. In other words, there may be just three key stages in the modelling cycle, usually advanced in a nonlinear way. For experienced data modellers, remaining activities could eventually be added: validating modelling (recommending changes) after answering questions; and preparing data after asking questions [28].

To attain successful realisation of these activities, teachers need to identify their main underlying skills, and provide modellers, especially novices, with support to complete such modelling as easily as possible. Some of these underlying skills are, for example: choosing relations to examine; identifying dependent and independent variables (asking questions); selecting charts to use; selecting measures to apply (visualising data); recognising regularities in charts produced; and connecting regularities observed with corresponding questions asked (answering questions). These and other underlying skills should be fostered through suitable scaffolding, taking into account potential modelling challenges and reasons for these challenges (discussed elsewhere [25], for example). As the three activities depend on each other, many scaffolds would

---

[1] Job candidates with data practice skills (in particular data science and analytics skills) will soon be preferred by most employers in the United States, for example (see http://www.bhef.com/sites/default/files/bhef_2017_investing_in_dsa.pdf, for reported figures).

connect their underlying skills (e.g. variables selection with charts production; charts production with regularities recognition). Of course, when interactive charts, especially dashboards, are created from scratch, data modelling becomes a design task, whose central activity of problem structuring [29] needs meticulous scaffolding, possibly with (special) attention paid to the role of context in doing so. To ease contextual challenges, the data to model may be coupled with a short description of the underlying context. Furthermore, modellers may be scaffolded to develop problem structuring skills (e.g. selecting variables, measures, table, and charts to use) while improving knowledge of context under scrutiny (e.g. clarifying what other issues to examine, how they have been measured, and for what points in time to use data available), and vice versa (derived from [30]).

3.3 Performing and Assessing Data Practice Through Modelling

As underlined above, CT should be cultivated within rich computational environments [17]. Regarding dashboards, Zoho Analytics is, for example, such an environment (https://www.zoho.com/analytics/).[2] Apart from using and combining various interactive reports, it supports data preparation by querying relevant datasets. It also enables collaborative work on dashboard projects, which, if skillfully managed (e.g. in designing, building and combining charts of increased structural complexity), would promote other valuable CT assets, such as computational strategies.

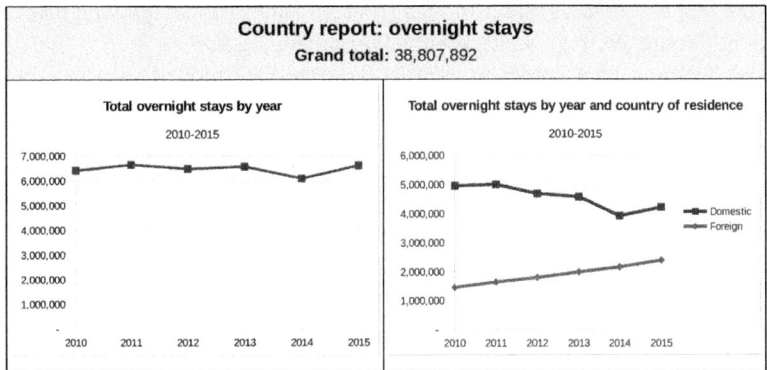

Fig. 1. Dashboard with two interactive charts and one summary measure: although not dominant, overnight stays by foreigners are increasing (modified from [25])

To illustrate some of these strategies, let us consider a dashboard presented in Fig. 1. Its design may be the result of decomposition (i.e. a divide and conquer strategy) of an issue under consideration (e.g. overnight stays in a country). This strategy is clearly applied in building each individual chart concerning its elements,

---

[2] Contrary to interactive charts, work with dashboards has only been supported by recent versions of some spreadsheet environments. To simplify dashboard creation, on-line publication and use, work with on-line dashboards has usually been realised in specialised, dashboard-tailored environments.

especially variables. Other strategies are top-down and bottom-up approaches. When we go from a dashboard as a whole to its individual reports as parts, a top-down approach is applied. When we start from some individual reports and combine them to create a dashboard, a bottom-up approach is used. (Instead of a single approach, we often apply a combination.) Furthermore, to get feedback and validation from peers and future users, building a chart or dashboard may make use of rapid prototyping, i.e. an iterative process through which we incrementally show what this display will look like. If we apply this interactive process to a chart, we may go from two variables (overnight stays by year) via three variables (overnight stays by year and country of residence) to four variables (overnight stays by year, country of residence and region, with values of the last variable used as a filter). In that way, we can examine whether the pattern of total overnight stays by year (the number of these stays is rather stable between six and seven millions in each year) holds true when we compare domestic and foreign guests, especially when we go from region to region.

As the dashboard development examines calls for simple system engineering, this development would only promote a basic understanding of these computational strategies. For a complex system, a top-down strategy could first be applied to identify its major units, followed by the main components of each unit. This strategy would then be repeated until the system is fully understood from top to bottom [31]. Note that contrary to decomposition, the three other strategies, especially rapid prototyping, have been under-represented in CT-related research (exceptions can be found [32, 33]; cf. CT facet named iteration [7]). For all these strategies to be put into practice, the use of a computing tool is indispensable, although some preparations for applying them may be done in an unplugged, paper-and-pencil environment.

Which learning path could be used to promote data modelling using interactive displays, and how may progression along this path be assessed? For work with digital artifacts in rich computational environments, Lee and colleagues [17] proposed applying the use-modify-create path (e.g. for our data practice, from playing with developed displays via modifying developed displays to creating displays from scratch). If we combine this path with the understand-debug-extend learning trajectory (i.e. from understanding a developed project via debugging this project to extending it [12]), we may arrive at the following learning path: *use displays* to understand or evaluate data modelling done – *modify displays* to debug or extend data modelling realised – *create displays* to perform full data modelling by yourself (cf. Dagstuhl perspectives, [34]). The evaluation of modellers' collaborative work may, as in Brennan and Resnick [12], be based on analysis of students' project portfolios, involving interviews with them about displays they have just evaluated, improved, or fully developed. To achieve this end, a rubric may be used with criteria that evaluate the success of pursuing each data modelling activity, making connections among them (e.g. in terms of major skills underlying these activities and links among them).

4 Closing Remarks

To empower learners for life in the digital age, various digital practices should be mastered. One of them, suitable for many (most) learners, especially in vocational education, is the data practice presented in this paper.

Although this practice is linked to CT in a mathematical context (and such studies are quite rare [35]), it may, embedded in other contexts with different learning cycles, contribute to the learning of computer science or statistics. For example, an extended context could ask for the preparation of data through a CT-based work with databases [36], whereby this practice becomes more relevant to computer science education where CT has become a critical component [37]. Or, instead of a modelling cycle, a data inquiry cycle could be used [23], making this practice relevant to statistics learning as well.

Apart from its relevance to developing CT, our approach seems to focus on CT pedagogy. Through considering a range of disciplines, it was recently proposed that pedagogical CT environments should primarily focus on interactive visualisations or simulations, modelling and troubleshooting of data sets, and searching for patterns in large data sets [38]. Clearly, our approach aligns with this focus.

To attain successful implementation of our approach in classrooms, professional development may primarily support teachers in realising and making connections between key data modelling activities in terms of their underlying skills (extrapolated from Niess and Gillow-Wiles [39]), being aware of potential challenges in this modelling and reasons for these challenges (e.g. [25]). To avoid some of these challenges (e.g. concerning data preparation and context understanding), teachers may be supported in preparing materials that will be given to students (e.g. data to model and short context descriptions). Detailed support may be provided for them to prepare scaffolds that would help students develop problem-structuring skills while improving context understanding, and vice versa. Professional development may also support teachers in applying particular learning paths and assessing their outcomes (e.g. *use displays* to understand or evaluate data modelling completed – *modify displays* to debug or extend data modelling done – *create displays* to perform full data modelling by yourself) [12, 17].

Apart from teachers and their appropriate professional development, successful implementation of our approach to data practice requires the support of other stakeholders (e.g. school administrators, policy makers, curriculum and assessment developers), who would eventually bring CT into classrooms and have it widely and skillfully applied (e.g. [13]). However, to support the claims that particular CT-interventions are beneficial to students, we need to improve assessment to provide solid evidence that specific CT components/facets were indeed promoted [7].

Acknowledgments. This contribution resulted from the author's work on the project "Improving the quality and accessibility of education in modernization processes in Serbia" (No. 47008), financially supported by the Serbian Ministry of Education, Science, and Technological Development (2011–2018). The author dedicates the contribution to his son Aleksandar.

References

1. Wing, J.M.: Computational thinking. Commun. ACM **49**(3), 33–35 (2006)
2. García-Penalvo, F.J., Mendes, A.J.: Exploring the computational thinking effects in pre-university education. Comput. Hum. Behav. **80**, 407–411 (2018)
3. Yadav, A., Hong, H., Stephenson, C.: Computational thinking for all: pedagogical approaches to embedding 21st century problem solving in K-12 classroom. TechTrends **60**(6), 565–568 (2017)
4. Wing, J.M.: Research notebook: computational thinking—what and why? Link Newsl. **6**, 1–32 (2011)
5. The Royal Society: Shut down or restart? The way forward for computing in UK schools. The Author, London (2012)
6. Voogt, J., Fisser, P., Good, J., Mishra, P., Yadav, A.: Computational thinking in compulsory education: towards an agenda for research and practice. Educ. Inf. Technol. **20**(4), 715–728 (2015)
7. Shute, V.J., Sun, C., Asbell-Clarke, J.: Demystifying computational thinking. Educ. Res. Rev. **22**, 142–158 (2017)
8. Mouza, C., Yang, H., Pan, Y.-C., Ozden, S.Y., Pollock, L.: Resetting educational technology coursework for pre-service teachers: a computational thinking approach to the development of technological pedagogical content knowledge (TPACK). Australas. J. Educ. Technol. **33**(3), 61–76 (2017)
9. Doleck, T., Bazelais, P., Lemay, D.J., Saxena, A., Basnet, R.B.: Algorithmic thinking, cooperativity, creativity, critical thinking, and problem solving: exploring the relationship between computational thinking skills and academic performance. J. Comput. Educ. **4**(4), 355–369 (2017)
10. Barr, V., Stephenson, C.: Bringing computational thinking to K-12: what is involved and what is the role of the computer science education community? ACM Inroads **2**(1), 48–54 (2011)
11. Computer Science Teacher Association, International Society for Technology in Education: Computational Thinking. Teacher Resources, 2nd edn. The Authors (2011). http://www.csteachers.org/page/CompThinking
12. Brennan, K., Resnick, M.: New frameworks for studying and assessing the development of computational thinking. In Proceedings of the 2012 Annual Meeting of the American Educational Research Association, Vancouver, Canada (2012). http://scratched.gse.harvard.edu/ct/files/AERA2012.pdf
13. Weintrop, D., et al.: Defining computational thinking for mathematics and science classroom. J. Sci. Educ. Technol. **25**(1), 127–141 (2016)
14. Kotsopoulos, D., et al.: A pedagogical framework for computational thinking. Digit. Exp. Math. Educ. **3**(2), 154–171 (2017)
15. National Research Council: Next Generation Science Standards: For States, by States. The National Academies Press, Washington, DC (2013)
16. Yadav, A., Mayfield, C., Zhou, N., Hambrusch, S., Korb, J.T.: Computational thinking in elementary and secondary teacher education. ACM Trans. Comput. Educ. **14**(1), 1–16 (2014)
17. Lee, I., et al.: Computational thinking for youth in practice. ACM Inroads **2**(1), 33–37 (2011)
18. Bell, T., Witten, I.H., Fellows, M.R., Adams, R., McKenzie, J., Jarman, S.: CS unplugged: an enrichment and extension programme for primary-aged students (2015). https://classic.csunplugged.org/

19. Román-González, M., Pérez-González, J.-C., Jiménez-Fernández, C.: Which cognitive abilities underlie computational thinking? Criterion validity of the computational thinking test. Comput. Hum. Behav. **72**, 678–691 (2017)
20. Wexler, S., Shaffer, J., Cotgreave, A.: The Big Book of Dashboards: Visualizing Your Data Using Real-World Business Scenarios, 1st edn. Wiley, Hoboken (2017)
21. Webb, M.E., et al.: Challenges for IT-enabled formative assessment of complex 21st century skills. Technol. Knowl. Learn. **23**(3), 441–456 (2018)
22. Davison, C.B.: Addressing the challenges of teaching big data in technical education. CTE J. **3**(1), 43–50 (2015)
23. Gould, R., Bargagliotti, A., Johnson, T.: An analysis of secondary teachers' reasoning with participatory sensing data. Stat. Educ. Res. J. **16**(2), 305–334 (2017)
24. Ridgway, J.: Implications of the data revolution for statistics education. Int. Stat. Rev. **84**(3), 528–549 (2016)
25. Kadijevich, D.M.: Data modelling with dashboards: opportunities and challenges. In: Engel, J. (ed.) Promoting Understanding of Statistics About Society. Proceedings of the Roundtable Conference of the International Association of Statistics Education (IASE), Berlin, Germany, July 2016. ISI/IASE, The Haag (2016). https://iase-web.org/documents/papers/rt2016/Kadijevich.pdf
26. Metz, S.: Editor's corner: Big data. Sci. Teach. **82**(5), 6 (2015)
27. English, L.D.: STEM education K-12: perspectives on integration. Int. J. STEM Educ. **3**(3), 1–8 (2016)
28. Kadijevich, D.M.: Data modelling using interactive charts. Teach. Math. **21**(2), 55–72 (2018)
29. Jonassen, D.H.: Toward a design theory of problem solving. Education Tech. Res. Dev. **48**(4), 63–85 (2000)
30. Restrepo, J., Christiaans, H.: Problem structuring and information access in design. J. Des. Res. **4**(2) (2004).
31. Faulconbridge, R.I., Ryan, M.J.: Systems Engineering Practice. Argos Press, Canberra (2014)
32. Kong, S.-C.: A framework of curriculum design for computational thinking development in K-12 education. J. Comput. Educ. **3**(4), 377–394 (2016)
33. Ozcinar, H., Wong, G., Ozturk, T.H. (eds.): Teaching Computational Thinking in Primary Education. IGI Global, Hershey (2018)
34. Brinda, T., Diethelm, I.: Education in the digital networked world. In: Tatnall, A., Webb, M. (eds.) WCCE 2017. IAICT, vol. 515, pp. 653–657. Springer, Cham (2017).
35. Hickmott, D., Prieto-Rodriguez, E., Holmes, K.: A scoping review of studies on computational thinking in K–12 mathematics classrooms. Digit. Exp. Math. Educ. **4**(1), 48–69 (2018)
36. Juxiang, R., Zhihong, N.: Taking database design as trunk line of database courses. In: Proceedings of the Fourth International Conference on Computational and Information Sciences, pp. 767–769. IEEE, Washington, DC (2012)
37. Webb, M., et al.: Computer science in K-12 school curricula of the 21st century: why, what and when? Educ. Inf. Technol. **22**(2), 445–468 (2017)
38. National Research Council: Report of a Workshop of Pedagogical Aspects of Computational Thinking. The National Academies Press, Washington, DC (2011)
39. Niess, M.L., Gillow-Wiles, H.: Expanding teachers' technological pedagogical reasoning with a systems pedagogical approach. Australas. J. Educ. Technol. **33**(3), 77–95 (2017)

Transformative Computational Thinking in Mathematics

A Comparison by Student Age

Andrew E. Fluck[1(✉)], C. K. H. Chin[2], and Dev Ranmuthugala[2]

[1] Faculty of Education, University of Tasmania, Launceston, Australia
Andrew.Fluck@utas.edu.au
[2] Australian Maritime College, University of Tasmania, Launceston, Australia

Abstract. The Calculus for Kids project showed how Year 6 (aged 12 years) students could master integral calculus through the use of multi-media learning materials and specialist mathematics software. When solving real-world problems using integral calculus principles and the software to perform their calculations, they demonstrated ability commensurate with university engineering students. This transformative use of computational thinking showed age-extension, because the students were enabled to redefine the curriculum by accessing content normally taught to much older children. To verify this was not an accidental finding, further work was undertaken with a relatively smaller cohort of (n = 44) Year 9 (aged 15 years) students. The results were similar to the earlier findings with an effect size of 24 (Cohen's d) recorded. The article explores the implications of these new findings, and the potential application to other subject areas and student age groups.

Keywords: Computational thinking · Transformative uses · Integral calculus · Students

1 Introduction

There is a problem with computers in schools. Schools can rarely guarantee every student access to a computer, so the curriculum is largely designed without assuming this equipment will be available. Yet outside school, students, citizens and professionals use digital technologies intensively. This study aimed to reconcile this incongruity, and to counter diminishing learning achievements in Australian schools.

School curricula change very slowly. They are not controlled by content experts, but by communities, politicians, educators and others. Therefore, new knowledge can take time to be adopted. In 2005, we celebrated the centenary of Einstein's special theory of relativity [1], but this is rarely found in primary schools. Technology and science continue to advance rapidly [2], often outstripping community discussion and legal controls. Disparities between the school curriculum and the lived world of children embedded in artefacts created from recent knowledge can lead to tension for them and their teachers. One way to bring new knowledge into schools may be to use computers. However, even computers are not making the desired impact in education.

An OECD report [3] showed a weak inverse relationship between computer investments in schools and student achievement in the Programme for International Student Assessment (PISA). This is, therefore, a wicked problem in education. When students regularly use computers to create text using keyboards, they are unlikely to develop the handwriting skills demanded in the current curriculum. So, these findings are not entirely unexpected. But how can learning achievements be improved and new skills and ideas enter the curriculum? A transformative perspective is necessary, looking beyond the current curriculum to new skills and higher order thinking [4]. These authors initially saw transformation as "an integral component of broader curricular reforms that change not only how students learn but also what they learn" and went on to suggest it could become "an integral component of the reforms that alter the organisation and structure of schooling itself" (ibid, p. 2).

It is suggested that new theoretical approaches are needed to compare transformative uses of computers in schools. Puentedura's Substitution, Augmentation, Modification, and Redefinition (SAMR) model [5] provides a framework for thinking about transforming school curricula with computers, but there is still neither a clear way of defining transformation, nor of measuring it. In this study, we tried using computers to change what students learnt in a very specific way. Material within the school mathematics subject is structured in a similar way across many jurisdictions. In particular, we could not find evidence of integral calculus being taught in primary school (up to age 12 years) in any widespread fashion. Therefore, the Calculus for Kids project used computers to teach this topic to both younger and older students. This article looks at the similarities and differences between the two groups.

2 Previous Work

Before explaining how this project could solve these entwined wicked problems, it is important to have an accepted way to measure the impact of an educational innovation. Meta-studies such as that by Hattie and Yates [6] have established 'effect size' (often using the statistical measure of Cohen's d) as a measure of innovation impact on learning achievement. A hinge point effect size of 0.4 has been identified as the minimum for a significant innovation [7]. Studies have shown that "supplementing traditional teaching… computers were particularly effective when used to extend study time and practice, when used to allow students to assume control over the learning situation… and when used to support collaborative learning" [3]. In these meta-studies, computer aided instruction was found to have an intervention effect size of 0.55 to 0.57.

When assessing the learning of any group of students, their achievements generally lie on a normal curve: a few do well; some under-perform; and most perform close to the average. After a group of students receives a successful teaching intervention, the group demonstrates higher achievement, so the distribution curve of achievement moves to the right. The quantum of the improvement is crucial to determining the effectiveness of the intervention. An effect size of 1.0 corresponds to an improvement of one standard deviation. Glass et al. [8] indicated that normal learning progress is about one standard deviation per year.

The Calculus for Kids intervention taught both Year 6 (aged 12 years) and Year 9 (aged 15 years) students to solve real-world problems using integral calculus with computer algebra software. This achieved a published intervention effect size between 1.85 and 25.53 [9] for the Year 6 students. The effect size of this transformative intervention was over four times the size of Hattie's hinge point (0.4) for a significant intervention [7]. The nearest other high effect size for new ways of using computers in class was reported by Puentedura [10] with 'redefinition' types of computer uses providing effect sizes of 1.6.

David Perkins provided the concept of 'person-plus' to embody the shared cognition of a learner assisted by their notebook [11]. In our project, we acknowledge this notebook could be a notebook computer, or any kind of specialised electronic assistive device. This 'person-plus' view supports arguments for open book assessment, because it is closer to real-world problem solving. The assistive device improves information retrieval and accuracy, and Perkins argues this leads to higher order knowledge. By extension, a student using modern digital technology can solve problems that are more complex. This models human adoption of other mind tools such as language, numbering systems and so on. Moursund's extension [12] divided problems into three groups: those which are more readily solved by humans alone; those best solved by computers alone; and those which are best solved by humans working in combination with computers. This project probed the transformative effects of students learning in partnership with their computers.

Computational thinking was popularised by Jeannette Wing [13] and encourages us to solve problems using method which can be automated. This approach promotes the application of computers beyond computer science. Wing sees computational thinking as recursive, parallel processing, choosing an appropriate representation for a problem, and modeling. Algorithms are explicitly labelled in computational thinking and involve decision steps. Many of these mental tools in computational thinking were used in Calculus for Kids, because the students had to decide how to represent problems in MAPLE and how best to model the real world.

This study grew from the Calculus for Kids work reported previously [9] with Year 6 students. That project trained teachers to use supplied multi-media materials to teach the core concepts of integral calculus and how to solve real-world problems using them. Students were provided with a copy of the MAPLE specialist mathematics software for learning and assessment. The assessment test was based on a first year engineering degree integral calculus examination.

While the overall results with Year 6 students have already been reported, some schools in our project undertook work with Year 9 students as well. This paper compares the performance of these older students with the younger ones.

3 Method

Schools were invited to become part of the project, with a teacher attending our university campus for one day of training. During the training day, we introduced the teachers to the animated Microsoft (MS) PowerPoint files they could use to teach each concept; introduced them to the ideas of integral calculus and trained them to use the

MAPLE computer algebra software. MAPLE was selected over Mathematica, Microsoft Mathematics and Maxima because it used conventional notation and because we were approached by a local re-seller of the product who supported our research.

We provided a MS PowerPoint slide deck for each lesson, together with a MAPLE worksheet and a Portable Document Format (PDF) page of example questions. Students were shown how to perform simple calculations using MAPLE, starting with those they already knew (addition, subtraction, area of a rectangle) and then moved immediately to the correct terminology for setting up algebraic expressions (see Fig. 1). Integral calculus was introduced as a tool for calculating the area under a function curve. This area might represent the distance travelled for a speed-time function curve. Our basic approach was to use the strips method, whereby a curve is approximated by successively shorter straight lines. The animated MS PowerPoint slides provided powerful visual representations to illustrate the techniques of integration. While this introduction to calculus as the area under a curve was very conventional, we skipped the task of calculating examples by hand. Students were shown the integral of the sum of any number of functions is equal to the sum of the integrals of the several functions. Some 'principles' of integral calculus were not taught, such as manipulation of trigonometric functions, since the MAPLE software could perform this activity. Nor was differentiation discussed, since it was outside the scope of the project. Teachers were provided with a comprehensive document with solutions to all the activities.

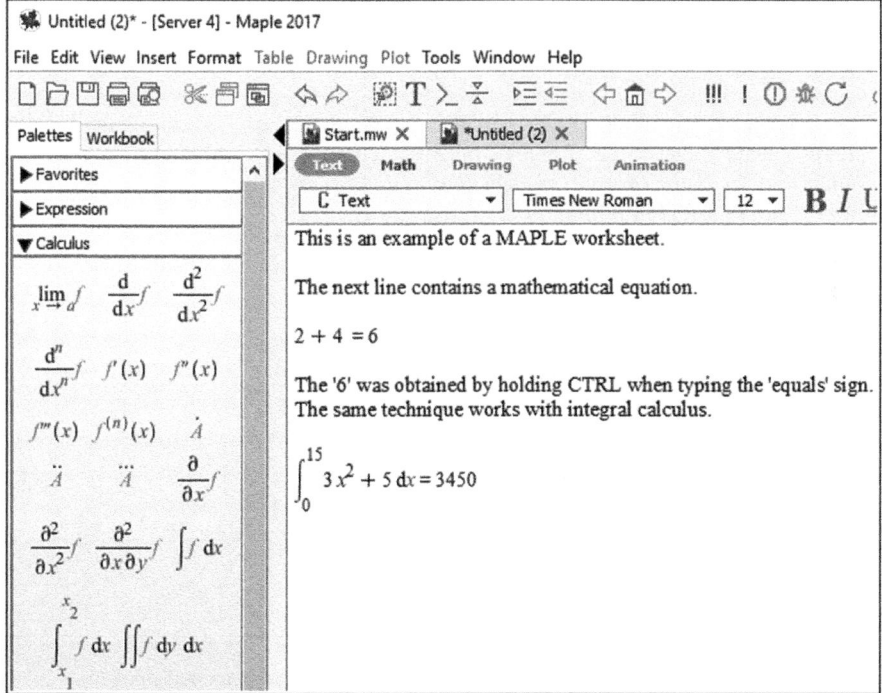

Fig. 1. Example of working in MAPLE with text and mathematical expressions

Figure 1 shows a screen from the MAPLE application. In the left-hand menu bar can be seen components for constructing mathematical expressions. The bottom-most left-hand icon is the template for a standard definite integral. When the user clicks on this icon, the template is transferred to the main page, whereupon the values of the lower bound (x_1) and upper bound (x_2) can be inserted. The mathematical expression for the target function 'f' can also be inserted to complete the definite integral. MAPLE recognises this notation and evaluates the numerical value of the integral when [CTRL] = is pressed. The MAPLE software is capable of symbolic manipulation in many other areas of mathematics. The advertising for the product claims "Maple has over 5000 functions covering virtually every area of mathematics, including calculus, algebra, differential equations, statistics, linear algebra, geometry, and much more" (www.maplesoft.com/products/Maple/features).

In the Calculus for Kids project, it is salient to recognise the software works with mathematically correct expressions and automates their calculation. From a student's point of view, a mathematically correct expression will generate a numerical result even if the expression does not fit the related real-world example. Similarly, a notationally deficient expression will not generate a numerical result, even if it has some semblance to the real-world situation. To obtain correct results, students need to use correct mathematical notation (on-screen) and frame their algebraic expressions to precisely match the real-world problem.

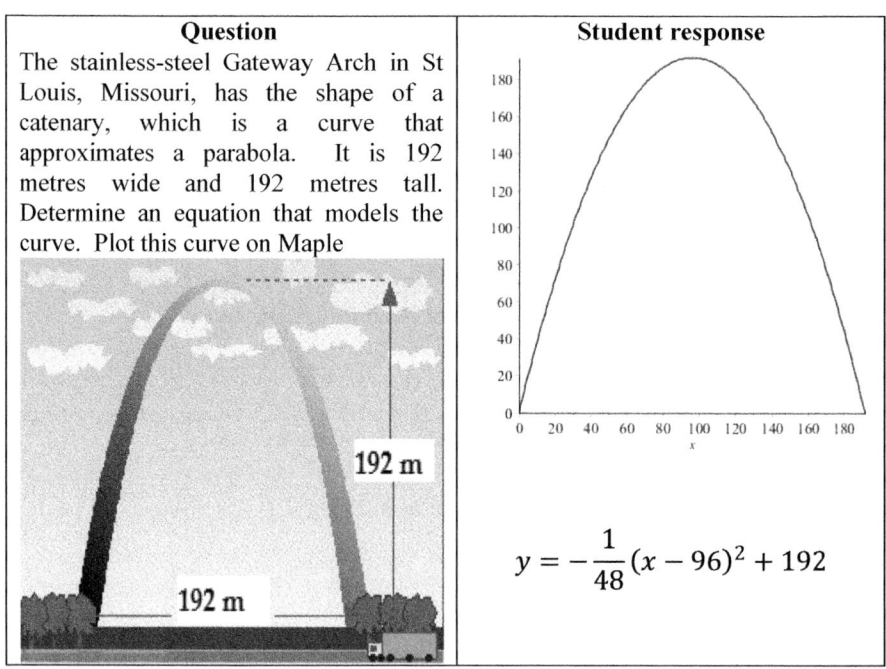

Fig. 2. A real-world problem to be solved in the Calculus for Kids project

Many of the activities contained real-world problems. Since our collaboration involved academics from the Australian Maritime College, such real-world problems often involved engineering or sailing boats. Other examples involved finding the area of a billboard to be covered with a poster, finding the amount of cloth to make a curtain for a stage, the amount of metal for a drain cover, and the quantity of grass seed for a curved garden path. Students calculated the area of a sail and the amount of fabric for the curved gable end of a tent. In some cases, students were expected to devise the parabolic equation representing a real-world situation. See Fig. 2 for an example of this question type, with a student response.

To solve these real-world problems, students needed to use their computational thinking skills of modelling to formulate the curves as a mathematical expression for MAPLE. It was important to select data points which correctly matched the limits of the function to be integrated, and ensure the correct units were applied to the result. One topic relevant to this discussion was that relating to parabolic curves. We used this as an early introduction to non-linear functions, and taught how the parameters of the descriptive equation could be found from two known points on the curve. It is important to remember that students did not have to work out the value of mathematical expressions by hand. Instead, they needed their computational thinking skills to put the right parameters and equations into MAPLE, so the computer could undertake the calculation for them. This provides a new way of understanding the skill of integral calculus, and shows how computational thinking can render old methods of learning redundant.

Moving now to ways in which our results could be compared with other teaching interventions, it was previously noted that effect size is the commonly accepted measure of the impact of an innovation. It is dimensionless, and therefore allows findings from different-sized cohorts to be compared fairly. However, in the context of transformative uses of computers in schools, it has some disadvantages.

The calculation of an effect size uses the following equation [14]:

$$\text{Effect Size} = \frac{[\text{Mean of experimental group}] - [\text{Mean of control group}]}{\text{Standard Deviation}}$$

When contemplating a transformative computer innovation, this equation can provoke speculation about the nature of the control group. Ordinarily, if students are randomly allocated to the experimental or control groups, the investigation would consider two different teaching methods. It goes without saying that the groups would be taught the same content in such a context, to show the difference in learning achievement between the two methods. However, in the current study, the definition of transformation that was adopted required new content to be taught; specifically, new content traditionally programmed for students at a much higher year level. Should the control group then comprise students in the higher year level? If so, there are two conflicting variables to consider: learning achievement and student age. If both groups are taught using the computer-based methods and tools, then it would not be easy to distinguish their impact on learning.

Another way to calculate an effect size without a control group is to compare learning achievement before and after the computer-based intervention. Where students are delivered content within the prescribed curriculum, standardised assessment tools can be used for this. However, age-accelerated transformative innovations cannot use such instruments. Therefore, Calculus for Kids used a method to calibrate each student to a notional academic year level scale. The initial measure was derived from national numeracy testing (www.myschool.edu.au), and effectively located each student as a bona-fide member of their chronological year group. Since the common post-test was derived from a first year university examination, it was possible to translate demonstrated learning achievement onto the same academic year level scale in the range Year 12–13 [9]. This study followed the same protocol. The mean numeracy score was used in conjunction with the Australia-wide mean numeracy score and standard deviation to deduce a pre-activity numeracy Year level for our students. A similar process was used to map the post-activity test score percentages onto the notional national numeracy scale, on the assumption that a 50% pass mark would map onto the Year 12/Year 13 boundary between high school and university. The demographics for the Year 6 and Year 9 samples are given in Table 1.

Table 1. Demographics for the two student groups

	Year 6 students	Year 9 students
N	434	44
Females	199	16
Lowest age at time of post-test	9.97	13.28
Highest age at time of post-test	13.82	14.95
Mean age (standard deviation)	11.96 (0.74)	14.27 (0.38)

There were more males in each cohort, with 54% males in the younger group, and 64% males in the older group. There was a slight overlap between the cohorts in terms of age, but at least 2 years between their mean chronological ages. This provided the opportunity to see if student age had any effect on the learning outcomes.

4 Results

Teachers of Year 9 students used the same protocols as for Year 6 students. Therefore, the three teachers attended a training session in Launceston, and then taught the material over 13 lessons (including a post-test lesson). The post-tests were sent to the research team and after marking were returned to the teachers with a community report for inclusion in newsletters to parents.

The data from each class were added to the national database for the project, and effect sizes extracted for the Year 6 and Year 9 cohorts (see Table 2).

Table 2 shows the numeracy aptitude for both cohorts was as expected for their respective ages. The older students demonstrated greater mastery of the high-end mathematics content than did the younger Year 6 students at the end of the intervention, but with greater variance among them.

Table 2. Effect size measures for younger and older students in the Calculus for Kids project

	Year 6 students	Year 9 students
Mean pre-treatment academic year level (s.d.)	6.47 (0.32)	9.49 (0.12)
Mean post-test academic year level (s.d.)	12.64 (0.12)	13.47 (0.39)
Pre/Post correlation (p)	0.56 (0.048)	0.69 (.000)
Effect size		
Cohen's d	25.53	13.79
Glass by annual maturation	6.17	2.98
Wiliam by annual maturation	1.85	0.89

The effect size has been calculated in three ways for each cohort. Firstly, the standard calculation using Cohen's d is given. Then, two annual maturation measures have been used. The first uses Glass et al.'s [8] supposition that one year of learning advancement corresponds to one standard deviation. Wiliam's refinement [15] showed annual growth in achievement between Grades 4 and 8 (as measured by standardised national testing) was 0.30 standard deviations. This has been used in the final part of the table.

5 Discussion and Conclusion

These very high effect sizes are unusual in the study of teaching innovations. However, they are derived from standard practice for comparing the effectiveness of different approaches to learning. When proponents make claims to have enacted a transformative change through the use of computers, the SAMR model predicts dramatic results, especially at the redefinition end. These very large effect sizes of 25.53 and 13.79, using Cohen's d, justify such claims. They are well above the 'hinge point' of 0.4 for an effective intervention, and greater than the intervention effect size of 0.57 ascribed to computer aided instruction. It can be deduced that computer use is highly effective in schools when used to teach transformative content, and much more so than when used to teach traditional content.

The Year 9 student cohort performed in a very similar way to the Year 6 cohort. This is promising in several ways. First, it shows the original Calculus for Kids project did not accidentally hit a mysterious 'sweet spot' which was only available for younger students for this topic of integral calculus. Second, the result validates the earlier work by showing a slightly different context does not change the outcome. Finally, it provides evidence this method of incorporating computational thinking [16] into the curriculum can be done at any age between 12 and 14 years with the same beneficial effect. Others may wish to see if these chronological boundaries can be expanded further.

To progress this work, we propose to continue working with Year 6 students using short and effective computer-based interventions involving specialist application software. Schools will be invited to participate in guided workshops that will generate specific plans appropriate for their own students. Key elements in each of the interventions will be:

- Short in duration (typically 5 to 7 lessons).
- Students to use a single computer software application for each intervention, generally free of cost to schools.
- Learning outcome will be a significant departure from the existing curriculum (4–6 years in advance of chronological age).
- Effect size will be calculated by comparing each student's National Assessment Program – Literacy and Numeracy (NAPLAN) ranking with a calibrated post-test of learning achievement accompanied by pre- and post-activity attitudinal surveys. We will modify the Attitudes toward Mathematics Inventory [17] to make it subject-generic and link with our previous work; also, the Mathematics and Technology Attitude scale [18, 19] will be similarly adapted.
- Participating schools will be drawn from a wide range, going beyond the 26 schools from 5 the states of Calculus for Kids, and drawing on mixed-ability classes from a range of ICSEA [socio-economic and loc ational status] backgrounds.

If we can demonstrate similar high effect size transformations by applying computational thinking in subjects across the breadth of the school curriculum, this would provide experimental evidence supporting curriculum change. We do not suggest every student should be taught in conjunction with a computer and powerful software in every lesson. However, there may be good reason to teach some topics, and perhaps introduce new knowledge into the curriculum where this is possible and desirable. Should we be able to demonstrate accelerated learning achievement of 4+ years with primary school students, similar processes can be put in place at other educational levels. For instance, first year undergraduates will be able to achieve learning outcomes at the Masters or even initial PhD candidate level. Year 10 students would be empowered to demonstrate understanding from first year degree courses. We seek to engender this quantum leap in learning in areas where humans working with computers can perform better than either alone. Our work with Year 6 students can be a lever for future work at all educational levels.

Acknowledgments. The authors would like to thank the Australian Research Council for supporting this study under LP130101088, the University of Tasmania and Australian Scientific & Engineering Solutions Pty Ltd. for financial assistance to support this study.

References

1. Einstein, A.: Zur Elektrodynamik bewegter Körper. Annalen der Physik **17**, 891 (1905). (English translation On the Electrodynamics of Moving Bodies by Megh Nad Saha, 1920)
2. Kurzweil, R.: Essay: The Law of Accelerating Returns (2001). http://www.kurzweilai.net/the-law-of-accelerating-returns
3. OECD: How computers are related to students' performance. In: Students, Computers and Learning: Making the Connection. OECD Publishing, Paris (2015)
4. Downes, T., et al.: Making Better Connections. Commonwealth Department of Education, Science and Training, Canberra (2002)

5. Puentedura, R.: Building transformation: an introduction to the SAMR model [Blog post] (2014). http://www.hippasus.com/rrpweblog/archives/2014/08/22/BuildingTransformation_AnIntroductionToSAMR.pdf
6. Hattie, J., Yates, G.C.R.: Visible Learning and the Science of How We Learn. Routledge, Abingdon (2013)
7. Hattie, J.: Visible Learning: A Synthesis of over 800 Meta-analyses Relating to Achievement. Routledge, Abingdon (2009)
8. Glass, G.V., McGaw, B., Smith, M.L.: Meta-analysis in Social Research. Sage, London (1981)
9. Fluck, A.E., Ranmuthugala, D., Chin, C.K.H., Penesis, I., Chong, J., Yang, Y.: Large effect size studies of computers in schools: *Calculus for Kids* and *Science-ercise*. In: Tatnall, A., Webb, M. (eds.) WCCE 2017. IFIP AICT, vol. 515, pp. 70–80. Springer, Cham (2017). https://doi.org/10.1007/978-3-319-74310-3_9
10. Puentedura, R.: SAMR: A Brief Introduction. [Blog entry] (2015). http://hippasum.com/rrpweblog/archives/2015/10/SAMR_ABriefIntro.pdf
11. Perkins, D.N.: Person-plus: a distributed view of thinking and learning. In: Salomon, G. (ed.) Distributed Cognitions: Psychological and Educational Considerations, pp. 88–110. Cambridge University Press, Cambridge (1993)
12. Moursund, D.: Introduction to Information and Communication Technology in Education. University of Oregon, Eugene (2005)
13. Wing, J.M.: Computational thinking. Commun. ACM **49**(3), 33–35 (2006)
14. Coe, R.: It's the effect size, stupid: what effect size is and why it is important. Paper Presented at the Annual Conference of the British Educational Research Association, University of Exeter, Exeter, England, 12–14 September 2002 (2002). http://www.leeds.ac.uk/educol/documents/00002182.htm
15. Wiliam, D.: Standardized testing and school accountability. Educ. Psychol. **45**(92), 107–122 (2010)
16. Webb, M.E., Cox, M. J., Fluck, A., Angeli-Valanides, C., Malyn-Smith, J., Voogt, J.: Thematic Working Group 9: Curriculum - Advancing Understanding of the Roles of Computer Science/Informatics in the Curriculum in EDUsummIT 2015 Summary Report: Technology Advance Quality Learning for All, pp. 60–69 (2015)
17. Tapia, M., Marsh, G.E.: An instrument to measure mathematics attitudes. Acad. Exch. Q. **8**(2), 16–21 (2004)
18. Barkatsas, A.: A new scale for monitoring students' attitudes to learning mathematics with technology (MTAS). Presented at the 28th Annual Conference of the Mathematics Education Research Group of Australasia (2004). http://www.merga.net.au/documents/RP92005.pdf
19. Pierce, R., Stacey, K., Barkatsas, A.: A scale for monitoring students' attitudes to learning mathematics with technology. Comput. Educ. **48**, 285–300 (2007)

Programming and Computer Science Education

Teachers' Perspectives on Learning and Programming Environments for Secondary Education

Riko Kelter[1(✉)], Matthias Kramer[2], and Torsten Brinda[2]

[1] Department of Mathematics, University of Siegen, Siegen, Germany
riko.kelter@uni-siegen.de
[2] Computing Education Research Group, University of Duisburg-Essen, Duisburg, Germany
{matthias.kramer,torsten.brinda}@uni-due.de

Abstract. Teaching and learning programming is a challenge. Although several learning and programming environments have been proposed for classes, there seems to be more dissent than consensus as to which tools are preferable over others. This paper investigates teachers' perspectives on popular learning and programming environments used in secondary computer science education in Germany. The environments investigated are: BlueJ, Scratch, Greenfoot, Eclipse, MIT App Inventor, Processing IDE, and Alice. Based on prior research, a catalogue of environment features supporting the learning processes of students was constructed. Using these criteria, an online-survey was conducted with computer science teachers in North Rhine-Westphalia, Germany. In the survey, the participating teachers evaluated the selected tools' adequacy for teaching object-oriented programming. The findings support the results of prior research conducted with students, stressing the importance of a simple and user-friendly graphical user interface (GUI) as well as the option to visualise classes and objects. Contrary to prior studies, the results show that teachers do not see the editor as equally important, as students do, and that there is no consensus about the role of the area of application for choosing an integrated development environment (IDE). Student-friendly debugging messages as well as a step-by-step execution of programs were identified as important features. Although no tool excelled for every criterion, the clear favourite was BlueJ.

Keywords: Educational programming environments · Teaching and learning programming · Object-oriented-programming

1 Introduction

Teaching and learning programming constitute a challenge. In Germany, a focus in secondary computer science education lies on object-oriented programming (OOP) in Java. While there is a variety of suitable learning and programming environments for this task, teachers are free to choose what best fits their personal preference. Given this situation, it is important to find out what exactly constitutes a beginner-friendly environment that supports the learning process. The advantages and problems of common integrated development environments (IDEs) have been discussed by Xinogalos et al. [1], Georgantaki [2] and Uysal [3], all of them focusing on students' perspectives. While the results show important features from the students' points of view, there is no information available about which features teachers regard as necessary to enhance the learning process. While students' perspectives are often based on a short period of use, most teachers use such environments for a long period of time and therefore have valuable knowledge about common fallacies or benefits of a given environment from a currently uninvestigated perspective. Therefore, teachers' perspectives are investigated in this paper, adding a new perspective to the debate about which aspects are important when selecting an educational OOP environment.

2 Background and Related Work

Extended research has been carried out investigating educational IDEs. To give a framework for orientation in computer science education research, Hubwieser et al. [4] constructed the so-called *Darmstadt model*, which defines "educational relevant areas". According to this paper, *teaching methods* and *media* are two crucial research areas in computer science education. Hubwieser et al. [5, p. 7] give a definition of what constitutes these areas: *"(12) Media: Technical Infrastructure, (…), Tools, Didactical Software, (…). Which (…) programming languages or environments, personal learning environments were found to support motivation (5), (…)?"* Nevertheless, no consensus has been established on what makes a good educational IDE. Xinogalos et al. [1] stress that there is no universally accepted framework for evaluating educational IDEs. Already in 2002, McIver [6] discussed how educational IDEs should be analysed. McIver [6, p. 2] points out that while there *"is some evidence that a well-designed programming environment can assist students learning to program (…) there have been few, if any, direct evaluations of whether the choice, or design, of programming development environments has a real impact on learning"*. Gross and Powers [7] additionally showed that the results even for environments which have been evaluated, cannot be replicated in a lot of cases. Georgantaki [2] built upon McIver [6] and investigated important features of IDEs. The results showed that the graphical user interface (GUI) and visualisation of program dynamics is important to students. Xinogalos [8, 9] showed in multiple studies that the educational IDE used does have an impact on learners' outcomes. To make analyses of environments more standardised, Uysal [3] proposed a framework for evaluating educational IDEs. Xinogalos [10] also isolated multiple important features of programming environments by conducting a study in which students compared a selection of IDEs in terms of effectivity and adequacy for different goals like programming in general, OOP or fundamental object-oriented concepts.

3 Goals

One key aspect missing in prior research is the influence of the learning or programming environment used on students' success compared to other factors. To judge the relevance of results, it is important to know which role the environment used plays at all. Also, while prior studies focused on isolating important features of such tools based upon students' views, the perspective of teachers has not currently been investigated. Therefore, direct evaluations of learning and programming environments – exploring which framework components are crucial, as well as benefits and disadvantages – from the perspective of teachers are missing. Additionally, there is a clear lack of knowledge about the spread and use of such tools in classrooms. Thus, four research questions have been formulated for the study:

- **RQ1:** What influence does the educational OOP environment have on students' learning success compared to other factors, according to teachers?
- **RQ2:** What features should an educational OOP environment have, according to teachers?
- **RQ3:** Which educational OOP environments are used and preferred for classrooms by teachers?
- **RQ4:** Which benefits and disadvantages exist for selected educational OOP environments, according to teachers?

To investigate the influence of the environments on students' successes in relation to other factors, **RQ1** was formulated. To answer **RQ2**, based upon the results from Xinogalos et al. [1], Uysal [3] and Georgantaki [2], a framework of six components for an educational programming environment was constructed for the study: graphical user interface (*GUI*), visualisation tools (*visual*), editor (*editor*), compiler and error messages (*compiler*), execution system and debugger (*debugger*), and area of application (*area*). Based upon the evaluated tools previously listed [2, 9, 10], six educational environments were then selected to answer **RQ3** and **RQ4**: BlueJ, Greenfoot, Scratch, Eclipse, MIT App Inventor, Processing, and Alice.

4 The Study

The chosen format of the study was an online survey, which was answered by 102 secondary education computer science teachers in North Rhine-Westphalia, Germany, from which 79 were filled out completely. The format was chosen to reach as many teachers as possible, as well as making the process of filling out the survey as easy as possible. The 79 questionnaires built the basis of the analysis, out of which 57 were filled in by male and 18 by female teachers (on 4 questionnaires no gender was selected). Fifty-two of the 79 teachers had mathematics as their second teaching subject, 12 had physics, with the rest split equally on other subjects.

4.1 Influence of the Environment on Learning Success Compared to Other Factors According to Teachers

The target of **RQ1** was to investigate whether, according to teachers, the environment plays a significant role for students' successes, compared to other factors. Teachers were asked to rate the importance of different factors for the learning success of students. The given factors were the used *API*, the used *textbook*, the used *IDE* as well as the student's (*student*) and teacher's personality (*teacher*). The used application programming interface (*API*) refers to the programming library used in class to enhance a student's learning process. Just as different textbooks and IDEs exist, there also exist a variety of available *APIs* for teaching OOP (e.g. GLOOP for Java), often with helpful examples and projects for classroom usage. Next to the *IDE*, teachers are free to choose an *API* for their lessons in Germany, so it is reasonable to investigate its influence compared to the selected *IDE* and textbook, as well as the personality of teachers and students. The answers were Likert-scaled, with 1 = unimportant, 2 = rather unimportant, 3 = rather important, and 4 = important. The results showed that while the used textbook seems to play a rather unimportant role according to the teachers, with a mean of 2.26, the used *IDE* and *API* have a definitive impact on students' outcomes (means of 2.84 and 2.90). In total, the student's and teacher's personality are the most important factors for teachers, with means of 3.60 and 3.69.

4.2 Evaluation of Framework Features

To answer **RQ2**, the identified framework features were evaluated. Teachers could agree or disagree to given statements about educational OOP environments on a Likert-scale including 1 (=don't agree), 2 (=rather don't agree), 3 (=rather agree) and 4 (=agree). The statements were constructed based upon the six selected components, which were based on prior research (see Sect. 3):

A programming environment for learning OOP should

- *have a simple, intuitive user interface,*
- *have the option to visualise objects and classes,*
- *have the option to execute a program step-by-step,*
- *have a code editor, which allows next to the entry of text also puzzle-like code snippets,*
- *provide comprehensive, beginner-friendly error messages instead of normal error messages of the compiler,*
- *have a wide area of application and therefore allow the development of different kind of program type (e.g. animations, web applications, apps).*

The results are shown in Fig. 1. The order of components on the x-axis in Fig. 1 follows no specific logic. The highest agreement can be found in the categories *GUI* and *visual* with means of 3.73 and 3.61. Similar is the rating for a debugger that allows step-by-step execution of the program (*debug*), with a mean of 3.46. Beginner-friendly error messages have a mean rating of 3.16 and the rating for the area of application (*area*) has a mean of 2.66. Nearly half of the teachers rather agree here, and the other half rather does not agree, so the opinion is split. With a mean of 2.20, the *editor* component has the lowest mean of all six components. Therefore, an editor supporting puzzle-like code snippets is not seen as a necessary feature, according to the teachers' perspectives, contrary to the students' points of view described in Xinogalos et al. [1], Uysal [3], and Georgantaki [2].

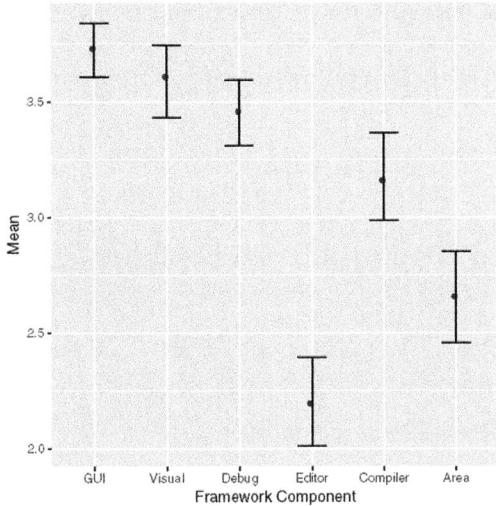

Fig. 1. Rating of framework components according to teachers

4.3 Use and Preference of Educational OOP Environments

Figure 2 shows that 85% of teachers already used BlueJ in class. Greenfoot and Scratch have been used by 58% and 59% respectively, and Eclipse has been used by 39%. There were plenty of other IDEs not listed in the survey, and 42% of the teachers did already use some other IDE. This underlines the vast dissent currently existing in the use of IDEs in classrooms. Teachers listed additionally Java Editor (16 teachers), Netbeans (7 teachers), Java Karol (4 teachers) or the Lego Mindstorms IDE (4 teachers).

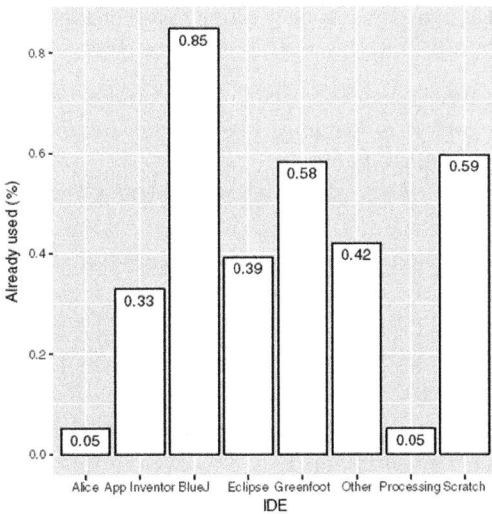

Fig. 2. Spread of different programming environments

When asked for their personal preference for classroom use, teachers' answers showed the distribution in Fig. 3. Clearly, BlueJ seems to be the most preferred OOP environment (48), while Eclipse (6) and Greenfoot (8) are preferred by a few teachers.

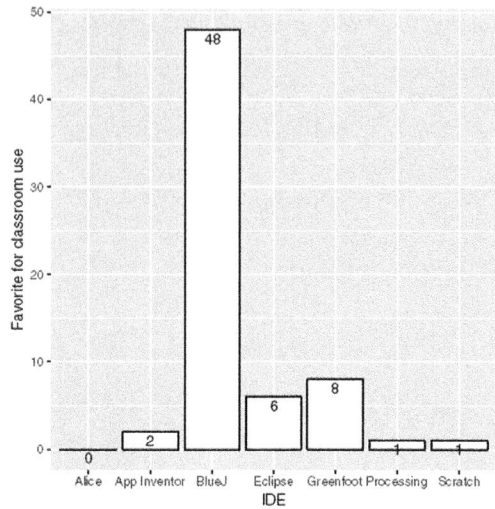

Fig. 3. Favourite programming environments of teachers for classroom use

4.4 Evaluation of the Selected Environments

Depending on the environments they already used in class, teachers had to answer additional questions. If a teacher selected BlueJ, he or she had to rate the following statements on a 5-point Likert-scale using 1 = do not agree, 2 = rather do not agree, 3 = neutral, 4 = rather agree, 5 = agree (and the same for every other environment, but with replacement of 'BlueJ' for the appropriate name in the following):

- *BlueJ has a structured, student-friendly user interface.*
- *BlueJ offers the option to visualise objects and classes supporting the understanding of the program dynamics.*
- *BlueJ offers the option to execute a program step-by-step to retrace the program flow.*
- *BlueJ offers a code editor which allows the use of puzzle-like codeblocks, to write a program.*
- *BlueJ shows student-friendly error messages easy to understand.*
- *BlueJ can be used for the development of a variety of program types, e.g. apps, web applications or animations.*

Table 1 shows the evaluation of the selected environments with regard to the framework components given in Fig. 1.

Table 1. Teachers' evaluation of the selected environments with regard to the framework components

IDE		GUI	Visual	Debugger editor		Compiler area	
Framework-components	3.73	3.61	3.46	2.20	3.16	2.66	
BlueJ	4.12	3.88	3.75	1.64	2.40	2.36	
Greenfoot	4.31	4.10	3,64	1.61	2.45	1.92	
Scratch	4.37	3.08	3.36	4.78	3.03	2.45	
MIT App Inventor	4.00	3.06	2.41	4.72	2.65	3.11	
Eclipse	4.84	3.00	4.44	2.04	2.42	4.84	

4.5 Evaluation of BlueJ and Greenfoot

The evaluation of BlueJ and Greenfoot can be seen in Table 1. The mean of every framework component is listed for the selected environment as well as the mean for agreement to the framework components themselves, as shown in Fig. 1.

BlueJ excels in most categories, especially the GUI, visualisation options and a step-by-step execution option. The environment lacks user-friendly compiler messages and a broad application area, but, especially in the last case, it is unclear if this component is necessary for a good educational OOP environment. BlueJ also offers no editor allowing puzzle-like statements, fitting into the results of Fig. 1.

The results for Greenfoot show a similar picture. According to the teachers, Greenfoot has a good GUI, visualisation options and step-by-step execution option. The editor here also allows no puzzle-like code blocks and therefore is rated poorly. However, there seems to be a consensus that such a component is not necessary at all for a good educational OOP environment (see Fig. 1). While the area of application is smaller than BlueJ's, the compiler seems to offer a degree of user-friendlier error messages.

4.6 Evaluation of Scratch and the MIT App Inventor

Scratch scores very high on the *editor* component with a mean of 4.78 (see Table 1). Offering its unique puzzle-like code-drag-and-drop system, it excels in this category. The *GUI* is structured and user-friendly according to the results. A weak point according to the teachers is the area of application (*area*). Taking a look at the step-by-step execution option (*debugger*), user-friendly error messages (*compiler*) and visualisation options for objects and classes (*visual*), Scratch is rated as 'good'.

The MIT App Inventor also has a very high rating in the *Editor* category, with a mean of 4.72 (see Table 1). However, it is only used by a few teachers, which may bias the results. The MIT App Inventor's editor seems to be highly capable of supporting students' learning successes by allowing the use of puzzle-like code blocks for building apps. Problematic indeed is the fact that most teachers do not see such an editor as a necessary feature for a good educational OOP environment (see Fig. 1 and compare the mean). The *GUI* is still rated 'good', with a mean of 4.06. While the area of application (*area*) still has a mean of 3.11, there is a slight tendency of teachers not to agree with the fact that the MIT App Inventor allows step-by-step execution to support students' learning processes, as can be seen by the mean of 2.41 of the *debugger* component.

4.7 Evaluation of Eclipse, Processing and Alice

Eclipse differs a lot from the teachers' general rating for the different framework components, as can be seen in Table 1. While its *GUI* and *debugger* are rated high, with means of 4.84 and 4.44, the error-messages (*compiler*) seem not to be beginner-friendly, with a mean of 2.42, and the visualisation options (*visual*) are also rated worse than every other environment with a mean of 3.00. The *editor* also is not capable of using puzzle-like code blocks; therefore its rating is quite low. A definitive strength can be seen with the high rating for the area of the application *area*, which has a mean of 4.84.

For Alice and Processing, there was so little data that summarising them would not have been useful. In total, 3 teachers gave feedback about the Processing environment. Alice was evaluated only by 2 teachers, who basically underlined that it is more appropriate for non-secondary education. Therefore, no data for Processing and Alice are included in Table 1.

5 Discussion and Conclusions

The study presented in this paper investigated the perception of secondary-school computer science teachers regarding seven popular educational learning and programming environments, with a focus on OOP, and the features that an ideal introductory environment should have. The study findings were based on an online questionnaire filled in by 79 secondary education computer science teachers in North Rhine-Westphalia, Germany. The results can be summarised as follows. Measuring the influence of the educational programming environment for learners' successes in OOP according to teachers was the target of **RQ1**. The results showed that while the textbook is seen as rather unimportant, the educational IDE used and the API used are seen as rather important. However, the personality of the student and teacher are regarded as even more important. Future research should further investigate how exactly the educational programming environment plays a role for students' successes and how the influence can be separated by the influence of the API used.

The necessary features of educational OOP environments were the target of **RQ2**. The constructed framework of six components was evaluated by the teachers. In summary, teachers did agree with the fact that the *GUI* and visualisation options are highly relevant for a good educational OOP IDE. Additionally, a step-by-step execution system and understandable error messages are regarded as important. Contrary to the results from Xinogalos [1], Uysal [3] and Georgantaki [2], the *editor* component was not seen as crucial and may not be a good candidate for the framework.

The use and preference of educational OOP environments was the target of **RQ3**. The most used OOP environment was BlueJ, but 42% of the teachers had also used other environments. When asked for preference in classrooms, the highest scorer was BlueJ.

The benefits and disadvantages of the environments were investigated in **RQ4**. Clearly, no single IDE excelled in every framework component. However, BlueJ and Greenfoot had 'good' to 'very good' ratings in most components. While Greenfoot seemed to be good as an introductory environment, BlueJ was also seen as a stable long-term solution by teachers, according to comments. Scratch (as well as the MIT App Inventor) were evaluated as 'good', especially with regard to the *editor* component, but they did not score as equally high as BlueJ or Greenfoot in other components. Eclipse was evaluated as the most professional, but also complex environment, and Alice and Processing had too few evaluations to construct meaningful results.

In the next step, the proposed framework of six components needs to be specified further by defining which features exactly make up a 'good' component. While an *editor* component supporting just puzzle-like code blocks is not regarded as necessary by teachers, there may be other features like auto-completion which may be regarded as helpful. Future work should further investigate these structures in detail.

References

1. Xinogalos, S., Satratzemi, M., Malliarakis, C.: Microworlds, games, animations, mobile apps, puzzle editors and more: what is important for an introductory programming environment? Educ. Inf. Technol. **22**(1), 145–176 (2017)
2. Georgantak, G.I.: Using educational tools for teaching object oriented design and programming. J. Inf. Technol. Impact **7**(2), 111–130 (2007)
3. Uysal, M.P.: Interviews with college students: evaluating computer programming environments for introductory courses. J. Coll. Teach. Learn. **11**(2), 59–70 (2014)
4. Hubwieser, P., Armoni, M., Giannakos, M.N., Mittermeir, R.T.: Perspectives and visions of computer science education in primary and secondary (K-12) schools. ACM Trans. Comput. Educ. **14**(2), 39–51 (2015)
5. Hubwieser, P., Armoni, M., Giannakos, M.N.: How to implement rigorous computer science education in K-12 schools? Some answers and many questions. ACM Trans. Comput. Educ. **15**(2), 5–17 (2015)
6. McIver, L.: Evaluating languages and environments for novice programmers. Presented in Fourteenth Annual Workshop of the Psychology of Programming Interest Group (PPIG), Brunel University, Middlesex, UK (2002)
7. Gross, P., Powers, K.: Evaluating assessments of novice programming environments. In: Proceedings of the First International Workshop on Computing Education Research, Seattle, WA, 01–02 October 2005, pp. 99–110 (2005)
8. Xinogalos, S., Satratzemi, M.: A Long-term evaluation and reformation of an object oriented design and programming course. In: Aedo, I., Chen, N.-S., Kinshuk, Sampson, D., Zaitseva, L. (eds.) Proceedings of the Ninth IEEE International Conference on Advanced Learning Technologies, pp. 64–66 (2009). https://doi.org/10.1109/icalt.2009.131
9. Xinogalos, S.: An evaluation of knowledge transfer from microworld programming to conventional programming. J. Educ. Comput. Res. **47**(3), 251–277 (2012)
10. Xinogalos, S.: Object-oriented design and programming: an investigation of novices' conceptions on objects and classes. ACM Trans. Comput. Educ. **15**(3), 13–34 (2015)

Multivocal Challenge Toward Measuring Computational Thinking

Bebras Challenge Versus Computer Programming

Yoshiaki Matsuzawa[1(✉)], Kazuyoshi Murata[1], and Seiichi Tani[2]

[1] School of Social Informatics, Aoyama Gakuin University, Tokyo, Japan
matsuzawa@si.aoyama.ac.jp
[2] Department of Information Science, Nihon University, Tokyo, Japan

Abstract. Towards the establishment of an evaluation platform for computational thinking (CT), in this paper, we use the "Bebras Challenge" coined by Dr. Dagienė as a measurement tool of CT skills. This paper presents a "triangle examination" which includes three kinds of testing methods (programming testing, traditional paper testing, and Bebras Challenges). Approximately one hundred and fifty non-computer science (CS) undergraduate students participated in the examination as a part of an introductory programming course. The result indicated a weak but positive correlation (.38–.45) between the three methods. Additional qualitative analysis for each task in Bebras showed that requirements of algorithm creation and interpretation, and explicitness of the description, are two critical factors to determine a high correlation between other testing methods. We conclude our research by showing a clear correlation between the Bebras Challenge and actual programming.

Keywords: Programming · Literacy · Computational Thinking · Bebras Challenge

1 Introduction

With the banner of "Computational Thinking (CT)" [1], a movement of promoting programming education as literacy for all citizens is increasingly growing all over the world. Following European and North American countries, the Japanese government issued a statement which includes compulsory programming education at elementary schools from 2020 [2]. The purpose of the education is not merely to increase computer science engineers in the future, but to increase 'good users' of computers. While advanced technologies have made a fundamental change in science practices over the past 50 years, a renovation of learning environments for both teachers and learners is required to empower computing [3]. Hence, the purpose of education is to develop citizens who can naturally employ new science practices and live in the knowledge society over the next 50 years.

However, the problem is how we can measure (or know) CT has been laid in front of teachers/researchers. Brennan and Resnick stated "there is little agreement about what CT encompasses, and even less agreement about strategies for assessing the development of computational thinking" on the basis of their long-term experiences in teaching children with Scratch [4]. Weintrop et al. [3] asserted that "much of the difficulty stems from the fact that the practices collected under the umbrella term CT [1, 5]". Recently, several studies on CT have been published under the IFIP umbrella (e.g. [6, 7]); however, in these papers, the discussion around assessment is limited. We think that a further clarification of CT needs a deeper discussion on assessment.

A number of research studies to evaluate student performance in undergraduate programming classes have been conducted using paper examinations. For example, Lister et al. [8] reported on reading and tracing, and Ford [9] tried to assess the achievement of classes incorporating tests used in cognitive studies in programming. However, there have been very few research studies that discuss methods of evaluating CT as formative problem-solving skills, instead of skills to tackle programming language elements.

Our purpose in this paper is the establishment of an evaluation platform for CT based on the "Bebras Challenge", a measurement tool of CT skills. A "triangle examination" is conducted, which includes three types of testing methods (programming testing, traditional paper testing, and the Bebras Challenge), and the correlation between them is analysed.

2 Theoretical Framework

2.1 Computational Thinking

There is some consensus between researchers that the movement of computing education is a revival of 1980s programing education with Logo [10]. The origin of this movement originated from Papert, who coined the term computational thinking [5], but was not primarily intended to develop programming skills but to open a new method of learning mathematics through programming. By working in situated environments, children could construct their ideas by directly operating these ideas in a situated world [11]. Papert criticised technocentrism of programming education, and he expressed the purpose as "to give children a greater sense of empowerment, of being able to do more than they could do before" [12].

More than 20 years after the first generation of programming education, as discussed above, Wing started to use the term CT [1] independently. Wing's CT has similarities with the term introduced by Papert, since both of them focus on the necessity of developing those general skills which are needed by all citizens in the knowledge society. Wing's CT was initially discussed in the computer science (CS) community, whereas Papert's term was considered from Piaget's constructivism perspective and has been discussed in the cognitive and learning sciences. This difference brought about a difference in focus: Wing's definition sounds like CS, technology-centric concepts; whereas Papert's use of the term is aimed to foster a greater sense of empowerment in solving problems through computing.

Weintrop et al. [3] offer a recent attempt to define CT by comprehending the literature over 30 years including the two generations of CT discussion, as mentioned above. They emphasised the change in science practices while advancing technology, and how to educate to develop a sensibility in order to literally survive in the world where changed practice is common sense. The higher level problem-solving skills are summarised as: "Data practices"; "Modeling and Simulation practices"; "Computational Problem Solving practices"; and "Systems Thinking practices". The practice to formulate a problem into computational models is defined as "Designing Computational Models", which is included in "Modeling and Simulation practices". "Computer Programming" or "Creating Computational Abstractions" is merely a part of "Computational Problem Solving". Accordingly, the large problem-solving cycle from the formulation of a problem to an evaluation of solutions was defined as "Computing" and then the competencies to conduct the process were defined as CT. Although the paper claimed it was originally designed for application of CT in science and mathematics, the definition is applicable to other disciplines.

2.2 The Bebras Challenge

The Bebras Challenge is an educational practice where students are challenged to do several small tasks, using CS/CT concepts to complete those tasks [13, 14]. It is also an international informatics contest where a large number of students participate from over 40 countries. Although the activity looks like quizzes that can be used in a classical classroom for grading students, we can see the difference in task design, being described as "wrap[ping] up serious scientific problems of informatics and the basic concepts into playful tasks, inventive questions thus attracting students' attention" [13]. Accordingly, the thoughtfully-designed tasks are playful and appreciated by students.

Bebras includes a "contest" where students can compete with each other through their scores, but that is not the main goal. The goal is "to motivate pupils to be interested in informatics topics and to promote thinking which is algorithmic, logical, operational, and based on informatics fundamentals" [13]. In other words, it can be explained as promoting the enjoyment of thinking, the learning of activities embedded in the procedure, and consequences performed as a formative evaluation of the learning process.

The Bebras international contest was created in 2004 by Dr. Dagienė, with a first report published in 2006 [14]. From the practice and research conducted over a decade, a review paper was published in 2016 [13], which included approximately 50 papers published during the previous ten-year period.

2.3 The Bebras Challenge as Assessment Tools

Although the Bebras challenge is not designed to assess students' knowledge or skills, Dr. Dagienė refers to the capability of Bebras as an assessment tool over a long time period [13]. One paper [13] describes how one of the most important and required cognitive operations in CSTA (Computer Science Teachers Association) K-12 Standards - using visual representations of problem states, structures, and data - investigates the "task-based assessment" approach to assess CT. Hubwieser et al. validated the use of item response theory, focusing on whether Bebras tasks could assess CT in CSTA [15, 16]. Dolgopolovas et al. [17] expanded on Hubwieser's work and tried a validation of Bebras as assessment tools of CT with first-year software engineering university students. This study included the following two research questions (RQs):

RQ1: How can the CT skills of novice software engineering students be evaluated independently of programming language?
RQ2: What is the relation between novice software engineering students' computational thinking skills and programming course results?

For RQ1, a study was attempted by Bebras with 65 university students. They succeeded in validating the test using item response theory, as described in a previous study [17]. However, for RQ2, they failed to find a correlation between Bebras and examination scores in the programming course. The paper [17] discussed how the failure resulted from the quality of questions in the examination, which asked for practical knowledge in programming (e.g. grammar and knowledge of a particular library) instead of algorithms, formalisation, or abstraction that are required in CT.

Djambong et al. [18] offers another influential study, which attempts a summative assessment of programming education where both grade 6 and grade 9 students engage in a robot programming activity using LEGO Mindstorms. Bebras was examined using a pre- and post-test after five hours (during a five-week period) in a classroom, but significant differences were not identified.

The study detailed in this paper can be seen as a revised version of this work. We conducted an experimental study using the same research question (RQ2), but we asked for actual programming construction in the examination in order to reveal any correlation between computer programming and Bebras activities with non-CS students.

3 Method

3.1 Research Question

Our research question is as follows:

RQ: Could we use Bebras as an assessment tool for computational thinking, and if so, to what extent? (What is the correlation between Bebras, the actual programming test, and the paper test?)

The aim of the RQ is an evaluation of Bebras as an assessment tool of CT by examining the correlation between Bebras, the actual programming test, and the paper test. Although the result of this question in the previous research [17] was negative, we hypothesised that a positive result could be achieved by improving the paper and programming tests by asking about CT instead of practical programming knowledge.

3.2 Experimental Study Environment

An experimental study was conducted in an introductory programming course designed for social informatics (non-CS) major students. The class was designed to develop language independent CT skills through the practical programming experiences with Visual Basic, and HTML (HyperText Markup Language) for all students in the major class (compulsory).

The time schedule of the class and the examination is shown in Fig. 1. The class was scheduled over 15 weeks (three hours per week), including an examination in the 16th week. Students engaged in programming with Visual Basic during the first nine weeks, and then engaged in web page authoring in HTML during the last four weeks.

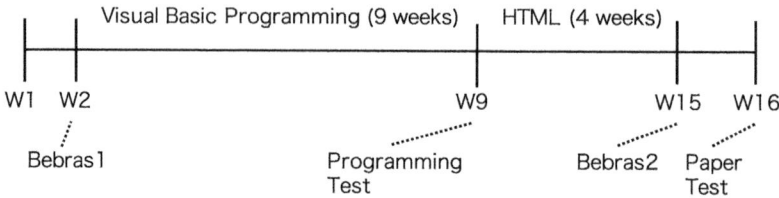

Fig. 1. Time schedule

The first trial of Bebras (Bebras1) was carried out in week 2 as a pre-test, and the second trial was carried out in week 15 as a post-test. The programming test was conducted in week 9 and the paper test was conducted in week 16. As there was a winter break in week 13, there was an approximate 10-week interval between the programming and paper tests. Despite this gap, we assumed the skill levels of the students were essentially the same, as the content of the class during the term was on web page authoring in HTML. As the Bebras trial was addressed as a part of the lectures, students were given as an incentive a maximum score of 10% of their grade.

3.3 Design of the Bebras Task

The Bebras task used in this study was from the senior level Japanese version of Bebras tasks. We considered that the difficulty of the senior tasks fitted well for first-year university students. Ten tasks were selected from Bebras 2015 and 2016 Challenges for the first trial (Bebras1). As a pilot trial had been carried out with a different student cohort one year earlier, the tasks which had a statistically high correlation were selected. Twelve tasks in all were selected from the Bebras 2017 Challenge for the second trial (Bebras2). All of the selected tasks are listed in the results section.

The time limit for the challenge was set to 40 min in both trials. The time was a little longer than that in the international challenge in order to encourage students to think deeply while doing each task. The web-based system used in the international challenge was used for the experiment. Students were given 10 min to practice the use of the system; consequently, there were no students who failed to answer the tasks.

3.4 Design of the Programming Test

The programming test examined during the 9th week of class was an examination to develop a program to meet the requirements presented to students using a specification sheet. All of the students were assigned a single computer, and then were asked to submit a workable code in Visual Basic. The students were allowed to access all course materials during the examination, although access to the Internet was prohibited.

Students were required to create four tasks, given on the specification sheets, within 85 min. The easiest task did not require using any loops, but to use branching. The most difficult task required using a collection (the course teaches Listbox for abstract data collection) and developing an algorithm to process inside the collection.

During the test, the students could use a development environment (Visual Studio). Therefore, the activity measured comprehensive skills of program construction: designing data structure and algorithms; correcting compilation errors; or debugging. Additionally, the time constraint required a certain level of fluency in their programming processes; we observed that some students gained full marks close to the time limit.

3.5 Design of the Paper Test

The paper test administered during the 16th week of the class was the traditional examination carried out using paper and pencil. Students could access all course materials during the examination as well as the programming test, while the use of all electronic devices was prohibited. The test was in six sections, lasting 85 min.

There were three kinds of tasks (code tracing, code complementing, and code ordering) among the sections analysed. Code tracing is a type of task where students read the code written in Visual Basic and then answer the outputs, values of variables at a particular state, or figures expected to be drawn by the code. Code complementing is a type of task where students complete a part of the code to complement the blanked, uncompleted code. Code ordering is a type of task where students initially order code fragments in random order to complete a workable code. In this manner, the tasks of the paper test were designed to assess algorithmic thinking, which is located within basic grammar knowledge.

4 Results

4.1 Descriptive Statistics

The study was conducted in our introductory programming class during the 2017 academic year. Approximately 200 students in the school are required to register for this course, with the students being randomly assigned to one of four separate classes in order to reduce the number of students in each class. Each of the four classes was managed by different teaching staff, but the course materials and examinations were the same.

Three of the four classes were randomly selected for the analysis. The descriptive statistics of the four examinations are shown in Table 1. In Table 1, "n" refers to the number of students, and the other number indicates the average score of the four tests: Programming; Paper; Bebras1; and Bebras2, respectively. A total of 137 students' data were used in the analysis. No significant differences in scores were found between the classes according to these descriptive statistics.

Table 1. Descriptive statistics

	n	Programming	Paper	Bebras1	Bebras2
Class A	43	49.2	50.5	64.9	55.4
Class B	45	53.3	50.4	71.6	57.4
Class C	49	44.7	44.0	62.3	55.3
	137	48.9	48.2	66.2	56.0

4.2 Correlation Analysis Between the Four Examinations

Figure 2 is a correlation table, showing the correlation and scatter plot between the four examinations. The correlation between Programming and Bebras was approximately 0.4. The correlation between Paper and Bebras was approximately 0.45. Although a strong correlation was not indicated, this is clearly a different result from the previous research [17], as no relationship was reported between the examinations in that study.

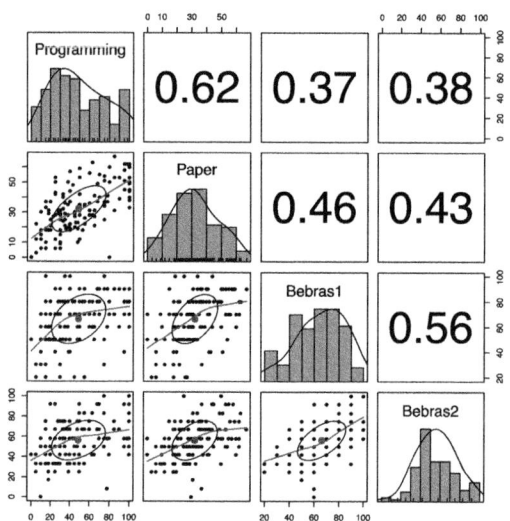

Fig. 2. Correlation table of the four examinations

Additionally, the correlation value can be considered as reaching a significant level when considering it in relation to the other correlations. The paired correlations between Programming and Paper, and Bebras1 and 2, respectively, are approximately .6. We assume the two pairs of tests were quite close in terms of methods, respectively. Therefore, these correlation values were high; however, they could be considered as not being higher than what we had expected. Notably, the correlation between Bebras1 and Bebras2 could be expected to be much stronger (.8–.9) if the validity of the tasks was improved. Accordingly, the correlation value between Bebras and other tests (.4–.45) can be considered sufficient to show a significant relationship between the actual programming and Bebras.

4.3 Detailed Analysis for the Tasks

A detailed analysis of the correlation between the programming test and each task in Bebras was performed. Table 2 shows the percentage of correct answers, and the significant differences between the paper test, programming test, and each task, respectively. The significant differences are indicated by the average scores between the group that answered correctly and the group that failed in answering for each task. The average score of the group that answered correctly was higher than the group that failed their answers in all the tasks.

Table 2. Percentage correct answers and average score significant differences by task

Q ID	Task ID	Name	Correct	Program	Paper
AQ1	2015-LT-04	Pencils alignment	0.78	**	**
AQ2	2015-JP-05	Ice Cream Shop	0.74	ns(p < .1)	*
AQ3	2015-CA-02	Fireworks	0.64	ns	ns
AQ4	2015-DE-05	Mobiles	0.39	ns	*
AQ5	2016-CZ-06	Finding the final state	0.76	ns(p < .1)	**
AQ6	2016-MY-02	Scanner code	0.85	*	**
AQ7	2016-NL-04	KIX Code	0.58	**	**
AQ8	2016-AT-06	Recursive painting	0.49	ns	*
AQ9	2016-JP-02	Paint it black	0.70	ns	ns(p < .1)
AQ10	2016-IT-02b	Red and blue marbles	0.69	ns(p < .1)	ns(p < .1)
BQ1	2017-RU-04	Grandmother's jam	0.42	ns	ns(p < .1)
BQ2	2017-JP-04	Colorful Building	0.64	ns	ns(p < .1)
BQ3	2017-AT-03	Files	0.67	ns	ns
BQ4	2017-MY-05	Moving Die	0.60	**	ns
BQ5	2017-IR-06	Bebragram	0.80	**	**
BQ6	2017-CH-01a	Exit the maze	0.73	ns(p < .1)	**
BQ7	2017-SK-12b	Robot	0.54	**	**
BQ8	2017-KR-07	Icon Image Compression	0.48	ns(p < .1)	**
BQ9	2017-KR-02	A Stray Baby Beaver	0.69	*	*
BQ10	2017-DE-09	BikeFun	0.72	ns	**
BQ11	2017-RU-02	Digit recognition	0.09	ns	ns
BQ12	2017-IT-10	Library	0.37	ns(p < .1)	ns

*$p < .05$, **$p < .01$

The result of a qualitative analysis for each task was conducted by the first author, although he was not a specialist in Bebras tasks, or in the interpretation of the results from the viewpoint of the correlation between Bebras, Programming, and CT.

Overall, the results of the programming and paper test indicate a similar tendency in the correlations. For example, significant differences were consistently found in AQ1, AQ6, AQ7 and BQ5, BQ7, BQ9, whereas no significant differences were consistently observed in AQ3, AQ9, AQ10, and BQ1, BQ2, BQ3, BQ11, or BQ12.

The tasks showing significant difference involved algorithm comprehension, creation, and abstraction. A typical example is AQ1 "Pencils alignment" where the task asks about the result of sorting algorithms written in natural language. There was a direct relationship to the topic of sorting algorithms that was taught in the lecture. Tasks which included an algorithm in a geometric field such as AQ5 "Finding the final state" or BQ6 "Exit the maze", were expected to show strong correlation. For the two tasks, only the paper test indicated significant differences, so further consideration is needed for this in terms of interpretation.

The tasks indicating no significant differences included relatively little algorithm comprehension, but also included other CT concepts, for example, data structure expressions, such as AQ4 "Mobiles." Although the lecture included basic data structure expressions with linear collection, further data structure expression, used to model the actual world, seemed to be difficult in introductory programming for non-CS students. For other examples, AQ2 "Ice Cream Shop" requires the concept of database structure, and BQ1 "Grandmother's jam" requires the concept of task scheduling.

Another possible deterministic factor to be considered was whether an expression of a task was explicit or not. For example, in BQ7 "Robot", the rule to be applied is simple and also clearly given by illustrations, whereas in BQ3 "Files" students have to construct a procedural algorithm by declarative rules. Another example, BQ12 "Library" was seen to create difficulty in description, although this may have been caused by local translation.

5 Discussion

The RQ of the study was "Could we use Bebras as an assessment tool for computational thinking? And if so, to what degree?" As shown in Sect. 4.2, the results indicate a positive correlation (.38–.45) between the three methods. As we discussed, this was an opposite result from previous research [17]. One notable difference of the two separate research studies is the design of the test; the test in this research required algorithm creation with actual programming, whereas the previous research required declarative information for a programming language. The results of the qualitative analysis for each task in Bebras support this consideration. The analysis revealed two critical factors: a requirement of algorithm creation and interpretation; and the explicitness of the description. Hence, we conclude here that the research showed clearly the difference between the Bebras Challenge and actual programming.

As was expressed earlier, a significant assumption in this research was that the actual programming requires a certain level of assessment ability in CT in higher-level problem-solving skills [3]. One significant criticism is that Bebras can be more accurate in measuring language-independent CT than actual programming. However, even if Bebras tasks enable users to operate CT concepts in a language-independent way, the concepts should be finally applied in practical situations: computer programming. Bebras Challenge trials lead to basic understanding of CT concepts, while subsequent programming experiences make the understandings deeper, and consequently they appear as a Bebras score. This cycle is expected in the design of Bebras. Accordingly, we believe our results will encourage all programming researchers/practitioners who are engaged in supporting language-independent and creative programming practices instead of conveying only syntax knowledge.

Acknowledgments. This work was supported by JSPS KAKENHI Grant Numbers 16K00488, and 17H06107.

References

1. Wing, J.M.: Computational thinking. Commun. ACM **49**(3), 33–35 (2006)
2. Prime Minister of Japan and His Cabinet: 26th Council for Industrial Competitiveness (2016). http://www.kantei.go.jp/jp/singi/keizaisaisei/skkkaigi/kaisai.html
3. Weintrop, D., et al.: Defining computational thinking for mathematics and science classrooms. J. Sci. Educ. Technol. **25**(1), 127–147 (2016)
4. Brennen, K., Resnick, M.: New Frameworks for Studying and Assessing the Development of Computational Thinking, Presented at the Annual Meeting of the American Educational Research Association (2012)
5. Papert, S.: Mindstorms: Children, Computers, and Powerful Ideas. Basic Books, New York (1980)
6. Angeli, C., et al.: A K-6 computational thinking curriculum framework: implications for teacher knowledge. J. Educ. Technol. Soc. **19**(3), 47–57 (2016)
7. Fluck, A., et al.: Arguing for computer science in the school curriculum. J. Educ. Technol. Soc. **19**(3), 38–46 (2016)
8. Lister, R., Adams, E., et al.: A multi-national study of reading and tracing skills in novice programmers. SIGCSE **2004**, 119–150 (2004)
9. Ford, M., Venema, S.: Assessing the success of an introductory programming course. J. Inf. Technol. Educ. **9**, 133–145 (2010)
10. Tedre, M., Denning, P.: The long quest for computational thinking. In: Proceedings of the 16th Koli Calling Conference on Computing Education Research, pp. 120–129 (2016)
11. Papert, S.: Perestroika and epistemological politics. In: Harel, I., Papert, S. (eds.) Constructionism, pp. 13–28. Ablex, Norwood (1991)
12. Papert, S.: A Critique of technocentrism in thinking about the school of the future. talk presented at children in an information age: opportunities for creativity, innovation, and new activities, Sofia, Bulgaria (1987)
13. Dagiene, V., Stupuriene, G.: Bebras a sustainable community building model for the concept based learning of informatics and computational thinking. Inf. Educ. **15**(1), 25–44 (2016)
14. Dagiene, V.: Information technology contests – introduction to computer science in an attractive way. Inf. Educ. **5**(1), 37–46 (2006)
15. Hubwieser, P., Mühling, A.: Playing PISA with Bebras. In: Proceedings of the 9th Workshop in Primary and Secondary Computing Education, WiPSCE 2014, pp. 128–129 (2014)
16. Hubwieser, P., Mühling, A.: Investigating the psychometric structure of bebras contest: towards measuring computational thinking skills. In: International Conference on Learning and Teaching in Computing and Engineering, pp. 62–69 (2015)
17. Dolgopolovas, V., Jevsikikova, T., Dagiene, V., Savulioniene, L.: Exploration of computational thinking of software engineering novice students based on solving computer science tasks. Int. J. Eng. Educ. **32**(3A), 1107–1116 (2016)

18. Djambong, T., Freiman, V.: Task-based assessment of students' computational thinking skills developed through visual programming or tangible coding environments. In: Sampson, D.G., Spector, J.M., Ifenthaler, D., Isaias, P. (eds.) Proceedings of the International Conference on Cognition and Exploratory Learning in the Digital Age (CELDA), pp. 41–51 (2016)

Investigating Learners' Behaviours When Interacting with a Programming Microworld

An Empirical Study Based on Playing Analytics

Fahima Djelil[1(✉)], Pierre-Alain Muller[1], and Eric Sanchez[2]

[1] University of Haute-Alsace, IRIMAS Laboratory, Mulhouse, France
{fahima.djelil,pierre-alain.muller}@uha.fr
[2] CERF, University of Fribourg, Fribourg, Switzerland
eric.sanchez@unifr.ch

Abstract. In our attempt to support Object-Oriented Programming (OOP) learning for beginners, we designed a novel microworld called PrOgO. It is based on a three-dimensional (3D) constructive game metaphor for describing OOP basic concepts and their implementation. In this paper, we describe a study about the use of PrOgO by beginners to investigate their behaviours when interacting with the programming microworld. The study is based on the collection, analysis and reporting of data about players (playing analytics). The data analysis allows the identification and the characterisation of different behaviours. From an educational perspective, the expected behaviour has been confirmed for a limited number of students. This enabled us to conclude that the design of the game needs to be improved. In addition, behaviours triggered by most students might have other educational values, which could be confirmed by other similar studies.

Keywords: Programming microworlds · Game-based learning · Learning analytics · Object-Oriented Programming · PrOgO

1 Introduction

Teaching and learning introductory Object-Oriented Programming (OOP) is recognised to be a difficult task [1]. Generally, abstract concepts describing OOP basics, and their implementation (coding) are the main difficulty faced by beginners [1]. This includes the concept of an "object", its properties and its relationship to the concept of a "class", as well as the relationship between classes. To overcome this educational difficulty, microworlds have often been used [2]. Representative OOP microworlds are Object-Karel, Alice and Greenfoot. A review of literature of these environments already exists [2]. These digital environments aim to give to beginners an intuitive and rapid understanding of abstract programming concepts, by allowing them to interact with representations of these concepts [2]. Following this trend and in our attempt to support OOP introduction for beginners, we created a new microworld called PrOgO. It is based on a three-dimensional (3D) constructive game metaphor and C++ programming language [3].

This paper reports on an empirical study on the use of PrOgO by beginners, to investigate its educational value. In particular, our goal is to know if the students' behaviours are relevant, by providing them with a good understanding of the addressed concepts. Playing analytics enables for the description of learners' behaviours. We collected and analysed interaction traces on the basis of event logs generated by PrOgO when students interacted with it. This work does not consider the link between learners' behaviours and their knowledge gain. This was carried out in another experiment which is already published [4].

The present paper is organised as follows. Section 2 gives a brief description of the PrOgO microworld. Section 3 is dedicated to the description of the study, including the addressed research question and the related hypothesis. Section 4 describes the methodology employed, including details of the context, as well as data collection and analysis. Results are summarised in Sect. 5 and then discussed in Sect. 6. Finally, conclusions are drawn in Sect. 7.

2 The PrOgO Microworld

PrOgO was created to address the needs of computer science teachers at the University of Clermont-Auvergne (France), where OOP is introduced in the C++ language. Teachers expressed a need for a playful tool, which is easy to use in a classroom with beginners, to represent abstract OOP basic concepts and their implementation in the C++ language. Therefore, PrOgO is designed with the intention to help beginners to understand the conceptual model triggering the OOP paradigm basics.

In terms of game purpose, it is expected that the player builds and animates 3D graphical robots or mechanical structures. In terms of metaphor and learning content integration, each 3D elementary graphic consists of a visual representation of a "computing object" (an instance of a "computing class"). A computing object has attributes and methods that define its appearance and also behaviours. This is what is represented, to be learned in the PrOgO interface with graphical blocks. Like a computing object, each 3D block has some properties, such as a position, a rotation and a colour. Thus, each 3D block is a constructive game piece and can be connected to another one. Connecting different blocks and operating some actions on them enables the building and animation of a 3D structure which represents an object-oriented system (Fig. 1a). Constructing and animating this structure is a metaphor of the OOP paradigm basics. Moreover, it has been demonstrated that analogies and metaphors are at the basis of human cognition [5]. Analogies and metaphors help learners to categorise and to capture the essence of concepts. We expect that such an approach will effectively help to overcome difficulties faced by students with OOP.

The PrOgO's interface includes a 3D scene synchronised with a code completion editor. Programming statements are generated when actions are performed on the 3D graphics. The code editor is exclusively based on auto-completion. It enables students to avoid syntax errors and to be focused on the relationship between concepts and their implementation (coding) (Figs. 1b and c). Moreover, the result of each completed statement is immediately visualised in the 3D scene.

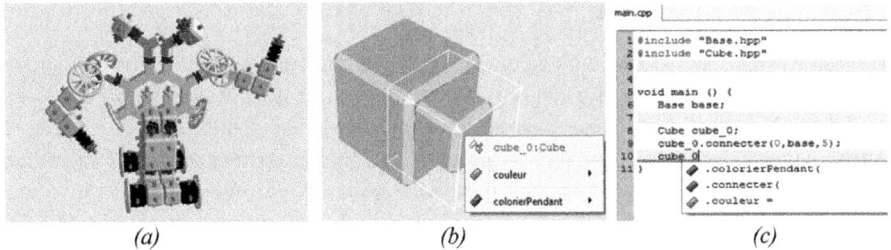

Fig. 1. (a) A 3D graphic built with PrOgO representing an Object-Oriented system; (b) and (c) Interactions with objects in PrOgO respectively within its 3D scene and code editor

3 Research Question and Objective

The objective of this empirical study consists of the identification and the characterisation of students' behaviours when playing with PrOgO. We want to know to what extent the students' behaviours may offer them the opportunity to understand the core concepts of OOP. We address the following question: What characterises the students' behaviours when playing with PrOgO?

We hypothesise that learners should spend time on the PrOgO interface, and manipulate most of the learning concepts both within the 3D scene and the code editor. Such behaviour should be triggered by students, to help us to verify the educational value of PrOgO regarding learning and teaching. This behaviour would help students to understand the link between the formal abstract basic concepts of OOP (the code editor) and the visual representations of the concepts through the PrOgO interface (the 3D scene). Consequently, learners would be able to analyse the OOP paradigm and to understand the addressed concepts.

4 Methodology

The study is based on playing analytics [6], which is an emerging sub-field of learning analytics. Learning analytics offers the opportunity to practitioners and researchers for measuring, collecting, analysing and reporting data about learners [7]. This enables monitoring of learners' activities and assessing innovative educational approaches. We conducted a statistical analysis of the actions performed by the students, based on their digital traces. They consisted of event logs that recorded learners' interactions with the PrOgO interface. By monitoring students' use of PrOgO we expected to investigate whether the game was used in a way that could help them learn, then to verify its educational value. In order to determine typical learners' behaviours, and the set of performed action types underlying similarities and differences between learners, we conducted a Principal Component Analysis (PCA) [8] and an Agglomerative Hierarchical Clustering (AHC) [9] on data built from the collected traces.

4.1 Context of the Study

The study was carried out with learners from two study levels: first year university learners in the Digital Imaging Degree (University of Clermont-Auvergne, France), and final year learners in a science and technology secondary school (Lycée Charles et Adrien Dupuy, France). Sixty-seven students (55 university students and 12 secondary school students) participated in the study in October 2015. They had all previously been introduced to procedural programming but had never been introduced to OOP.

The experiment lasted for one hour. Learners were given access to a tutorial describing the game objective, the interface details, and how they could perform different tasks both in the 3D scene and the code editor of PrOgO. They were asked to play individually with PrOgO and to express their creativity for constructing and animating a virtual robot or a machine. During the experiment, learners' actions were recorded and log files were enabled to keep track of their use of PrOgO.

4.2 Data Collection and Analysis

Players' interactions were recorded in log files, which included timestamped interactions in relation to the learning basic concepts of OOP: creations of objects; modifications of objects' attribute values; and method calls. These interactions could be performed both inside the 3D scene, and the code editor (code selections and code completions). In order to prepare the data analysis, we built a new data file of aggregated data. For each participant, we stored the number of different interactions, as well as the time spent on the game. This included the number of interactions performed both inside the 3D scene, and the code editor such as the code completion actions. PCA was conducted with this aggregated data (Table 1).

Table 1. PCA input variables.

PCA variable	Signification
NB of Instanciate-Connect	Number of class instantiation and objects connection actions
NB of setAttributeColor	Number of attribute colour setting actions
NB of setAttributeRotationAngle	Number of attribute rotation angle setting actions
NB of callFuncColorFor	Number of calls to the method colorForaDuration()
NB of callFuncTurnFor	Number of calls to the method turnForaDuration()
NB of CodeSelection	Number of code selection actions
NB of CodeCompletion	Number of code completion actions
Total time	Time spent by the student

The key objective with PCA is to reduce the dimensionality of a dataset with a large number of interrelated variables, while retaining as much as possible the variation present in the dataset [8]. This reduction is achieved by converting the initial variables into a new set of uncorrelated variables, called principal components. Principal components are ordered so that the first few retain most of the variation present in the dataset [7]. The principal components are also called PCA axes or factors. This reduction of variables enables the user to find the two-dimensional plane through the high-dimensional dataset in which the data are most spread out. So, data can be plotted with respect to those two dimensions, and to produce a visual representation of the data. The PCA returned the principal components with their corresponding eigenvalues, reflecting the variability of the reduced initial data. Ideally, a small number of factors with high eigenvalues are retained to ensure good visual representations of data [8]. A second important PCA result is the correlation circle. This circle shows a projection of the initial variables in a 2-dimensional space with respect to two chosen factors that are ideally the first two. Correlation refers to the degree of dependence between two variables. In our case, it is measured according to Pearson's correlation coefficient, giving a value between −1 and +1 inclusive. The closer the coefficient is to −1 or +1, the greater is the correlation between the variables. To ensure a good interpretation of the meaning of the axes, variables should be far from the centre of the circle. A variable is well linked to an axis when the absolute value of its coordinate on the axis is high. The greater the coordinate absolute value, the greater is the link with the corresponding axis.

In order to achieve our ultimate goal, which is to identify groups of learners, we conducted an AHC on the new observations' coordinates in the sub-space containing the chosen factors. Then, we conducted a second PCA on the same initial dataset to which we added the observations groups returned by the AHC, as a supplementary qualitative variable. We obtained a 2-dimensional map. To complement the visual results from this map, we looked at the coordinates of the classes' centroids with respect to the chosen factors. Centroids are the most typical observations. They have very similar characteristics to observations within the same category but are significantly different from observations belonging to a different category. Therefore, centroids can give us a general idea of the trends inside a whole class.

5 Categories of Students

The PCA returned 8 factors estimated from the initial variables listed beforehand (Table 2). The first three eigenvalues represent 61.45% of the initial variability of the data. We retained the first three factors and ignored the last ones, since the fourth factor had an eigenvalue quite similar to the third one and the last ones had very low eigenvalues.

Table 2. Principal components returned by the PCA.

	F1	F2	F3	F4	F5	F6	F7	F8
Eigenvalue	2.36	1.48	1.08	1.04	0.79	0.73	0.3	0.22
Variability (%)	29.45	18.54	13.45	13.03	9.89	9.13	3.69	2.8
Cumulative %	29.45	47.99	61.45	74.48	84.37	93.5	97.2	100

The correlation circle showed that the horizontal axis (F1) is linked with variables NB of Instantiate-Connect, NB of CodeSelection and NB of CodeCompletions, while the vertical axis (F2) is linked with the variable Total time (Fig. 2).

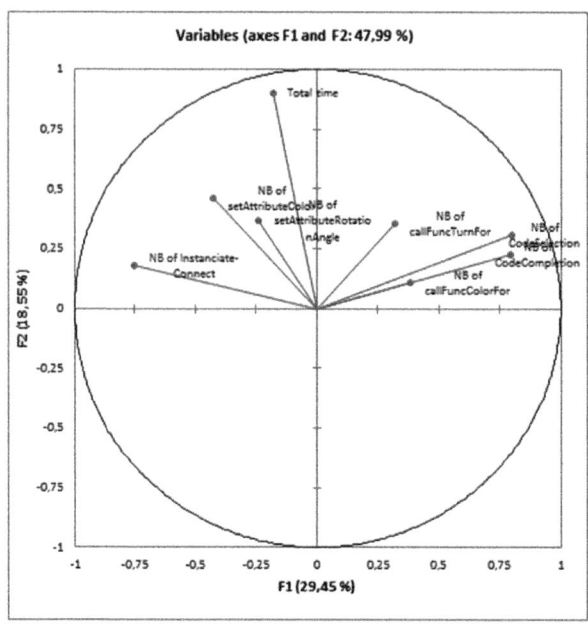

Fig. 2. Correlation circle showing the variables defining the axes F1 and F2.

Results from Table 3 confirm the set of variables defining the different axes. Variables that scored high on the factor F1 are the same listed above, with respective correlation values of −0.75, 0.79, and 0.79. F2 is positively correlated with Total time with the value 0.90, and F3 is significantly correlated with the variables NB of call-FuncColorFor, and NB of callFuncTurnFor. Correlation values between these variables with F3 are respectively 0.66 and 0.62.

Table 3. Correlations between the PCA variables and the first three factors.

Variables	F1	F2	F3
NB of Instanciate-Connect	**−0.75**	0.18	0.01
NB of setAttributeColor	−0.43	0.46	−0.17
NB of setAttributeRotationAngle	−0.24	0.37	−0.01
NB of callFuncColorFor	0.39	0.11	**0.66**
NB of callFuncTurnFor	0.32	0.36	**0.62**
NB of CodeSelection	**0.79**	0.31	−0.32
NB of CodeCompletion	**0.79**	0.29	−0.34
Total time	−0.18	**0.9**	-0.03

Based on the statistical analysis, we can conclude that it is possible to distinguish students: (1) by the number of actions performed with the code editor as well as the number of class instantiation actions; (2) by the total time spent on the PrOgO interface and; (3) by the actions performed to animate the robot of the 3D-scene.

The AHC was conducted on the new observations' coordinates in the 3-dimensional space with respect to the chosen factors F1, F2, and F3. The algorithm returned four homogeneous groups showing, for each participant, the group the user belongs to. After running a PCA for a second time on the same initial variables with a supplementary qualitative variable (the group to which an observation belongs to), we obtained a 2-dimensional map (F1−F2) of the observations, coloured according to the category they belong to (Fig. 3).

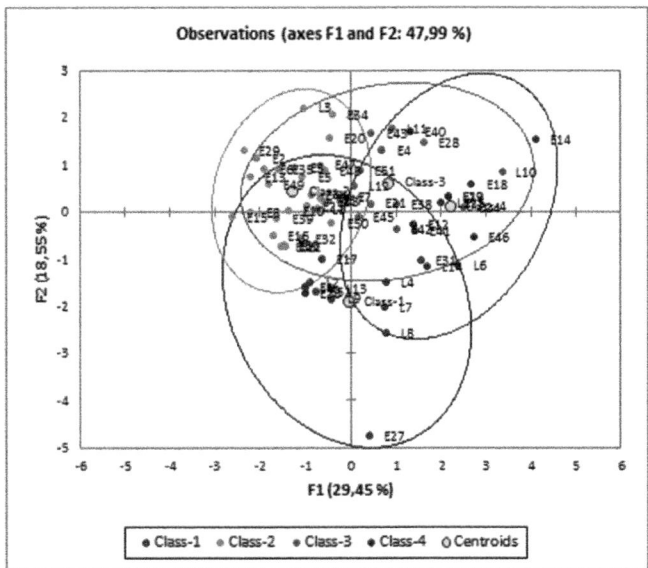

Fig. 3. Map showing the partition of the participants into 4 groups. (Color figure online)

Table 4 supplements Fig. 3. It shows the percentage of observations for each class and gives the 3-dimensional coordinates of the classes' centroids with respect to the axes F1, F2, and F3.

Table 4. Class size and central object coordinates in the subspace (F1, F2, F3).

Class	Objects (%)	Centroid (F1, F2, F3)[a]
1	18.18	(−0.42, −1.83, −0.04)
2	42.42	(−0.96, 0.13, −0.07)
3	21.21	(0.21, 0.89, 1.35)
4	18.18	(2.15, 0.31, −1.08)

[a]Class central object coordinates in the subspace (F1, F2, F3).

Class-1 objects (the blue points) are plotted in the negative semi-plane of the F2 axis, which is highly correlated with the Total time variable (Fig. 3). This indicates that class-1 members are students who have spent little time playing with PrOgO. They have low coordinate absolute values on the F1 axis, which means that they performed a small number of actions, both within the code editor and the 3D scene. Few students belonged to this class. The class-1 centroid is defined by the coordinates (−0.42, −1.83, −0.04) in the subspace (F1, F2, F3), indicating first, that the user has performed a small number of actions linked to the factors F1 and F3, and second, has spent little time playing with PrOgO (−1.83 on the F2 axis). Thus, class-1 is covered by learners who performed a small number of actions, since they have spent little time playing with PrOgO. They represent 18.18% (Table 4) and may correspond to learners who were not very interested in playing with PrOgO.

Class-2 objects (the green points) are plotted in the negative semi-plane of the F1 axis and mostly in the positive semi-plane of the F2 axis (Fig. 3). This indicates that these class members performed a high number of instantiation actions in the 3D scene, and no or very few actions within the code editor. The central object from Table 4 is defined by the coordinates (−0.96, 0.13, −0.07) in the subspace (F1, F2, F3). It represents a student who created a lot of objects in the 3D scene and connected them to each other without using the code editor. The user also played close to the mean time of the experiment and performed no or very few animation actions (as the coordinate is close to 0 on F3). As a result, class-2 members are students who constructed a 3D robot, without using the code editor. They are numerous (42.42%) and have nearly used all the time allocated to the experiment without animating their realisations.

Class-3 objects (the magenta points) are plotted in the positive semi-plane of F1 and F2. According to the F1 axis, they have lower values compared to class-4 members, and greater values compared to class-2 members. They are also located near to the variables related to the animation actions, namely NB of callFuncColorFor, and NB of callFuncTurnFor. Therefore, class-3 members stand out by having: (1) not a high number of coding actions compared to class-4; (2) not a high number of construction actions compared to class-2; (3) and finally a high number of animation actions compared to class-2 and class-4. This can be confirmed by the central object having the coordinates (0.21, 0.89, 1.35). It represents a student who used the code editor, has spent time playing with PrOgO and has animated his construction. Class-3 members are also not numerous, they represent 18.18% (Table 4).

Class-4 members (the red points) are located in the positive semi-plane of F1. They have high values on the F1 axis and moderate absolute values on F2. Class-4 members are students who performed the highest number of coding actions and had a limited use of the 3D scene. The central object is defined by the coordinates (2.15, 0.31, −1.08), representing a student who has performed most of his actions on the code editor, has used the allocated time and has performed very few animation actions. Therefore, class 4 contains participants that are differentiated by the highest number of coding actions compared to the rest of participants.

6 Discussion

Based on the statistical analysis, we obtained four categories of learners who play differently with PrOgO. A first important result is that a majority of students had mostly accepted to play with PrOgO, since those who had spent little time on its interface represented a low percentage of students (Class-1) (Table 4). The majority of students used most of the time allocated to achieve the game's objective in three different ways: students who were focused on the 3D scene with the goal to construct a meaningful 3D structure (Class-2); those who were both focused on the 3D scene (high number of animations) and the code editor (a high number of coding actions) (Class-3); those who performed the highest number of code completion actions, and low construction and animation actions within the 3D scene (Class-4). Thus, one group of learners was focused on constructions within the 3D scene, whereas another was focused on the code editor with a varying number of code completion actions.

One important result is that only a few students manipulated most of the learning concepts (Class-3). These participants performed a high number of animation actions (method calls concept), in addition to actions of construction within the 3D scene (objects' creation concept and modification of objects' attributes values concept). They were also characterised by code completion actions. From an educational perspective, this behaviour is expected. Indeed, making links between connected and animated 3D-objects, as metaphors of most of the represented OOP concepts and their coding, should help beginners to understand these concepts and how they are coded. Consequently, the hypothesis that learners should spend time playing with PrOgO to manipulate most of the represented learning concepts is confirmed for a limited number of students (Class-3). This may be due to the fact that students can perform the goal's game both by graphics and by code. They can master easily the interface while focusing only on graphics (Class-2) or on code (Class-4). From an educational perspective, these behaviours might have other values. Further studies are needed to enable this to be identified and assessed. In addition, as a design improvement of PrOgO, further usage scenarios enabling the expected behaviour should be strengthened.

7 Conclusion

In this work, we have presented the PrOgO microworld dedicated for learning OOP to beginners. We have described our methodology and the results of a study we conducted to investigate learners' behaviours when interacting with the programming concepts represented in this microworld. Our methodology is based on playing analytics, by recording and analysing the interactions of players. We processed a PCA and an AHC in the analysis of data, leading to the characterisation of different groups of learners on the basis of their behaviours when playing with PrOgO. The results showed that the behaviour which is expected from an educational perspective, was triggered by a limited number of students. Behaviours triggered by most students might have other educational values which need to be identified and assessed in further similar studies. Moreover, improvements in the design of PrOgO is needed to strengthen the expected behaviour for which the educational value is known.

The contribution of the paper also consists of the methodology used for the evaluation of the use of PrOgO. This responds to the lack of standardised methodologies for evaluating tools that support computer science education and programming in particular [10]. It is also in line with the current concerns of the computer science education research community. Indeed, querying the ACM Digital Library database with the expression "Programming Learning Analytics" returns 16,562 results (query performed in March 2018). We perceive a high interest in this methodology, since it considers a learners' attitudes analysis, instead of collecting learners' points of views or observing their score progression by means of knowledge tests or questionnaires. Moreover, this methodology is an alternative to comparatist approaches: instead of comparing the efficiency of a digital learning environment, we proceed with the analysis of learners' use of the environment.

Acknowledgments. The authors would like to thank Jeane Fine for her advice in the statistical analysis, Dominique Moncorgé, Adélaïde Albouy-Kissi and Benjamin Albouy-Kissi for the scheduling of the experiment, and Delphine Huguel for the development of the PrOgO microworld. This work has been financed by the French Ministry of National Education, Higher Education and Research within the Tactileo E-Education project (2013–2016).

References

1. Börstler, J., Nordström, M., Kallin Westin, L., Moström, J.-E., Eliasson, J.: Transitioning to OOP/Java—a never ending story. In: Bennedsen, J., Caspersen, Michael E., Kölling, M. (eds.) Reflections on the Teaching of Programming. LNCS, vol. 4821, pp. 80–97. Springer, Heidelberg (2008). https://doi.org/10.1007/978-3-540-77934-6_8
2. Djelil, F., Albouy-Kissi, A., Albouy-Kissi, B., Sanchez, E., Lavest, J.-M.: Microworlds for learning object-oriented programming: considerations from research to practice. J. Interact. Learn. Res. **27**(3), 265–284 (2016)
3. Djelil, F.: Conception et évaluation d'un micromonde de Programmation Orientée-Objet fondé sur un jeu de construction et d'animation 3D. Ph.D. thesis, University of Clermont Auvergne (2016)
4. Djelil, F., Sanchez, E., Albouy-Kissi, B., Albouy-Kissi, A.: Acquisition de connaissances de programmation en fonction des stratégies d'apprentissage: une étude empirique du micromonde PrOgO. Environnements Informatiques pour l'Apprentissage Humain (EIAH), Strasbourg, France, pp. 41–52 (2017)
5. Hofstadter, D., Sander, E.: Surfaces and Essences: Analogy as the Fuel and Fire of Thinking. Basic Books, New York (2013)
6. Sanchez, E., Mandran, N.: Exploring competition and collaboration behaviors in game-based learning with playing analytics. In: Lavoué, É., Drachsler, H., Verbert, K., Broisin, J., Pérez-Sanagustín, M. (eds.) EC-TEL 2017. LNCS, vol. 10474, pp. 467–472. Springer, Cham (2017). https://doi.org/10.1007/978-3-319-66610-5_44
7. Siemens, G., Long, P.: Penetrating the fog: analytics in learning and education. EDUCAUSE Rev. **46**(5), 30–38 (2011)
8. Jolliffe, I.: Principal Component Analysis. Springer, Heidelberg (2002). https://doi.org/10.1007/b98835
9. Day, W.H., Edelsbrunner, H.: Efficient algorithms for agglomerative hierarchical clustering methods. J. Classif. **1**(1), 7–24 (1984)
10. Djelil, F., Boisvert,C., Peter, Y., Sceq, Y., Broisin, J., De La Higuera, C.: Vers une massification de l'apprentissage instrumenté de l'informatique et une intégration des instruments de l'informatique et de leur évaluation, Orphée Grand Challenges (2017)

A Semi-automated Approach to Categorise Learning Outcomes into Digital Literacy or Computer Science

Stefan Pasterk[✉], Max Kesselbacher, and Andreas Bollin

Department of Informatics Didactics, Alpen-Adria-Universität Klagenfurt,
Klagenfurt, Austria
{stefan.pasterk, max.kesselbacher,
andreas.bollin}@aau.at

Abstract. Computer science related curricula, standards and frameworks are designed and implemented in many countries to incorporate informatics education in schools, already starting with kindergarten and primary education. A recurring point of discussion addresses the focus of those educational models concerning the different fields of computer science - the topics related to the scientific subject of computer science, or digital literacy (the set of skills and competencies needed in everyday life in the digital age). In this paper, we present a semi-automated approach to categorise learning outcomes of computer science related curricula into one of those two categories. Categorisation is performed with linguistic metrics computed for nouns and verbs of representative curricula of each category. The categorisation is compared against classifications of nine experts of computer science teaching and research. The results show a matching categorisation for 70% of all learning outcomes and 90% of learning outcomes uniformly classified by the experts.

Keywords: Curriculum · Computer science · Digital literacy · Natural language processing · Primary education

1 Introduction

The incorporation of topics, skills and competencies related to computer science and computer literacy in primary education is currently in focus worldwide [1]. Curricula, standards and frameworks related to computer science are designed and implemented in many countries. The developed curricula differ in many aspects. A possible distinguishing factor of comparison is the focus between computer science and digital literacy categories. The former typically includes topics related to the scientific subject of computer science, while the latter includes skills and competencies needed in everyday life in the digital age. Experts are still in discussion about how the two terms should be correctly classified, which of the two should be focused, and where to draw the distinguishing line between the two categories regarding the formulation of learning outcomes. One of the problems that arises from those open discussion points is that the number of formulations and learning outcomes overwhelms researchers and curricula developers who seek to determine the focus of a curriculum. Curricula often include between dozens and hundreds of formulations and learning outcomes, and manually classifying them is a tedious work [2]. This paper describes a semi-automated approach to categorise learning outcome formulations into computer science or digital literacy categories. Natural language processing (NLP) techniques [3, 4] are applied to analyse learning outcomes and extract categorisation features of representative curricula for both categories, building dictionaries of verbs and nouns with their respective fraction of occurrence in learning outcome descriptions. The approach is evaluated by categorising four computer science related curricula and comparing the results to a classification of experts of computer science research and teaching. The results show that it is possible to determine the focus of a curriculum with the NLP-based categorisation approach.

The remainder of the paper is structured as follows. Section 2 presents related work and contrasts the presented approach. Section 3 covers the educational models used for analysis and evaluation. Section 4 presents the experimental setup and the results. Section 5 discusses the results, an application and possible implications. Section 6 summarises the contribution of the paper.

2 Related Work

With the recency of digital technology emergence, the concepts of computer science are in the focus of researchers worldwide, especially for primary education. Most of the resulting articles concerning computer science related curricula focus on one single curriculum and describe this, possibly new, approach in a detailed way. A few other publications analyse and compare different curricula for either primary or secondary education, although most curricula combine those two levels. The article from Barendsen et al. [1] focuses on computer science concepts in K-9 education (from kindergarten to school level 9) and considers curricula from England, Italy and the United States (US). To analyse the curricula, the learning outcomes of the documents are grouped into knowledge categories with the help of open coding. The occurrences and distribution of the codes within the knowledge categories are calculated and presented to compare the curricula. With the goal of designing a primary school curriculum for computer science and programming, Duncan and Bell [5], in a first step, compared different related curricula. For this purpose, they chose the main English-language curricula for the primary school level, the Computer Science Teachers Association (CSTA) K-12 Computer Science Standards [6], the England computing curriculum, and the Australian Digital Technologies curriculum [7]. To identify possible key ideas and to show similarities as well as differences, the elements of the curricula were categorised into six content themes [5].

An overview of the global situation of K-12 education is given by Hubwieser et al. [8]. They use articles that discuss the situations in different countries as a corpus. Following the steps for qualitative text analysis, the corpus is categorised using the tool MaxQDA. They collected 249 competence statements and analysed knowledge elements like 'Algorithm' regarding the verbs used in combinations with them; as we will see later, this was a step that was also relevant for our work. The statements of the 'Goals' category were manually preprocessed and collected into content categories. Afterwards, they compared those new categories and showed which were covered in which countries [8]. The authors used a manual qualitative analysis approach to extract, categorise and summarise text passages with different topic foci from research texts. In this paper, we present an approach for semi-automatic extraction and categorisation of learning outcome descriptions from curricula documents. Instead of a categorisation considering computer science topics, we focus on the comparison of learning outcomes regarding computer science and digital literacy categories.

3 International Educational Models

Different educational models vary in organisational circumstances, learning goals, topics and teaching methods [9]. With a high number of educational models, the number of basic pedagogical approaches used also rises. Some of them are based on learning objectives or statements. Most of them differ in formulation, details and volume. In this contribution, the umbrella term 'learning outcome' is used to collect all the statements, and the following definition is used: "Learning outcomes are statements of what the individual knows, understands and is able to do on completion of a learning process [10]." This definition suffices for the purpose of this contribution as the focus is on the used words and word combinations, not the structure or the volume.

3.1 Selected Curricula, Educational Standards, and Competency Models

Following the related work, two of the main English-language educational models for computer science in primary education, the CSTA Computer Science Standards from 2011 and the Australian national curriculum for Digital Technology [5] are selected for this contribution. As a recent update, the new CSTA Computer Science Standards from 2017 [11] and due to locality, the curriculum 21 from Switzerland [12] were added. The selected curricula, educational standards and competency models are briefly described.

CSTA K-12 Computer Science Standards (2011). The CSTA K-12 Computer Science Standards from 2011 [6] are well known and often referenced in relevant literature [1, 5, 9]. They start with the kindergarten and last until the twelfth grade. A combination of the levels K-3 and 3–6 covers an age range comparable to primary education. These levels include 45 standards, 16 for levels K-3 and 29 for levels 3–6.

Australian Curriculum (AC). As part of the learning area 'Technologies', the subject Digital Technologies was presented in Australia in 2013 [7]. It is an obligatory subject from the first school year called Foundation (F) until the eighth year. The ninth and tenth year is elective. The learning outcomes are described for each level, representing two school years. That means levels F-2, 3–4 and 5–6 cover the age range of primary education. For this range, 22 learning outcomes can be found, six of them belong to level F-2, seven to 3–4, and nine to 5–6 [13].

Curriculum from Switzerland (21). In Switzerland, the new curriculum for primary and lower secondary education called 'Lehrplan 21 (curriculum 21)' was presented and established in 2014 by 21 of 26 cantons with the possibility of individual adaptations [12]. It includes the subject 'Medien und Informatik (Media and Informatics)' from the first school year on. The levels of this curriculum are represented by 'cycles' containing three to four school grades. For primary education, it contains overall 44 competence levels, 14 for cycle 1 and 30 for cycle 2.

CSTA K-12 Computer Science Standards (2017). The reworked CSTA K-12 Computer Science Standards were presented in 2016 as a draft version and published in 2017. They differ from the older version in a lot of aspects, such as the levelling system and the strands. Considering primary education, the level 1A (age range from five to seven years), and level 1B (age range from eight to eleven years), are of interest. It contains 39 standards for primary education, 18 in level 1A and 21 in level 1B [11].

3.2 Categorisation of Learning Outcomes

The categorisation of the learning outcomes is an often-applied method to compare educational models [1, 5]. In most cases, the categories represent areas of interest, like 'Algorithms'. This contribution looks at two more general categories to identify the focus of the selected educational models: 'computer science' and 'digital literacy'.

Considering the different terminology used in computer science related educational models, it is necessary to clarify and define the term 'computer science' (CS) for this contribution. In English-language countries 'computer science' is a common term, especially in the US and Australia. In Europe, the term 'informatics' is frequently used. For this contribution, we use these terms synonymously, following the definition from the UNESCO/IFIP Curriculum 2000 [14]: "The science dealing with the design, realization, evaluation, use, and maintenance of information processing systems, including hardware, software, organizational and human aspects, and the industrial, commercial, governmental and political implications of these." This contribution builds on this definition of computer science and uses the abbreviation CS.

The terms 'digital literacy' and 'digital competence' can be used synonymously. In the 'DIGCOMP Framework for Developing and Understanding Digital Competence' in Europe [15], 'digital competence' is defined as "the confident, critical and creative use of [information and communication technologies] ICT to achieve goals related to work, employability, learning, leisure, inclusion and/or participation in society. Digital Competence is a transversal key competence which enables acquiring other key competences (e.g. language, mathematics, learning to learn, cultural awareness)". In the following sections, this contribution will use this definition of digital literacy and refer to it as DL.

4 The Experiment

This contribution presents a semi-automated approach to categorise learning outcomes of different educational models with the aim of gaining information about their foci. To evaluate our approach, in a first step, experts were asked to categorise the learning outcomes into CS and DL using a questionnaire. The process and first results of this step have already been described by Pasterk and Bollin [2] and are summarised and extended in Sect. 5.1. In a second step, a categorisation with the help of natural language processing based on linguistic features is applied on the same learning outcomes. This process, the results and a comparison to the results from the experts' categorisation are presented in Sect. 5.2.

4.1 Learning Outcomes Classified by Experts

As described by Pasterk and Bollin [2], a group of nine experts, consisting of four computer science teachers and five researchers in the field of computer science education, participated in a survey to categorise the learning outcomes of three selected educational models. To get a larger basis for the evaluation of the semi-automated approach, the survey was repeated with the same group of experts and with two additional educational models, the CSTA computer science standards from 2011 and from 2017. Every expert completed a questionnaire including all learning outcomes of the selected models for primary education in a random order and had to choose one of the following categories: 'CS', 'DL', 'Both' or 'None'. Further, they were asked to describe their strategy for the categorisation process.

Experts' Strategy. Considering the answers of the experts regarding their strategy, seven out of the nine experts referred to the definitions of CS or DL. Six experts used keywords that they assigned to either CS or DL. Finding keywords or key terms was the way to categorise for two experts. Two other experts focused on the topics of the learning outcomes and the combined objectives, which were often defined by keywords. Eight out of nine experts took keywords into account during categorisation.

Results of Classification. First results have already been presented by Pasterk and Bollin [2] and are summarised and extended in Table 1. The added results for the CSTA curriculum from 2011 and from 2017 can also be found in Table 1. The general categories CS and DL were determined by majority votes. Because of the possibility to choose 'Both', this method can lead to undecided learning outcomes. However, this concerned only a few learning outcomes, as can be seen in Table 1. Additionally, the learning outcomes where there was a strong agreement between the experts are included in Table 1. For those, at most, a single expert disagrees with the common classification. Overall, the inter-rater agreement value (Fleiss's kappa) is 0.43 and shows a 'fair to good' agreement, following the interpretation guidelines of Fleiss [16].

Table 1. Summary of the results from the experts' categorisation

	AUS	21	CSTA 11	CSTA 17
Number of LOs	22	44	43	39
CS	10	10	10	20
CS (Strong Agreement)	7	3	0	9
DL	11	32	32	18
DL (Strong Agreement)	2	19	16	5
Undecided	1	2	1	1

Discussion. The results of the experts' categorisation show that the selected educational models can be grouped into the two types 'focus on digital literacy' and 'balanced orientation'. As can be seen in Table 1, the Australian curriculum and the CSTA standards from 2017 have nearly a uniform distribution between CS and DL. Whereas, more than two-thirds of the learning outcomes from the curriculum 21 from Switzerland and the CSTA standards from 2011 were categorised into DL. Following the majority of the experts, those two educational models focus on DL.

4.2 Categorisation by Linguistic Features

We now present an automated categorisation approach based on linguistic features to assign a category, either CS or DL, to each learning outcome of the four analysed curricula. The categorisation results are evaluated against the expert classification.

Linguistic Processing for Analysis. The analysed curricula are available as portable document format (PDF) documents. Manual preprocessing was done by extracting the texts of the learning outcomes. The extraction is implemented in Python. The process of extraction of the linguistic features included the following basic techniques: normalisation of words to improve comparability (lowercase, lemmatising); stop word removal with a list of English stop words; and word tokenising to produce term lists. Each learning outcome text constitutes a single element, called document, in the analysis. Tagging is applied with a trained part-of-speech tagger [17] to extend the words with part of speech categories. The learning outcome text is tagged in full sentence form - 'the students will be able to' is added at the beginning. Tags are grouped; one of the following categories is assigned to each word: noun, verb, adjective, adverb, and other. After tagging, the sentence start is removed, and the tag category and lemmatised words are stored as term list for each learning outcome.

Categorisation Process. For the categorisation, linguistic frequency measures of curricula representative for CS and DL education are computed, following the same linguistic processing, and stored in two dictionaries. The 'Computer Science Curricula 2013' (AIE) [18], created by a cooperation of the Association for Computing Machinery (ACM) and the Institute of Electrical and Electronic Engineers (IEEE) members, contains a set of curriculum guidelines for undergraduate CS programmes and is used to build the dictionary for CS. For DL, the dictionary is built from three curricula. 'The Digital Competence Framework for Citizens' (Dig) [19] designed by the European Union in 2017, 'British Columbia Digital Literacy Framework' (BC) [20] from the Province of British Columbia, and 'Digi.Komp' (DK) [21] from the Austrian initiative for digital competencies and informatics education.

The considered linguistic features include term frequency (TF), term frequency over inverse document frequency (TF-IDF) and document frequency (DF) [3, 4]. The metrics TF and TF-IDF performed poorly for the categorisation because of size differences in the dictionaries. For categorisation, the DF value is used. In context, this value describes in which fraction of learning outcomes a term occurs.

For each learning outcome to be categorised, the sum of the DF values of the occurring tagged terms in the two dictionaries was computed. Insights from the experts' strategies suggested that content terms (nouns), cognitive activity terms (verbs) and their combinations should be considered. In this contribution, individual terms tagged as nouns and verbs are counted. The highest value determines the category. When both sums are within 10% of the highest value, a third category 'undecided' is assigned. Figure 1 shows an example of this process.

"The students will be able to recognize that software is created to control computer operations."

↪ *[recognize, software, create, control, computer, operation]*

CS value: 0.0054 + 0.0928 + 0.0018 + 0.0180 + 0.0243 + 0.0180 = **0.1603**
DL value: 0.0000 + 0.0294 + 0.0441 + 0.0059 + 0.0765 + 0.0088 = **0.1647**

⇩

Automatic categorization: undecided
Expert categorization: 4 CS, 4 DL, 1 Both

Fig. 1. Example for learning outcome processing from CSTA standards from 2011 [6]

Comparing Categorisation Results to Experts' Classification. The automated categorisation results are compared to the expert classifications in two ways. First, the categorisation is compared against the expert classification regarding all learning outcomes of the curricula. The results show the categorisation performance for a wide range of learning topics. Second, the categorisation is separately compared against the classification of learning outcomes for which the experts showed a strong agreement.

Table 2 summarises results of all possible combinations of different sets of the curricula used for building the dictionary for DL categorisation. The results show the fraction of matching categorisations. E.g., row five shows the approach achieves a match with expert ratings for 74% of all learning outcomes of CSTA 11 using BC and DK for the DL dictionary. For the categorisation of uniformly classified learning outcomes, this configuration matches in 94% of the DL learning outcomes, and 94% of all those learning outcomes. CSTA 11 does not contain uniformly classified CS learning outcomes, indicated with '—'. No single dictionary performs best for the categorisation of all analysed curricula. The best overall categorisation scores are achieved by DK for a single curriculum dictionary, with scores in the range .64 to .75 and a mean score of .70, and by the combination of BC and DK for a multi-curriculum dictionary, with scores in the range .68 to .74 and a mean score of .70. Notably, these two dictionaries perform best for two different sets of analysed curricula.

Regarding categorisation of uniformly classified learning outcomes, again no single dictionary performs best. Measured with the sum of matching categorisation scores, the dictionary built with BC performs best for categorising CS learning outcomes and overall uniformly classified learning outcomes, with mean scores of .81 and .90, respectively. The dictionary built with all three curricula performs best for categorising DL learning outcomes, with a mean score of .99, mismatching one learning outcome.

Table 2. Comparison of results

[a]Curricula for DL dict.	AUS, all Agreement			21, all Agreement			CSTA 11, all Agreement			CSTA 17, all Agreement		
BC			.73			.70			.65			.64
	1.0	**1.0**	**1.0**	.86	.67	.89	.88	—	.88	**.86**	**.78**	**1.0**
Dig			.73			.57			.67			.67
	.89	**1.0**	.50	**.64**	**.67**	.63	**1.0**	—	**1.0**	.71	.56	**1.0**
DK			.73			**.75**			.70			.64
	.89	.86	**1.0**	**.91**	**.67**	**.95**	**.94**	—	**.94**	.79	**.78**	.80
BC, Dig			.73			.64			.72			.64
	.89	**1.0**	.50	.73	.34	.79	**1.0**		**1.0**	.71	.56	**1.0**
BC, DK			.68			.70			**.74**			**.69**
	.89	.86	**1.0**	.81	**.67**	.84	**.94**	—	**.94**	**.86**	**.78**	**1.0**
Dig, DK			.73			.70			.67			.64
	.89	.86	**1.0**	.77	**.67**	.79	**1.0**	—	**1.0**	.71	.71	**1.0**
Dig, BC, DK			.68			**.75**			.72			.67
	.89	.86	**1.0**	**.91**	**.67**	**.95**	**1.0**	—	**1.0**	.79	.67	**1.0**

[a]The header denotes analysed curricula. Results rounded to two decimal places use the format [All CS DL] to show overall relative match of categorisation and relative match for competencies with strong expert agreement. Best scores per column and category are marked bold

5 Discussion

With the help of the experts' categorisation, it was possible to identify the foci of the selected educational models. For automated categorisation, the best performing sets of dictionaries with an accuracy of 70% are AIE for CS and DK for DL or the combination of DK and BC for DL. To identify the foci of the educational models, the numbers and fractions of categorised learning outcomes are presented in Table 3.

Table 3. Application of categorisation with two different dictionaries

		AUS		21		CSTA 11		CSTA 17	
CS	Experts	10	.45	10	.23	10	.23	20	.51
	AIE/DK	7	.32	7	.16	8	.19	19	.49
	AIE/BC, DK	8	.36	7	.16	9	.21	17	.44
DL	Experts	11	.50	32	.73	32	.75	18	.46
	AIE/DK	15	.68	35	.80	31	.72	15	.39
	AIE/BC, DK	9	.41	34	.77	31	.72	17	.44
Undecided	Experts	1	.05	2	.04	1	.02	1	.03
	AIE/DK	0	.00	10	.23	4	.09	5	.12
	AIE/BC, DK	5	.23	7	.16	3	.07	5	.12

As can be seen for the Australian curriculum (AUS), the dictionary based on AIE/DK tends to identify a focus in DL (.68 compared to .32 in CS). Following the results of the dictionary based on AIE/BC, DK this curriculum is balanced (.41 for DL and .36 for CS). This balanced view corresponds to the results from the experts' choices. For the curriculum 21 from Switzerland, a clear focus on DL can be identified with both dictionaries having similar results (.77–.80 in favour of DL). This result corresponds to the experts' categorisation. A similar situation can be seen for the CSTA standards from 2011 where a focus for DL is visible (.72 in favour of DL). Here again, the results from the experts also indicate a focus on DL. Following the experts' results, the CSTA standards from 2017 tend to be balanced, which is also reflected by the semi-automated generated results (.39–.49 for CS and .44 for DL). Summarising, the semi-automated categorisation matches the experts' opinions in the identification of the focus for the majority of the analysed educational models. In three cases, both dictionaries of the semi-automated approach identified the same foci as the experts did. In one case, only the results from the dictionary based on AIE/BC, DK corresponded with those of the experts. An important conclusion is that the quality of categorisation is highly dependent on the curricula used for building the categorisation dictionary.

The semi-automated approach presented in this contribution shows a few threats to validity. The translation of the learning outcomes from the German-language curriculum can lead to the use of different terms. This can result in a lower frequency of important terms. Because all of the experts were from Austria, it can also be the case that they are biased by the local, well-known 'digikomp (DK)' competency model which was chosen to build the dictionaries. This could be a factor resulting in the higher performance of the dictionary based on DK. Another threat can be that expert categorisation can arise from misinterpretation, invalidating the comparison.

6 Conclusion and Future Work

Educational models are designed and implemented on different levels in many countries. These models include national curricula, workgroup recommendations, competency frameworks and guidelines. There is ongoing discussion about whether this newly implemented education trend should focus on topics related to the scientific subject of computer science or the development of skills and competencies needed in everyday life in the digital age. In this paper, we present an approach to semi-automatically categorise learning outcomes of computer science related curricula into computer science or digital literacy categories. For each of the categories, a dictionary of noun and verb terms of curricula representative for the category was built. The value of relative frequency of each term in all learning outcomes of the dictionary was used as a categorisation metric. The categorisation was applied to four computer science related curricula, and results were compared against classifications from nine experts of computer science teaching and research. The best performing dictionaries achieved a matching categorisation of 70% of all learning outcomes of the analysed curricula. Furthermore, for learning outcomes which were uniformly classified by the experts (at most one expert disagreed), the best performing dictionary achieved a matching categorisation of 90% of those learning outcomes. The results suggested that the focus of a curriculum regarding the two categories, computer science and digital literacy, can be identified with the application of the approach. Our goal for future work is an automatic classification of computer science related curricula and the individual learning outcomes regarding different categories. Going forward, we intend to take into account the verb and noun phrases for categorisation, following the general strategy of the experts. Additionally, we want to compare our approach of categorisation with machine learning classification and with sets of additional linguistic features. We also plan to evaluate them against a larger set of expert ratings, including additional experts.

Acknowledgments. The authors would like to thank Günther Fliedl for his feedback on the natural language processing methods and on preliminary studies.

References

1. Barendsen, E., et al.: Concepts in K-9 computer science education. In: ITiCSE-WGR 2015, pp. 85–116 ACM, New York (2015)
2. Pasterk, S., Bollin, A.: Digital literacy or computer science: where do information technology related primary education models focus on? In: Jakab, F. (ed.) Proceedings of the 2017 ICETA, pp. 1–7. IEEE, Stary Smokovec, Slovakia (2017)
3. Han, J., Kamber, M.: Data Mining: Concepts and Techniques, 2nd edn. Morgan Kaufmann, San Francicso (2006)
4. Bird, S., Klein, E., Loper, E.: Natural Language Processing with Python, 1st edn. O'Reilly Media, Sebastopol (2009)
5. Duncan, C., Bell, T.: A pilot computer science and programming course for primary school students. In: Proceedings of the 2015 WiPSCE, pp. 39–48. ACM, New York (2015)
6. Seehorn, D., et al.: CSTA K-12 Computer Science Standards: Revised 2011. Technical Report. ACM, New York (2011)
7. Falkner, K., Vivian, R., Falkner, N.: The Australian digital technologies curriculum: Challenge and opportunity. In: Proceedings of the Sixteenth Australasian Computing Education Conference, Australian Computer Society, vol. 148, pp. 3–12 (2014)
8. Hubwieser, P., et al.: A global snapshot of computer science education in K-12 Schools. In: ITiCSE-WGR 2015, pp. 65–83. ACM, New York (2015)
9. Hubwieser, P., et al.: Computer science/informatics in secondary education. In: Adams, L., Jurgens, J. (eds.) ITiCSE-WGR 2011, pp. 19–38. ACM, New York (2011)
10. ECTS: Users' Guide (2015). https://ec.europa.eu/education/ects/users-guide/docs/ects-users-guide_en.pdf
11. CSTA: Standards (2017). http://www.csteachers.org
12. Lehrplan 21: Lehrplan 21 (2014). http://v-ef.lehrplan.ch
13. Australian Curriculum: Digital technologies in focus (2013). http://www.australian curriculum.edu.au/
14. Anderson, J., van Weert, T., Duchâteau, C. (eds.): Information and Communication Technology in Secondary Education: A Curriculum for Schools and Programme of Teacher Development. UNESCO, Paris, France (2002)
15. Vuorikari, R., Punie, Y., Carretero Gomez, S., Van den Brande, G.: DigComp 2.0: The Digital Competence Framework for Citizens. Update Phase 1: The Conceptual Reference Model. Publication Office of the European Union, Luxembourg (2016)
16. Fleiss, J.L.: Statistical Methods for Rates and Proportions, 2nd edn. Wiley, New York (1981)

17. Toutanova, K., Klein, D., Manning, C., Singer, Y.: Feature-rich part-of-speech tagging with a cyclic dependency network. In: Proceedings of HLT-NAACL, Association for Computational Linguistics, Stroudsburg, pp. 173–180 (2003)
18. Joint Task Force on Computing Curricula, Association for Computing Machinery (ACM) and IEEE Computer Society: Computer Science Curricula 2013: Curriculum Guidelines for Undergraduate Degree Programs in Computer Science. ACM, New York (2013)
19. Ferrari, A.: DIGCOMP: a framework for developing and understanding digital competence in Europe. IPTS, Seville, Spain (2013)
20. British Columbia: Digital Literacy Framework (2013). https://www2.gov.bc.ca/gov/content/education-training/k-12/teach/teaching-tools/digital-literacy
21. Digi.komp: Die Initiative (2011). https://www.digikomp.at/

Teachers' Education and Professional Development

Who's Teaching the Teachers?

Viewing the ICT Content of a Teaching Degree Through the Eyes of Pre-service Teachers

Amber McLeod[✉] and Kelly Carabott[✉]

Monash University, Melbourne, Australia
{amber.mcleod,kelly.carabott}@monash.edu

Abstract. The myth of the "digital native", pedagogical beliefs about ICT and its place in education, and the reality of a teacher as an ICT role model each contribute to the attitudes school students develop about ICT. All Australian teachers, regardless of discipline, are required to incorporate ICT in their lessons. The way pre-service teachers (PSTs) are educated has a direct impact on their ability and desire to teach digital competence to school students. Using 482 first year PSTs' experiences and expectations as a lens, teaching degrees at an Australian university were investigated, using a mixed methods approach, to find out whether the ICT content was appropriate to prepare graduate teachers to implement the national curriculum. Findings indicated that the teaching degrees did not meet all PSTs' needs. PSTs wanted more explicit instruction in the practical and pedagogical implications of using ICT in the classroom, and some even wanted training to navigate the university's online systems. These findings indicate that assumptions implicit in universities about digital competence may be invalid. Recommendations include suggestions that universities review their expectations of PST digital competence and consider including both embedded and explicit methods of teaching ICT in teaching degrees.

Keywords: Initial teacher education · Digital competence · Pre-service teachers · Information and communication technology

1 Introduction

In order to prepare students for the future, the current Foundation to Year 10 Australian Curriculum includes digital competence in two ways. The first is as a discipline area - the digital technologies strand - taught either as a separate subject or embedded across the curriculum. The second is as a general capability in information and communication technology (ICT) which is taught by all teachers regardless of their discipline areas. The ability of teachers to successfully implement the curriculum, however, is varied [1] and this phenomenon appears to be worldwide [2]. One problem is that institutions that deliver teaching degrees hold inaccurate assumptions about pre-service teacher (PST) digital competence and so do not cover this area properly. Upon graduation, these new teachers may be unable to teach school students the basic digital literacy expected in today's society.

In addition, to be effective, teachers require more than just the technical skills needed to deliver the curriculum. As digital technology advances at a rapid rate, it is not always possible to keep up with the latest developments and risk-taking skills need to be developed, leading to courage and a confident attitude when presented with new digital technologies. Teachers are socialisers who transmit their values, attitudes and priorities to their students regardless of the curriculum [3]. Teaching degrees should build PSTs' digital competence to the point where they become positive ICT role models if the envisaged outcomes of the curriculum are to be achieved. This is particularly pertinent for female teachers, who make up 86% of primary school teachers and 62% of secondary school teachers in Australia, as females are underrepresented in the ICT field [4]. Research in the field of initial teacher education in ICT has mainly focused on problems of practice, but, as highlighted by Tondeur, Roblin, Van Braak, Voogt and Prestridge [5], the links between graduate teacher digital competence and future success of their students remains an area in the literature which needs further review. The adequacy of one Australian university's teaching degrees' ICT content is investigated in this paper.

2 Literature Review

Digital competence is more than knowing how to use computers, tablets and smartphones. Ferrari [6] suggested that being digitally competent not only encompasses an understanding of technical operations, but should also include information management, collaboration, communication and sharing, creation of content and knowledge, ethics and responsibility, evaluation and problem solving. Mishra and Koehler [7] proposed the Technological Pedagogical Content Knowledge (TPACK) model for effective incorporation of technology into teacher education. The model suggests that educators not only need Technological Knowledge, but an understanding of Pedagogical Knowledge and Content Knowledge (of both the ICT aspects of the curriculum and the discipline area) as well. In order to successfully integrate technology in education, there needs to be an intersection between these three knowledges. These researchers highlight the breadth of digital competence and the importance of understanding how ICT fits within every lesson, no matter what the discipline.

2.1 Teachers as Role-Models

Students are socialised into their attitudes about ICT by teachers, parents, peers, and the media [8, 9]. Students themselves have reported that when making decisions about future studies or careers these same groups are the main influencers [10]. Teachers affect the way students see themselves [11]. Females, in particular, have been found to develop self-efficacy through vicarious modelling in their relationships with teachers [12]. Encouraging, passionate teachers, and good student-teacher relationships have been reported as making students' sense of belonging to an ICT environment stronger [13]. A good teacher can significantly improve a child's school performance [14].

Butler [15] argued that teachers can give messages to girls, sometimes unconsciously, that they do not need to participate in digital technology. Teachers' stereotypical beliefs and attitudes about appropriate behaviour and roles for boys and girls, and technology, have been found to distort their perception of actual student abilities [16] and subtly steer girls away from ICT [17]. Similarly, researchers have claimed that student performance can be predicted by examining teachers' expectations and beliefs about student ability [18].

2.2 Teaching Degrees and ICT as a Cross Curricular Priority

While governments, the community and PSTs themselves expect that by participating in teaching degrees students will increase their digital competence, this does not seem to match with what is actually happening in universities [19]. A lack of preparation in terms of teacher education has been blamed for slowing the journey to digital competence [20, 21]. This is problematic as teaching degrees are a vital motivator and contributor to future integration of ICT by PSTs [5]. In order to explore the complexities of preparing PSTs, there first needs to be an appreciation of their digital education prior to university, which for most undergraduates, is school.

The Australian National Assessment Program in Information and Communication Technology (NAP-ICT) results showed that only 52% of Year 10 students reached proficiency level and, notably, there was a statistically significant drop in digital competence since the last assessment across all cohorts of students [22]. It is unsurprising then, that Murray and Perez [23] found that 72% of the students in their university course could not be considered digitally competent. Studies into the ICT competence of first year university students suggested that they tended to use a limited range of technologies in ways which did not correspond with institutional expectations, with significant variations in digital competence across the university student body [24]. These results add weight to previous findings that so-called "digital natives" [25] do not share new ways of working and learning linked to ICT and have failed to achieve the digital competence levels expected [26].

The importance of ICT in teacher education is recognised in the Australian Professional Standards for Teachers [27], which explicitly mention ICT competence. Graduate level teachers are expected to "implement teaching strategies for using ICT to expand curriculum learning opportunities for students", "Demonstrate knowledge of a range of resources, including ICT, that engage students in their learning", and "Demonstrate an understanding of the relevant issues and the strategies available to support the safe, responsible and ethical use of ICT in learning and teaching" (standard 4.5). The Professional Standards for Teachers form part of the criteria against which teacher education programmes are accredited.

PST education is directly related to school students' results [14]. Clearly, as teachers are the ones teaching digital competence, their teacher education programmes should be preparing them for that [28, 29]. Alarmingly, however, many teacher education degrees are not designed to have a strong influence on the technology use of PSTs and fail to explicitly address digital competence [23, 30].

Buabeng-Andoh [31] suggests that the lack of educational opportunities and support for developing ICT skills was one of the barriers to digital competence. While education degrees may include a single technology unit [32], the units are usually deemed insufficient for PSTs to be adequately prepared for the complexities involved in integrating ICT [33]. Although at many universities the ICT requirements for accreditation have been achieved by embedding digital literacy across the curriculum [23], discipline units often demonstrate or require little to no technology integration [32]. Consequently, after graduation, PSTs may be unable to deliver the Australian Curriculum as envisaged.

Black and Smith [34] found that when PSTs were asked how well they thought their lecturers in education modelled ICT in their units, only 26% thought it was done well with 9% indicating they did not think their lecturers had embedded ICT at all. Even where the focus had been on becoming skilled in using applications, little was done to help the students understand how to include the technology in their own teaching or facilitate subject learning [34].

3 Methodology

For entry into teaching degrees at this Australian university, students must demonstrate they have achieved minimum levels of numeracy and English language competence [35] and have particular personal and professional characteristics [36], which the teaching degree builds upon. Demonstration of a minimum level of digital competence is not required, and so the university has simply assumed a level of digital competence, which informs the ICT content of the degree.

Using PSTs as a lens, this study investigated whether the ICT content of teaching degrees in an Australian university was adequate. This was explored through two questions:

1. How digitally competent do PSTs believe they are, and does this indicate a minimum level which can be assumed by universities?
2. Do PSTs reflections indicate that the ICT content of their degrees are adequate?

This study was conducted using qualitative and quantitative methods interwoven in a mixed methods approach [37]. Ethics for the study were obtained through the Monash University Human Research Ethics Committee.

From 2015 to 2018, during O-week sessions promoting opt-in ICT classes, first year students who were enrolled in either a Bachelor of Education (Foundation-12), Bachelor of Education (Early Childhood/Primary), a Masters of Teaching (Primary/Secondary) or a Masters of Teaching (Primary) were invited to be part of this study. Students were asked to complete a survey that was available online or on paper, according to student preference. Completed surveys were returned to the researchers immediately after the one-hour information sessions. The survey included a question inviting students to take part in follow-up group interviews. Surveys were returned by 482 students (366 females, 110 males, 6 unknown) and three group interviews were conducted with 10 students.

The survey included questions addressing digital self-efficacy as well as confidence with, interest in and attitudes towards ICT based on a five-point Likert scale. The responses were coded as 1 = Strongly disagree to 5 = Strongly agree, or 1 = Low to 5 = High. One sample t-tests were used to determine whether attitudes were statistically significantly different to the middle value, "Unsure" or "Moderate". The p-value was set at .05 for significance [38].

Group interviews were conducted towards the end of the first semester and explored some of the themes which emerged from the quantitative data. The sessions were audio taped and the tapes were later transcribed for analysis. Thematic analysis of the qualitative data were conducted using *Nvivo*.

4 Results and Discussion

4.1 How Digitally Competent Do PSTs Believe They Are, and Does This Indicate a Minimum Level Which Can Be Assumed by Universities?

From the quantitative data, one sample t-test results indicated that for all but one statement (If something goes wrong with digital technologies I panic, M = 3.15, which is statistically significantly different to 3, "unsure") PSTs were, on average, positive about digital technologies and their own digital competence. However, as every teacher is required to competently deliver the ICT components of the curriculum, a measure of the average response is not enough. It is important to gauge the percentage of responses indicating negative attitudes or lack of self-efficacy in order to investigate the minimum level of digital competence that can be assumed. The lower two response categories and the higher two response categories for the questions have been combined and presented in Table 1.

Table 1. Percentage of student responses for each response category.

Statement	% Low	% Moderate	% High
Please indicate what you think is the priority given to computer education within schools	5.6	31.0	63.3
How would you rate your skills with digital technologies?	12.1	46.6	41.4
How would you rate your enjoyment of using digital technologies?	4.5	27.1	68.4
How would you rate your enjoyment of using digital technologies in classrooms?	7.3	31.0	61.7
If something goes wrong with digital technologies I panic	33.4	22.3	44.2
I find it easy to teach myself how to use a new program	11.2	22.7	66.1
I feel nervous when I have to learn something new on the computer	59.4	16.6	24.0
I don't understand how some people can get so involved with digital technology	61.6	22.2	16.2
I enjoy thinking up new ideas and examples to try out on digital technology	15.3	27.8	56.9
I would like it if people thought of me as a computer geek	38.3	34.9	26.8
If I can avoid using digital technologies, I will	67.7	15.5	16.9
I am good at fixing problems with digital technology	27.8	29.5	42.8
I think it is important to use digital technologies for learning	4.2	6.8	89.0

Table 1 shows large differences in PSTs' evaluation of their own digital competence, and attitudes towards ICT. Only 41.4% of students communicated that they had high or moderately high digital technology skills with 12.1% of students actually self-identifying as having low skills. Answers indicating negative attitudes or low self-confidence ranged from 4.2% to 44.2%. This suggests that an emphasis on ICT components of teaching degrees would be beneficial for a sizeable minority of PSTs.

4.2 Do PSTs' Reflections Indicate that the ICT Content of Their Degrees Are Adequate?

Towards the end of the first semester, PSTs had some experience of the ICT content and expectations of the degree. While some PSTs interviewed were clearly very digitally competent, others appeared to have trouble coping and were concerned that the course content did not match their expectations. A thematic analysis of the qualitative data were conducted and four key themes emerged as discussed below:

(1) Not all students have the digital self-efficacy assumed

The university's expectation of students is that they have the digital competence to engage in the risk-taking associated with navigating new digital technologies such as the university's online enrolment and learning management systems. As summarised earlier in Table 1, at least 12% of students surveyed rated themselves as having low skills, found it difficult to teach themselves new programs, felt nervous when they had to learn something new, did not feel they could fix problems and panicked if something went wrong, and would avoid using digital technologies if they could.

These sentiments were echoed by participants in the group interview who indicated that they had wasted a considerable amount of time learning to navigate the online systems, which they found very stressful. They believed the university should run introductory sessions for the students, suggesting that they would attend weekend sessions or even pay for a workshop. Students also expressed concerns that the changes in digital technologies were so fast they found them overwhelming. They did not feel able to sort out which new developments they should focus their energy on and wanted more instruction from teacher educators. Some participants also revealed how little experience they had with ICT, finding the jump in expectations from high school to university surprising. As teachers model behaviours to students, and if teachers do not have the confidence to engage with new technologies, this will be picked up by their students [39].

(2) Digital technologies need to be explicitly modelled by lecturers, but also played with

PSTs signalled that competence with digital technologies was not something that came naturally and needed to be worked on. They compared it to learning a new language that had to be studied and practiced, because not only is it a new concept, but they also have to learn how to use it and when and why it is appropriate. In addition, PSTs found learning on their own was not enjoyable and were looking for alternative ways to gain this knowledge. They believed that use of ICT must be modelled and explicitly demonstrated by the teacher educators and that unless the PSTs themselves were able to play with the technologies in a meaningful way in the workshops, they were unlikely to adopt them for their own classes. If PSTs were left to learn to use digital technologies on their own, they found it a chore. This reflects findings shown in Table 1 where around 16.2% of students indicated that they could not understand how people can become so involved with digital technologies.

Comments from students also suggested that unless the pedagogical implications of programs that they had seen modelled in lectures and tutorials were explicitly discussed, students had difficulty imagining how programs could be adapted to be used in other disciplines, year levels, or other educational contexts.

(3) Digital technology education is an extra

As shown Table 1, the results of the questionnaire showed that 11% of students were unsure or did not agree that it was important to use digital technologies for learning. In addition, 36.6% of students believed schools gave a low or moderate priority to computer education. This was reflected in comments from the group interviews where postgraduate students in particular suggested that they believed that their own education, which did not include ICT, was sufficient and that digital technologies were not a requirement of education, rather an add-on to keep students interested. They indicated that they thought of digital technologies as an optional extra that could be used as a tool if the teacher chose to do so. While they conceded that digital competence was important, they believed that students could learn this outside of school, as indeed they had done themselves, albeit painfully. Students also expressed concern that digital technologies in schools were getting in the way of a "proper" education and that they would make classroom management more difficult. These attitudes do not reflect the Australian Curriculum, and if modelled to school students, could result in school graduates without the level of digital competence envisaged. At one extreme the curriculum would be subverted and at a lesser level it would be compromised.

5 Conclusion

The results of this study indicate that while the current structure of the teaching degrees at this university may be adequate for the majority of first year students, university assumptions have meant that the way digital competence is taught in teacher education programmes may not address the needs of all students, as approximately 12% of students have self-identified as having low self-efficacy or negative attitudes towards ICT. While this percentage may not seem large, imagine if 12% of PSTs graduated without the literacy or numeracy skills expected.

The qualitative and quantitative data collected for this study suggest a variety of perceived abilities and a range of attitudes towards ICT among PSTs. This indicates that universities need to carefully consider their assumptions about the minimum level of digital competence PSTs have. Worryingly, at this university, some PSTs struggled to access and understand basic university systems. When instruction is required at this level, it is unlikely that these PSTs will gain a comprehensive understanding of the technological and pedagogical knowledge required to incorporate ICT into their teaching without extensive explicit instruction.

These results show that students' concerns are, perhaps, not presently being addressed in this university's teaching degrees and some students could benefit from, and are actively asking for, more ICT content and opportunities to play with digital technologies as part of their degree. It is clear from their comments and concerns that PSTs felt the pedagogical implications of using technology in classrooms had not yet been adequately addressed. While it must be kept in mind that these were first year PSTs who had only participated in one semester of their degrees, for many, their expectations were not being met. If teaching degrees are to truly prepare PSTs to deliver the envisaged Australian Curriculum, then instruction in ICT needs to happen throughout their degree. Existing assumptions about the way PSTs become digitally competent need to be re-examined and degrees restructured to reflect this, otherwise graduate teachers may not be able to use ICT across the curriculum to support the digital competence of their own students.

References

1. Selwyn, N., Nemorin, S., Bulfin, S., Johnson, N.F.: Left to their own devices: the everyday realities of "one-to-one" classrooms. Oxford Review of Education, pp. 1–22 (2017)
2. Haydn, T.: Lessons learned? Teaching student teachers to use ICT in their subject teaching: view from the UK. Aust. Educ. Comput. **24**(2), 35–41 (2010)
3. Whittle, R.J., Telford, A., Benson, A.C.: The 'Perfect' Senior (VCE) secondary physical education teacher: student perceptions of teacher-related factors that influence academic performance. Aust. J. Teach. Educ. **40**(8) (2015)
4. Australian Government Department of Jobs and Small Business: Australian Jobs 2017 - Occupation Matrix (2017). https://web.archive.org/web/20180226083930/. https://docs.jobs.gov.au/system/files/doc/other/australianjobs2017occmatrix.pdf
5. Tondeur, J., van Braak, J., Sang, G., Voogt, J., Fisser, P., Ottenbreit-Leftwich, A.: Preparing pre-service teachers to integrate technology in education: a synthesis of qualitative evidence. Comput. Educ. **59**, 134–144 (2012)
6. Ferrari, A.: DIGCOMP: A framework for developing and understanding digital competence in Europe. IPTS, Seville (2013)
7. Mishra, P., Koehler, M.: Technological pedagogical content knowledge: a framework for teacher knowledge. Teach. Coll. Rec. **108**(6), 1017–1054 (2006)
8. Clayton, K.L., von Hellens, L.A., Nielsen, S.H.: Gender stereotypes prevail in ICT: a research review. In: Proceedings of the Special Interest Group on Management Information System's 47th Annual Conference on Computer Personnel Research, pp. 153–158. ACM (2009)
9. Multimedia Victoria: Reality bytes: An in depth analysis of attitudes about technology and career skills. Victoria State Government, Melbourne (2001)
10. Roger, A., Duffield, J.: Factors underlying persistent gendered option choices in school science and technology in Scotland. Gend. Educ. **12**(3), 367–383 (2000)
11. Margolis, J., Fisher, A.: Unlocking the Clubhouse: Women in Computing. MIT Press, Cambridge (2002)

12. Zeldin, A.L., Britner, S.L., Pajares, F.: A comparative study of the self-efficacy beliefs of successful men and women in mathematics, science, and technology careers. J. Res. Sci. Teach. **45**(9), 1036–1058 (2008)
13. Furrer, C., Skinner, E.: Sense of relatedness as a factor in children's academic engagement and performance. J. Educ. Psychol. **95**(1), 148–162 (2003)
14. Department of Education and Early Childhood Development: From New Directions to Action: World class teaching and school leadership (2013). http://ncee.org/wp-content/uploads/2016/12/Vic-non-AV-6-DEECD-2013-From-New-Directions-to-Action.pdf
15. Butler, D.: Gender, girls, and computer technology: what's the status now? Clear. House **73**(4), 225–229 (2000)
16. Eccles, J.S.: Understanding women's educational and occupational choices. Psychol. Women Q. **18**(4), 585–609 (1994)
17. Barker, L.J., Aspray, W.: The state of research on girls and IT. In: Cohoon, J.M., Aspray, W. (eds.) Women and Information Technology. The MIT Press, Cambridge (2006)
18. Eccles, J.S.: Families, schools, and developing achievement-related motivations and engagement. In: Grusec, J.E., Hastings, P.D. (eds.) Handbook of Socialization: Theory and Research. Guilford Press, New York (2006)
19. Tondeur, J., Pareja Roblin, N., van Braak, J., Voogt, J., Prestridge, S.: Preparing beginning teachers for technology integration in education: ready for take-off? Technol. Pedagog. Educ. **26**(2), 157–177 (2017)
20. Wang, S.K., Hsu, H.Y., Campbell, T., Coster, D.C., Longhurst, M.: An investigation of middle school science teachers and students use of technology inside and outside of classrooms: considering whether digital natives are more technology savvy than their teachers. Educ. Technol. Res. Dev. **62**(6), 637–662 (2014)
21. Sweeney, T., Drummond, A.: How prepared are our pre-service teachers to integrate technology? A pilot study. Aust. Educ. Comput. **27**(3), 117–123 (2013)
22. National Assessment Program: National Assessment Program ICT Literacy, Years 6 & 10, Report 2014. Australian Curriculum, Assessment and Reporting Authority (2015)
23. Murray, M.C., Pérez, J.: Unraveling the digital literacy paradox: how higher education fails at the fourth literacy. DigitalCommons@ Kennesaw State University (2014)
24. Elsden-Clifton, J., Jordan, K.: The pre-service teachers' ICT toolkit: expertise and expectations. In: Proceedings of EdMedia: World Conference on Educational Media and Technology, pp. 1743–1748 (2013)
25. Prensky, M.: Digital natives, digital immigrants. On Horiz. **9**(5), 1–6 (2001)
26. Duncan-Howell, J.: Digital mismatch: Expectations and realities of digital competency amongst pre-service education students. Australas. J. Educ. Technol. **28**(5), 827–840 (2012)
27. Australian Institute for Teaching and School Leadership: Australian professional standards for teachers (2017). https://www.aitsl.edu.au/teach/standards
28. Svensson, M., Baelo, R.: Teacher students' perceptions of their digital competence. Procedia Soc. Behav. Sci. **180**, 1527–1534 (2015)
29. de Silva Joyce, H., Feez, S., Chan, E., Tobias, S.: Investigating the literacy, numeracy and ICT demands of primary teacher education. Aust. J. Teach. Educ. **39**(9), 111–129 (2014)
30. Banas, J.R., York, C.S.: Authentic learning exercises as a means to influence preservice teachers' technology integration self-efficacy and intentions to integrate technology. Australas. J. Educ. Technol. **30**(6), 728–746 (2014)
31. Buabeng-Andoh, C.: Factors influencing teachers' adoption and integration of information and communication technology into teaching: a review of the literature. Int. J. Educ. Dev. Using Inf. Commun. Technol. **8**(1), 136–155 (2012)

32. Brown, D., Warschauer, M.: From the university to the elementary classroom: students' experiences in learning to integrate technology in instruction. J. Technol. Teach. Educ. **14**(3), 599–621 (2006)
33. Lawless, K.A., Pellegrino, J.W.: Professional development in integrating technology into teaching and learning: knowns, unknowns, and ways to pursue better questions and answers. Rev. Educ. Res. **77**(4), 575–614 (2007)
34. Black, G., Smith, K.: Hot Topic: ICT in Pre-Service Teacher Training. Strategic ICT Advisory Service, Adelaide (2009)
35. Australian Council for Educational Research: Literacy and Numeracy Test for Initial Teacher Education. (2018). https://teacheredtest.acer.edu.au/
36. Altus Assessments: Discover CASPer (2019). https://altusassessments.com/discover-casper/
37. Creswell, J.: Educational research: Planning, Conducting, and Evaluating Quantitative and Qualitative Research, 5th edn. Pearson, Boston (2015)
38. Tabachnick, B.G., Fidelll, L.S.: Using Multivariate Statistics, 6th edn. Pearson Education, Boston (2013)
39. Clayton, K., Beekhuyzen, J.: Engaging girls in ICTs: mind the gap! In: Proceedings of the 2004 Australian Women in IT Conference, pp. 41–50 (2004)

Exploratory Study on the Effort Perceived by In-service K-12 Teachers from Subject Areas not Specialising in Computer Science Who Are Complete CS Novices

Paolo Tosato and Monica Banzato[✉]

Department of Linguistics and Comparative Cultural Studies,
Ca' Foscari University, Venice, Italy
{ptosato,banzato}@unive.it

Abstract. Due to the shortage of IT teachers in Italian schools, the teaching of computational thinking is carried out by in-service K-12 teachers from scientific areas not specialised and by novices in computer science (CS). It is crucial to investigate not only the training of teachers in digital skills, but also how their beliefs, attitudes and behaviours can affect, in detail, their implementation in the classroom. From these premises, the present exploratory study investigates the self-efficacy beliefs, intrinsic motivation and perceived effort of a group of 46 teachers who, on a voluntary basis, engaged in a 20-h workshop on CS teaching. The results show a significant improvement in self-efficacy, despite their perception of strong effort to master the subject.

Keywords: Teacher training · Computer science education · Self-efficacy · Intrinsic motivation · Perceived effort

1 Introduction

The educational policies of the last few years have been decisive in promoting the inclusion of computational thinking (hereafter CT) in the school curriculum in several European countries and the rest of the world. The aim is to prepare students for a world strongly influenced by information technology [1, 2], encouraging in the new generations a culture of creation and production rather than the mere consumption of technology.

In Italy, CT has been introduced in primary and secondary schools since 2015 [3]. This educational reform, albeit accompanied by a certain initial enthusiasm, nevertheless presents considerable difficulties for primary and secondary schools (hereafter K-12), among which are: the lack of teachers with sufficient knowledge of the subject as well as complete novices; educational activity in computer science (hereafter CS) carried out by non-specialist teachers or, in some cases, replaced by external IT experts; and insecurities on the part of teachers studying this new subject. A similar situation has been reported in other countries, including: the United States of America (USA) [2], the United Kingdom (UK) [4], Israel [5], and others (see Sect. 2).

The reforms in Italy (as in other countries in the world) have to deal with the lack of CS teachers capable of covering the needs of the entire national school territory. The situation in Italian primary schools, which appears to be the most delicate, has the following peculiarities: 69% of teachers have only a high school diploma; the remaining ones have a higher degree mainly in the science of primary education; and 96.5% are women with an average age of 54.3 years [6]. Nearly all of these teachers are complete novices in CS. Turning to Italian middle schools, we find that there are practically no teachers of CS due to a normative problem: information technology can be taught by engineers or architects; while science is taught by graduates in biological, geological, natural, environmental, agricultural, mathematical and physical sciences (also by some engineers). The average age of teachers in these schools is 53 years, of which 22% are male [6]. The presence of CS teachers in the middle schools is not common (these teachers are specialist subject teachers but not specialised in CS); while CS graduates can teach mathematics, applied mathematics and CS in some high schools. As a result, almost all teachers who are involved in training in CS in middle schools are non-CS scientific area teachers. Even if there were to be a change in the current legislation, it seems a remote possibility that the few graduates in computer science in Italy would be attracted to work as teachers in K-12 schools, both because of the low salary remuneration compared to other school roles, and the high job insecurity in the teaching profession.

Unfortunately, at the moment, there is little research on this precise group of K-12 teachers working in scientific areas not specialised in CS (mainly present in middle schools) or novices at CS (present in primary schools). From research carried out in other countries (USA [2], UK [4], Israel [5]) there are numerous critical issues related to the training of K-12 teachers, also shared in Italy. These include fragmentation and discontinuity of training courses throughout the year, to which is added the heterogeneity of the background of teachers who take training for these courses (both the starting degree and the level of the school where they work). There are CS certification programmes for teachers, recognised by the Italian Ministry of Education, but they have "no tangible relationship with what you need to teach in a computer room" [5]. Unfortunately, there is very little research literature on the beliefs about difficulties, obstacles and perceived efforts that teachers meet in this initial update phase, which requires shifting from information and communication technologies (ICT) to computer science education (see Sect. 2). In Italy, as well, this type of analysis is still an unexplored territory. For this reason, the present exploratory survey aims to investigate the beliefs of self-efficacy, intrinsic motivation and perceived effort required for K-12 teachers involved in CT training courses. In particular, the research questions which we will try to answer are: (1) what are the self-efficacy beliefs of K-12 teachers in-service involved in programming workshop activities?; (2) what perception do K-12 teachers have regarding the intrinsic motivation and effort required and the skills involved in programming activities?; and (3) based on their training-workshop experience, would teachers be able to imagine themselves confidently performing similar classroom activities with their students? The objectives of the research are: (1) to establish the factors that influence the self-efficacy and intrinsic motivation beliefs of K-12 teachers who are studying how to teach programming in the classroom; and (2) to determine the impact of the beliefs of K-12 teachers regarding their ability to teach programming in the classroom.

The exploratory survey was carried out in the course of a 20-h programming laboratory for 46 K-12 teachers. Teachers' participation in the workshop was free and purely on a voluntary basis (no credits or scores were expected).

2 Related Work

The Royal Society [4] has reported that "There are simply not enough teachers with sufficient subject knowledge and understanding to deliver a rigorous Computer Science and Information Technology curriculum in every school at present". In parallel, the European Commission has expressed serious concern that "digital literacy is taught mainly by specialist teachers at secondary level but in approximately 50% of countries it is also taught by other specialist teachers such as mathematics or science teachers" [7]. "Information Technology is not taught by specialist teachers in Ireland, France, Italy, the Netherlands, Sweden, Liechtenstein and Norway – even at secondary level" [4]. Yadav et al. [2] record a similar situation in the United States: "efforts to increase the number of CS teachers have predominantly focused on training teachers from other content areas". There have been several research inquiries that document the experience of computer scientists who teach other scientific subjects in schools. By contrast, there has been little study of the experiences of scientists not specialised in computer science who are asked to teach CS in K-12 schools. Also as pointed out in a number of studies [2, 4, 5], little is known about the difficulties of teachers with no scientific background who must be trained in CS in order to teach it in the classroom. Some studies [2, 8, 9] identify several obstacles which are faced by teachers in CS who teach outside their discipline, such as feeling isolated, teaching in multiple disciplinary areas, class management and insufficient planning time. Veenman [9] identifies 24 crucial problems by means of a meta-analysis work of 83 studies. Among these are difficulties in evaluating student work, a heavy teaching load that leads to reduced planning time, problems in lesson planning, inadequate knowledge of the subject matter and insufficient assistance and support. Other studies report that novice teachers are faced with other challenges such as: loneliness, isolation [2, 10] the lack of adequate IT background and limited resources for professional development [2]. "The researchers argued that these teachers need support during the first years of teaching to increase their content and pedagogical knowledge, self-efficacy and beliefs about what it means to be a successful teacher" [2]. This support should be extended as well to novices and scientists non-specialised in CS K-12 teachers, in both pedagogy and content, taking into account the different educational backgrounds (scientific and not) and the students' education level, as precisely these teachers are facing the first impact of the introduction of CS in K-12. Unfortunately, there is a lack of research documenting what is needed to respond to the needs of these teachers. For this reason, the objective of this exploratory study is to begin an investigation of the critical difficulties faced by K-12 teachers of CS with regard to their self-efficacy beliefs and their perceived effort. "The efficacy beliefs of teachers are related to their instructional practices and their students' achievement" [11].

3 Methods and Instruments: Self-efficacy, Intrinsic Motivation and Perceived Effort

Based on the research questions and objectives presented in Sect. 1, the exploratory survey analysed the results of self-efficacy, intrinsic motivation and perceived effort, according to the following independent variables: gender, age, length of service, diploma or degree, level of education in which the teacher works, subject of teaching, and previous experience of teaching CS courses. The aim was to verify if these matters have a statistically significant impact on the dependent variables. For this reason, a programming workshop was organised, which was preceded and followed by the administration of: (1) pre-test and post-test questionnaires on the beliefs of self-efficacy and intrinsic motivation; and (2) a brief unstructured interview, post-laboratory, aimed at investigating the perceived effort.

The first questionnaire was based on the New General Self-Efficacy scale [12]. This instrument is dedicated to understanding the self-confidence of teachers regarding their learning of CS and their competence to master specific academic domains concerning programming in CS. Pajares [13] found that there was a "strong relationship between teachers' educational beliefs and their planning, instructional decisions, and classroom practices". The self-efficacy questionnaire was based on 8 items on a 5-step Likert scale: from 1, on the "completely disagree" pole, to 5, on the "completely in agreement" pole. The questionnaire investigated the following aspects: the level of self-efficacy in activities of teaching and learning about the subject; expectation of success in the CS workshop; mastery of the computer skills required; work commitment required; teachers' abilities in relation to the programming activities; the achievement of the educational objectives; and the security of managing the evaluation of teaching activities with students.

The teachers' intrinsic motivation, based on a 5-step Likert scale (as with the previous questionnaire), was measured by a selection of 11 items from the Intrinsic Motivation Inventory (IMI) [14]. The original questionnaire consists of seven sub-scales. For this research, three subscales were selected: (a) "interest" to teach programming: this refers to teachers' general intrinsic motivation; (b) "perceived competence" to teach programming: this is theorised to be a positive predictor of intrinsic motivation; (c) "perceived effort" required to teach programming: this is a separate variable which seeks to reveal teachers' needs. This instrument required teachers to imagine themselves teaching programming activities to students.

The third tool employed unstructured interviews aimed at exploring in depth teachers' perceptions of effort: (1) effort required for updating in CS and degree of satisfaction; (2) required effort for personal study of CS; (3) self-assessment of progress in one's CS competence level based on the teacher's experience; (4.1) if the teacher has already taught students programming, what are the perceived difficulties of educational activities in the subject?; and (4.2) if the teacher has not yet taught students programming, what are the expectations and when does he or she plan to start teaching? The study was conducted during a 20-h teacher update workshop that aimed to explore and test elementary programming concepts with the following tools: Lego WeDo, Scratch and Rospino.

4 Research Results

A total of 46 teachers, comprising 17 primary school teachers and 29 lower secondary school teachers, enrolled in this pilot study. The teachers were aged from 35 to 63 years (mean age 47 years). The teachers from scientific areas (mathematics, science and technology) were 34, while the teachers from humanities areas (Italian, history, religion, music, foreign language) were 12; the majority had never experienced programming laboratories (30 teachers), while 16 had participated in at least one laboratory on this topic. According to gender, the participants comprised 12 males and 34 females, while according to their academic degree, the majority of teachers were college graduates (32 participants) compared to high school graduated teachers (12 participants).

4.1 Results Regarding Changes in Self-efficacy

To verify whether the educational activities had produced an improvement in the sense of self-efficacy, a t-test for dependent samples was performed on data from 46 teachers; this revealed that the change (Pre: $M = 3.65$, $SD = 0.54$, range from 2.14 to 5.00; Post: $M = 4.16$, $SD = 0.56$, range from 2.71 to 5.00) was statistically significant ($t(45) = -5.14$, $p < 0.01$). Subsequently, in order to answer the research questions, the data collected from the questionnaires were more deeply analysed to understand if the increment of self-efficacy was uniform in the group of participants or particularly relevant in a specific category of teachers. For this reason, some independent variables were identified (gender, age, years of service, educational qualification, programming experience, subject taught), and based on these variables, the impact of the laboratory on teachers' self-efficacy was assessed.

Groups by Gender. Grouping data by gender importantly indicated how the change in the sense of self-efficacy was statistically significant in female teachers ($t(33) = -4.93$, $p < 0.01$), moving from a mean of 3.61 to a mean of 4.17. By contrast, the change in the sense of self-efficacy was not statistically significant in male teachers ($p > 0.05$), moving from a mean of 3.76 to a mean of 4.12.

Groups by Age. To analyse the change in self-efficacy, 4 groups were created: from 30 to 39 years old, from 40 to 49 years old, from 50 to 59 years old and from 60 to 69 years old. The most numerous groups were those aged 40–49 years (24 teachers) and those aged 50–59 years (13 teachers). In these groups the increment of self-efficacy was greater than the other groups and was also statistically significant. A deeper analysis of these two groups (40–49 and 50–59 years old), found out that the increase in self-efficacy was particularly relevant and statistically significant in teachers who taught science subjects, were college graduated and were women.

Groups by Years of Service. To analyse the change in self-efficacy, 5 groups were created: from 0 to 9 years, from 10 to 19 years, from 20 to 29 years, from 30 to 39 years and from 40 to 49 years. Confirming the results obtained by grouping data by age, teachers with 10–19 years of service obtained the more significant increase in self-efficacy, from a statistical point of view, moving from a mean of 3.74 to a mean of 4.24, $t(23) = -3.39$, $p < 0.01$.

Groups by Educational Qualification. Grouping data according to teachers' degrees, it was possible to notice how the increase in self-efficacy was statistically significant both in college graduated teachers ($p < 0.01$) and in high school graduated teachers ($p < 0.01$). A deeper analysis of these groups revealed that the increase in self-efficacy was more significant in women and in teachers who taught science subjects.

Groups by Programming Experience. Grouping data according to programming experience, it was possible to notice how the increase in self-efficacy was statistically significant both in teachers with experience ($p < 0.01$) and in teachers with no experience ($p < 0.01$). A deeper analysis of these groups revealed that the increase of self-efficacy was more significant, from a statistical point of view, in female, college graduated teachers and in teachers who taught science subjects, according to the findings of the previous section.

Groups by Subject. Grouping data according to the subject taught, it was possible to notice how the increase in self-efficacy was statistically significant both in teachers who taught humanities ($p < 0.01$) and teachers who taught science subjects ($p < 0.01$). As noted in previous sections, the increase in self-efficacy was greater and statistically significant in female and college graduated teachers.

4.2 Results Regarding Changes in Intrinsic Motivation

To verify whether the educational activities had produced an improvement in intrinsic motivation, a t-test for dependent samples was performed on data from 46 teachers; this revealed that the change (Pre: $M = 4.04$, $SD = 0.41$, range from 3.00 to 5.00; Post: $M = 4.13$, $SD = 0.49$, range from 3.00 to 5.00) was not statistically significant ($t(45) = -1.72$, $p > 0.05$). In order to answer the research questions, the data collected from the questionnaires were more deeply analysed, grouping by different variables. This made it possible to compare the results regarding intrinsic motivation with the results of self-efficacy and to understand if the change in intrinsic motivation was particularly relevant in a specific group of teachers.

Groups by Age. Using the same groups identified for self-efficacy (Sect. 4.1), the change in teachers' motivation was analysed. In these groups, the change of motivation was not statistically significant, but it is interesting to highlight that in teachers aged 30–39 and 60–69 years the motivation decreased, while in teachers aged 40–49 and 50–59 years it increased, moving from a mean of 4.07 to a mean of 4.18 (40–49 years old) and from a mean of 3.95 to a mean of 4.14 (50–59 years old). A deeper analysis revealed that the increase in intrinsic motivation was greater and statistically significant in teachers aged 40–49 with programming experience, moving from a mean of 4.26 to a mean of 4.60, $p < 0.05$. Nothing statistically significant can be said grouping teachers aged 40–49 years by gender or educational qualification, even if the increase in motivation was particularly important in female teachers (from a mean of 4.05 to a mean of 4.18, $p = 0.077$).

Groups by Programming Experience. Grouping data according to programming experience, the increase in motivation was statistically significant only in teachers with experience ($p < 0.05$). Nothing statistically significant can be said grouping teachers with experience and without experience by gender. Instead, by grouping data according to their degree, there was a significant increase in motivation in college graduated teachers with experience, moving from a mean of 4.09 to a mean of 4.36, $p = 0.066$.

Groups by Subject. Grouping data according to the subject taught, there was no statistically significant change in motivation, even if the change in teachers who taught science subjects was greater (from a mean of 4.08 to a mean of 4.21) than teachers who taught humanities (from a mean of 3.91 to a mean of 3.93). Nothing statistically significant can be said grouping teachers by gender or educational qualification. Instead, it is important to highlight the increase of motivation in teachers who taught science subjects with programming experience (from a mean of 4.13 to a mean of 4.38, $p = 0.072$), partly supporting the findings of the previous section.

4.3 Results Regarding Changes in Perceived Effort

To verify whether the educational activities had produced an improvement in perceived effort, a Wilcoxon test was performed on data from 46 teachers; this revealed that the change (Pre: Median = 4.00, Q1 = 3.50, Q3 = 4.50; Post: Median = 4.00, Q1 = 3.50, Q3 = 4.13) was not statistically significant ($z = -0.94$, $p = 0.347$). It is important to underline that the higher mean values indicate a lower perceived effort, therefore a better teacher response. As with self-efficacy (Sect. 4.1) and intrinsic motivation (Sect. 4.2), a deeper analysis for perceived effort was also performed, grouping data by different factors.

Groups by Age. Using the same groups identified for self-efficacy (Sect. 4.1) and intrinsic motivation (Sect. 4.2), the change in teachers' effort was analysed. In any groups the change of effort was not statistically significant, but it is interesting to highlight that in teachers aged 40–49 and 50–59 years the perceived effort increased less than teachers aged 30–39 and 60–69 years. The values are respectively: teachers aged 30–39 years: from 4.00 to 3.67; teachers aged 40–49 years: from 4.04 to 3.98; teachers aged 50–59 years: from 4.00 to 3.96; teachers aged 60–69 years: from 3.83 to 3.67. Grouping data according to the years of service, the perceived effort increases, or remains the same, in all groups, except in teachers aged 40–49 and 50–59 years having 10–19 years of service. Although the change in effort is not statistically significant, in teachers aged 40–49 years with 10–19 years of service the perceived effort decreases from 4.00 to 4.04, while in teachers aged 50–59 years with 10–19 years of service the perceived effort decreases from 3.83 to 4.08. A similar result is obtained grouping data by programming experience.

Groups by Programming Experience. Grouping data according to the programming experience, there is not a statistically significant change in perceived effort, although in teachers without experience the effort increases (from 3.92 to 3.75), while in teachers with experience the perceived effort decreases (from 4.19 to 4.22). A deeper analysis highlights that the reduction in perceived effort among teachers with experience is particularly relevant in college graduated teachers (from 4.05 to 4.25), while among high school graduated teachers the perceived effort increases both in teachers with experience and without experience in programming.

Groups by Subject. Grouping data according to the subject taught, there is no statistically significant change in perceived effort. Grouping data by subject and programming experience, perceived effort increases in all groups, except among teachers who teach science subjects and have experience in programming (from 4.23 to 4.27). The change is not statistically significant, but it confirms what was highlighted in the previous section, where teachers were grouped according to programming experience.

5 Interview on Motivation and Perceived Effort

The transcribed interviews were codified and on the basis of a subsequent re-elaboration some categories were extrapolated to provide the conceptual structure that allowed us to select the results reported here. Whereas, in general, we have found a shared accord in the opinions of the teachers, we report the answers as cumulative percentages. From the analysis of the unstructured interviews, to which 96% voluntarily responded, it emerged that many teachers (80%) expressed a determined intention to master the subject and a willingness to continue learning, despite the difficulties that they were encountering. Nevertheless, 73% expressed uneasiness about the training on offer to them. Although characterised by many valid and interesting offers, they found it difficult to form a satisfactory overall picture of what was available to them. Another crucial point is that teachers asked for their commitment to training in this new discipline to be recognised by the schools. They believe that in the future they will be asked to teach their specialised subject and CS at the same time, and will have to keep up-to-date with developments in both of them. The teachers interviewed manifested a good ability: to analyse the commitment required (80%); to reflect on their self-assessment of progress in the discipline (70%); but they considered that they did not yet possess appropriate criteria for assessing the subject; to maintain a proactive attitude, advancing proposals and alternative solutions to existing training (80%); and to show willingness to assume the responsibilities for teaching CS at school (80%). Far fewer teachers expressed their strong disagreement with the current training (7%) or did not wish to continue because the subject was too difficult and complex (9%). Most teachers wondered how many years it would take to master the discipline. Ninety-one per cent expressed concern that they did not feel as expert in CS as in their own disciplines, which they had been teaching for years, and 36% believed that the students knew more than they did. The proposals advanced by 80%, mentioned above, were all oriented to informal learning and to classroom practice, such as: having opportunities to share and discuss problems and learning solutions with colleagues in CS who, unfortunately, are not present in their school; to observe a CS colleague when teaching programming lessons to students; and to start their own programming lessons in co-teaching with a more experienced colleague. They expressed a desire: to analyse the various alternative ways of teaching CS (68%); to review their choices and solutions with colleagues in the subject (73%); and to discuss with expert colleagues the management strategies needed to face any difficulties (80%). The percentage of teachers who were aware of their strengths and weaknesses in the CS area was also high (95%). Many had shown the ability to predict the difficulties they might encounter in the implementation of CS with students in the classroom (66%), even if only a few (25%) were able to think positively about the possibility of failure and to recognise the typical causes of their own mistakes, due to lack of experience. Most of the novices in CS (93%) believed that they would not begin teaching programming in less than a year; while those who already taught it stressed that they did not feel expert in the subject and were proceeding very cautiously with small workshops with pupils. It was therefore too early for them to analyse the educational difficulties.

6 Conclusions and Limitations of the Research

From the results of the questionnaire, we can deduce that the course in programming completed by the researchers led to an increase in their sense of self-efficacy. To answer the first research question, we can state that the most significant improvement is in female teachers who were college graduated and taught science subjects. These groups of teachers also reported increased motivation and no worsening of perceived effort, which remained almost the same in pre- and post-tests (these improvements were particularly notable among teachers with programming experience). The groups that appeared to be the weakest were the younger and older teachers: this appeared to be a consequence of inexperience in the young and lack of energy in the old. However, we must not forget the problematic context that creates the difficulties and obstacles these teachers have to face (Sect. 5). To answer the first two research questions, it is important to note that self-efficacy and intrinsic motivation have increased in some groups despite the fact that a high level of perceived effort was required. Moreover, in the interviews they demonstrated a high level of analysis, critical reflection and professional self-assessment in carefully evaluating their present and future actions. From their reflections, we conclude that immediate intervention measures are needed to support teachers who are facing genuine challenges. This is especially important in this delicate period in which the teaching of CS is being introduced in schools. "It has been demonstrated that students generally learn more from teachers with high self-efficacy than from those whose self-efficacy is low. In fact, teachers' beliefs in their instructional efficacy is a very strong predictor of academic attainment in young children" [15]. Confirming other evidence reported by other authors [2, 5, 16] in Sect. 2, and answering the third question, these teachers demonstrated that: (1) their perceived effort increases especially because they have difficulty in re-elaborating the subject teaching on their own. The training courses are not intended to be established as an organised system of learning, but they are fragmentary and unrelated to each other; therefore, it is difficult for teachers to draw up a systematic overall picture of CS and its pedagogical aspects; (2) based on their teaching experience, they believe this "adventure" is absolutely new (it does not have anything similar to their past work) and unexpectedly puts into question their professional role (as some teachers have said: "At this moment, the children know more than we do"); and (3) the teachers have analysed their commitment as perceived by the school and believe that it does not have the deserved recognition because colleagues often confuse it with a training in general ICT, rather than with a specific disciplinary area, computer science education.

The principal limits of this exploratory study are: the selection of the group of participants is based on criteria of convenience (volunteer teachers participating in a training course); and is subject to bias. Finally, it should be observed that as these teachers are Italian, the problems identified by them may not be relevant in other contexts. This exploratory study has investigated only some characteristics and criticalities; however, if we take into account the multidimensionality of teacher professionalism and the constant pressure to which it is subjected (in this phase of digital innovation in the schools), it is necessary to expand and deepen the investigation to further dimensions.

Note: For reasons of national assessment of Italian university research, the authors must declare which sections each has written, in spite of the fact that work is entirely the result of continuous and intensive collaboration. Sections 1, 2, 3, 5 and 6 are by M. Banzato. Section 4 is by P. Tosato. Our thanks to Matthew Hoffman.

References

1. National Research Council: Committee for the Workshops on Computational Thinking: Report of a workshop of pedagogical aspects of computational thinking. National Academies Press, Washington, DC (2011)
2. Yadav, A., et al.: Expanding computer science education in schools: understanding teacher experiences and challenges. Comput. Sci. Educ. **26**(4), 235–254 (2016)
3. MIUR: Riforma del sistema nazionale di istruzione e formazione e delega per il riordino delle disposizioni legislative vigenti. LEGGE 13/07/ 2015, n. 107 (2015)
4. The Royal Society: Shut down or restart? The way forward for computing in UK schools. The Royal Society, London (2012)
5. Gal-Ezer, J., Stephenson, C.: Computer science teacher preparation is critical. ACM Inroads **1**, 61–66 (2010)
6. OECD: Education at a Glance 2016: OECD Indicators. OECD Publishing, Paris, France (2016)
7. Eurydice: Key data on learning and innovation through ICT at school in Europe 2011. EACEA, Brussels, Belgium (2011)
8. Feiman-Nemser, S., Schwille, S., Carver, C., Yusko, B.: A conceptual review of literature on new teacher induction: National partnership of excellence and accountability in teaching. National Partnership of Excellence and Accountability in Teaching, East Lansing, MI (1999)
9. Veenman, S.: Perceived problems of beginning teachers. Rev. Educ. Res. **54**, 143–178 (1984)
10. Corley, E.L.: First-year teachers: Strangers in strange lands. Paper presented at the Mid-Western Educational Research Association, Chicago, IL, pp. 1–43 (1998). https://files.eric.ed.gov/fulltext/ED424216.pdf
11. Tschannen-Moran, M., Hoy, A.W., Hoy, W.K.: Teacher efficacy: its meaning and measure. Rev. Educ. Res. **68**(2), 202–248 (1998)
12. Chen, G., Gully, S.M., Eden, D.: Validation of a new general self-efficacy scale. Organ. Res. Methods **4**(1), 62–83 (2001)

13. Pajares, F.: Teachers beliefs and educational research: cleaning up a messy construct. Rev. Educ. Res. **62**, 307–332 (1992)
14. Ryan, R.M., Deci, E.L.: Intrinsic and extrinsic motivations: classic definitions and new directions. Contemp. Educ. Psychol. **25**(1), 54–67 (2000)
15. Mulholland, J., Wallace, J.: Teacher induction and elementary science teaching: enhancing self-efficacy. Teach. Teach. Educ. **17**(2), 243–261 (2001)
16. Qian, Y., Hambrusch, S., Yadav, A., Gretter, S.: Who needs what: recommendations for designing effective online professional development for computer science teachers. J. Res. Technol. Educ. **50**(2), 164–181 (2018)

Hanging Pictures or Searching the Web

Informing the Design of a Decision-Making System that Empowers Teachers to Appropriate Educational Resources to Their School's Infrastructure

N. Yiannoutsou[1,2(✉)], N. Otero[3,4], W. Müller[5], C. Neofytou[1], M. Miltiadous[1], and T. Hadzilacos[1,6]

[1] Open University, Nicosia, Cyprus
{chrystalla.neofytou,Thanasis.Hadzilacos}@ouc.ac.cy,
miltos.miltiadous@st.ouc.ac.cy
[2] University College London – Knowledge Lab, London, UK
n.yiannoutsou@ucl.ac.uk
[3] Linnaeus University, Växjö, Sweden
nuno.otero@lnu.se
[4] ISCTE-IUL, CIS-IUL, Lisbon, Portugal
[5] University of Education Weingarten, Weingarten, Germany
mueller@md-phw.de
[6] The Cyprus Institute, Nicosia, Cyprus

Abstract. In this paper, we report work in designing a decision-making system that aims to support teachers in appropriating to their practice innovative scenarios that employ uses of information and communication technologies (ICT) in teaching and learning. To this end, we break down educational scenarios into micro-activities, and connect them to required and alternative infrastructure. We argue that micro-activities is a unit of analysis of educational scenarios that is compatible with the role of teachers as designers who select, decompose, combine, enact and revise different pieces of resources. This paper offers a reflective viewpoint on integrating ICT in existing scenarios and investigates how teaching objectives make use, or not, of the potential of digital technologies.

Keywords: Educational scenarios · Micro-activities · Educational innovation

1 Introduction

Educational technology moves much faster than pedagogical innovation. This leads to the paradox of schools never having enough information and communication technology (ICT) while this very ICT is underutilised. Teachers willing to at least try out innovative technology-enhanced educational scenarios are often stopped by perceived lack of necessary equipment. However, the question "can I do this with my existing school infrastructure?" may be unnecessarily getting negative answers, as obvious and non-obvious substitutes exist. While most teachers know about open source alternatives to a piece of software they do not have, they may need to be told that a shared document (e.g., Google Docs, cryptpad) can play the role of an interactive whiteboard, thus representing a not-so-obvious replacement for a piece of hardware described as being essential in a learning scenario identified by a teacher as desirable. In this paper, we present a systematic approach to answer the question "Can I do this (ICT-enhanced lesson) with my school's infrastructure?" We start with a structural analysis (break up) of the educational scenario, leading to a sequence (or web) of 'micro-activities', where alternatives with other equipment may exist for each. It is up to the teacher, and depends on the learning context and goals, whether each of these alternatives is an acceptable alternative or not. Our analysis is backed by an ontology-based knowledge base system that provides the means to propose alternative implementations of scenarios on the technical level, potentially allowing for more sophisticated inference mechanisms in the future.

2 Theoretical Background

In early discussions about integration of ICT in education, availability of resources was one of the contextual forces impeding the use of digital technologies in the classroom [1]. Today, the situation is very different, as teachers are exposed to numerous learning resources through platforms, be they open (PhET, i2geo, LeMill, Curriki, EduTags), from textbook or learning tool publishers, or more social network oriented (e.g., OpenDiscoverySpace, eTwinning, YouTube for Schools, Canvas LMS). While these platforms offer widely-available learning scenarios and, sometimes, reports of experiential use in different contexts, their current impact on schools and teachers remains low [2]. Our observation is that each of these contributions is quite isolated and the deployment within the school infrastructure is often inexplicit. Lack of infrastructure used to be, and in some cases still is, a problem for ICT integration [3]. However, today, the problem of infrastructure has been transformed to an issue regarding type of infrastructure available and teachers' access to it, making infrastructure an issue of school and/or national policy [1, 3, 4].

The paradox of choice (i.e., *more is less*) that applies in the availability and use of resources has another facet, which is related to the grain size of resources available, and the way teachers use these resources [5]. A fully-fledged scenario (lasting several hours) or a lesson plan, may be difficult to implement in another classroom for reasons related not only to curriculum and context (i.e., classroom, school, country), but also to a teacher's personal epistemologies and pedagogies (such as factors influencing the use of resources by the teachers [5]). Furthermore, appropriation of this type of resources is often time-consuming and requires a lot of effort to overcome cultural, contextual and methodological barriers. This is not to say that a scenario or a lesson plan is not useful as a resource; instead, for the teachers to be able to use it, we argue that it is important to address teachers as designers, and not just as users.

These observations are backed by the work of Gueudet and Trouche [6], which highlights that the use of resources by the teachers does not simply involve implementation of what they (the teachers) find available. Instead, it is a complex and demanding process involving a continuous dialogue between design and enactment. More specifically, teachers, using existing knowledge and influenced by the institution and the community they belong to, select resources, combine different pieces of resources together, test them in their class and revise the initial use (ibid). To capture this complexity, Gueudet and Trouche (ibid), describe the use of resources in practice as **documentational genesis**. Documentational genesis consists of two elements: (a) the resource; and (b) the development of a utilisation scheme. The latter involves a process of appropriation and transformation of the resource in order to solve a specific problem or to achieve a type of task (ibid). Documentational genesis is mediated by two intertwined processes. Instrumentalisation: where teachers appropriate and shape the resources (i.e., in our case educational scenarios/lesson plans) using their existing knowledge. Instrumentation: where a teacher's interaction with the resources (e.g., inspection, appropriation) enriches and shapes a teacher's knowledge and practice.

Our approach for the structural analysis of scenarios and the design of the recommendation system, is informed by the theoretical analysis of teachers' use of resources, in the following ways:

- We break up the scenario into micro-activities (which can lead back to the initial scenario) in order to facilitate the process of appropriation, selection and combination of different pieces of resources;
- We provide connections of micro-activities to different types of infrastructures in order to facilitate the instrumentalisation process (i.e., adaptation of resources by the teacher);
- We design recommendations for adaptation of micro-activities based on technology functionalities and different contexts of use, aiming to support the instrumentation process (enrichment of teacher knowledge). The purpose of the latter is to attend to the creative dimension of teaching and address teachers (also) as designers.

Fischer et al. [7] highlight that creativity can emerge in contexts where people experience breakdowns (i.e., when they experience something they cannot do). Considering that our overarching question "Can I do this?" is also a fertile ground for creativity [8], we do not provide ready-made solutions, but instruments to trigger a teacher's creativity, i.e., choosing one or more micro-activities from a scenario, showing how the same micro-activity can be transformed in different contexts and supporting the investigation of alternatives.

3 Motivation

The motivation for our work stems from two observations. First, the use of ICT in the classroom being tool-centred – as opposed to affordances-centred – very often results in short-sighted and trivial uses of digital technologies, which could be replaced by 'low tech' alternatives if seen from the point of view of the instructional goal they support. Second, looking into tool affordances - instead of specific pieces of software - can help facilitate the implementation of ICT scenarios with the available infrastructure, and also support teachers in harnessing the potential of ICT in the scenarios they apply in their classroom.

Based on these two observations, we argue that in order to answer the question "Can I do this" we need to adopt a critical stance both when we look at the uses of ICT in educational scenarios and when we look at the instructional goals underlying each activity. Next, we use the example of a simple activity, that of hanging pictures on the classroom wall, to demonstrate how focusing on the affordances of a tool and being critical of the instructional goals supported by the specific tool, can lead to a number of feasible (in terms of infrastructure available) and suitable (in terms of tool affordances) uses of technology.

3.1 Hanging Pictures on the Classroom Wall – An Outsider's View

We adapt an outsider's view to discuss the activity of hanging pictures on the classroom wall. Being an outsider that observes a classroom activity through the window of the class frees us from accepting contextual assumptions about the instructional goals, and directs us to explore the context by asking a very important question: why are they doing this? The exploration of possible answers to this question allows us to create a "locus of potentiality" populated with various instructional goals behind a single micro-activity, each of which is re-examined in relation to the infrastructure it requires to be achieved. In our example, the micro-activity is the following: "The teacher asks the student to put up the picture on the class wall". The necessary infrastructure for this activity is: (a) a framed picture; (b) a hammer; and (c) a nail.

Now let us investigate "why are they doing this", i.e., what are the potential instructional goals behind this activity. In a kindergarten class, each pupil is asked to put a picture on the wall for the whole class to see everybody's work. In this context, the required infrastructure to perform this activity is shaped as follows: the picture does not need to be framed; pupils can use blue tack to put an unframed picture on the wall; hammer and nail are not necessary.

In a vocational education setting, the goal might be to show what type of hanging is suitable for each type of wall surface. In this case, the absolute specific infrastructure is needed (i.e., framed picture, nail and hammer), as they are essential for achieving the goal of the specific learning activity. A screw and a screwdriver might provide a useful alternative in terms of infrastructure, depending on the type of wall, or it could be used as a counter-example of what should not be done.

In a high-school classroom, the picture might be needed on the wall in order to analyse its content in a whole class discussion. In this case the goal is to make the picture visible to the whole class for the duration of the specific lesson. To achieve this goal, we might use a stone and a nail, instead of a hammer, a screw and a screwdriver if they are available, blue tack, or a computer and a projector. In this case the nail, hammer and framed picture are not essential.

In an examination context, at high school, the picture needs to be put up on the wall in order for the students to analyse it individually, responding to one or more test questions. In this case, the goal again is to make the picture visible to the whole class for the duration of the examination. All the solutions to replace hammer and nail mentioned in the previous paragraph are applicable here. Furthermore, considering the context of the examination, we might prefer to provide students with a printed picture allowing them to observe it closely and to comment on it in order to structure their response to the test. Alternatively, and if students have their computers or mobile telephones with them, they could access a common digital picture or slightly different pictures slightly changing the initial scenario. Again, nail, hammer and framed picture are not essential.

4 Method of Work: Reverse Engineering of Educational Scenarios

We mentioned earlier in this paper that our aim is to design a recommendation system supporting teachers to adapt existing scenarios to their classroom infrastructure. To this end we built a knowledge base consisting of 200 educational scenarios (accessible at: www.esit4sip.eu) drawn from the web and provided by the schools we are collaborating with. The next step was to select certain scenarios and ICT tools to focus on, in order to be able at a later stage to create a more general model to be applied in all the scenarios of the knowledge base. At this first stage, we chose scenarios of sufficient complexity based on teacher suggestions and on diversity of educational contexts. We analysed the selected scenarios using qualitative research methods and tools as to how and why ICT is used in each one. For this, we broke down the scenarios extracting ICT micro-activities, which are smaller units of learner and teacher ICT activity. The way ICT is used in a micro-activity corresponds to ICT tool affordances. The educational effect to which ICT is used in a micro-activity corresponds to educational functionality. For each micro-activity, we considered technological alternatives with educationally equivalent functionality (Fig. 1).

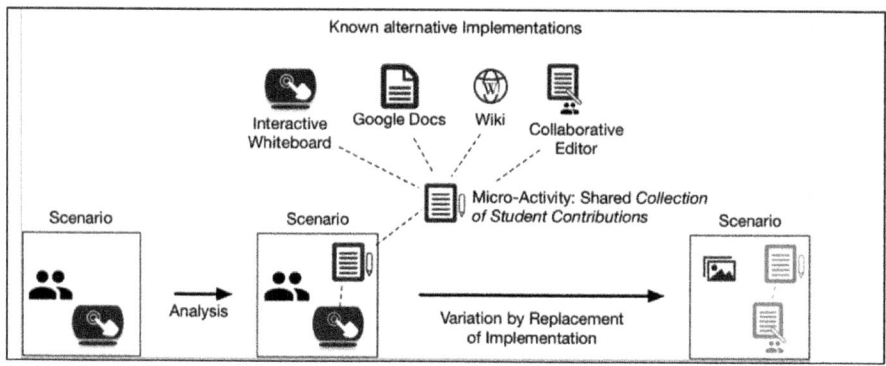

Fig. 1. Method of scenario analysis - example of micro-activity with whiteboard

As long as "Can I do this?" refers to whole educational scenarios, answering it remains very complex. By breaking up a scenario into micro-activities, we reduce the question to finding equivalent and alternative micro-activities using different ICT infrastructure. Educational equivalence depends on the exact context and learning goals. A stone can replace the hammer for driving the nail in the wall, except if the purpose of hanging the picture was the very use of the hammer. Another word processor can replace Microsoft (MS) Word for writing a text, except if the purpose of writing the text was learning the specific characteristics of MS Word 2016.

We would need to know the educational rationale of the micro-activity in order to find proper equivalents using alternative infrastructure. But the educational rationale may be hidden and certainly not explicitly stated in an educational scenario. What our system can do is discern patterns of use (instructional approaches) and propose alternatives for the teacher to decide if they are sufficiently suitable substitutes - some may be unacceptable, others may modify the learning results, others may be equivalent, still others may offer something quite different but quite acceptable. To better demonstrate our methodology, we present in the following the procedure we follow to generate recommendations:

1. **From the scenario abstract micro-activities** ("hang a picture") and related 'infrastructure' (hammer, nail, picture)
2. **Consider diverse possible instructional rationales** of each micro-activity (diverse educational contexts): "why would you want students to hang pictures on the wall?"
3. **Analyse functionality/affordances of infrastructure** - Hammer: can drive nails into walls; Nail: can hold framed pictures on walls; Picture on wall: can be seen by whole class
4. **Consider other infrastructure with** similar functionality (stone ~ hammer, screw ~ nail) or similar result (glue ~ hang, project digital ~ hang physical, directly observe single physical object ~ through ICT observe digital copies)

Next, we show how we use these steps to analyse an ICT-based scenario in order to provide recommendations for equivalent and alternative activities for one of its micro-activities (collect material).

5 "Searching the Web": Analysis - Recommendations for Equivalent and Alternative Activities

The work we report here takes place in the context of the Erasmus + project "eSIT4SIP" (empowering the School IT infrastructures for the implementation of Sustainable Instructional Patterns, www.esit4sip.eu). In Sect. 4, we mentioned that part of the project's outputs is an ontology-based knowledge-base consisting of 200 scenarios. From this knowledge-base, we extracted the scenario: "How to revive the story" (Authors: Nada Stojičević, Nikola Ćurčin). The scenario is designed for 15–18-year-old students. The subject matter is not mentioned. Following the analytic scheme presented in Sect. 4, our analysis of this scenario takes the following form:

Micro-activities: The micro-activities (coded as MA) extracted from the scenario are the following - MA1: Prepare a story that triggers student interest about QR codes and animated maps; MA2: Discuss the story with the students; MA3: Create groups of students (different roles: photographers, researchers, coordinators, animators, web designers); MA4: Taking pictures of selected sites (topics in the original); MA5: Collect material [interpretation: information for the locations] that will be integrated in the animated map; MA6: Create animated maps. [Subject: students]; MA7: Upload the finished materials to the site (Wordpress); MA8: create and print quick response (QR) codes [Subject: students]; MA9: Students present their work [Subject: students].

Infrastructure: The infrastructure mentioned in the scenario involves: at least 15 computers with internet access; mobile telephones with cameras and QR code scanner; digital photo cameras; software: Animaps, Wordpress, Panorama, QR code generator.

Functionalities/affordances of infrastructure: Web-search: Find information around a subject using relevant keywords, offer access to various types of information regarding the topic of interest and sort the information found from the most relevant to the least relevant.

Other infrastructure. Similar result: take interviews, use information from an accredited source. Similar functionality: use teacher laptop and projector instead of computer laboratory.

To demonstrate our approach, we will focus only on the "Collection of information" micro-activity (MA5). We chose this activity for two reasons. The first is that collection of information is a common element of a wide variety of scenarios, especially in social sciences and humanities. The other reason is that information seeking is part of a new set of skills acknowledged as digital competences [9]. In the next two sub-sections, we show how we generate recommendations for alternative and equivalent activities based on an analysis of the affordances of technology (i.e., what is its potential) in relation to the teaching objectives it serves (i.e., what a teacher would intend to do with this technology).

5.1 Diverse Instructional Rationales (Alternative Activities)

The scenario mentions that students collect information to add to the interactive map without specifying the means or the type of the collected material. However, in the introductory session, the authors describe the actual output of students' work: "*In addition to photography, the user will be reading an explanation of the museum building, centre, municipal building, park, church....*". Situating this in the context of the overall scenario - i.e., the creation of an interactive map - helps us to assume that the collected information will consist of short texts describing the sites of the map.

The scenario neither explains the means nor the tools students are going to use to collect information. Two assumptions are drawn from this: (a) the use of web search is so widespread that it is not necessary to be mentioned; (b) the type of information collected is not that important because the emphasis is on adding content (photographs, text) on the map. If we accept the first assumption, then web-search is a "legitimate" learning activity. In this case, the infrastructure required for this micro-activity is: computer laboratory, computers connected to the internet, browser. Next, we provide two examples of instructional goals related to the micro-activity involving web-search and respective settings.

Setting 1 - Instructional goal 1: Identify differences between search engines and between devices (owned by different users) - the filter bubble [10]. The infrastructure mentioned in the micro-activity is the same, but the instructional goal involves the development of digital competences. The micro-activity can be implemented with the same age group in the context of IT lessons.

Setting 2 - Instructional goal 2: Seek, evaluate, select and appropriate information from the web. Here the emphasis would be for the students to learn how to refine their keywords (seek information), evaluate the sources of the information provided and appropriate the information they select to their purposes. The micro-activity can be implemented across subject topics, with younger audiences (age 12–15 years), using the same infrastructure (as in the initial MA).

5.2 Infrastructure with Similar Functionality or Similar Result (Equivalent Activities)

In this section, we present how the focus on the technological affordances in terms of results and/or functionalities can support the implementation of the micro-activity "Collection of information" in the classroom with different types of infrastructure.

Infrastructure with similar result 1: Take an interview from someone who has the information or ask people who live or work next to the sites that are going to be included in the map, to describe the site of interest with a relevant representative phrase. The infrastructure needed here is a notebook or a sound recording device. From an instructional point of view, the use of this infrastructure will allow students to collect the information they need. This choice can be "instructionally acceptable" in the following situations: (a) if the means students use to collect information does not really matter for the specific learning scenario (i.e. there are no implicit or explicit objectives regarding this activity); (b) if the teacher would like to explore with the students the interview as a medium for collecting information. If a teacher decides to take this path, then he/she should envisage a time slot for the students to work on appropriating this information to be integrated in a digital map. A final step would be for the students to delve into the differences between the information collected and that existing in other digital maps. From an instructional perspective, this option might offer rich learning opportunities regarding the use of digital information, especially if compared to unstructured web-search where students type a keyword and copy-paste information from the first result coming up.

Infrastructure with similar result 2: The teacher provides each group with printouts containing information about the sites they are going to include in their map. Their job is to appropriate this information so as to be interesting for the users of the map and to record it on a piece of paper. Infrastructure: printouts and notepad. From an instructional point of view this option can be acceptable if the teacher does not want, or does not have the time, to emphasise the aspect of including information on a digital map or wants her/his students to work on specific information, e.g., taken from an accredited text book. The appropriation of information, however, should consider the functionalities of a digital map (length and type of information shown). From an instructional point of view, this activity, though not making direct use of digital technologies, is done with reference to digital technologies (i.e., the functionalities of a digital map) and allows for focused work on the editing and appropriating information, which often is overlooked when simple web-search is involved.

Infrastructure with similar functionality: Students work in groups, each group being responsible for one site of interest, and take some time to think about the keywords they could use in order to search information on the web. When they are ready, each group takes turns in dictating their keywords to the teacher who types them on his/her laptop and the teams see the results through a video projector. Then the group, with the help of the teacher and the other groups, review the results and refine their search if necessary. The teacher goes through the information found (i.e., reading it aloud) and the group responsible for the specific site takes notes to use them for the construction of information to be included in the map. Alternatively, the teacher can print out the information for the groups to adapt it for the map. The infrastructure that is necessary here is one computer connected to the internet, a browser, and a projector. From an instructional point of view, the use of the same technology in a different orchestration (from the computer laboratory to the teacher laptop) makes salient in the whole class a process which usually happens in a group or individually. This transfer results in a qualitatively different process, as it offers opportunities for refinement from different viewpoints (i.e., the viewpoints of the other groups), which is rarely pursued when web-search is just a small step for something else (e.g., to use the information found to construct a map).

The analysis of this scenario aimed to show the application of our analytic framework and the production of recommendations by domain experts. The recommendations stemmed from a critical-reflective analytic approach on the uses of technology. This approach involved a focus on learning objectives and technology affordances. In the example we analysed above, we found that there are uses of ICT which do not harness the potential of digital technologies to support learning (in the sense that the same learning objectives can be pursued effectively without technology). Furthermore, looking at the technology from the point of view of affordances allows us not only to rethink the infrastructure needed but also to come up with new educational activities which rely on what the technology can actually do.

6 Concluding Remarks

In this paper, we described our approach in empowering teachers to integrate available resources (i.e., ICT enhanced scenarios and lessons in their practice) by making use of existing infrastructure in their schools. Our work is informed by two theoretical underpinnings. One is the role of infrastructure in impeding teachers to try innovative educational scenarios in their class. The second involves the role of the teacher as designer. In order to facilitate the appropriation process, we break down the educational scenarios into micro-activities, each explicitly connected to the infrastructure mentioned or implied in the scenario and to other equivalent solutions. Furthermore, considering that the use of resources is also a creative process enriching and shaping a teacher's knowledge, we explore diverse instructional rationales around the use of infrastructure exploring alternative micro-activities. We used a quite general example to illustrate the implementation of this analytic framework and to show how this analysis can be used to inform the design of an ontology and a knowledge base supporting a decision-making system for teachers.

Currently, the decision-making system provides alternatives for the 200 scenarios of the knowledge base which are tagged manually according to parts of the analysis presented here. The implementation of the system at this stage looks only at the tools and their affordances in a scenario, and based on these affordances, provides suggestions for alternative tools. The next step is to refine our system so as to include the micro-activities, the educational functionalities and a set of technology-enhanced learning design patterns. The latter are recurring ICT-based solutions for recurring educational problems in diverse educational contexts, which will be used to conceptually group scenarios, thereby allowing integration of contextual knowledge in our system related to the use of the tools and not only on their affordances. The question "Is this alternative acceptable, i.e. does it serve the learning goals?" was put to teachers. It is the teacher of course who decides if the learning goals are met with the proposed replacements/substitutions. Seeing an active role for the teachers in this process, we expect to create a vibrant community with teachers and other stakeholders, sharing learning scenarios, providing advice regarding the implementation of the different scenarios, or even suggesting alterations based on their own experiences.

Acknowledgments. The research has been conducted in the context of the eSIT4SIP project, co-funded by the Erasmus+ programme of the European Union. The European Commission support for the production of this publication does not constitute an endorsement of the contents, which reflects the views only of the authors, and the Commission cannot be held responsible for any use which may be made of the information contained therein.

References

1. Mumtaz, S.: Factors affecting teachers' use of information and communications technology: a review of the literature. J. Inf. Technol. Teach. Educ. **9**, 319–342 (2000)
2. Mavroudi, A., et al.: Let me do it: towards the implementation of sustainable instructional patterns. In: Spector, J.M., Tsai, C., Sampson, D., Huang, K.R., Chen, N., Resta, P. (eds.) IEEE 16th International Conference Advanced Learning Technologies (ICALT), pp. 414–415 (2016)
3. Vrasidas, C.: The rhetoric of reform and teachers' use of ICT. Br. J. Educ. Technol. **46**(2), 370–380 (2015)
4. Tondeur, J., van Braak, J., Valcke, M.: Curricula and the use of ICT in education: two worlds apart? Br. J. Edu. Technol. **38**, 962–976 (2007). https://doi.org/10.1111/j.1467-8535.2006.00680.x
5. Gueudet, G., Pepin, B., Trouche, L. (eds.): From Text to "Lived" Resources. Mathematics Teacher Education. Springer, Dordrecht (2012). https://doi.org/10.1007/978-94-007-1966-8
6. Gueudet, G., Trouche, L.: Teachers' work with resources: documentational geneses and professional geneses. In: Gueudet, G., Pepin, B., Trouche, L. (eds.) From Text to "Lived" Resources. Mathematics Teacher Education, pp. 23–41. Springer, Netherlands, Dordrecht (2011). https://doi.org/10.1007/978-94-007-1966-8_2
7. Fischer, G., Giaccardi, E., Eden, H., Sugimoto, M., Ye, Y.: Beyond binary choices: integrating individual and social creativity. Int. J. Hum Comput Stud. **63**, 482–512 (2005). https://doi.org/10.1016/j.ijhcs.2005.04.014
8. Nelson, C.: Generating transferrable skills in STEM through educational robotics. In: Barker, B., Nugent, G., Grandgenett, N., Adamchuk, V. (eds.) Robots in K-12 Education: A New Technology in Learning. Inf. Sc. Ref. (IGI Global), pp. 54–65 (2012)
9. Vuorikari, R., Punie, Y., Carretero, S., Brande, L.V. den: DigComp 2.0: the digital competence framework for citizens. JRC-Science Hub - EC, Luxembourg (2016)
10. Pariser, E.: The filter bubble: how the new personalized web is changing what we read and how we think. Viking (2011)

Designing an Educational Action Task Force for MOOCs and Online Course Production

Halvdan Haugsbakken[1(✉)] and Inger Langseth[2]

[1] Department of Sociology and Political Science, Norwegian University of Science and Technology, Trondheim, Norway
Halvdan.Haugsbakken@ntnu.no
[2] Department of Teacher Education, Norwegian University of Science and Technology, Trondheim, Norway
Inger.Langseth@ntnu.no

Abstract. Although the research literature on online courses, such as massive open online courses (MOOCs), has proliferated, surprisingly few studies have explored the organisational approach to a generic institutional strategy for supporting educators when developing online courses in higher education (IIE). The goal of this paper is therefore to describe and conceptualise the outline of an infrastructure for organising the production of online courses in continuous and further education. Central to the infrastructure is the Educational Action Task Force (EATF), a network consisting of employees with complementary competences (c.f. technical, pedagogical and multimedia) that can coach, mentor and support educators through the entire online course production process in designated teams. In this article, we outline the design of the online course production process in the EATF teams. The design is stepwise and collaborative, and aims to contribute to a seamless and quality-assured strategy that caters for the various goals that content creators may have within the scope of the strategic goals in the organisation.

Keywords: Online courses · MOOC · Organisational design · Network · Coaching

1 Introduction

The rationale for designing an Educational Action Task Force "EATF", a flexible, collaborative and networked support unit that will support faculty to make online courses, is based on research and experiences acquired at a large Norwegian university. This research shows the increased need for putting focus on how online courses are made [1, 2]. There is a demand for a technological infrastructure, and pedagogical support for faculties that wish to make high-quality online courses. At our university, MOOC initiatives are short-lived and significantly rely on project funding and enthusiasts to survive. Even so, there has been no centralised strategy for producing certified online courses and MOOCs for continuous education. Such factors inhibit scalability and flexibility in online course production. Consequently, the need for an institutional support unit that can assist educators and assure the quality in (massive, open) online course production, other than ordinary courses delivered on the learning management system (LMS), has emerged.

2 Inspiration for Establishing an EATF

In research on MOOCs, we find few studies focusing on the essential requirements and conditions for supporting faculty in their production of a quality-assured MOOC for the first time. For example, little research addresses the implications related to the collaborative production process, the choice of platform, the planning of the course design and the video production time involved, which are essential. In fact, a MOOC production is a collaborative activity that can last for months. Moreover, we argue that ideas about making high-quality MOOCs are often scrapped, partly due to the commitment that educators must make and partly due to the lack of technical and pedagogical support in higher education (HE). Instead, a prolific MOOC research literature has emerged, focusing on the analysis of the *activities* and *outputs* in MOOCs, like decomposition of user groups [3], video engagement among learners [4], drop-out rates [5] etc., overlooking the efforts to make one. In a recent research review, Sanchez-Gordon and Luján-Mora [6] suggest that researchers need to redirect their focus towards developing clearer strategies and standards for MOOC course design, which supports our claim that the strategic and organisational aspects of faculty's MOOC production processes must be highlighted. Their argument is supported in a recent study on the design of online learning opportunities associated with MOOCs where they found that the quality of instructional design across 76 MOOCs was limited [7].

The proposed outline for the EATF for MOOC and online course production is a lasting, non-project based organisational construct that can support faculty, who will share their subject-specific expertise in a MOOC or an online course. The EATF is organised around three core principles: collaboration; distributed network online; and a stepwise production process design.

First, the adoption of cloud-based services for teaching and learning facilitates scalable and flexible courses. The EATF is a *collaborative endeavour*, based on a formalised partnership between the educator(s) and designated EATF-team members during the production period. Together, they form a network of some 3 to 7 participants, meeting at regular intervals to discuss, learn and inform stakeholders at different stages in the MOOC production process. Each meeting has a fixed agenda to ensure progress. Second, the EATF performs all internal and external activities and assignments in a *distributed network online*. This implies that the EATF is mainly cloud-based and that meetings and collaboration are largely online. This allows for a more flexible and transparent workflow. An overall goal is to coach and mentor faculty in digital collaborative spaces (Office 365, Skype, etc.) instead of having many face-to-face meetings on campus. Consequently, the EATF networked design is closely related to what Groth calls "ad-hoc organizations" [8]. Third, the EATF aims to establish and maintain a coherent and stepwise course *production process design*, a "virtual assembly line" that contributes to transparency and course content quality assurance. Transparency is also a cornerstone for continuity and quality performance in the EATF over time.

In the EATF, we aim at using *coaching techniques* to uncover faculties' initial motivation and intentions in order to support their aims and objectives. Coaching is an emerging research field that has been successfully used in health care, sports and private business to make performers stay on target, enhancing performance, self-esteem and intrinsic motivation [9]. Very little research has been conducted on the gains from coaching in formal educational [10, 11]. We also aim at using mentoring to inform faculty of online course design, video production and platform technicalities. The details about how we envision our approach is outlined in the next section of the paper.

3 The EATF Support Process

Our experience, from MOOC production since 2013, is that online course production easily drags out in time terms. Educators tend to underestimate the workload and focus too quickly on video production. They base their idea of the online course on previous experience from teaching on campus and have little understanding of the pedagogical limitations of the platforms and of the difference between online and on-campus teaching. The latter is also reflected in studies that we have previously referred to in [7].

To enhance the quality of the instructional design and make the online course production process more efficient, the EATF works in a streamlined production process consisting of seven steps. The main goal is to form a growth spiral where the educator and the EATF team members collaborate in a network to complete the course production. The network typically consists of 3 to 7 members with complimentary competences in: (1) online course design and pedagogy; (2) multimedia production; (3) front-end representation and platform functionalities; and (4) expertise in the course content area. In each step, the network collaborates to understand and carry out tasks that have to be completed, before the team moves on to the next step in the production process. Information about the tasks in the various steps is also available online to support the educators between the meetings in the network, with a form that shows an overview of the activities and progress made.

The EATF makes use of coaching and mentoring as well as reflection-on-action [12] to motivate educators and help them understand the actions required to make an online course. Coaching is an emerging research field and can be described as questioning and listening techniques that may help educators see more clearly where they are, where they want to be when the online course is finished, and how to get there. Coaching is a method that has the capacity to motivate educators to stay on track to reach their goals. Research from the Erasmus+ COACH project [10] shows that coaching has positive benefits in educational environments. An important strength is what may emerge in terms of increased reflectivity, stronger cultures of collaboration, sharing of knowledge and greater engagement with professional development [9]. The GROW model, which is an acronym for *Goal, Reality, Options and Will*, has been used with great success in sports and corporate business. It is an approach that can be used to aid educators to positively reach their final goal through a series of supported steps. Mentoring is rooted in Vygotsky's theories of the "zone of proximal development" and can be understood as adult learners engaged in new learning and relearning in changing educational contexts that demand a new view on education [13].

Following, we outline some initial ideas of the potential content and composition in the EATF support process.

Step 1, Initial clarification of goals and motivation: The first step is to invite the educators to an initial meeting. The meeting intends to raise their awareness of the educational context and help them clarify the goal and the steps that will have to be taken to reach their goal by means of coaching techniques. Also, the objective is to form an EATF team that can support the educators in the best way. The conversation initiates a formalised, collaborative networked process to support the educators so that they can reach their goal.

Step 2, Selection of platform and work flow: In this step, the educators make various decisions that are supported by mentoring. First, the educators are introduced to the EATF-team members and the result from the first meeting is discussed to contribute to further specify the conditions for the course production and inform all stakeholders. Second, the educators get a better understanding of the potential and limitations of the various course platforms and the nature of the support the other team members can offer. Third, the educators select an appropriate platform for the course. An important activity is to introduce the educators to a course on the platform, which serves as an example of what the course might look like. Fourth, the educators decide upon a work flow to commit to a timeline for the course production and to decide upon online collaboration software and when to meet next and whether to meet face-to-face.

Step 3, Course design: In this step, the educators are introduced to online instructional design. They are invited to reflect on learning objectives, the number of modules, types of activities and forms of assessment in the context of their chosen course platform. They explore the selected platform and discuss possibilities and limitations with more experienced platform users. An important activity in this process is to discuss what type of content is better suited as text, picture or video. At the end of the meeting, the educators have a clearer idea of what the MOOC will look like and is able to go to the next step with a draft or overview of how many pictures, animations and videos they will create and content that can be reused in the course.

Step 4, Multimedia workshop: In this step, the educators are invited to a multimedia workshop. The focus is on preparing the educators for the video production and support the multimedia course content. In the workshop, they are first introduced to video-production methodology and how to visualise knowledge in a video for an online audience. Educators come to the workshop with a written text, a treatment or a *draft that will be completed with multimedia content in collaboration with the team.* They will typically discuss different concepts like a talking head, two-dimensional (2D) animation, voiceover, slide layout, illustrations, etc., to support the written content that will be read on a teleprompter. In the workshop, the team finally outlines a detailed video production schedule for the next step.

Step 5, Video production: In this step, the focus is on the actual video production process. The project team strives to create an atmosphere of trust, where uncomfortable and inexperienced educators are supported to make the best possible product.

Step 6, Uploading content to platform: In this step, the course content production is completed, and the educators are ready to start uploading the course to the platform. The EATF team informs the educators about technical platform support depending on the educators' technical competence. The team also discusses how to proceed with user testing, piloting, and feedback from peers on content quality when the course is online.

Step 7, Evaluation: In the last step, the team meets to finalise the online course and support the educators for launching and possible marketing. The educators are also invited to evaluate the EATF and pertaining pedagogy, methods and technologies to contribute to quality assurance. Feedback is essential, to improve the supportive network.

4 Conclusion

This paper intends to address a missing link in the MOOC research literature – how to organise support for educators who want to make MOOCs. Researchers have examined student user patterns and outputs but seldom cast lights on the efforts involved in making them. This paper attempted to outline some initial ideas on how HE institutions can organise support for educators, who want to produce MOOCs, in a conceptual framework for MOOC and online course production. The seven steps outlined contribute to a scaffolded technical, pedagogical and quality-assured process, which contributes to efficiency in online course production and quality enhancement for online learners. The introduction of an organisational approach to structuring support for online course production contributes to closing the gap in the MOOC research literature.

References

1. Langseth, I., Haugsbakken, H.: Introducing blended learning MOOC – a study of one bMOOC in Norwegian teacher education. In: Brinda, T., Mavengere, N., Haukijärvi, I., Lewin, C., Passey, D. (eds.) SaITE 2016. IAICT, vol. 493, pp. 59–71. Springer, Cham (2016). https://doi.org/10.1007/978-3-319-54687-2_6
2. Jacobsen, D.Y.: Dropping out or dropping in? A connectivist approach to understanding participants' strategies in an e-learning MOOC pilot. Technol. Knowl. Learn. **24**, 1–21 (2017)
3. Kizilcec, R.F., Piech, C., Schneider, E.: Deconstructing disengagement: analyzing learner subpopulations in massive open online courses. In: Suthers, D., Verbert, K., Duval, E., Ochoa, X. (eds.) Proceedings of the ACM International Conference on Learning Analytics and Knowledge, Leuven, Belgium (2013)
4. Guo, P.J., Kim, J., Rubin, R.: How video production affects student engagement: an empirical study of MOOC videos. In: Proceedings of the First ACM Conference on Learning @ Scale Conference, pp. 41–50, Atlanta, GA. ACM (2014)
5. Clow, D.: MOOCs and the funnel of participation. In: Suthers, D., Verbert, K., Duval, E., Ochoa, X. (eds.) Proceedings of the ACM International Conference on Learning Analytics and Knowledge, Leuven, Belgium (2013)
6. Sanchez-Gordon, S., Luján-Mora, S.: Research challenges in accessible MOOCs: a systematic literature review 2008–2016. Univ. Access Inf. Soc. **17**(4), 775–789 (2018)
7. Margaryan, A., Bianco, M., Littlejohn, A.: Instructional quality of massive open online courses (MOOCs). Comput. Educ. **80**, 77–83 (2015)

8. Groth, L.: Future Organizational Design: The Scope for the IT-based Enterprise. Wiley, Chichester (1999)
9. Horn, T.S.: Coaching effectiveness in the sport domain. In: Horn, T.S. (ed.) Advances in Sport Psychology, pp. 239–267, 455–459. Human Kinetics, Champaign (2008)
10. Erasmus+: COACH (Coaching SchOols to fAce Change aHead). European Union, Brussels, Belgium (2017)
11. van Nieuwerburgh, C., Loma, T., Burke, J.: Editorial. Coach. Int. J. Theor. Res. Pract **11**(2), 99–101 (2018)
12. Schön, D.A.: The Reflective Practitioner: How Professionals Think In Action. Basic Books, New York (1983)
13. Fletcher, S., Mullen, C.A.: Sage Handbook of Mentoring and Coaching in Education. Sage, London (2012)

A Teaching Process Oriented Model for Quality Assurance in Education - Usability and Acceptability

Elisa Reçi[✉] and Andreas Bollin[✉]

Department of Informatics-Didactics, Alpen-Adria-Universität Klagenfurt,
Universitätsstraße 65-67, Klagenfurt, Austria
{Elisa.Reci,Andreas.Bollin}@aau.at

Abstract. The lack of standards to objectively assess the quality of teaching opened a new path of research. Teaching involves a lot of different tasks and activities that should be explored, so, consequently, when talking about quality of teaching, it makes sense to look at teaching as a process and to assess its maturity. This contribution briefly looks at existing approaches, and introduces the idea of a teaching maturity model (TeaM) for school and university teachers. Such a framework, even though it proves helpful from a measurement perspective, might not be acceptable by teachers, so this paper presents the results of a study for testing the TeaM model in respect to its usability and acceptability with informatics lecturers at the Alpen-Adria-Universität Klagenfurt. The results show the interest of our teachers in the model, but also some of the impediments that have to be dealt with when applying the model on a larger scale.

Keywords: CMMI · Teaching quality · Maturity model · Higher education

1 Introduction

Quality assurance in relation to the educational system is a path of research, aiming to provide standards to assess that quality. Researchers have already presented models within this scope. These models assess quality by covering only one or two teaching factors (like, teachers, curricula, etc.). Studies by Chen et al. [1] emphasise the fact that a better quality of teaching is achieved when managing the whole teaching process. Their work is based on the concept of a maturity model from the Software Engineering Institute (SEI) of Carnegie Mellon University. The SEI addresses the quality for software development by assessing and managing the process for producing that software. The process is defined by a framework called Capability Maturity Model Integration (CMMI) [2]. In this model, levels of maturity are assigned to processes based on their performance. The model of Chen et al. is based on CMMI, and, like Chen et al., we also believe that quality is related to the management of the teaching process. Spurred by their results and the concept behind CMMI, a Teaching Maturity Model (TeaM) covering all educational levels was created. The TeaM model differs from the work of Chen et al., as it considers not only university teachers but primary and secondary teachers as well.

The basic components of the TeaM were constructed by following the strategy of SEI. The TeaM's practices and the other specific elements were created by observing experts in teaching, and by collecting best practices. The TeaM was additionally assessed by a CMMI expert. All our evaluations so far show that the TeaM seems to be consistent and contains all aspects of the teaching process [3].

On the other hand, the introduction of the model in the educational domain raises the question of how to integrate it in one's daily (teaching) life. Another issue is how to integrate the TeaM in educational institutions so that teachers can use it for assessing the quality of teaching in their lectures. This requires testing of the model and improving it based on feedback that we get, and, with it, also to look at its usability and acceptability. The objective of this paper is to describe our results in checking for the applicability of the TeaM.

Within the scope of the paper, we collected opinions of informatics lecturers at the Alpen-Adria-Universität Klagenfurt when using the model, and the paper reports on the most important findings.

The rest of the paper is organised as follows: Sect. 2 describes related work by giving an overview of how models like CMMI-Services and others are related to the educational system in respect to their usability and acceptability. A detailed description of how the TeaM is tested and the feedback from the lecturers is presented in Sect. 3. In Sect. 4, the results of the study in respect to our model are discussed. Future work and the findings are described in Sect. 5.

2 Background

This section gives a short description of related models. It introduces briefly how CMMI is structured and discusses, for related models, their applicability and usability in practice.

2.1 Related Work

Traditional forms for addressing quality of teaching, such as student evaluations, feedback, peer evaluation and inspections are seen as quite subjective. This opened up a path for research for assessment models that rely on standards. In this, a lot of authors address the quality of teaching by mainly focusing either on teachers (preparation, communication, engagement), or pupils/students, or course content or the environment. Taking a closer look at existing work, these models can be divided into several groups.

There are models that, to address the quality of teaching, focus only on teachers. The AQRT model addresses quality of teaching by assessing teacher teaching practices [4]. In this case, Chen et al. applied the model in thirty physical education lessons with nine elementary physical teachers. The results emphasised the applicability of the model. The competence-based model is another model that assesses teaching quality through teacher-licensure tests [5]. Mehrens's study is more an investigation and analysis of licensure and teachers' competency tests. A similar model is the competence-based model for teachers on how to teach [6], and based on this, it assesses quality.

There are other approaches that consider pupils/students and the teachers' interactions for addressing quality. The CEM model is one of them, which assesses teacher quality based on students' outcomes [7]. Azam and Kingdon applied their model to compare students' results of examinations from the tenth-grade to the twelfth-grade. Based on the results (improved or not) the teacher contribution was estimated. The National Education Association uses a standards-based learning and assessment system to show how student learning standards can be connected with teacher education and assessment [8]. Although there is no concrete implementation in practice, this is how they suggest measuring quality of teaching. The assessment of teacher competences and students' learning and feelings is integrated into another model presented by Snook et al. [9], where they run an investigation in the New Zealand school system. The Angebots-Nutzungs Model is another model used to address quality based on teacher-student interaction (results, feelings, and environment) [10], while TEQAS is a model where quality is addressed by assessing teaching education [11]. Dilshad showed the applicability of the latter model by covering five quality variables through interviews (questionnaire) with 350 students on MEd programmes.

Furthermore, there is the TALIS model, which assesses quality based on the working conditions of teachers and the learning environment [12]. This OECD article was a technical report where they applied this model in a pilot test (which was successful) with five volunteered countries: Brazil, Malaysia, Norway, Portugal and Slovenia.

Beyond traditional forms and assessment methods mentioned above, some maturity models based on the CMMI's principles have been created. Researchers in the field of computer science education adapted and created maturity models to assess and to improve the curricula or the institution itself [13–15]. In these cases, validation of models is referred to at a later stage, but so far, no results have been published. Ling et al. applied their model through a case study in a private institution of higher learning (IHL) in Malaysia and mentioned that a larger participation of IHLs will be used in the future for a better validation of the model [15].

The adaption of CMMI in the educational domain is seen also in course design, either in a classroom environment [16] or online [17, 18]. The model of Petri is not validated yet [16], but Neuhauser did validate the model in relation to usability, and the answers from the questionnaires revealed that 88% of the respondents found themselves in a cell within each process area [18]. Similarly, Marshall and Mitchell validated the processes and the model in the analysis of an e-learning module at New Zealand University [17].

Likewise, in primary and secondary schools, some CMMI-like implementation models focus on the institutional level or on the syllabus [19–21]. Montgomery applied her model in six schools for defining the level of using computers and technologies in schools. The model provided goals and practices for making improvements [19]. Solar et al. conducted a pilot study to test the validity of their model and its associated web-support tool [20]. They tested the applicability of the model in different schools and obtained positive feedback from them.

Only Chen et al. established a maturity model for observing the teaching process. The model is limited to a subset of possible process areas and focusses on tertiary teachers [1] only. In their paper, Chen et al. address the implementation of a model for primary and secondary schools, but to the best of our knowledge, such a model has not been implemented and/or yet published.

We believe that the quality of teaching is more than just focusing on the teacher or on the students, and it is more than just looking at the institution or the course content. It is rather a process that includes all the above and more. So, unlike the aforementioned models, like Chen et al., we address the quality of teaching by looking at the teaching process as a whole. However, in contrast to Chen et al., our model considers not only tertiary teachers but primary and secondary teachers as well. A more elaborated (tabular) overview about the differences between CMMI, TeaM and the T-CMM models can be found in the work of Reçi and Bollin [3, p. 7] where the authors compare the different process areas tackled and include these in the respective model.

2.2 Maturity Model in Practice

The application of maturity models is straightforward for engineers, but for teachers, such an assessment might be new. This section describes the application of a maturity model in practice, and briefly discusses usability and acceptability concerns.

The Capability Maturity Model Integration (CMMI) stemmed from the need to assess and improve the quality of products. After many years of research, the SEI collected and grouped together some relevant tasks and activities (by naming them Process Areas (PAs)). These tasks were further split into basic ones (named Specific Goals (SGs)) and their related activities (named Specific Practices (SPs)). The specific tasks and activities are unique to a PA. When talking about the generalisation and standardisation of processes, then some general tasks (named Generic Goals (GGs)) and related general activities (named Generic Practices (GPs)) were also defined. The latter tasks and activities are common for all PAs [2]. The assessment of the process for producing a product (software/service, etc.) with this model has a twofold meaning. It can focus on different PAs and defines at which level (Capability Level (CL)) the correlated specific tasks and activities are fulfilled, or it controls the fulfillment of tasks and activities on a predefined group of PAs that correspond to a Maturity Level (ML). Such outputs reveal at which maturity level a process for producing a product is. Further improvement for the process means fulfillment of the group of PAs corresponding to a higher ML [2].

Naturally, the question of how an assessment with maturity models looks might arise. For conducting the assessment, CMMI has specific models, which consist of steps of implementations. The assessment is conducted by a CMMI institute certified assessor. The steps of the assessment start with the analysis of the requirements, which determine what processes (sectors) a company wants to assess. This is followed by an appraisal plan development and a selection and preparation of a team for doing the assessment. The PAs are selected and a catalogue with questions is prepared. CMMI-Services contains a total of 24 PAs and each of them has corresponding goals and practices. This means that a catalogue with several questions needs to be answered by the interviewees. For this, considerable time is required, and the quality and quantity of questions is important as it might influence the results for ranking the company at the appropriate maturity level. In the last steps of the implementation, artifacts are obtained and the appraisal is conducted [2].

One major problem when addressing the quality of maturity models is related to time consumption for planning, answering and conducting the appraisal. It is also related to the quality and quantity of the questions, and consequently that a rating to the maturity model might influence the company (in terms of money, success, etc.). However, the published "appraisal results directory" from the CMMI institute manifests the usability and applicability of the CMMI model [22].

The Software Engineering Institution puts much effort in coming up with a consistent version of CMMI, involving a long process of studies and improvements within the last 30 yrs. Nowadays, although the model is applied in practice, there are still parts of it being improved. It is a continuous process of improvements. The same problem holds for the TeaM model. Several studies are required to produce a better version of the model.

3 Validating the TeaM

The TeaM is built up from the necessity for some standards to address the quality of teaching. The particularity of the model is on addressing quality by considering the teaching process as a whole with regard to teachers at university, primary and secondary schools. Making use of the model then either helps the educational institution in evaluating and improving its quality of teaching (by, when required, producing a ranking), or it helps teachers to evaluate and improve their teaching process on their own. Within the TeaM, the teaching process is composed of four phases:

- *Initialisation* - where administrative issues are managed;
- *Preparation* - where the course is planned and prepared by teachers;
- *Enactment* - where the implementation of the teaching unit takes place;
- *Quality and Incident Control* - where possible incidents and the teaching process itself are observed, analysed and refined.

For each of these phases, factors related to the quality of teaching are determined, and in the TeaM terminology they are called Process Areas (PAs). Each PA contains a collection of goals and activities (practices). The implementation of these goals and practices indicates which PA is satisfied. In TeaM this is called "reaching a Capability Level". When a predefined group of PAs is satisfied, until the maximum Capability Level is reached, then also a Maturity Level is reached. The latter expresses how mature the teaching process is. Achieving a higher Maturity Level (so improving the teaching process) means satisfying all the PAs associated with that Maturity Level.

A detailed description of the TeaM and its related PAs can be found in the paper of Reçi and Bollin [3], where also a first assessment related to its consistency is presented. For the validation as presented in this study, another survey (including two questionnaires and one interview) were conducted. For this, the practices of the TeaM were mapped to 76 questions in the first questionnaire (comparable to CMMI appraisals), helping us to assess the quality of the model. The second questionnaire (containing 7 questions) then focused on applicability considerations.

3.1 Study Objectives

Having the size of the TeaM and the time-requirements (when applying it in practice) in mind, the objective of the study was to test the TeaM in terms of usability and acceptability with teachers at the University of Klagenfurt. In the context of this paper, we tried to answer the following question: how is the applicability of the TeaM perceived by lecturers at the Alpen-Adria-Universität Klagenfurt?

To deal with the objective and for answering the question, a structured interview accompanied by a questionnaire were performed.

3.2 Research Settings

A survey (including questionnaire and interviews) was used as a research instrument to assess the applicability of the TeaM in practice. The assessment was planned in a similar way to CMMI appraisals, and at first, we identified potential lectures and lecturers at our university. At random, 30 informatics courses from our bachelor and master programmes at Alpen-Adria-Universität were selected. The experimental subjects were the lecturers of these courses who were then interviewed. From 30 informatics courses that were selected for the study, only 13 lecturers participated and answered the questionnaire. The lecturers varied in their experience in teaching, from 3 yrs to 25 yrs. Only one lecturer was female, but all of them were specialised in the field of informatics and are teaching in the bachelor and the master programmes.

In comparison to CMMI, the TeaM has a total of 12 PAs with related goals (31) and practices (76). The practices of each PA were taken and a catalogue with questions was provided. The catalogue contained 76 "yes/no" questions representing the 76 practices of the TeaM. For instance, the practice "SP1.2.1.2 Arrange the Classroom Atmosphere" is mapped to the questionnaire as the question (translated to English): "7. Do you attempt to provide an adequate atmosphere in the classroom?" The same strategy is applied to all the other practices. For supporting the appraisal process, the 76 questions were provided in an electronic format using Google forms. This makes the questions public and accessible by those who are interested to use such a model. Moreover, the participation remains anonymous as no personal data are collected. The link to the questionnaire is maintained on the website of our Department (in the project section with the name "TeaM model"). On the project website, you find both the link for the questionnaire and the file containing the detailed description of the TeaM Version 1.6 (including the 76 practices) [23]. Teachers and educators are invited to join the project and to report on their personal experience with it.

For performing the appraisal, two non-expert assessors (members from the Informatics Didactic Department of the Alpen-Adria-Universität Klagenfurt) were involved in the interviews. During the interviews, the teachers were given two questionnaires. The first questionnaire contained 76 questions related to 76 practices of the TeaM. This was necessary in order to introduce the model to the teachers (by applying it in practice). The second questionnaire (with 7 questions) then focused on the two dimensions, usability and acceptability, and it was given to teachers after applying the TeaM. The questions focused on:

- (Q1) Time to fill out the TeaM questionnaire
- (Q2) The understandability of the questions
- (Q3) How much they liked filling out the questionnaire
- (Q4) The assumed benefit of the model in the future
- (Q5) The relevance of the model for assessing the quality of teaching
- (Q6) Whether the model would criticise the teachers' way of teaching
- (Q7) Other observations or ideas to share

The results are presented in detail in Sect. 3.3, while the presentation of the results from the first questionnaire (the TeaM assessment) is not in the scope of this paper. In a next step, however, the results from applying the TeaM in practice will be analysed to see if there is a correlation between the generated TeaM's maturity levels for each course with the feedback provided in the ZEUS system at the University of Klagenfurt.

3.3 Study Results

The 13 lecturers participating in the questionnaire worked through all the "yes/no" questions about the practices of the TeaM, and at the end they provided their opinion about missing/relevant practices of the model. Additionally, a questionnaire with 7 questions was given to them to better understand their perceptions about usability and acceptability of the model.

(Q1) The first question was related to the time required to fill out the questionnaire. The average time was 30 min to answer the 76 questions. Only one interview lasted longer (56 min) because the assessor read the questions and the interviewee read the questions himself one more time.

(Q2) The second question dealt with the understandability of the questions from the first questionnaire. We were looking for any ambiguities. Five questions needed explanation from the assessor, because their structure was misleading for the interviewees. Basically, these questions were connected with "and/or" conjunctions and they confused the interviewees. Examples of such questions were: "Do you consider other requirements that might come from students/pupils (like explanation of a new term, repetition of an exercise, etc.), OR administration (like substituting a colleague in one teaching hour because she/he is sick?)"; "Do you consider AND document problems during units' delivery?" Another problem was a set of questions related to existing curricula. As there are courses which are not based on only one curriculum, a correct answer was impeded as well.

(Q3) The third question produced a ranking from unpleasant (1) to wonderful (10) of the process for filling out the questionnaire. The interviewees rated it with 6. This was related to the unclear structure of the sentences and due to the fact that they had to think about their teaching process for the first time. This created a little tension for them and they were trying to explain the reason why their answers were "no" or why "bad" things happened in their course. The assessors think that the TeaM questionnaire might work better without the presence of an assessor. However, the interviewees expressed their deep interest in the model.

(Q4) The benefit in using this model for the future was the fourth question. The interviewees liked the idea of thinking about the questions that helped to improve their teaching, so they thought that it was an advantage to use the model. The only problem identified was related to documentation practices that were required by the model.

(Q5) The fifth question revealed if the TeaM is relevant or appropriate to be used in order to assess the quality of teaching. None of interviewees raised a concern that any of the questions was not related to the quality of teaching. They saw it as a good collection of standards to follow for addressing the quality.

(Q6) The sixth question looked closer at the fear of the interviewees if such an assessment could criticise their way of teaching. In a way, the answers were "yes". They expressed this response even in question 3. There, they expressed worries about some questions that they could only answer with "no", and this was in a major way related to the documentation practices.

(Q7) Last but not least, they were asked about other observations or ideas to share. They thought that providing more information on the questions in such a way that no assessor had to participate during the assessment would make them answer with less tension. Most questions were well understandable and also interesting to think about. Already the process of trying to answer the questions and thinking of their own process was felt to be worthwhile.

4 Discussion

By analysing the collected feedback, it is noticeable that the model somehow surprised the interviewees. It made them think (maybe for the first time) about teaching as a process. If we go back to the questionnaire, it is obvious that, in comparison to the CMMI questions catalogue, answering the questions concerning the TeaM takes not so much time (referring to Q1). This is worthwhile when thinking about the model as a part of assessing and improving your work.

Based on the results (Q2), we see that the TeaM needs to be improved regarding the structure of its "and/or" sentences, even though splitting them will yield a slightly larger number of questions and consequently lead to a higher time consumption.

When answering the main question related to the objective of this paper, the TeaM is perceived as interesting from the general point of view of the lecturers at Alpen-Adria-Universität. Providing an improved version of the model (with clearer questions and with no assessor) will further motivate the teachers to use it in practice. Clearly, at least within the scope of the study, the model is applicable by the teachers at Alpen-Adria-Universität Klagenfurt. Another benefit to be considered is: by just introducing the TeaM, the idea of seeing their own teaching process in more detail was planted into the heads of the participants. When perceiving TeaM more as a self-assessment framework rather than as a raking generator, then its integration in practice in the educational domain could be greater.

5 Summary and Future Work

The TeaM is an ongoing project running at the Alpen-Adria-Universität Klagenfurt. At first, it can be seen as a model for ranking. This might create doubt with teachers as to whether to use it or not. However, the main aim of the TeaM is not to create a ranking between teachers or educational institutions (even though one might do so). TeaM aims at providing a framework that helps teachers to assess the quality of teaching and to tell them how to improve.

After a lot of theoretical research, the TeaM is now consistent, and its applicability in practice was tested for the first time. Based on the results presented in this paper, it seems that it can be used by teachers to assess their teaching process.

As to future work, we plan to test the model in other courses at the University and schools and to produce stable maturity levels based on the results. Further future work will be the extension of the TeaM by an advisory framework. The practices of the models will then be presented in a form of a checklist, clearly defined and annotated, and future users will not need the presence of an assessor to apply the appraisal.

References

1. Chen, C.Y., Chen, P.C., Chen, P.Y.: Teaching quality in higher education: an introductory review on a process-oriented teaching-quality model. Total Qual. Manag. Bus. Excell. **25**, 36–56 (2014)
2. Forrester, E.C., Buteau, B.L., Shrum, S.: CMMI for Services: Guidelines for Process Integration and Product Improvement, 2nd edn. Pearson Education Inc., Fort Worth (2011)
3. Reçi, E., Bollin, A.: Managing the quality of teaching in computer science education. In: Pieterse, V., van Eekelen, M., Michalis Giannakos, M. (eds.) Proceedings of CSERC 2017: The 6th Computer Science Education Research Conference, pp. 38–47, Helsinki, Finland (2017)
4. Chen, W., Mason, S., Stainszewski, C., Upton, A., Valley, M.: Assessing the quality of teachers' teaching practices. Educ. Assess. Eval. Account. **24**(1), 25–41 (2012)
5. Mehrens, W.A.: Assessing the quality of teacher assessment test. Assessment of teaching: purposes, practices and implications for the profession, pp. 77–136. The Buros-Nebraska Series on Measurement and Testing at DigitalCommons at University of Nebraska, Lincoln, NE (1990)
6. Sekretariat der Ständigen Konferenz der Kultusminister der Länder in der Bundesrepublik Deutschland: Standards für die Lehrerbildung: Bildungswissenschaften. Beschluss der Kultusministerkonferenz. Ständige Konferenz der Kultusminister der Länder in der Bundesrepublik Deutschland, Germany (2004)
7. Azam, M., Kingdon, G.: Assessing the teaching quality in India. IZA Discussion Paper (2014). https://ssrn.com/abstract=2512933
8. National Education Association: Framework for Transforming Education Systems to Support Effective Teaching and Improve Student Learning (2010). http://www.nea.org/home/41858.htm
9. Snook, I., Neill, J., Birks, S., Church, J., Rawlins, P.: The Assessment of Teacher Quality: An Investigation into Current Issues in the Evaluating and Rewarding Teachers. Institute of Education, Massey University, Auckland, New Zealand (2013)

10. Helmke, A.: Studienbrief Unterrichtsdiagnostik. Projekt EMU (Evidenzbasierte Methoden der Unterrichtsdiagnostik) der Kultusministerkonferenz. Landau: Universität Koblenz-Landau (2011)
11. Dilshad, R.M.: Assessing quality of teacher education: a student perspective. Pak. J. Soc. Sci. **30**, 85–97 (2010)
12. OECD: TALIS Technical Reports. Teaching and Learning International Survey (2008). http://www.oecd.org/education/talis
13. Lutteroth, C., Reilly, A., Dobbie, G., Hamer, J.: A maturity model for computing education. In: Mann, S., Simon (eds.) Proceedings of the 9th Australasian Conference on Computing Education, vol. 66, pp. 107–114. Australian Computer Society, Ballarat (2007)
14. Duarte, D., Martins, P.: A maturity model for higher education institution. J. Spat. Organ. Dyn. **1**(1), 25–44 (2013)
15. Ling, T., Jusoh, Y., Abdullah, R., Hayati Alwi, N.: A review study: applying capability maturity model in curriculum design process for higher education. J. Adv. Sci. Arts **3**(1), 46–55 (2012)
16. Petrie, M.L.: A model for assessment and incremental improvement of engineering and technology education in the Americas. In: Second LACCEI International Latin American and Caribbean and Conference for Engineering and Technology, Miami, FL (2004). https://www.researchgate.net/publication/254888917
17. Marshall, S., Mitchell, G.: Applying SPICE to e-learning: an e-learning maturity model? In: Lister, R., Young, A. (eds.) Proceedings of the Sixth Australasian Conference on Computing Education, vol. 30, pp. 185–191. Australian Computer Society, Ballarat, VA (2004)
18. Neuhauser, C.: A maturity model: does it provide a path for online course design. J. Interact. Online Learn. **3**(1), 1–17 (2004)
19. Montgomery, B.: Developing a technology integration capability maturity model for K-12 schools. Published Diploma Thesis. Concordia University, Montreal, Canada (2003)
20. Solar, M., Sabattin, J., Parada, V.: A maturity model for assessing the use of ICT in school education. J. Educ. Technol. Soc. **16**(1), 206–218 (2013)
21. White, B., Longenecker, H., Leidig, P., Yarbrough, D.: Applicability of CMMI to the IS curriculum: a panel discussion. Presented in the Information Systems Education Conference, EDSIG, San Diego, CA (2003). http://citeseerx.ist.psu.edu/viewdoc/download?doi=10.1.1.586.2876&rep=rep1&type=pdf
22. CMMI Institute: Published Appraisal Results (no date). https://sas.cmmiinstitute.com/pars/pars.aspx
23. IID: Research projects (2018). http://iid.aau.at/bin/view/Main/Projects

Games-Based Learning and Gamification

Collaboration Platform for Public and Private Actors in Educational Games Development

Jaana Holvikivi[1(✉)], Leenu Juurola[2], and Maija Nuorteva[3]

[1] Metropolia University of Applied Sciences, Helsinki, Finland
jaana.holvikivi@gmail.com
[2] Science Centre Heureka, Vantaa, Finland
leenu.juurola@heureka.fi
[3] University of Helsinki, Helsinki, Finland
maija.nuorteva@helsinki.fi

Abstract. This paper describes innovation platform development for co-creation of serious games. Innovation platforms offer modes of collaboration for schools, universities, citizens, and companies. The main actors of this project are three universities and two science centres in Finland. Several modes for collaboration have been tried in order to discover permanent structures that would benefit various stakeholders. Interests of different stakeholders have been analysed in order to find conditions for successful co-creation. Problems that prevent efficient collaboration have been identified, which are predominantly financial issues. Moreover, some more game-specific issues have been discovered: the understanding of use of games in education and pedagogical goals and methods are not necessarily shared between game developers and educators. Game developers seek to create games that are entertaining, whereas educators want tools that support curriculum goals and enhance learning. However, the idea of collaborative design practices in learning has been welcomed by all stakeholders. In particular, the co-creation in science centres has started successfully, bringing small start-up companies and school students together around educational application development where science centres act as facilitators. Recommendations for best practices in universities are drafted in order to find efficient ways of implementation.

Keywords: Serious games · Co-creation · Innovation platforms · Games firms

1 Introduction

This paper aims at analysing conditions and boundaries for collaboration between various stakeholders on an intended innovation platform for development of educational games. This research follows the methods of innovation action research [1], which is an obvious choice for a study where researchers follow and act as part of the development. The data are based on several projects and experiments that have been implemented in Metropolia and Oulu Universities of Applied Sciences, the University of Helsinki, and the science centres Heureka and Tietomaa in Finland. The efforts of the Edudigi project to create an innovation platform are analysed, and data from similar endeavours are compared with this particular process. The main focus is on collaboration patterns and how successful different ways of implementing co-creation have been. There is already many years of accumulated experience of development of serious games with various partners in these institutions, but the changing situation in the games and mobile applications marketplace needs continuous reassessment.

The project has been implemented as part of the European Union (EU) sponsored Six City strategy, which is described as follows: "The Six City Strategy runs between 2014 and 2020 with the aim of creating new know-how, business and jobs in Finland. It is funded by European Regional Development Fund, European Social Fund, the Finnish Government and the participating cities. The Six City Strategy has three focus areas: open innovation platforms, open data and interfaces, and open participation and customership" (p.n.p.) [2].

This paper first briefly discusses use of games in the classroom and the current research on educational games. Next, the idea of an innovation platform and different stakeholders in educational games development are presented, and the current situation for each stakeholder is analysed. Next, several efforts in collaboration between public and private actors in forms of projects are described, major obstacles are analysed, and some lessons learnt during the projects are listed. Finally, conclusions on collaboration patterns are drafted.

2 Educational Games in the Classroom - Current Research

In Finland, the new National Core Curriculum (2014) emphasises using games and gamification in learning [3, 4]. Playful learning is seen to advance learning and as a motivational factor in both information and communications technology (ICT) skills and in different subjects such as mathematics or languages. While digitalisation has entered children's lives, there is still a huge variation in how digitalisation and digital games are being used in classrooms: more than 80% of the teachers report that they need additional training for ICT use [5]. Many teachers are having difficulties in implementing digitalisation in schools so that it would truly support and advance the ways that the students use ICT. However, gaming has been shown to motivate students, spark interest towards new knowledge, as well as to build bridges between formal and informal learning [6].

The use of educational games is increasing both in primary schools and in higher education. Additionally, many virtual learning environments increasingly offer "gamified" features such as badges and points, without really ensuring that they enhance learning. The assumption has been that gamification is good as such, because it is presumed to motivate students. Several studies on the usefulness of games in learning have been published, including a meta-study in 2012 by Kapp [7]. Kapp had collected six carefully chosen meta-analysis studies that each examined a large amount of studies that attempted to resolve the issue of effectiveness of games in education. The studies compared reported learning outcomes of game use to other methods, but the result was inconclusive. Overall, in more than half of the cases games were found somewhat beneficial. Kangas et al. conducted a meta-study on teacher involvement in game-based learning in 2017, noticing that there still is a scarcity of research in this field [8]. Plass et al. recently presented ideas for viewing game-based and playful learning through cognitive, affective, behavioural and sociocultural levels of learner engagements, which offer foundations for analysing successful learning both from the features of the game and its pedagogical context [6]. Much depends on the type of game, how it is supported in the classroom, and what kind of learning it is designed to produce.

Research in serious games and gamification spans various disciplines, and it is still at a nascent stage, as concluded above. There are journals that are inclusive to games research such as the International Journal of Serious Games (online) but most research is published across various platforms including educational technology conferences. The research results from academia are therefore hard to locate, and have not yet fully reached the commercial world or schools.

3 Methods

Kaplan [1] outlined a version of action research that engaged the researcher in an explicit programme to develop new solutions, and to evaluate and improve the solution in a research cycle that he called innovation action research. In the research that is presented in this paper, the method seems a natural choice, as the researchers follow and act as part of the development effort, where publishing intermediate steps also works as an evaluation tool. Action research is a form of field research, largely descriptive and qualitative, consisting of a set of cases for analysis and testing theories. The data in this study are based on several projects and experiments that have been implemented in three universities in Finland, with the authors as members of development teams or observers.

4 Stakeholders on Innovation Platforms

4.1 Innovation Platforms

Innovation platforms are defined as environments that enable the development of new products, services and markets, allowing the entire city community to work together to create new services, solutions and businesses. This indicates that innovation platforms are tools that cover the entire life cycle of a service, from idea to testing and from testing to product. Innovation platforms were created to offer effective and functional services for agile trials, user-oriented joint development, and controlled user-testing of new innovations and technologies [2].

The Edudigi project in the cities of Espoo, Vantaa, and Oulu is an experiment to create a platform for collaborative development of educational games. The actors of the project are three universities and two science centres in those geographical areas. Several modes for collaboration have been tried and analysed in order to discover permanent structures that would benefit various stakeholders, including universities, primary schools, games companies, and science centres. Figure 1 explains the intended setup of the innovation platform, showing the stakeholders in the city of Oulu.

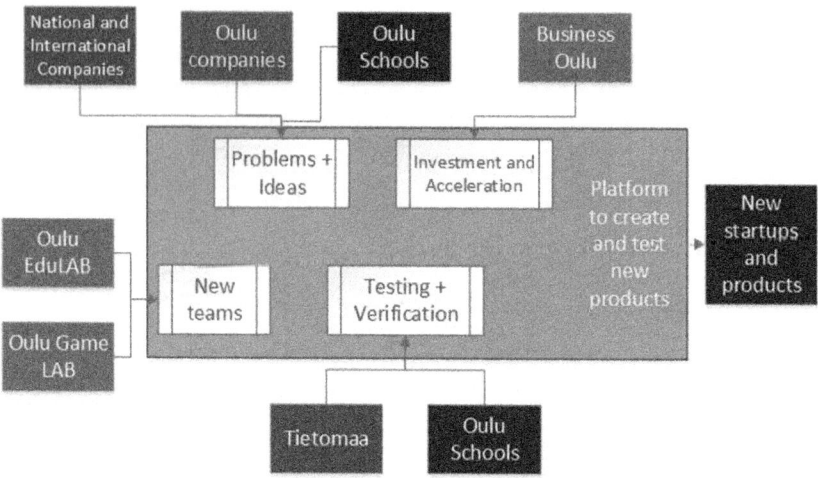

Fig. 1. Oulu educational game development platform

4.2 Games Companies

Games companies are predominantly small, often start-ups. According to a survey by the national Finnish funding agency TEKES, there were around 80 companies that were developing serious games in 2016 [9]. However, in an effort to map their activities in 2017, only less than ten firms were found to be continuously developing and selling games for public use. Most were producing games and other software as a service, or had stopped functioning. On the other hand, over 30 other companies have started since then. Many firms are start-ups with one game or a family of games. About a half of the games that were brought to the market were free, whereas 26% were sold as a direct purchase (premium model). Some of the games had a more complex earning model such as yearly or monthly subscription, school licence or a freemium model. The freemium model is dominant with commercial mobile games where players pay for extra services or goodies during the game. These games have been developed to hold the attention of the player, or even to create an addiction. This kind of model is seen as unethical when children are concerned, and therefore should be avoided in educational games [10].

According to the above-mentioned survey, financial problems are the most important impediment for the growing of the firms. One large problem is with the earning model compared to developers of entertainment games, where the players are customers and pay for the games. The question arises, who is the paying client when a game is used in school? Schools favour open source, free software because of lack of funds. Most of the above-mentioned free games had been developed in some project with public funding. Unfortunately, the development and maintenance of the game usually stops when project funding ends, and the products soon disappear from the market. A few financially successful products have been developed without a connection to school curricula, such as Yousician (where you can learn to play a musical instrument) and the language game WordDive. Language teaching applications abound for mobile devices and personal computers (PCs) also globally. Additionally, there is a category of educational games that has been developed by enthusiastic school teachers or university educators. Many mathematical and science games belong to this category, as well as learning environments based on map-related activities [11].

One of the ideas of the innovation platform for serious game development was to connect educators and pedagogical experts with game developers. However, the games firms do not seem to feel a strong desire to get help neither in usability or pedagogical issues, nor in game development as such. This was obvious in the TEKES survey [9], and it is illustrated by responses to later efforts to contact the firms and to market pedagogical knowledge to them. Money matters are most urgent for small businesses. Moreover, the market for classroom materials and textbooks is dominated by a couple of large publishers who can also provide gamification as part of the teaching material.

4.3 Schools and Teachers

Education departments in municipalities have an active policy to encourage digitalisation of schools according to national strategies [3]. In practice, the most popular measurements locally have been purchases of tablets, computers, and other hardware. On the national level, there are several government funded projects to enhance digitalisation, such as trials of virtual reality gear in some school districts. Teacher unions have conducted surveys among their members and complain that teacher training in digitalisation has not been a priority, and very little time has been allocated to the training [12]. Recent studies show that teachers have difficulties in implementing new practises of ICT in schools [13]. In fact, even though teachers reported to use ICT in schools, most of the use in classrooms is teacher-driven and the main aim has only been to show students facts, for example, using Microsoft (MS) Power Point. Internet is mainly used as a source of information. According to the students, ICT was used less than what the teachers reported.

However, an active cohort of teachers participates in networks that develop uses of virtual and digital tools. Some act as mentors for their colleagues, who are less knowledgeable. Teachers who are willing to participate in development efforts, can be found through the existing networks.

4.4 Educational Institutions: Higher and Vocational Education

Since the remarkable global success of the local commercial entertainment games industry in 2010, universities in Finland have been involved in game developer education and various projects to develop new games. The ministry of education as well as the board of education have granted funds for the projects, many of which are also funded from European sources. Currently, 6 universities and 11 universities of applied sciences have some kind of degree specialisation that has "game" in its name. The first students from these programmes graduated in 2016 [14, 15]. Additionally, education is provided by 10 vocational schools. The games industry was worth 2,400 million euros in 2015 (turnover). However, it only employed 2,700 people [15]. Those figures indicate that the investment in the education for professionals in that field is very strong.

Despite the strong interest in educating games experts and creating company contacts, universities have not shown that much interest in using games as part of the educational toolkit. Exceptions are business and industry games that are widely used in business schools and other universities. Fields that evidently would be suitable for educational games such as engineering, have developed astonishingly few educational games.

A thesis that surveyed the attitudes of vocational school teachers and students in construction, heating, ventilation, and air-conditioning (HVAC) teachers in particular, found that the instructors did not see any use for mobile game applications in their education, even though most students expressed interest in learning through the games. Teacher answers showed lack of knowledge of mobile application use, and reluctance to devote time to something new and unknown. If the games were part of the textbook materials, they would have accepted them. The respondent population in this survey covered about half of the vocational teachers in HVAC in Finland, 96 people [16]. A newly-designed game prototype in a related area, namely electric installations, has just been released and was tested by two groups of students, vocational and engineering students. The six engineering students who were already certified electricians found this three-dimensional (3D) game on PCs useful and interesting. According to the electricians, practicing electric installations in reality is slow, and going through alternative solutions takes considerable time. A game offers quickly many challenges and a safe environment to fail and retry.

4.5 Students

Currently, most young people play mobile or computer games daily, at least in Finland. According to the nationwide survey on playing habits, 80% of the population between 10 and 30 years play some kind of digital games regularly [17]. The age group 10 to 19 years is most active, and 52.2% of respondents from that group play some kind of digital game daily, and 81.6% weekly. This part of the population plays digital games on average 12 h per week. In fact, 25% of them report having some kind of time management problems because of the game playing. The modes of playing vary between ages and gender, as girls and young women play more mobile or social games such as Candy Crush and Hay Day, whereas boys and young men play more car driving and fighting games on game consoles. However, it seems clear that playing digital games is a common activity among the student population, also internationally [6], and young people have no aversion against games.

5 Modes of Collaboration in Game Development

5.1 Co-creation of Games in Science Centres

School groups regularly visit science centres to heighten interest in science. Science centre exhibitions are planned to support active learning and participation. New modes of presentation and latest innovations in science and technology are attractively presented. Nowadays, tinkering is an important aspect of the ideology of a modern science centre; challenges in the exhibition are open-ended, and visitors can create and experiment with various alternative solutions. Therefore, science centres are well suited to be collaboration hubs for co-creation in game development.

The two science centres in this project have developed a procedure to contact games companies and schools in their surrounding areas, and have created a platform for testing and collaboration sessions. School groups can combine a game session to the science centre visit, or they come particularly for a game development and evaluation session. Game companies can pose their questions to the students, let them try to use their prototype applications, or generate ideas for new educational games. The companies have direct access to young people's feelings, and moreover, they get teacher insights into the educational value of their products. The types of games have not been limited into any particular variety and have included mobile applications as well as virtual reality games.

This service has proven to be popular among game companies as they can avoid the bureaucratic procedures of contacting schools and acquiring permissions from parents for evaluation sessions. The facilitators of the science centre support the co-creation process by motivating the school group. Students learn about the innovation process by practicing it themselves. Different kinds of brainstorming tasks are an essential element in the session. It has to be emphasised that the students are the actual experts in the co-creation process (see Table 1).

Table 1. Structure of the co-creation process

1st visit *Science centre* facilitators motivate pilot users; problem solving tasks; pilot groups' own innovation process begins Introduction to co-creation session, start-up presentation, co-creation and feedback
2-3 weeks break *Schools:* Homework *Start-up:* Further development based on feedback
2nd visit Pilot groups' own innovation process continues; presentations Introduction to co-creation session, start-up's greetings, co-creation and feedback

Around 700 school students have participated in co-creating products of 15 different companies in one science centre. The evaluation methods have been tailored for each company. Sessions have been observed and sometimes videotaped, and participants have answered questionnaires after the session. This has given the researchers a great amount of data on children's approaches to games. The companies have participated in co-creation sessions to a varied degree. Additionally, they have received summary reports of the findings from the facilitators. The service has been provided for free due to various sources of project funding. Whether companies will be willing to continue to use the service when they will be charged, is yet an open question.

Student eagerness to participate in co-creation has been positive, even though their learning has not been ensured. Students have been offered a glimpse into the game development process, and a chance to influence the resulting products, which they have found inspiring. The real interaction between the entrepreneur and the student is a cornerstone of the process. If the entrepreneur is deeply interested in the feedback, the co-creation process is an empowering experience for students. Evaluations by teachers reveal what kind of skills teachers believe their students learned during the process. Product development process, teamwork, brainstorming, causal relationships, and argumentation are often mentioned.

5.2 Games Development in Universities

Universities have a variety of collaboration units, some with purely educational goals, and some with commercial interest. There are separate development laboratories, called Game labs, Games Studios, or the like, which offer students a chance to get involved in real projects ordered by outside firms or organisations. In those laboratories, methods of team software or games development are applied, and students have an opportunity to learn industry practices [15]. They might also get support in founding start-up businesses, which usually takes place in business incubators that are attached to universities. One university also has a game-related learning centre that gives start-up businesses a chance to participate in a couched six-month accelerator programme.

As long as the game development activities are mainly geared towards educational goals, the experiences and outcomes have been positive. However, when commercial interests are counted, more ambiguous results are shown. University projects seldom can produce outcomes that fulfil commercial requirements, and they function best for idea generation and prototype creation.

Universities have been involved in various student projects where gamification of educational content has been explored in collaborative settings [18]. We have earlier reported trials of collaboration between primary schools and various groups of university students, which have been successful in educational terms, but no commercial product was ever delivered. Additionally, there has been educational game development together with large enterprises and, on the other hand, with start-up companies. The fields of application involved health care and health education, engineering education and simulations [19].

6 Discussion

Crucial problems that prevent efficient collaboration have been identified, such as different timespans and periods of activity in educational institutions and private companies. Large enterprises are more tolerant with time issues, as the activity is only of minor importance for them, and they can afford a small investment without quick turnover. Small start-ups work on very short timespans, and the delays that are caused by school semesters and terms, and timing of project activities, can be restrictive. Experience has shown that when the school or university was ready for the collaboration, the start-up had already been engaged in something else. On the other hand, financial issues are always central. Firms have to take the most lucrative deals, therefore they might abandon a school project that had been started in favour of a well-paid project.

Another set of difficulties involves questions concerning privacy, especially when minors are involved. Public projects and institutions have to act openly, and the intellectual property rights are granted to students when they are involved; moreover, public grants demand open sharing of results. Companies would like to keep business secrets and secure their own intellectual property rights (IPRs). However, these could be seen as practical problems that can be solved by careful drafting of contracts. Many universities have developed their own contract forms for these situations. In case of underage children, permissions need to be acquired from parents for activities that make them test subjects or targets for photographing or videos. Because school districts act locally, there are many different models for this.

Aside from these general concerns in collaboration, some more game-specific issues have been identified: the understanding of use of games in education and pedagogical goals and methods are not necessarily shared between game developers and educators. Moreover, organisational cultures in the game development world and in public education are far apart. The views could be summarised simply as follows: game developers seek to create games that are addictive and fun whereas educators want tools that support curriculum goals and enhance learning. For example, a new educational game Big Bang Legends has many entertaining and addictive elements, but it offers high school physics to primary school age children. Therefore, schools have little interest in it, but it might function as a commercial success as a game.

7 Conclusion

Certain basic requirements have to be met in order to have a functional innovation platform for co-creation. Before creating or maintaining the platform itself, there has to be a clear shared vision across all parties. How are the different parts of the concept seen and how have the meanings been negotiated? The main actor or centre for the platform has to be reliable and easy to reach by all parties. The platform needs constancy and continuity, which is achieved when there is a strong commitment to it among the major parties. As was detected in this study, personal relations and individual interests cannot be forgotten as, after all, everything works through people. Finally, a sound earning or funding model has to be established, otherwise financial pressures will make the operation impossible.

References

1. Kaplan, R.S.: Innovation action research: creating new management theory and practice. J. Manag. Account. Res. **10**, 89–118 (1998)
2. 6Aika: Smart Cities Work Together (2019). https://6aika.fi/in-english/
3. Ministry of Education and Culture (2019). https://minedu.fi/en/frontpage
4. Krokfors, L., Kangas, M., Kopisto, K., Rikabi-Sukkari, L., Salo, L., Vesterinen, O.: Learning. Creatively. Together. Educational Change Report. University of Helsinki, Helsinki, Finland (2015)
5. Jalava, T., Selkee, J., Torsell, K.: Peruskoulujen ja lukioiden tietotekniikkakartoitus 2013. Kysely kunnille ja kuntayhtymille. Kuntaliitto, Helsinki, Finland (2014)
6. Plass, J.L., Homer, B.D., Kinzer, C.K.: Foundations of game-based learning. Educ. Psychol. **50**(4), 258–283 (2015)
7. Kapp, K.M.: The Gamification of Learning and Instruction: Game-Based Methods and Strategies for Training and Education. Pfeiffer, Hoboken (2012)
8. Kangas, M., Koskinen, A., Krokfors, L.: A qualitative literature review of educational games in the classroom: the teacher's pedagogical activities. J. Teach. Teach. Theory Pract. **23**(4), 451–470 (2017)
9. TEKES: The Finnish Serious Games Industry Report 2016 (2016). https://www.tekes.fi/en/whats-going-on/news-2016/serious-games-are-promising-but-need-more-investments/
10. Kimppa, K., Heimo, O., Harviainen, T.: First dose is always freemium. ACM SIGCAS Comput. Soc. **45**(3), 132–137 (2015). Special Issue on Ethicomp
11. Kiili, K., Devlin, K., Perttula, A., Tuomi, P., Lindstedt, A.: Using video games to combine learning and assessment in mathematics education. Int. J. Serious Games **2**(4), 37–55 (2015)
12. OAJ: Trade Union of Education (2018). http://www.oaj.fi/cs/oaj/public_en
13. OKM: Tilannekatsaus perusopetuksen digitalisaatioon julkaistu (2017). http://minedu.fi/artikkeli/-/asset_publisher/10616/tilannekatsaus-perusopetuksen-digitalisaatioon-julkaistu-digitutor-jo-valtaosassa-peruskouluista
14. Theseus: Theseus (2019). http://www.theseus.fi
15. Neogames: Hub of the Finnish Game Industry (2019). http://www.neogames.fi
16. Haavisto, J.: Kartoitus mobiilioppimisen soveltamismahdollisuuksista toisen asteen talotekniikan koulutuksessa. Metropolia, Helsinki (2015)
17. Mäyrä, F., Karvinen, J., Ermi, L.: Pelaajabarometri 2015: Lajityyppien suosio. Tampereen yliopisto (2016)
18. Holvikivi, J., Toivanen-Labiad, T.: Health-game development in university – lower secondary school collaboration. In: Tatnall, A., Webb, M. (eds.) WCCE 2017. IAICT, vol. 515, pp. 45–54. Springer, Cham (2017). https://doi.org/10.1007/978-3-319-74310-3_6
19. Koivisto, J-M.: Learning clinical reasoning through game-based simulation: design principles for simulation games. University of Helsinki, Helsinki, Finland (2017)

Students' Conducts During a Digital Game-Based Museum School Visit

Eric Sanchez[1(✉)], Elsa Paukovics[1], Sylvia Müller[2], Nicolas Kramar[3], and Antoine Widmer[4]

[1] CERF, University of Fribourg, Fribourg, Switzerland
{eric.sanchez,elsa.paukovics}@unifr.ch
[2] HEP Valais, Saint-Maurice, Switzerland
sylvia.mueller@hepvs.ch
[3] Musée de la Nature, Sion, Switzerland
Nicolas.Kramar@admin.vs.ch
[4] HES-SO Valais-Wallis, Sion, Switzerland
antoine.widmer@hevs.ch

Abstract. This paper deals with a preliminary empirical study carried out during a museum school visit. The study aims to understand the influence of a game on students' conduct in the museum. We address the use of digital games for personalising experiences in museums and for fostering visitors' interactions with the museum exhibition. The paper describes the design-based methodology and the collaborative design and testing of a digital game dedicated to help young museum visitors address the consequences of their relationships with nature and to understand the concept of anthropocene. Students were videotaped and the data collected enabled the identification of different conducts and situations depending on the gameplay performed by students.

Keywords: Gamification · Game-based learning · Museum school visit · Anthropocene · Nature Museum

1 Introduction

To educate visitors about the concept of anthropocene, a new relationship with nature and a global human impact of human behaviour, the Nature Museum of Valais (Switzerland) is seeking innovative approaches to offering young visitors engaging experiences and meaningful encounters with the museum's collections and exhibitions. Within this context, the PLAY Project addresses a specific question: how can we link conceptual knowledge with embodied and gameful experiences in the museum space?

This paper aims to describe how this issue has been collaboratively addressed by researchers and the staff museum. Different game-based approaches have already been proposed for the use of digital technology as a means for personalising experiences in museums. For the PLAY project, we applied *ludicisation* to convert the museum visit into a gameful experience dedicated to help secondary school students to re-think their relationships with nature.

In the following sections, we describe the first iteration of the project. We also discuss the preliminary results of an empirical work carried out in the museum with 3 classes of secondary school students. These results deal with students' behaviours and students' interactions with the museum collection and also with the digital technology, peers and the museum staff. In the first section, we present the context, the concept of *ludicisation* for museums and the research objectives. A second section is dedicated to describe the methodology of the study and *Pearl Arbor*, a game dedicated to help young museum visitors to address the consequences of their relationships with nature and to understand the concept of anthropocene. In the last section, we discuss the results and the lessons learned from this study.

2 Museum Exhibition Ludicised

2.1 Understanding Human Relationships with Nature During a School Visit

The Nature Museum of Valais (Switzerland) is a natural history museum which gives a broad space to the topic of the relationship between man and its environment. In particular, since 2013, anthropocene has been the backbone of many of its activities offered to the public. As a result, since 2014, a room is dedicated to present the concept of anthropocene. The room concludes the museum path of the permanent exhibition, which is mainly based on anthropological knowledge presenting evolution during the time period covering the relationship between humankind and its environment.

The concept of anthropocene expresses the idea that humankind has become a geological force with direct and strong effects on geochemical cycles and on biodiversity [1, 2]. More precisely, the name anthropocene refers to the international chronostratigraphic chart also named geological timescale. Currently, there is a controversy to make anthropocene a new official geological period and there is strong debate on this in the scientific community.

Despite its controversial nature, anthropocene has been considered in the Nature Museum of Valais to have great potential for many reasons in both communication and science education. In terms of communication, the concept is more and more used in the media and, as a result, more and more known by a large audience. In terms of science education, it first offers the opportunity to present an overview on all ecological problems and to focus not only on climate change, that is certainly serious, but is definitely not the only problem.

From a school curriculum point of view, anthropocene enables perspectives on the borders of school disciplines. As it deals with topics like history, geography, anthropology and philosophy, anthropocene is not limited to the natural sciences. Anthropocene is a new idea, but is not a single and well-defined concept and many discourses are proposed. The project developed by the Museum can be affiliated on what is called "the bad Anthropocene" which does not mean that the vision is purely pessimistic but basically means that the concept has a strong cultural dimension. From this point of view, basic anthropological and philosophical topics are questioned, because the anthropological ascertainments are not limited to population overgrowing or bad use of technology. It also has cultural dimensions; for instance, the myths and stories that societies have about their relation with nature or the classical modern ontology making a strong difference between nature and culture. Those cultural dimensions are contingent to space and time and must also be addressed.

Anthropocene is not mentioned in the Romand Swiss Secondary School Curriculum. However, in this official document, this concept precisely relates to the first sentence of the introductory text for social sciences and humanities: "Discovering cultures and ways of thinking through space and time; identifying and analysing the system of relationship that join each person and each social group to the world and the other". By combining diverse knowledge from disciplines as different as the physical, natural sciences, engineering, social sciences and humanities, anthropocene is a great opportunity for combining knowledge from many school disciplines and addresses both multi-disciplinarity and complexity. However, for secondary school students, addressing anthropocene is a big challenge and specific educational strategies might help. Thus, we decided to use digital learning technologies to implement a *ludicised* learning scenario for school visits.

2.2 Ludicisation of School Visits

Museums are considered ideal environments for experimenting with learning technologies [3], and, recently, a multitude of game-based programs have been designed for different media, platforms, and visitor types. Current approaches entail the use of mobile devices, guiding families' explorations of collections through treasure hunting and mystery solving [4, 5] or tasks that scaffold students' problem-solving across school and museum contexts [6–8]. In designing learning games that both engage and support inquiry across school and museum contexts, mobile social media, 'smartphone' technologies, and ubiquitous Internet access have been pivotal developments [9, 10]. However, technology is not an objective per se and experts agree on the need to increasingly focus on personalising experiences in museums [11].

Given this context, *ludicisation* [12] may offer an opportunity for designing game-like experiences for museum school visits. *Ludicisation* is now proposed as an alternative concept to gamification. Indeed, initial definitions of gamification are focused on the use of game elements and game mechanics for non-game contexts. Since no specific elements belong to games [13], recent definitions describe gamification in more psychological terms. Gamification is grounded on motivational affordances, the actionable properties between an object and an actor [14] and gamefulness or 'gameful experience', the experiential condition that is unique to games [13]. The concept of *ludicisation* is a new step forward to recognise the subjective and performative nature of play. The suffix –icisation emphasises that it is not possible to "make" the game, as suggested by the suffix "-fication" (facere) of gamification, but mainly, that it is possible to *change* the meaning of an ordinary situation with the implementation of affordances grounded in game-design principles, to foster gamefulness [12] and to personalise experiences.

2.3 Research Objectives

By using *ludicisation* techniques, we expect to foster students' engagement into meaningful encounters with the museum's collections and exhibitions. We expect that *ludicisation* will enrich students' experience in the museum. We also expect that the students will take advantage of this experience by developing knowledge related to the concept of anthropocene and their relationships with nature. This paper deals with a preliminary study based on the experimentation of the very first version of the game. It focuses on students' behaviour in the museum when they play the game and we address two main research questions:

1. Does *ludicisation* foster new types of encounters with the museum's collections and exhibitions? How do we foster students' interactions that help them to identify their relationships with nature and to rethink these relationships?
2. Which element, or which methods, should be taken into account for the *ludicisation* of a museum school visit?

For the first question, we examine students' behaviours and hypothesise that a specific gameplay should have specific consequences on students' behaviours and knowledge in terms of:

a. interactions with the museum's collections and exhibitions;
b. interactions with peers, teachers and museum staff;
c. self-identification of their relationships with nature.

For the second question, we want to elaborate on concrete experiences gained through the concrete implementation of *ludicisation*.

3 A Design-Based Research Project

3.1 A Collaborative, Iterative and Contributive Methodology

The study is grounded on a design-based research methodology (DBR) [15] and strong collaboration between researchers and practitioners [16]. Design-based research (DBR) consists of conducting an iterative process [17] dedicated to game design, taking advantage of the museums as educational resources [18]. This design process is combined with the analysis of the data collected during experimentations carried out collaboratively by researchers and practitioners (museum educators and software engineers) in naturalistic contexts (museums) [19]. Thus, DBR aims to address theoretical issues with targeted research based on interaction design with digital artifacts and empirical studies performed in naturalistic contexts [16].

The methodology used in this project can be described based on the five following characteristics of DBR [15]:

- *Contributive*: Practice is considered to be a condition but also a means for carrying out research [20]. A game (called *Pearl Arbor*) has been designed during a one-week workshop organised in the Museum. Four Master-level students participated in the workshop in 2015. In 2016, one of the Master-level students was hired for the

writing of the final version of the specifications of the game. In 2017, the first version of the game was developed by students from a Swiss computer science vocational school.
- *Collaborative*: For the design of the game, the Master-level students were assisted by 2 researchers (scholars in game-based learning and museums). During the one-week workshop, specific meetings, focus groups or interviews were organised with stakeholders: the director of the museum, museum visitors, museum educators and other museum staff. The design of the game was grounded on Agile [21] and user-centred [22] methodologies and thus used a collaborative process aimed at designing visitors' personalised experiences adapted to the museum's objectives.
- *Iterative*: the design of the game and the scenario were iterative. The preliminary version designed by the Master-level students was modified. Some changes were made to the writing of the specifications and new changes were decided during a workshop organised after a first experiment in the museum. The design of the game and the scenario resulted from several steps that combined design and analysis for flexible design revisions.
- *Experimentation in naturalistic contexts* [19] was enabled by the participation of museum staff for the whole process. DBR considered the complexity of the studied context without restricting it to a few variables only [23]. Three experimentations were carried out in the museum with the presence of the researchers, the software engineer and the museum staff.
- *Diffusion of the results*: The theoretical issues and the gameplay tended to be communicated through papers and presentations to the scientific community and practitioners. Informal learning contexts of museum needed to be documented to raise and improve existing practices [18]. All the participants in the project were involved in the writing of this paper.

In the following sub-section, we describe the game designed by the Master-level students and re-engineered during the writing of the specifications and the software development.

3.2 Pearl Arbor, a Metaphor of Relationships with Nature

Pearl Arbor is a mobile game accessible on digital tablets. Using augmented reality (AR), the game is playable by teams of students. The game encompasses two parts, representing a shift of relationship with nature. In the first part, players are asked to virtually capture animals using AR. They try to gain as many points as possible. The museum has a large collection of stuffed animals. For this first part of the game, each player can point the camera to a stuffed animal. The mobile application (app) recognises the animal and asks the player what she wants to do. At this stage, the player can choose if she wants to domesticate the animal using a finite stock of food or tools or if she wants to capture the animal through a combat with an animal from her collection already captured. The outcome of the combat is based on statistics, computing the chance of winning depending on the kinds of animal faced during the battle. For example, a bear has a better chance to win against an ermine than the opposite. If the battle is won, the animal is captured and placed in the player collection and can be used in future combats. Each time an animal is domesticated or captured, a collective life gauge representing the amount of natural resources is lowered. This gauge starts at 100%. It is visible on all mobile apps. When the life gauge is close to 0, the first part of the game ends. Then, a short debriefing session is conducted by the museum educator. Players are made aware that the game ended due to the lack of natural resources that was collectively lowered by players when they captured animals.

The second part of the game leads players to better understand nature by answering a set of multiple choice questions (MCQs) to collectively set the nature resources back to normal. The set of MCQs is based on pieces of information available in the museum exhibition. One good answer increases the life gauge of a few points and one bad answer has no effect on the life gauge. When all players have answered the set of questions, they get information about the level of the final life gauge.

The two parts of the game are a metaphor of a shift of our relationships with nature and the consequences of this shift on the sustainability of natural resources. We expect that the game will help students to get an embodied experience of these relationships through gameplay. After the end of the game, the students are grouped in the main room of the Museum. This final step consists of a debriefing session conducted by a museum educator. The objective of the debriefing session is to deconstruct the metaphor and to make the knowledge explicit. The discussion is based on the experience that the students get through the game. It offers the opportunity to introduce core ideas in which the concept of anthropocene is grounded.

3.3 First Experimentation and Data Collected

During autumn 2017, three experimentations were carried out with 3 classes of secondary school students. The whole scenario encompasses different phases: (1) explanations about the museum, security rules and objectives of the game; (2) the first part of the game played by the students; (3) a debriefing session and explanation of the second part of the game; (4) the second part of the game played by the students; and (5) the final debriefing session. The whole scenario was orchestrated by the museum staff according to the decision previously taken by the team.

Three categories of data were collected:

- Notes taken during the workshop dedicated to discussing the first experimentation of the game. Different stakeholders participated in the workshop: researchers (scholars in game-based learning and science education, and a PhD student) and practitioners (2 museum educators, the museum director and a computer scientist). The workshop took the form of a focus group, where the knowledge gained by the different participants through the participation in the experimentation were gathered and discussed. The discussion occurred at two levels that formed a praxeology [20]: practice (What was done? What should be done in the future in order to increase the visitor experience and learning?); and theory (How can we understand what was observed? What did we learn from the experiment conducted in the Museum?).
- Field notes taken about students' behaviours and specific events.
- Videotaping of the students with 3 digital cameras (2 fixed and 1 mobile).

The videos were analysed with HyperRESEARCH, a software which enables tagging of specific events. Specific attention was paid to students' conduct during the school visit. A preliminary analysis consisted of the identification of students' conduct during the visit for one selected class. Three variables were used to describe a students' conduct. The first variable was the spatial distribution of students for a given team. Are they grouped? Are they separated from each other and do they act individually? The second and third variables were the terms that described an action performed in the museum. Do they take a picture of an animal? Do they interact with peers? Do they interact with the museum exhibition? The terms are a verb ("to take", "to discuss with") and direct or indirect objects of the performed action ("a picture", "with peers"). Students' conducts enabled researchers to define different situations with different values regarding what we can learn from the museum visit.

4 Students' Conduct and Lessons Learned

4.1 Students' Behaviours and Interactions

The analysis of the video recorded for one class of students enabled researchers to identify 13 different situations for the first part of the game and 18 for the second part. The situations differed according to the spatial distribution of students and the performed action. This preliminary result might not be exhaustive. However, it shows the large diversity of situations permitted by the game in the museum.

Table 1. Different categories of interactions observed for the same class (one camera)

Part of the game	Interaction with...							
	Peers only		Museum		Tablet (picture)		Tablet (questions)	
	P1	P2	P1	P2	P1	P2	P1	P2
Individual	0	0	1	2	0	0	0	0
Individual + museum educator	0	0	0	0	1	0	0	0
Team	0	1	1	4	4	0	0	3
Team + museum educator	0	1	0	1	2	0	0	2

Table 1 summarises the observations performed with the videos recorded for one class and information is given in terms of students' interactions. Interactions are categorised depending on the spatial organisation of students (individual, group, with or without the museum educator) and depending on what they interact with (digital tablet or museum exhibition). The numbers from Table 1 indicate how many times a situation was enabled for a given type of interaction. These preliminary results are too limited to be conclusive. However, they tend to show that interactions are different for the 2 parts of the game. During part one, the majority of the situations observed and reported concern students who mainly interact with the digital tablet. For the second part of the game, we observed a majority of situations where the students interact with the museum exhibition. These results are coherent with the hypothesis of our project. Different gameplays should enable different types of interactions and *ludicisation* makes possible the influencing of attitude and/or behaviour by implementing motivational affordances [13]. Indeed, the results are also coherent with the game metaphor: a shift from relationships based on the exploitation of natural resources for part 1 (the students take as many photographs as possible without really paying attention to the museum exhibition), to a novel way of interacting with nature based on the understanding of the museum exhibition for part 2 (the students try to get information for being able to answer questions and to get points).

Data analysis was continued and these results tended to be confirmed by a more systematic and larger analysis and data collected by all cameras. During phase 1, a group of students (Gr. 1) was mainly involved in taking pictures or other interactions with the tablet (n = 17) and direct interactions with the exhibition were limited (n = 2).

4.2 Lessons Learned from the Focus Group

The focus group that was held after the experiment was carried out in the museum enabled the collection of data from the different participants to the project that were useful to address game-based informal learning issues. These issues are:

- *The roles of museum educators during the school visit.* For game based learning, debriefing has already been recognised as a crucial step regarding metacognition [24]. This issue was already taken into account for the first iteration of the project with two debriefing sessions that took place after the 2 parts of the game. However, we learnt that the debriefing should be grounded in the data collected when the students play. Depending on their behaviour in the museum, depending on the success or errors that they make when they answer questions, a specific approach should be followed by the museum educator. Thus, we plan to offer the museum educator the opportunity to visualise data that might be useful. We also learnt that the role of the museum educator was not limited to the debriefing session. The way she introduced the game to the students was also crucial. We decided to call this introductory part "constructing the metaphor". It consisted of offering the students the opportunity to understand the game narrative and to give a different meaning to the school visit by identifying themselves as autonomous actors.
- *The roles of teachers during the school visit.* It has been underlined that the role of the teachers should be clarified. Indeed, it was observed that, depending on the class, the teachers were inactive and appeared not concerned by the school visit (the responsibility was transferred to the museum educator) or, in contrast, were active and participated in the tutoring of students and in the debriefing sessions. It was also mentioned that active teachers faced difficulties for participating due to their lack of knowledge about the game. *Ludicisation* needs to be orchestrated and, for the next steps, we will explore two possibilities: (1) the teacher will act as a game-master and will get specific responsibilities; and (2) the teacher will be a player with a specific

role within the game. In order to address this issue, we also plan to involve voluntary teachers in the research team.
- *The design of the game*. The game-based museum school visit was to an extent recognised to be a success in terms of students' behaviours and students' engagement. However, a lot has still to be done in terms of learning content. The limited number of questions that are not totally adapted to the students' school level did not enable the learning objectives to be fully addressed. In addition, it was mentioned that the feedback was not totally clear and, for the students, it was difficult to link the decisions that they took to the consequences in the game. The game design was complex. It did not only consist of integrating learning content with game mechanics. The design of a good metaphor of the learning content and the design of motivational affordances is important for fostering desired behaviour and learning.

5 Conclusion

Implementing *ludicisation* for a museum school visit does not only consist of creating a game. It is essential to address the complexity of the context by designing a scenario where the game is important but also only one element among many other elements that should be taken into account. In particular, the roles taken by the museum educators and the teachers are crucial. In addition, the learner should be taken into account and his lusory attitude [25] fostered with motivational affordances. *Ludicisation* can be seen as managing players' behaviours and designing epistemic interactions.

This issue can be addressed by design-based research. The collaborative design enables gathering of the needed expertise from different stakeholders. Experimentation in naturalistic contexts and collecting data make it possible to learn from concrete field experiments and to envisage a new iteration enabling improvement of the existing scenario. Thus, the design of the innovative scenario and the digital artefact become a means for carrying out education research.

References

1. Steffen, W., et al.: Planetary boundaries: guiding human development on a changing planet. Science **347**(6223), 736–746 (2015)
2. Waters, C.N., et al.: The anthropocene is functionally and stratigraphically distinct from the Holocene. Science **351**(6269), 137–148 (2016)
3. Pierroux, P., Bannon, L., Kaptelinin, V., Walker, K., Hall, T., Stuedahl, D.: MUSTEL: framing the design of technology-enhanced learning activities for museum visitors. In: Trant, J., Bearman, D. (eds.) Toronto: Archives & Museum Informatics (2007). http://www.archimuse.com/ichim07/papers/pierroux/pierroux.html
4. Cabrera, J., Mu, H., Frutos, H., Stoica, A., Avouris, N., Liveri, K.: Mystery in the museum: collaborative learning activities using handheld devices. In: Tscheligi, M., Bernhaupt, R., Mihalic, K. (eds.) Proceedings of the 7th International Conference on Human Computer Interaction with Mobile Devices & Services, Salzburg, Austria, pp. 315–318 (2005)

5. Dini, R., Paternò, F., Santoro, C.: An environment to support multi-user interaction and cooperation for improving museum visits through games. In: Cheok, A.D. (ed.) Proceedings of the 9th International Conference on Human Computer Interaction with Mobile Devices and Services, Singapore, pp. 515–521 (2007)
6. Bakken, S.M., Pierroux, P.: Framing a topic: mobile video tasks in museum learning. Learn. Cult. Soc. Interact. **5**, 54–65 (2015)
7. Charitonos, K., Blake, C., Scanlon, E., Jones, A.: Museum learning via social and mobile technologies: (how) can online interactions enhance the visitor experience? Br. J. Educ. Technol. **43**(3), 802–819 (2012)
8. Pierroux, P., Krange, I., Sem, I.: Bridging contexts and interpretations: mobile blogging on art museum field trips. J. Media Commun. Res. **50**, 25–44 (2011)
9. Tallon, L., Walker, K. (eds.): Digital Technologies and the Museum Experience, Handheld Guides and Other Media. Altamira Press, Plymouth (2008)
10. Wishart, J., Triggs, P.: MuseumScouts: exploring how schools, museums and interactive technologies can work together to support learning. Comput. Educ. **54**, 669–678 (2010)
11. Freeman, A., Becker, S.A., Cummins, M., McKelroy, E., Giesinger, C., Yuhnke, B.: NMC Horizon Report, Museum edn. Horizon, Austin (2016)
12. Sanchez, E., Young, S., Jouneau-Sion, C.: Classcraft: from gamification to ludicization of classroom management. Educ. Inf. Technol. **20**(2), 497–513 (2016)
13. Huotari, K., Hamari, J.: A definition for gamification: anchoring gamification in the service marketing literature. Electron. Mark. **27**, 21–31 (2017)
14. Gibson, J.: The theory of affordances. In: Shaw, R., Bransford, J. (eds.) Perceiving, Acting, and Knowing: Toward an Ecological Psychology. Erlbaum Associates, Hillsdale (1977)
15. The Design-Based Research Collective: Design-based research: an emerging paradigm for educational inquiry. Educ. Res. **32**(1), 5–8 (2003)
16. Wang, F., Hannafin, M.J.: Design-based research and technology-enhanced learning environments. Educ. Technol. Res. Dev. **53**(4), 5–23 (2005)
17. Anderson, T., Shattuck, J.: Design-based research: a decade of progress in education research? Educ. Res. **41**(1), 16–25 (2012)
18. Reisman, M.: Using design-based research in informal environments. J. Mus. Educ. **33**(2), 175–185 (2008)
19. Cobb, P.: Supporting the improvement of learning and teaching in social and institutional context. In: Carver, S., Klahr, D. (eds.) Cognition and Instruction: 25 Years of Progress, pp. 455–478. Lawrence Erlbaum Associates, Mahwah (2001)
20. Sanchez, E., Monod-Ansaldi, R., Vincent, C., Safadi, S.: A praxeological perspective for the design and implementation of a digital role-play game. Educ. Inf. Technol. **22**(6), 2805–2824 (2017)
21. Highsmith, J.: Agile Software Development Ecosystems. Addison-Wesley Professional, Boston (2002)
22. Norman, D., Draper, S.: User Centered System Design: New Perspectives in Human-Computer Interaction. Lawrence Erlbaum Associates, Hillsdale (1986)
23. O'Donnell, A.M.: A commentary on design research. Educ. Psychol. **39**(4), 255–260 (2004)
24. Garris, R., Ahlers, R., Driskell, J.E.: Games, motivation, and learning: a research and practice model. Simul. Gaming **33**(4), 441–467 (2002)
25. Henriot, J.: Le jeu. Presses Universitaires de France, Paris (1969)

Assessing Social Engagement in a Digital Role-Playing Game

Changes over Time and Gender Differences

Guillaume Bonvin[1(✉)], Eric Sanchez[1], Pierre-Antoine Champin[2], Rémi Casado[2], Nathalie Guin[2], and Marie Lefevre[2]

[1] University of Fribourg, CERF, Fribourg, Switzerland
{guillaume.bonvin,eric.sanchez}@unifr.ch
[2] University of Lyon, CNRS, Lyon, France
{pierre-antoine.champin,remi.casado,nathalie.guin,
marie.lefevre}@univ-lyonl.fr

Abstract. Classcraft is a digital role-playing game dedicated to classroom management. Teachers can create teams and assign an avatar to students, as well as points and 'powers' as rewards for desired behaviour. We conducted a study in 4 classrooms from Switzerland. The study aimed at assessing to what extent the game fosters the social component of students' engagement. The detection of socially-engaged behaviours is based on the monitoring of players' behaviours. We collected and analysed players' digital traces with kTBS4LA, a platform dedicated to playing analytics. The data collected shows that social engagement varies across time or gender. This variation seems to be linked to specific features of the game and also depends on how the game is played.

Keywords: Playing analytics · Gamification · Classroom management · Social engagement · Classcraft

1 Introduction

1.1 Managing the Classroom with a Role-Playing Game

Classcraft is a digital role-playing game dedicated to classroom management [1]. The objective of Classcraft is to transform the classroom into a role-playing game for the duration of the school year. Teachers can create teams and assign avatars to students. They also assign points and 'powers' as rewards depending on students' behaviour, defined by specific game rules. In order to acquire powers, a player must demonstrate behaviour expected by the school, such as doing homework or being on time for class. The students play as warriors, mages or healers and, depending on their avatar, they can acquire and use specific powers that have impact on real life. For example, a student being late to class may be saved from punishment if one of his teammates uses the power called "Protect_1". The teacher is the game-master. He deducts points or rewards depending if students' behaviours fit (or not) the classroom rules. Collaborative behaviours are expected from students, and players own individual or collaborative powers.

1.2 Classcraft as Ludicisation of Classroom Management

Classcraft aims to convert an ordinary class into a playful situation. Each player, depending on his avatar, plays a specific role and owns specific powers. Players are rewarded or punished by the game master. Each week, a random event provokes positive or negative consequences, such as acquiring or losing powers. This use of game features, in order to convert non-game context into a game, is called gamification [2]. However, Classcraft is not limited to the use of game features in a mechanical way. Classcraft is based on a metaphor that changes the meaning of the action performed by the students. The actions themselves are not altered. The students attend class on time, do their homework or collaborate for learning activities. However, the meanings and the motives of these actions are changed when Classcraft is played. The classroom becomes a battle, where players have to overcome difficulties and to develop specific skills. Sanchez et al. called *ludicisation* [1] the conversion of a non-game context into a playful situation aiming at fostering gameful experiences and students' engagement.

2 Objectives of the Study: Assessing Students' Social Engagement

There is an ambiguity about the concept of players' engagement. Different definitions have been provided [3] and, due to the ambiguity of the related concepts and their context-dependent definitions, assessing players' engagement might be difficult. Our approach is based on Self-Determination Theory (SDT) [4], which states that motivation results from innate psychological needs. Based on SDT, Bouvier et al. [3] consider that players' engagement encompasses four components: the environmental component in relation to autonomy needs; the self-component that relates to autonomy needs; the action component linked with competence and with autonomy needs. The social component is in relation to relatedness.

By playing Classcraft, students are expected to help other students and to collaborate with teammates. Thus, Classcraft aims to foster players' social engagement. As a result, the objective of our study aims at assessing the social component of the players' engagement. For this study, we examine the evolution of the student's social engagement during a school year. We also examine gender differences.

3 Methodology of the Study

3.1 Monitoring the Player: Playing Analytics

In order to assess a player's social engagement, we developed a specific methodology based on playing analytics [5]. We detect engaged-behaviours by monitoring players. Players' digital traces are players' actions performed during a digitally-mediated activity. *Obsel* (observed elements) are automatically collected. *Obsels* [6] are elementary players' actions (like buying or using powers). Each *obsel* is characterised by a type of event, a timestamp (beginning and end of the event) and information that is useful to derive meaning (attributes and relations with other *obsels*). Some *obsels*, like using collaborative versus individual powers, are inherent to players' social engagement. Indeed, we consider that the use of collaborative powers (powers that have a positive impact on a teammate) brings information on the participation of the player to a collaborative play, where the outcomes of the game depend on the capacity of players to take their teammates into consideration. Thus, we consider that the use of collaborative powers demonstrates that a player is socially engaged with his/her teammates.

3.2 Data Collection and Data Processing

The data collected come from 11 classes in Switzerland. For each class, the data consist of 8 JavaScript Object Notation (JSON) files. The main file (logbook.JSON) is a list of *obsels* collected during a session dedicated to play. The logbook.JSON file is completed with information coming from the other files: gender of the players; different teams involved; and game-levels reached by a given player. These operations are carried out with the data collected from the different classes. However, four sets of data have been selected for this exploratory study. The data analysis is performed with a specific digital platform called kernel Trace Based System for Learning Analytics (kTBS4LA) [7]. The data collected are uploaded, and different functionalities dedicated to data processing are available. Some of them were developed for the needs of this study. First, a kTBS4LA export model is created. This model gives a precise description of the digital traces uploaded on the platform. The platform allows for selecting specific *obsels* from the data collected. The *obsels* that are considered to be relevant for the study are extracted from the whole dataset. kTBS4LA enables the visualisation of these *obsels* along a timeline and different colours and shapes can be used for making apparent specific features. In order to obtain consistent results, the same protocol is applied to each dataset. We designed and recorded several scenarios for the visualisation of *obsels* such as the use of collaborative powers or individual powers according to gender and teams.

4 Results and Discussion

The 4 classes selected for this preliminary study have an average of 16 students, 7 girls and 9 boys, and 3 teams per class. We collected data for 4 to 7 months, depending on the different classes. Table 1 shows that 'the activity' of the different classes (measured by the number of *obsels* collected and powers used by students) varies a lot. Class 4 is a specific case. The data collected show that the teacher gave all the powers to everyone, right from the beginning of the game.

Table 1. Information about the different classes of the study

Traces	Class 1	Class 2	Class 3	Class 4
Obsels	640 *obsels*	568 *obsels*	2352 *obsels*	7923 *obsels*
Use of powers	44 powers	52 powers	184 powers	467 powers

4.1 Variation of Players' Social Engagement During the School Year

Figure 1 represents collaborative (green) versus individual (red) powers used by the students during the school year (time line). For classes 1, 2 and 4, collaborative powers are increasingly used during the school year. However, it is not the case for class 3. For this class, there is a balance between individual and collaborative powers used by the students. As a result, for 3 classes, students' social engagement increases during the school year. The students are increasingly involved in collaborative play. The game seems to have the expected influence on students: fostering collaborative behaviours. However, the differences observed with class 3 show that the influence of the game is complex, and might depend on different factors. Students' social engagement also probably depends on how the game is played by the students and orchestrated by the teacher.

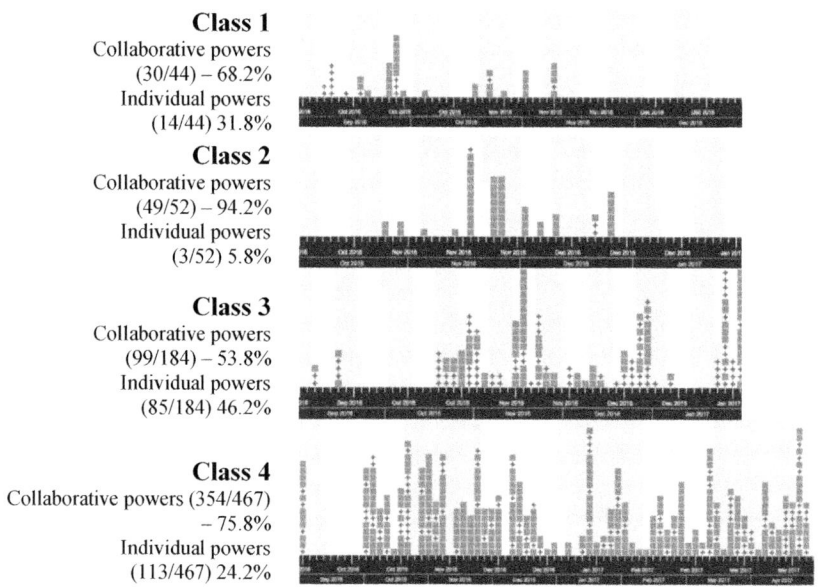

Fig. 1. Powers used by the students from the different classes during the school year (Color figure online)

Playing analytics do not provide information regarding this issue, so further classroom observations or/and teachers' and students' interviews are needed.

4.2 Variation of Social Engagement Depending on Students' Gender

The data collected from the 4 classes selected for the preliminary study also show differences between how girls and boys play. While boys use more collaborative than individual powers, they still use a lot of individual powers in comparison to girls. Girls are less active but more efficient, and use few individual powers (see Table 2). Social engagement varies according to the students' gender. Girls are more involved in collaboration than boys.

Table 2. Uses by gender: collaborative powers versus individual powers

	Male	Female
Collaborative	(304/493) - 61.7%	(228/254) - 89.8%
Individual	(189/493) - 38.3%	(26/254) - 10.2%

5 Conclusion

Based on the data collected from this preliminary study, there are arguments to state that the ludicisation of classroom management with Classcraft helps students to develop positive classroom behaviour. The game influences how students collaborate with their teammates and, therefore, fosters students' social engagement. Changing the meaning of the situation experienced by the students helps to take into account their teammates. Students' social engagement varies along the school year and according to gender. However, the differences observed for different classes also show that the way the game is orchestrated by the teacher influences how the game is played by the students. Playing analytics do not offer any information regarding this issue and further investigations are needed. Thus, we plan to continue to address this issue with a mixed methodology. The project will consist of collaborative work with voluntary teachers for the implementation of the game in different classes. The combination of learning analytics and classroom observations should enable the characterisation of students' social engagement and the identification of the game elements that foster students' collaboration. Therefore, we expect to gain a better understanding of how ludicisation might be applied for classroom management.

References

1. Sanchez, E., Young, S., Jouneau-Sion, C.: Classcraft: from gamification to ludicization of classroom management. Educ. Inf. Technol. **20**(5), 497–513 (2016)
2. Kapp, K.: The Gamification of Learning and Instruction. Pfeiffer, San Francisco (2012)
3. Bouvier, P., Lavoué, E., Sehaba, K., George, S.: Identifying learner's engagement in learning games - a qualitative approach based on learner's traces of interaction. In: Foley, O., Restivo, M.T., Uhomoibhi, J.O., Helfert, M. (eds.) Proceedings of the 5th International Conference on Computer Supported Education, Aachen, Germany, pp. 339–350 (2013)
4. Ryan, R.M., Deci, E.L.: Self-determination theory and the facilitation of intrinsic motivation, social development, and well-being. Am. Psychol. **55**, 68–78 (2000)

5. Sanchez, E., Mandran, N.: Exploring competition and collaboration behaviors in game-based learning with playing analytics. In: Lavoué, É., Drachsler, H., Verbert, K., Broisin, J., Pérez-Sanagustín, M. (eds.) EC-TEL 2017. LNCS, vol. 10474, pp. 467–472. Springer, Cham (2017). https://doi.org/10.1007/978-3-319-66610-5_44
6. Cordier, A., Lefevre, M., Champin, P., Mille, A.: Connaissances et raisonnement sur les traces d'interaction. Revue d'Intelligence Artificielle **28**(2–3), 375–396 (2014)
7. Casado, R., Guin, N., Champin, P., Lefevre, M.: kTBS4LA: une plateforme d'analyse de traces fondée sur une modélisation sémantique des traces. Papier présenté lors de l'Atelier ORPHEE Rendez-Vous, Font-Romeu, France (2017)

A Learning Analytics Approach in Web-Based Multi-user Learning Games

Matthias Ehlenz[✉], Thiemo Leonhardt, and Ulrik Schroeder

Learning Technology Research Group,
RWTH Aachen University, Aachen, Germany
{Ehlenz,leonhardt,schroeder}@cs.rwth-aachen.de

Abstract. As technology changes, learning games are adapted to target audience and available devices. Analytics methods must keep up with keeping the learner in focus. This work presents the Multi-Touch Learning Game (MTLG) framework, designed to implement cross platform educational games with support for cooperative, collaborative and competitive settings. It shows adaption of a user-centred learning analytics data model, the learning data context model, to fit circumstantial requirements of multi-user settings on a shared device in games implemented using the MTLG framework. A first field study has been conducted, and the results, challenges and lessons learned are discussed.

Keywords: Game-based learning · Learning analytics · Multi-touch · Educational games · Learning context

1 A New Style of Learning

Learning nowadays requires educators around the globe to understand current developments of everyday habits of their students to provide methods of knowledge transfer via alternative channels, for example, game-based learning. To avoid unnecessary overheads in development processes, the method of choice for producers is often web-based. Hypertext markup language (HTML) and JavaScript based content can be viewed on a range of devices and can even be compiled without much effort in native applications (apps) for nearly all the common target platforms. Though this is carried out on an everyday basis, most learning analytics standards do not reflect those different settings. This paper aims to fill the gap between context awareness in learning analytics and their application in game-based learning. This challenge is approached by extending the Learning Context Data Model to fit modern collaborative contexts of "playing together" and specifics regarding educational games, to offer a broad range of analytic possibilities in game-based learning.

The paper has three parts. First, we explain the Multi-Touch Learning Framework to integrate learning analytics in web-based educational games and applications. Second, we introduce the Learning Context Data Model as an alternative to the Experience Application Program Interface (API), as it focuses on the learner and not only on the learning event. Third, we present our first field study as a proof of concept.

2 Multi-Touch Learning Games

Educational games play an important role in modern education. It is widely accepted that engaging games enhance learning in a wide variety of ways [1]. As progress leads to a wide spread in platforms, developers are often either forced to stick with their area of expertise, thus limiting the reachable audience, gather an expensive team, or risk the time-consuming effort of getting accustomed to new areas. An alternative is to follow the more modern path of a cross-platform approach.

Most of those used on an everyday basis by the target audience of educational games, mainly children and teenagers, are not desktops or notebooks but tablets and smartphones are dominating this area [2]. Touch interaction has outrun keyboard and mouse and a big share of newly-introduced notebooks feature touch functionality. Thus, educational games make use of the possibilities of gestures and ten finger input that students have grown accustomed to. Furthermore, technology has advanced and produced touchscreens in growing sizes and capabilities. This opens up opportunities far beyond single learners behind their own devices and enables content creators to provide true collaborative learning environments where all users have per definition equal rights and chances of participation.

The Multi-Touch Learning Game framework (MTLG) developed by the Learning Technologies Research Group at RWTH Aachen University aims to assist university students, teachers and other developers to create suitable user experience on devices and for their demanding clientele, while maintaining core features of educational games [3]. In this paper, we focus on discussing the analytics component, as it represents the foundation of understanding behavioural patterns in multiuser multi-touch learning environments, and describe the challenges those collaborative settings bring.

3 Intention of the Learning Context Data Model

Learning analytics is a current trend, but is not a new and revolutionary topic. Since Learning Management Systems (LMSs) have been around, educators have striven to understand their learners and improve their systems to optimise user experience and, in the long run, maximise learning efficiency.

After early approaches to standardise a data format for interchange and storage of learning records like Tin Can API, the successor, Experience API (xAPI) has become a de-facto standard for learning record stores and is implemented in all major LMSs.

xAPI represented a huge improvement compared to Tin Can regarding support of game-based learning, platform transitions and learning in teams, but still is mostly fitting for traditional e-learning scenarios. xAPI is a specification with the set main goal of interoperability in mind and providing a widely generic "one size fits all" solution which proves applicable in most settings.

Using xAPI to store the whole context of a user's learning environment stretches the bounds of this ambiguity beyond the point of good conscience, especially when interoperability is not the priority in the intended project. Thus, during the Prime Project, Thüs et al. [4] developed the Learning Context Data Model (LCDM), which is a learning record data definition aiming to provide a structural way to collect information not only on the learning process itself but also on the context of the learner [5, 6]. Furthermore, this model is not only platform agnostic, it provides a structured pattern for storing the platform, source, session, action and general learning setting (work, academic, private); it introduced a hierarchical category system, with entities to model user interests [7] and generic entities.

The LCDM was implemented for usage in professional settings, but with the intention to allow self-reflection on daily tasks and learning activities [8]. Thus, it is not an event-centric or application-centric data model, but focuses on the learner. This user-centric idea emphasises applicability of this data model in multi-user settings as context might play an important role in analysis of gathered data. For use in MTLG games, the LCDM has been ported by a Representational State Transfer (REST)-Interface using a simple token-based authentication system. During implementation, an adaptive REST endpoint was created to facilitate exports of all events in xAPI format to keep future opportunities for using analytics toolkits, relying on the said standard.

4 First Field Studies and Challenges

As proof of concept and a first research prototype, a four-user learning game for the introduction of regular expressions (a central topic in theoretical computer science and foundation for formal languages), has been implemented as the first game using the data collector and the LCDM back end.

The basic idea shown in Fig. 1 is that each player has her/his own drop area, associated with a regular expression. In the common area of the screen, word cards appear, either matching (one of) those regular expressions or not. Players have to touch matching cards and drop them in their drop area. Correctly assigned cards are awarded two points, while mismatched cards reduce the score by one. Depending on the setting, there are either individual scores or a team score, individual expressions or the same for all players, and the play modes consist of two versus two and cooperative playing.

One goal of the study was to explore the practicability of the data model in real usage scenarios and investigate reliability of the produced data set. Information gathered for each touch interaction consisted of the result (success or not), drop area, regular expression on the drop area, timestamps and duration as well as session identifier (id).

Random sample checks comparing event data with the video recording of those sessions suggests that the data set is complete, and no interaction events have been lost. Nevertheless, there is a good amount of unassigned word card interactions since the first approach was guessing player id from the drop area, and cards moved in the common area could not be resolved that way, thus being assigned to the unknown player "John Doe" for later assignment in post-processing.

Another problem surfaced during observation, and shown by analysis of the visual recordings. Both in cooperative and competitive settings (less in the former, often in the latter), cards have been dropped in areas of different players, in the first case usually during the process of mutual explanation, and in the second, in taking advantage of the score malus for wrong cards for the opposite team for dropping those cards across the table. While this could be seen from a mostly negative perspective, some researchers

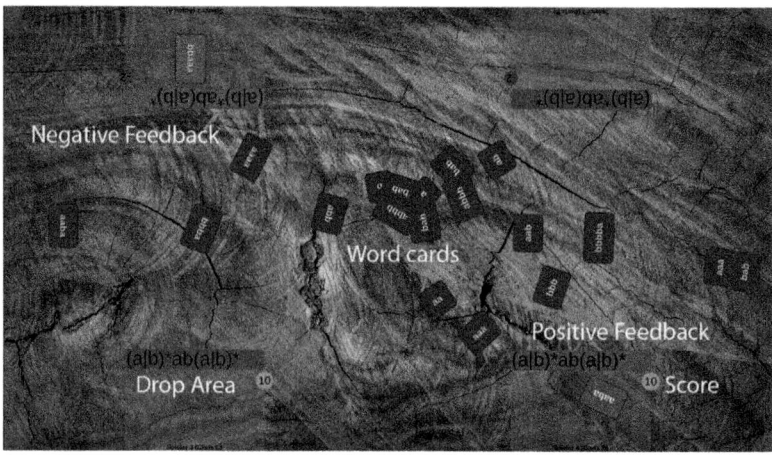

Fig. 1. PoC prototype (Source: Own work - http://tabula-content.informatik.rwth-aachen.de/games/dem1-RegEx/)

[9] indicate that such a change in behavioural pattern can be interpreted as emotional involvement and thereby immersion in the playing experience. Still, this renders the collected data effectively useless in an unprocessed state in the attempt of user-centric analysis and demands of approaches either in post-processing or future data collection.

While this first field study merely aimed, from the technological perspective, at showing the capabilities of the data collector and back end, it left us with valuable insights and optimism regarding the planned approaches on the expected challenges.

Regarding further field studies in laboratory conditions, post-processing in regard to user assignment will be rendered obsolete. The TABULA Project enrichens learning experiences with so-called tangibles [10], objects that can be detected by any capacitive touchscreen device and adds a haptic aspect to the process.

While the users in our first case study have already been using the first version of passive tangibles for comparable user experiences, those tangibles are not distinguishable from each other. In the next, those tangibles will become active. By adding a microcontroller board with Bluetooth capabilities, the tool in the hands of each student will provide options like a direct and discreet feedback channel to each user, uniquely identifiable and linked (in the context of this prototype) to a specific user for the whole game session, which will empower us to assign "cross reaching" events as well as "unassigned" events to a specific user.

5 Conclusion and Outlook

The first field study shows that the LCDM fulfils the needs of multi-user multi-touch learning games. There are adjustments to make to fit specific use cases, but mostly at a semantic level, like extending the range of values for a platform (by a MTTABLE value), or minor categories (by touch interaction events). Introducing a fourth category type GAME is in discussion. Software tools are currently being implemented enabling analysts to synchronise a recorded video with an LCDM event stream for easy, time-efficient post-processing for general study use without availability of tangibles.

The next iterations will collect an advanced set of interaction data including the start and end coordinates of each touch interaction, opening up the possibility to answer straightforward questions like "Does this user collect from the whole common area or just from within arm's reach" to sophisticated ones like "Does a user become more hesitant over [time/failed attempts/difficulty]?" by looking at pixel distance to duration ratios. Further research will be done, aiming to implement automated, personalised feedback, continuing and transferring the groundwork laid in a previous study [11].

Acknowledgments. The authors acknowledge the financial support by the Federal Ministry of Education and Research of Germany in the call ELE (Project TABULA).

References

1. Hamari, J., Shernoff, D.J., Rowe, E., Coller, B., Asbell-Clarke, J., Edwards, T.: Challenging games help students learn: an empirical study on engagement, flow and immersion in game-based learning. Comput. Hum. Behav. **54**, 170–179 (2016)
2. Medienpädagogischer Forschungsverband Südwest mpfs: JIM-Studie 2017. Jugend, Information, (Multi-) Media. Basisuntersuchung zum Medienumgang 12- bis 19-Jähriger. Medienpädagogischer Forschungsverband Südwest mpfs, Stuttgart (2017)
3. Ehlenz, M., Leonhardt, T, Schroeder, U.: Spielend leicht Lernspiele entwickeln - Ein Framework für Multitouch-Lernspiele. In: Igel, C., Ullrich, C., et al. (Hrsg.) Bildungsräume 2017, pp. 297–302. Gesellschaft für Informatik, Bonn (2017)
4. Thüs, H., et al.: Mobile learning in context. Int. J. Technol. Enhanc. Learn. **4**(5/6), 332–344 (2012)
5. Thüs, H., Chatti, M.A., Greven, C., Schroeder, U.: Kontexterfassung, modellierung und auswertung in Lernumgebungen. In: Trahasch, S., Plötzner, R., et al. (eds.) Proceedings der 12. e-Learning Fachtagung Informatik, pp. 157–162. DeLFI, Gesellschaft für Informatik, Freiburg (2014)
6. Thüs, H., Chatti, M.A., Schroeder, U., Kammer, T.: Kontexterfassung zur Anreicherung mobiler Anwendungen. Presented at the Mobile Learning Workshop. DeLFI, Bremen (2013)
7. Thüs, H., Chatti, M.A., Brandt, R., Schroeder, U.: Evolution of interests in the learning context data model. In: Conole, G., Klobučar, T., Rensing, C., Konert, J., Lavoué, É. (eds.) EC-TEL 2015. LNCS, vol. 9307, pp. 479–484. Springer, Cham (2015). https://doi.org/10.1007/978-3-319-24258-3_43
8. Thüs, H., Soworka, M., Brauner, P., Schroeder, U.: Smart experience sampling in Android. In S. Rathmayer, H. Pongratz (eds.) Proceedings of the Mobile Learning Workshop, pp. 213–221. DeLFI, München (2015)
9. Jabbar, A.I.A., Felicia, P.: Gameplay engagement and learning in game-based learning: a systematic review. Rev. Educ. Res. **85**(4), 740–779 (2015)
10. Voelker, S., et al.: PERCs: persistently trackable tangibles on capacitive multi-touch displays. In: Proceedings of the 28th Annual ACM Symposium on User Interface Software and Technology, Charlotte, NC, pp. 351–356. ACM, New York (2015)
11. Herding, D.: The tutor-in-the-loop model for formative assessment. Dissertation, RWTH Aachen University, Aachen, Germany (2013)

Learning in Specific and Disciplinary Contexts

The Role of Audiovisual Translation in Mediating Foreign Language Learning

Activity Theory Perspective

Rasha AlOkaily[✉]

Lancaster University, Lancashire, UK
rashaokaily@gmail.com

Abstract. This is a case study of a specific learning environment in the Intensive English Language Program, characterised by technical, spatial, temporal, and motivational restrictions that impede students' progress. Activity Theory was used to describe the situation, and to design an intervention in the form of a new activity system. A dubbing project was designed and implemented in the Listening and Speaking Course. It utilised students' mobile devices in an anywhere, anytime type of learning, and their native language and cultural background as a starting point to engage them in a collaborative effort that led to the production of eight dubbed videos. The resulting videos were entered in an internally-organised video competition which added a further motivational element to the project. To evaluate the project's effect on students' perceptions and motivation, data were collected using 5 focus group interviews. Results show high levels of motivation, increased learning, increased confidence and sense of achievement and pride in the resulting work.

Keywords: Audiovisual translation · Dubbing · Activity theory · Language learning

1 Introduction and Context

The dubbing project is a mobile learning project that was carefully designed to fit a specific learning context characterised by a number of restrictions. This paper reports a case study that took place over one academic semester where the learning context was first analysed using Activity Systems Analysis and tensions were identified as temporal, motivational, spatial, and technical. An intervention in the form of a new activity system was designed and implemented by the researcher.

This study was conducted in the Intensive English Language Program (IEP) in a semi-private university in the United Arab Emirates where students are required to demonstrate their English language proficiency by sitting a standardised English language proficiency test (IELTS). Students who do not obtain the required score enrol in the IEP to improve their language proficiency. The programme is in 4 levels, starting from level 1 for false beginners, i.e. students who studied English language before but have little command of the language, up to level 4 for intermediate students. Each level is taught over a period of one academic semester. Students are placed in each level, based on the results of a placement test. Those who miss the placement test prior to programme entry are placed in level 1 regardless of their actual level. All students are allowed to drop out of the IEP as soon as they achieve the required score; therefore, students make multiple attempts to take the standardised test during the semester.

The dubbing project was implemented in two sections at level 1, taught by the researcher. One section had 18 female students and the other had 16 female students. Eight short videos were dubbed to English and were entered in an internally-organised competition to choose the winning video. The winners were chosen by a panel of judges who were four IEP instructors.

This study asked the following questions:

1. How did the video dubbing project remediate English language learning for false beginners and mixed ability classes?
2. What was the impact of this remediation on students' perceptions and motivation?

These questions are significant in that they test dubbing projects in a context different to contexts documented in previous studies (see Sect. 2.2).

2 Literature Review

This section provides a short review of Activity Theory (AT), which is used to problematise the context, followed by a review of relevant literature on practices and concepts that form the theoretical framework for this study. Dubbing as a language learning activity is reviewed, followed by mobile learning. Both of these constitute the basis for the proposed activity system that was designed to overcome the above-mentioned constraints.

2.1 Activity Theory

AT provides a suitable lens for conceptualising learning environments [1–3]. It offers the language for description and addresses the situation using a manageable unit of analysis: the activity [4, 5]. It is a cultural historical theory where context is integral to the activity itself and is seen to influence the mind and action of people [6]. An activity is an action directed towards an object and is motivated by the need to change the object into an outcome [1], which means reaching this object is purposeful and leads to achieving an outcome.

AT studies the activity in its natural context, taking into consideration all variables within the environment of the activity. These variables are the *subject* or actor, the *object* or objective which the subject needs and is motivated to achieve, and the *tools* and artefacts that mediate the activity. All these are governed by *rules,* and exist within a *community* where there is a *division of labour* among community members to ensure the achievement of the objective. These elements are depicted in a triangular form (in Fig. 1).

Including the community in the system of interaction came as a later development by Engeström [7], who extended Vygotsky's and Leontiev's understanding of the social mediation of activity to include social mediators within a community. Engeström

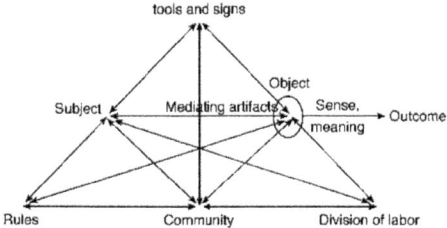

Fig. 1. The structure of a human activity system [7]

explains that the *tool* mediates the relationship between the subject and the object, the *rules* mediate the relationship between the subject and the community and the *division of labour* mediates the relationship between the object and the community.

The variables are seen to interact either in an enabling manner, or in a manner that causes tensions and contradictions, also referred to as obstacles [4]. There are four levels of tensions within AT: primary, secondary, tertiary, and quaternary [7] (see Sect. 3). By identifying these relationships and the tensions, improved activity systems can be designed to enhance the activity by overcoming them.

According to Engeström, Bateson's Learning 3 is relevant here. He refers to it as expansive learning and defines it as learning by constructing a new activity and expanding the context. He explains:

> 'Learning by expanding or learning 3 is very much going beyond the information given to construct a new set of criteria, a broader picture, a broader object for your activity which liberates you from the constraints of the particular setting in which you are functioning and enables you to create new settings.' [8] (minute 8.18 of interview)

This came after Engeström's revision of AT when he suggested the possibility of expansive transformations, stating that 'an expansive transformation is accomplished when the object and motive of the activity are re-conceptualised to embrace a radically wider horizon of possibilities than in the previous mode of activity' [9, p. 137].

2.2 Dubbing and Audio-Visual Translation

There are three main types of audio-visual translation: dubbing (or lip-sync); subtitling; and voice-over [10]. All three types involve a recount of both image and sound of the original video, either in the form of written text at the bottom of the screen, as in subtitling, or in the form of audio voice-over.

The empirical studies that are available show that all three types have been experimented with in the field of language learning. Danan explains how dubbing from L1 (native language) to L2 (target language) has many benefits which he attributes to the combined use of translation and technology. He asserts that the return of the pedagogical role of translation along with the ubiquity and growing versatility of technological tools have opened up an array of possibilities for language learning, one of which is dubbing activities [11]. His approach of implementing the L1 to L2 dubbing activity is interesting, and his findings are promising; therefore, they influenced the design of the new activity system in this study.

Other studies suggest different dubbing activities ranging from intralingual (L2 - L2) to interlingual (L1 - L2/L2 - L1). First, there is the repeat/verbatim activity (intralingual) where learners simply repeat the original speech of the characters [12–17]. Such studies report improvement in learners' pronunciation, intonation, speed and fluency. Another type involves free translation, i.e. to paraphrase for gist [11, 12], or translation but with concision since literal, faithful translation may not be possible due to register difference or time constraints or learners' slower speeds of speaking [11]. This point proved to be particularly significant in this study because it highlighted areas of difference between L1 and L2 in terms of register, and encouraged students to attempt more fluent speech. Reported benefits of these studies are similar to those of the intralingual activities with additional benefits ranging from the improved overall language skills, grammar, awareness of register, language variation, intercultural awareness, paralinguistic elements (such as expression of emotions through voice and facial expression). Other important behavioural benefits were reported such as motivation, autonomy, collaboration, enjoyment, ownership and pride of finished product. In general, all mentioned studies report high levels of student enjoyment of the projects and a desire to do similar projects in the future.

Researchers have reported that within the available body of literature, little has been done on the use of audio-visual translation in relation to productive skills and autonomous learning [11]. There is also a call for empirical evaluation of the effect of dubbing in the foreign language learning context [16]. Avila and Talavan report on dubbing projects used with advanced learners and speculate about the suitability of these projects with beginners [17]. None of the available studies have linked dubbing projects with mixed-ability classes or with class management, nor has it been implemented with beginners/false beginners. This study is an attempt to fill these gaps by providing an empirical study to evaluate the use of dubbing projects for language learning with false beginners and mixed-ability classes.

2.3 Mobile Learning and Bring Your Own Device (BYOD) Policy

The UNESCO report on 'Mobile Learning and Policies' identifies a popular definition of mobile learning to be 'education that involves the use of mobile devices to enable learning anytime and anywhere' [18]. This anytime and anywhere feature relates to the physical and temporal spaces making mobile learning possible for people who face restrictions in terms of time and space as in the context of this study. Palalas identifies five essential spaces - temporal, physical, transactional, technological, and pedagogical - explaining that it is the *blending* of these spaces that:

> 'can produce a combination of resources (information and actors), contexts, processes and supports that promote learning. [...] Hence, with facilitation and guidance of experts, mobile tools can effectively mediate the interplay of these elements toward successful learning outcomes' [19, p. 87].

This is an important part of the theoretical framework that underlies this study.

3 The Problem Statement - Constraints

Level 1 of the IEP programme is best explained using AT. By examining how variables relate to each other, contradictions were identified. The information below stems from the researcher's insider knowledge of the programme as a faculty member and as the instructor of level 1 classes. These contradictions are categorised into three types of restrictions or systemic tensions (see Fig. 2) and are explained below.

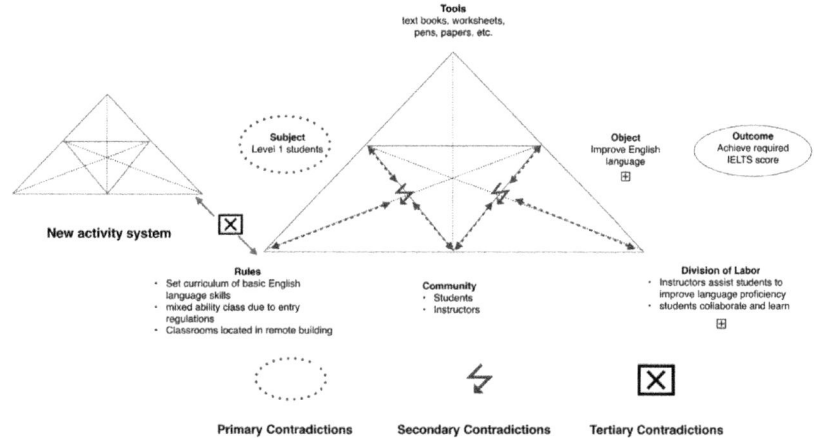

Fig. 2. Systemic tensions in level 1 activity system

3.1 Primary Tensions: Motivational and Temporal Restrictions

Engeström explains primary contradictions to be relevant to the values 'within each corner of the triangle of the activity [7, p. 102]. In this case, the contradiction is within the students' value system. Although they value the outcome of the activity, they do not value the time they need to spend to achieve that outcome. Therefore, students tend to not comply with the timeframe of the original activity system by engaging in several attempts of the standardised test. When they do not achieve the required score, they experience feelings of frustration. This has a noticeable negative effect on students' motivation and engagement, which threatens the activity system since the subject needs to be motivated to reach the object (a motivational constraint).

3.2 Secondary Tensions: Institutional Constraints

'The secondary contradictions are those appearing between the corners' [7, p. 102], i.e. 'between the constituents of the central activity' [20]. The *rules* within the IEP stipulate that the curriculum is designed for a *community* of false beginners when in fact the same rules allow students to enter level 1 without a placement test which causes the *community* of the level to be more mixed ability, hence, causing a contradiction between *rules* and *community*. This also affects the *division of labour,* which mediates the relationship between *community* and *objective*. Because some students are of a higher level, they tend to dominate group work activities or simply disrupt them. In other words, the *rules* cause inconsistency in the *community* and cause tension in the *division of labour,* which reduces its ability to mediate the relationship between *community* and *object*.

3.3 Tertiary Tensions: Technology Related Restrictions and Spatial Restrictions

Engeström clarifies that the tertiary contradiction appears when teachers who represent culture introduce a new, more advanced activity system with a new objective and motive [7]. The new activity system, the dubbing project, designed by the researcher/instructor had a new object (dubbing a video), a new motive (the dubbing competition), and new tools (a short video, dubbing software, etc.), i.e. technology. This new activity system faced tensions caused by the *rules* of the previous activity system. All classes of level 1 were located relatively far from the computer laboratory which made it difficult to arrange for computer laboratory classes where students can have access to required software tools, causing spatial and technological restrictions.

4 Theoretical Framework

The theoretical framework for the intervention is based on AT, dubbing as a language learning activity, mobile learning and BYOD. AT was used to identify tensions in the learning environment. An intervention was designed to overcome these tensions. The new activity system is the activity of translating and dubbing an Arabic video clip into English using personal mobile devices as mediators and an internally-organised competition as motivator. As indicated earlier, dubbing activities have been used previously for language learners and studies report positive results. In addition, mobile learning studies show that mobile learning is capable of blending spaces to overcome the temporal, spatial, technological and motivational restrictions of the old activity system and BYOD helps overcome lack of classroom technology.

The change in object, motive, tools, rules and division of labour can lead to collective transformation. Engeström explains that:

> 'expansive learning theory is concerned with collective transformation, rather than individual learning. Although changes in the collective are initiated by individuals within the community, the transformation itself is a change in the collective system. The object of expansive learning activity is the entire activity system in which the learners are engaged. Expansive learning activity produces culturally new patterns of activity. Expansive learning at work produces new forms of work activity.' [9]

5 The New Activity System

In the 'Listening and Speaking' class, a multi-stage project was designed. The main *outcome* for it, other than language learning, being to re-enforce students' self-confidence to communicate in English, an act they had been resisting. The rules of this new activity system were the set of instructions given to the students. The division of labour enabled the more advanced students to do the more advanced linguistic tasks (translation) and helped weaker students with new vocabulary and pronunciation.

Initially, students were instructed to choose any short Arabic video they particularly liked. This stage was designed to engage students through something they were familiar with and enjoyed, while at the same time alleviating the pressure of the foreign language by starting from L1. Students used their own mobile devices to view, save, and share these videos with group members. Then, they collaborated to translate the script into English and handed it in for evaluation. Translations needed to be reworked more than once until it finally reached an acceptable state. The next stage was the division of roles, and practicing performing the parts.

In the recording stage, the instructor/researcher functioned as a tool along with iMovie App and a personal mobile telephone. This was to monitor students and ensure that pronunciation, intonation, fluency, etc. were all correct. Each recording session turned into a personalised lesson on pronunciation, intonation, grammar and register. This was a valuable stage of the project because it ensured paying attention to each student individually by giving personalised guidance along with mini-lessons on language register and paralinguistic elements.

The result was 8 dubbed videos that were entered in an internally-organised competition for the two sections. All IEP students and staff were invited to the auditorium where the dubbed videos were shown on the big screen. This competition heightened students' *motivation*, increased their self-confidence and gave them a sense of achievement.

6 Methodology

This study adopted a constructivist research paradigm since AT is a constructivist-based learning theory. Constructivism aligns with AT because 'Both Cultural Historical Activity Theory (CHAT) and Dewey's idea-based social constructivism bridge the gap between the dualism of mind and world' [21, p. 38]. Moreover, it provides an understanding of 'the world of human experience' [22, p. 36] through the 'participants' views of the situation being studied' [23, p. 8]. Contrary to post-positivists, the study does not start with a theory, but inductively develops patterns of meaning [23].

The methodology followed was a case study approach to provide a holistic description [24] and explore students' perceptions of the dubbing activity as an alternative to the prevailing activity system. It was a study of a 'bound system' through detailed data collection using multiple sources within a rich context [25].

Case studies benefit from a variety of data collection methods to arrive at a more detailed description of the case [26]. Data were collected through focus group interviews, a questionnaire to collect demographic data and my personal observations as an insider researcher (who is part of the educational institute, the instructor of the participants and the designer of the new activity system). This required some measures to reduce researcher bias and influence, mainly by delaying data collection until the participants completed the course and moved on.

7 Participants and Procedure

The dubbing project was assigned to two sections of level 1 in the 'Listening and Speaking' class. There was a total of 34 female students aged 18 to 21 years, mostly fresh graduates of Arabic public secondary schools. Around half of the students were placed in level 1 because they missed the placement test.

Data were collected through 5 Focus Group (FG) interviews where students were required to reflect on their experience of the dubbing project, describe, and evaluate it. Twenty students responded to the FG invitation and 5 groups were formed in two different ways. Two groups constituted students who worked together on the same video and three groups contained students who worked on different videos. Although Cohen et al., among others, advise that FGs should be rather heterogeneous so that discussion can be enriched [24], Cousin tends to disagree, stressing that group members should have something in common to gain a certain sense of cohesion [26].

Each group interview went through three stages and lasted around one hour. Initially, the dubbed video(s) of the group members were played to remind students and stimulate detailed discussion. The second stage was answering a questionnaire to gather some demographic data, including their IELTS examination results before and after the project. This served as a good reminder of the project, particularly because the interview took place three months after the end of the project. Finally, the interview stage was introduced with an explanation of the purpose of the research.

8 Data Analysis

The group interviews were transcribed, translated and thematically analysed using open coded analysis [27]. Apart from the unanimous expression of how much fun and enjoyable the project was, six main themes emerged and are here discussed in order of the emphasis given to them by students.

8.1 Group Work and Collaboration

This emerged as a strong theme. Students expressed in different ways how group work enriched them and helped them learn. Two groups mentioned how they got together after class to work and how tasks were divided and redistributed if one student faced difficulty. A student remarked that she could not have understood much on her own without the help of her group. The following comments show this meaning: "If one of us did not understand something, other group members would explain it to her" and "When in a group, everyone participates with ideas. When I did not notice something, someone else in the group drew my attention to it."

Group 4 mentioned that they did not need the dictionary much because they had a classmate who knew English well enough and asked her for meanings. One student, however, expressed how she did not like to work with a group and that she would have rather worked on her own or used the help of people from outside. This was a point of disagreement in one of the mixed focus groups and generated discussion among group members. Eventually, the student who disagreed acknowledged the need for others in this kind of project, but expressed her preference to work with outsiders for a more enriching experience. These findings show how the community of the new activity system became more harmonious, and division of labour was more effective in reaching the outcome.

8.2 The Competition as a Motivating Factor

This was a prominent theme that emerged strongly without prompting. It was mentioned when asking for general impressions. Words such as 'enthusiastic', 'motivated', 'encouraged', 'competitive', and 'want to win' were quite recurrent. One student said that for her, it was only after announcing the competition that the interest started. "This is when the interest and drive for hard work kicked-in. This is when ideas started to come" she said. Another expressed that the competition made them more serious about the work, especially after knowing that the dubbed videos would be shown to an audience and a panel of judges. "We started to work hard when we knew that other instructors will be on the panel of judges to choose the winner." Two groups remarked that when you work hard on something, you want people to see it. Others said that they finally dared to speak in English after being very reluctant to do so. They said that now they do not mind speaking in English and feel more confident and motivated. They also indicated that they felt honoured to be called on stage and presented with achievement certificates and awards. One student said that she immediately shared her certificate with her family. It is quite clear here that the new activity system was effective in changing students' perceptions and motivating them, which answers the second research question.

8.3 Achievement, Pride, and Sense of Ownership

A general sense of pride and achievement was prevalent. Students repeatedly asserted that doing this project was a big achievement for them since it was their first semester in the university, especially for being able to speak as fluently as they did in the videos. Having it on video was a proof of their improvement. Most students said that they shared the videos with family and friends, except one student who said she did not share it because she felt that she could have done better. This was the same student who did not prefer group work, giving the impression that she could have produced a better video on her own.

Many students expressed repeatedly that they never thought they could speak like that. "I don't know how, but I dared to speak! I don't speak much, not even in Arabic! Now I'm more confident and I don't mind speaking as I used to before" one student commented. They also mentioned that they showed it to their other instructors: "they were impressed, told us how well we did and encouraged us to keep it up." One student mentioned a significant remark from one of their instructors. She said that this instructor turned around while the video was playing and said to her: "So you do speak English!" This remark from the instructor is an indicator of how resistant students were to communicating in English, even in their English classes.

8.4 Difficulties

One common difficulty mentioned around 8 times was the fact that they had to speak in English and how they struggled with accepting the idea. They said that seeing others speaking and making mistakes made them feel that it was fine to make mistakes and gave them some confidence. Other remarks varied about the difficulties they faced and different students pointed to different aspects of the project. Students mentioned difficulties such as:

- dealing with Arabic words that do not have English equivalents: "Some words were hard to translate and had no equivalent, so we had to describe them instead";
- lip synching, speaking speed, editing and re-recording: "the duration of our pronunciation was different from the character's lip movement, so we had to re-record and change some of the dialogue as we were recording";
- acting and changing the voice according to the role: "Sometimes we had to practice a lot just to get the right voice for the character. Acting with your voice is not easy";
- pronunciation of new words.

One student said: "the more difficulties there are, the more you would want to overcome them and it drives you to do more". Finding a suitable, quiet place to do the recording was noted as a challenge, but because the recording was done with a mobile telephone, the location shifted according to availability.

8.5 Learning

Although this might be a difficult aspect to measure, students indicated that they learned a number of new vocabulary words. As students were watching the video at the beginning of the interview, they were prompted to jot down any word they learned in this project. They produced lists of words that ranged from 4 to 11 words per video. There was a correlation between the number of words and the length of dubbed video. The longer the video was, the more words were learned. Moreover, in the interviews they mentioned learning pronunciation and register: "Some Arabic expressions do not fit in the same context in English". This was linked to the difficulty of translating some expressions. Repeating the recording for the sake of proper lip-synching was pointed out as the main reason they improved their pronunciation and fluency. One group specifically said: "this project was good to learn language, vocabulary, pronunciation, how to say things [intonation]… When you translate, you also learn grammar." This relates to the first research question showing that the dubbing project remediated learning for false beginners and mixed ability classes.

8.6 Suggestions

When asked if they recommended this project for other classes and what suggestions they had, they all recommended it. Most said that the project was good as it was, a few suggested dubbing whole episodes or plays. One student suggested individual productions but others in the group did not agree, saying that if they had to act or perform on their own, they would not have done it.

9 Discussion and Conclusion

Students' comments and reflections were overwhelmingly positive and indicated a high level of engagement within the activity of dubbing. This is seen as a significant change to the disengagement, disruption, and frustration that were prevailing in the old activity system. As for motivation, a positive change in students' attitudes towards learning was noted. The activity catered for different levels of language learners. On the one hand, it encouraged collaboration between students. On the other hand, by breaking away from the set curriculum, each student found a task suitable to her level. Stronger students helped weaker ones, while all of them were motivated to do everything they could to win the competition.

Part of the demographic information students provided in the questionnaire was their score in the speaking component in the IELTS examination before and after level 1. Ten students indicated taking the IELTS both before and after level 1. The speaking component score improved for seven of them. Although this cannot be attributed to the dubbing project alone, it can still be suggestive of improvement. These results answer the first research question and provide evidence that this new activity system remediated language learning for false beginners in mixed-ability classes. It also answers the second question by showing students' increased motivation and confidence. Although the dubbing activity proved to be successful and enjoyable, results of the study need further verification in other contexts. For example, in the recording stage, students could be guided to do their own recording, video editing and publishing with less interference from the instructor.

References

1. Issroff, K., Scanlon, E.: Using technology in higher education: an activity theory perspective. J. Comput. Assist. Learn. **18**(1), 77–83 (2002)
2. Scanlon, E., Issroff, K.: Activity theory and higher education: evaluating learning technologies. J. Comput. Assist. Learn. **21**(6), 430–439 (2005)
3. Kaptelinin, V., Nardi, B.A.: Acting with Technology: Activity Theory and Interaction Design. MIT Press, Cambridge (2006)
4. Yamagata-Lynch, L.C.: Activity Systems Analysis Methods. Springer, Boston (2010). https://doi.org/10.1007/978-1-4419-6321-5
5. Nardi, B.: Some reflections on the application of activity theory. In: Nardi, B. (ed.) Context and Consciousness: Activity Theory and Human-Computer Interaction, pp. 235–246. MIT Press, Cambridge (1996)

6. Edwards, A.: Cultural historical activity theory (2011). https://www.bera.ac.uk/researchers-resources/publications/cultural-historical-activity-theory-chat
7. Engeström, Y.: Learning by Expanding: An Activity-Theoretical Approach to Developmental Research. Orienta-Konsultit Oy, Helsinki (1987)
8. Engeström, Y.: University of Lancaster interview [Video] (2002). http://csalt.lancs.ac.uk/alt/engestrom/
9. Engeström, Y.: Expansive learning at work: toward an activity theoretical reconceptualisation. J. Educ. Work **14**(1), 133–156 (2001)
10. Díaz-Cintas, J.: Audiovisual Translation, Subtitling. Routledge, New York (2014)
11. Danan, M.: Dubbing projects for the language learner: a framework for integrating audiovisual translation into task-based instruction. Comput. Assist. Lang. Learn. **23**(5), 441–456 (2010)
12. Sokoli, S.: Audiovisual translation for foreign language learning. Presented at the TISLID Conference, University of Salamanca, Ávila, Spain (2014)
13. Kumai, W.N.: Karaoke movies: dubbing movies for pronunciation. Lang. Teach. Online **20**(9) (1996). http://jalt-publications.org/old_tlt/files/96/sept/dub.html
14. Casas-Tost, H., Rovira-Esteva, S.: Clipflair: the use of captioning and revoicing for TCFL. Presented at the First International Conference on Teaching Chinese as a Foreign Language, Hong Kong (2013)
15. Burston, J.: Video dubbing projects in the foreign language curriculum. Calico J. **23**(1), 79–92 (2005)
16. Chiu, Y.: Can film dubbing projects facilitate EFL learners' acquisition of English pronunciation? Br. J. Educ. Technol. **43**(1), 24–27 (2012)
17. Avila, J.J., Talavan, N.: The role of dubbing in foreign language learning. Presented at the AESLA 31st International Conference, Alicante, Spain (2013)
18. Vosloo, S.: Mobile learning and policies: key issues to consider. UNESCO, Paris (2012). http://unesdoc.unesco.org/images/0021/002176/217638E.pdf
19. Palalas, A.: Blended mobile learning: expanding learning spaces with mobile technology. In: Tsinakos, A., Ally, M. (eds.) Global Mobile Learning Implementations and Trends, pp. 86–104. China Central Radio & TV University Press, Beijing (2013)
20. Weibell, C.J.: Expansive learning and activity theory (Engeström – 1987), principles of learning [Blog] (2011). https://principlesoflearning.wordpress.com/
21. Postholm, M.: Cultural historical activity theory and Dewey's idea-based social constructivism: consequences for educational research. Outlines: Crit. Pract. Stud. **10**(1), 37–48 (2008)
22. Cohen, L., Manion, L.: Research Methods in Education, 4th edn. Routledge, London (1994)
23. Creswell, J.W.: Research Design: Qualitative, Quantitative, and Mixed Methods Approaches, 2nd edn. Sage, Thousand Oaks (2003)
24. Cohen, L., Manion, L., Morrison, K.: Research Methods in Education, 7th edn. Routledge, London (2011)
25. Creswell, J.W., Maietta, R.C.: Part 4: qualitative research, the case study. In: Miller, D.C., Salkind, N.J. (eds.) Handbook of Research Design and Social Measurement, pp. 142–197. Sage, Thousand Oaks (2002)
26. Cousin, G.: Researching Learning in Higher Education: An Introduction to Contemporary Methods and Approaches. Routledge, London (2008)
27. Flick, U.: An Introduction to Qualitative Research, 4th edn. Sage, Los Angeles (2009)

Innovation in Language Teaching and Learning

What Do We Need to Make a Massive Open Online Course (MooC) for Language Learning Genuinely Innovative?

Veruska De Caro-Barek[✉]

University of Science and Technology (NTNU), Trondheim, Norway
`Veruska.de.caro@ntnu.no`

Abstract. By sharing experiences from the process of making Massive Open Online Courses (MooCs) in second language at NTNU, this paper aims to raise awareness about the need for improved technology solutions with a critical look at how course developers can build more innovative and interactive language MooCs within the frame of self-instructed courses using new convergent technologies such as Web Real Time Communication (WebRTC).

Keywords: MooC · Language teaching and learning · Oral interaction · WebRTC technology

1 Introduction

In 2005, Siemens argued the need for a new theory of learning in the digital age [1]. In the past decade, access to worldwide information in the form of continuous streaming from social media and fast developing new convergent technologies have radically changed our way to connect and interact with the world around us and our approach to learning. New emergent technologies offer different models and structures to support learning, and disrupt the notion that learning should be controlled by educators and educational institutions [2].

Following the enthusiasm for "The year of the MooC" (Massive Open Online Courses) as highlighted in a well-known article in the New York Times in 2012 [3], we have seen a fast-growing interest in MooCs connected to language learning. For example, the MooC provider FutureLearn enrolled over 370,000 students on the preparatory course to the English language proficiency test, IELTS. This is so far the biggest MooC in the world [4].

While the general research literature on MooCs is fast-growing, the emergent body of specific research literature on MooCs for language learning is still very limited [5, 6]. MooCs is a 'hot topic' in the context of online teaching and learning research and practice, with numerous ardent supporters as well as fervent opponents.

Among the arguments set forth by the opponents, high dropout rates have, for instance, been interpreted as an indication that barriers to persistent learning in MooC environments are present and are a steep wall to climb and conquer for course developers, independent of the subject field [5]. The wider lay-audience of the general public has also argued that this situation could well manifest a symptom of an exaggerated hype around MooCs and an overrated and overestimated focus on supposed teaching and learning innovations [7, 8].

This paper is framed within the field of second language didactics and is a result of my work on two Language MooC projects at the Norwegian University of Science and Technology (NTNU). The first project (2016) was a collaboration with the Ministry of Foreign Affairs to produce a self-instructed introductory Norwegian language MooC on Open EdX for the foreign embassy employees around the world. The second project (2017 18) was a wider and updated version of the Norwegian MooC, which has now been launched internationally on FutureLearn.

In this paper, I wish to readdress the topic of innovation in language teaching and learning that supporters of MooCs and providers of MooC platforms predicate. Working with both Open EdX and FutureLearn, I experienced that the provided technology can limit the possibilities for a developer to construct a MooC for language learning, defining and somehow constricting the teaching approach in a more traditional manner. Specifically, I will try to raise awareness about the technological limitations for language MooCs' development as presented by most MooC platform providers, with special attention to oral production and interaction. I will then address the need for improved technology solutions, with a critical look at how MooC platform providers and course developers can build more innovative and interactive language courses by integrating new convergent technology such as Web Real Time Communication (WebRTC) in order to promote genuine oral interaction, especially in the case of self-directed learning.

2 Are MooCs Really Just a Hype?

The challenges facing the higher education (HE) sector in meeting technology are multiple, the foremost being how to adapt a static institutional system and traditional teaching and learning patterns to the new dynamics offered by technology services. The paradoxical result is that even in the presence of technological availability for implementing newer and more effective learning processes, historical and cultural barriers from a bygone era of education philosophy and practice create hindrances to innovation processes [9–11]. This creates somewhat dysfunctional learning and teaching environments where technology is applied, yet not fully understood, nor is it used to its fullest [ibid].

The journey to real innovation in MooC developmental technology is just at its beginning [11]. In the words of George Siemens [11, 12], there are two types of MooCs: cMooCs and xMooCs. The "cMooC model emphasizes creation, creativity, autonomy and social networking learning" while the xMooC model emphasises "a more traditional learning approach through video presentations and short quizzes and testing. Put another way, cMooCs focus on knowledge creation and generation whereas xMooCs focus on knowledge duplication" [ibid.].

However, despite the claims of innovation, disruptive learning technology methods and a revolution in learning approaches, several meta-studies [11, 13, 14] reviewing the existing research literature on MooCs and investigating the pedagogical approaches applied seem to confirm that the pedagogical practices in MooCs are neither entirely new nor radically innovative [14]. The general teaching setups in most MOOCs seem to rely on a classic behaviouristic teaching paradigm, with pre-produced and teacher supervised study paths and fairly linear learning sequences. Knowledge is passed on to a mostly passive audience through video presentations or streaming from classroom practices. This seems to occur both in teacher-supervised learning environments, as in most xMooCs, and in self-teaching or autonomous learning environments oriented to a more connectivist approach, as in cMooCs - the connectivist side being the student fora available on the MooC platform [13, 14].

The above-mentioned problems are certainly true for language courses as well.

3 The Case of Language MooCs

With regard to the worldwide development of 'Language Massive Open Online Courses' or 'Language MooCs' (as termed hereafter), Spain and the United States of Amercia (USA) are in the lead with a solid academic legitimacy but also an extensive commercial production. It is therefore not surprising that the most prolific Language MooCs are in Spanish and English. In the rest of Europe, including Norway [15, 16], the situation is quite different and Language MooCs are often developed under the umbrella of smaller, specific research projects.

Platform selection and technical functionality vary greatly according to funding and this impacts correspondingly on the final product. The kind of Language MooCs which have been developed, whether these are meant to be self-instructed courses or tutored, also imposes specific didactical and technical choices, along with cost management strategies.

In a very first attempt to gather and categorise research on learning and teaching experiences in the emerging field of Language MooCs, Bárcena and Martín Monje have edited a pioneering and insightful meta-study that covers paramount topics relevant to any language MooC developer. The conundrum for language courses, irrespective of their possible categorisation as cMooCs or xMooCs, is defined as follows:

> "language learning is not only knowledge-based, in the sense that it requires the rather passive assimilation of vocabulary items and combinatory rules, but is mainly skill-based, in that it involves putting into practice an intricate array of receptive, productive and interactive verbal (and non-verbal) functional capabilities, whose role in the overall success of the communicative act is generally considered to be more prominent than that of the formal or organizational elements" [13].

How does the technology available on MooC platforms cater with such a challenge?

Even if MooC platforms in general undoubtedly offer a considerable improvement on online language course development, the technological advancements are not sufficiently developed to meet the specific requirements of language didactics. For example, it is a fact that none of the existing platforms has embedded technology which can enable course participants to fully develop their oral interaction skills. Most of the course content relies on written interaction, with the exception of fully-tutored Language MooCs, where feedback on the participants' oral performance takes place with the aid of external technological resources such as videoconferencing. In self-instructed courses there is neither the possibility for oral interaction nor external feedback on the platform [13, 14].

3.1 Oral Interaction Issues in Language MooCs

According to the Common European Framework of Reference for Languages (CEFR), which is increasingly also being used in countries outside Europe, the categorisation of the language learner and user's linguistic competence is based on real-life language use and grounded in interaction and co-construction of meaning. Activities are presented under four modes of communication: reception, production, interaction and mediation in written *and* oral context [17].

In the CEFR, *proficiency* is a term encompassing the ability to perform communicative language activities stated as *"can do-s"*, while drawing upon communicative language competences (linguistic, sociolinguistic, and pragmatic), and appropriate communicative strategies [ibid.]. When one of these primary competences fails to be represented within the language learning environment, as for instance in the case of the technological inadequacy of MooC platforms to support solutions which cover oral production and interaction, a question arises concerning the learner's actual possibility for fully developing the range of linguistic competences necessary in order to master the target language. Similarly, a concern becomes apparent about the integrity and validity of the language course and the possibility for future assessment and accreditation. These are indeed pressing demands which need to be addressed by MooC-developing institutions and MooC platform providers for and within HE.

Regarding the allegedly interactive environment present on MooC platform solutions, there is a growing consensus that "most of the MooLC (language MooCs) initiatives don't offer a highly interactive environment where the learners are interconnected to a language learning community and collectively build their language skills" [14]. Learners are still studying language in a traditional way, following courses based on a cognitive behavioural pedagogical model with extended use of instructional videos and pre-formatted learning sequences [14, 18].

Even in the case of two of the largest and most successful MooC providers, Open EdX and FutureLearn, platform limitations in structure and functionalities are present. Especially, FutureLearn is constricted by a rigid platform setup and few functionality options (video, article, audio, quiz and poll/discussion). The underlying connectivist pedagogy, enhanced in the form of supported collaborative learning tasks among student participants, also seemed to be limited too frequently by the technology options available on the platforms and solely bound to discussion fora. The inspirational vision of connectivist MooCs is too often proving elusive. While it is possible to follow the course participants' interaction on tutored Language MooCs, it is very difficult to monitor whether the course participants will interact with each other in a self-instructed Language MooC [18, 19]. Neither is it possible to know for certain whether the participants will be able to build a learning community outside the platform and beyond the platform resources by utilising external digital services for language learning to instigate collaborative knowledge building [19]. It is important to note that many Language MooCs are indeed self-instructed and based on the concepts of autonomous learning. In this case, platform technology is not necessarily synonymous with better teaching or learning. For instance, even the use of synchronous tools for written communication on MooC platforms can be counterproductive. It is indeed extremely difficult to foster high-level cognitive interactions in long multiple-threaded forum conversations on a MooC platform; it is even more difficult to keep track of participants' actions when compulsory tasks, based on communicative or collaborative tools, are external to the platform [18 in 13, 19]. *Who* is doing *what*, *why* and *how* are crucial questions to ask when in the process of learning a language. It is already a challenging task for the course facilitator/instructor trained in language didactics to create a sense of logic communication flow on the platform for tutored Language MooCs. It could be a virtually impossible task for the well-intentioned but not necessarily trained volunteer mentors and curators possibly emerging from the learning community of a self-instructed Language MooC.

Is it then possible to create better learning environments on MooC platforms which can support the development of oral interaction so critically important to language teaching and learning?

4 Towards Better Technological Solutions

It is not easy to answer why such an important feature like oral interaction on Language MooCs has yet not been a priority for MooC platform developers. Especially so, since the technology which could make this possible is ready available and in use on popular Language Exchange Apps like *Bilingua*, *HiNative* and *HelloTalk*.

Language Exchange Apps like the ones mentioned above offer the opportunity to communicate with other language learners as well as native speakers through chat and videoconferencing. Using matching algorithms, they select the best possible learning matches to your profile. As a common denominator, these apps display integrated learning tools like translator, vocabulary lists and grammar checker, but foremost they make language learning a pleasant experience keeping learners motivated. *Bilingua* has even included gamification features in the app with a reward system to stimulate language learning through gaming and competitions among learners.

Would it be possible to recreate this kind of productive and interconnected learning environment on Language MooC platforms? Would it be possible, for instance, to integrate videoconferencing technology on OpenEdX or FutureLearn and open up for oral communication directly on the platform, without having to rely on external programs and resources?

4.1 WebRTC Technology

Videoconferencing has traditionally required installing a dedicated application, such as Skype. In 2011, Google released WebRTC (Web Real Time Communication) as an open source project to bring video conferencing to browsers. As a result of its addition in popular browsers such as Chrome and Firefox, numerous web-based videoconferencing services were launched.

WebRTC enables real-time communication over peer-to-peer connections and applications such as video conferencing, file transfer, chat, or desktop sharing without the need of either internal or external browser plugins or external software. As an example, Appear.in was launched in Norway by the national telecommunication company Telenor as an online collaboration tool that supports videoconferencing with multiple participants (up to 12) with no required registration. At the core of its functionality is WebRTC.

In order to integrate this technology on a MooC platform, the platform itself must support customisation using HTML and Javascript. An example is the Xblock-functionality on OpenEdX.

Xblocks are fully customisable extensions or plug-ins that add functionality to OpenEdX platform and can provide interactive content to the learning objects in the course. In this case, a bespoke Xblock provides access to an external WebRTC platform through an Application Program Interface (API). The implementation of WebRTC can be done by integrating existing conferencing services. Suppliers of such services are, for instance, the American *Tokbox*, the Singapore-based *Temasys* or open source providers like *Jitsi*. These suppliers offer Javascript APIs which are used on web sites together with a "conference bridge" which browsers will then connect to in order to deploy videoconference functionality. At NTNU, we are currently experimenting with building XBlocks to implement WebRTC (by using *Jitsi*) on our Open EdX installation, so that we will be able to provide Language MooCs with real-time oral interaction for our learners.

It is, however, important to underline that even in the case of Open EdX, this is not something course designers will be able to do on their own. This bespoke functionality requires the dedicated efforts of a team, including computer programmers and web designers, and it comes with a cost that will impact on the project budget. Nonetheless, OpenEdX is the only platform that allows the necessary customisation to integrate this technology.

Unfortunately, at the moment, FutureLearn does not offer course developers the possibility to include such convergent technology for tailoring learning objects' functionalities, as the platform is rigidly preformatted and does not support custom extensions. In this respect, any attempt to include oral interaction in the course design of self-instructed language courses on FutureLearn is currently precluded.

4.2 WebRTC for Language MooCs

Integrating ad hoc technology to enable oral interaction on MooC platforms is a first step. Most crucial, though, is integrating the technology in the language course design. How is it possible to use WebRTC technology in a meaningful way for large classes that are common to MooCs? And how can such activities be assessed fairly and equally?

The implementation of WebRTC on Language MooCs could give rise to different learning scenarios and entail different levels of cooperation. In the following, I will describe some possible courses of action that can work on Open EdX, as this is currently the MooC platform which offers the best technological functionality.

4.3 The Participants

The first logical approach will be to match the existing course participants so that they can start to practice their oral skills with each other. In the matching process different variables must be considered as with Language Exchange Apps mentioned in previous paragraphs. Such variables include personal interests, level of proficiency in the target language, time of dedicated effort a week and different time zones.

In language didactics, there is an unequivocal consensus that small groups work better than large classes. The platform should therefore include functionality for creating smaller learner groups, such as "cohorts" on Open EdX. Cohorts will then be assigned language tasks according to their level of proficiency. It will be possible, for instance, to create guided video-chats where learners have to solve problems or enact a role play in the target language.

In order to foster genuine oral interaction on Language MooCs, though, the pivotal feature of the course design will be to open up for interaction with native speakers. Only through feedback provided by native speakers can a language learner fully develop his/her range of communication skills. It is then necessary to build a database of participants which comprises native speakers willing to learn and help others learn languages. But how to recruit such participants?

On Open EdX, for instance, it is possible to recruit in interdisciplinary ways, from other courses on the platform, during the enrollment process. When the participants receive their enrolling mail to a course, it is possible to ask them whether they want to join the platform's tandem language learning community. It is also possible to create a separate enrollment dedicated only to the platform's tandem language community. This could have been displayed as a platform feature on an institution's main page. Educational institutions could cooperate with local community initiatives, or themselves initiate local community projects, like inviting retired language teachers to the tandem community. In this way, language courses can be guaranteed the necessary experience of native speakers and at the same time the language tandem project can have a positive impact on a segment of society whose resources are underestimated.

4.4 Assessment, Certification and Accreditation

Certification and accreditation are notoriously a challenge for MooCs. In Language MooCs, I think the challenge is even greater.

Utilising existing technology and integrating functionalities on MooC platforms to support linguistic oral interaction have simply not been a priority for MooC providers so far. However, this is certainly something that they will need to take into consideration in the future, especially when having to front the pressing demand for course accreditation in the HE sector. How is it possible to give credits or provide certificates of accomplishments when a course is simply not teaching the learners one of the most important skills they need to know when learning a language?

When integrating WebRTC in Language MooCs, new forms of assessment can come to light and offer interesting solutions, particularly in self-instructed courses.

Open Response Assessments (ORA) are, for example, flexible assignment types on Open EdX in which learners submit different text responses to open questions or assignments. Responses can be submitted in different file formats and learners are guided through a series of assessment steps that can include a training step, peer assessment, self-assessment, and even staff assessment in fully tutored courses. In self-instructed courses, course designers set forth constraints and conditions and can define the assignments in ORA. For instance, a learner can be required to deliver 30 to 45 min of work/week in oral communication skills. In this case, each video conference session is recorded in the MooC platform's analytics system, which means that the platform registers the learner's participation, and the learning task is then marked as completed for future certification/accreditation. In the same way as other language exercises, it will be possible to integrate several video conferences in the curriculum and adjust these according to language learners' level and progression.

What ORA functionality allows particularly in self-instructed courses is the emergence of a learning community, where learner's tasks are not simply collected and stored in analytics, as happens with regular multiple-choice or predefined exercises, but it is an intrinsic part of a learner's development. The ORA's cornerstone on a Language Mooc is peer-to-peer assessment. The learner is required to perform a language task and get peer evaluation on his/her performance while at the same time having to evaluate the responses of other course participants. In addition, the learner also gets evaluation from his/her *virtual tandem partner* (VTP), that is, the native speaker or speakers with whom he/she regularly engages in conversations. In this way, the scaffolding so crucial to language learning [20] fluctuates organically between the expert support given by the native speakers and the peer support presented by other course participants, offering the learner the possibility to explore and test language skills in his/her zone of proximal development [ibid.]. In the same way, the rigid boundaries between informal and formal assessment fluctuate; the learner's assessment of his/her own achievements is continuous and progressive thanks to the feedback from the VTP, the learning community and the automated analytics functionality on the platform.

Only when platform functionality and course design are able to cover for all these aspects can a Language MooC genuinely claim to foster language learning.

5 Discussion and Conclusion

The need for successful Language MooCs, which can present learners with quality ad hoc technological solutions and appropriate language didactics, is high, due to multilingualism and multiculturalism being paramount aspects in our modern globalised society. The journey to reach that target is just at the beginning; there are still issues which are neither being fully addressed nor perhaps fully understood in the MooC-platform providers' community.

Language MooCs have to deal with the same ontological, conceptual and practical challenges of regular MooCs, like the evolving nature of teaching and learning in digital networks, the redefinition of the teacher's role as facilitator, time and implementation costs, as well as assessment and accreditation issues. In addition, Language MooCs necessarily face specific challenges intrinsic to language didactics, such as how to enable oral interaction on the platform among the course participants but also within the authentic context of oral communication with native speakers. This is particularly important for self-instructed Language MooCs. However, most Language MooCs so far do not offer oral interaction functionality.

Without pretending to have a solution to a complicated matter, which involves several levels of theoretical and technological understanding, I wish, however, to conclude this paper by mentioning that it is indeed possible to utilise existing convergent technology such as WebRTC and integrate functionalities on MooC platforms to support linguistic oral interaction. This aspect has simply not been a priority for MooC providers so far, but it certainly is an issue which needs to be addressed, especially concerning the pressing demands for course accreditation in HE. MooC platform providers and language course designers could find inspiration in their search for a solution to this problem by looking at developments in non-MooC language learning environments, such as in the case of Language Exchange Apps.

Implementation of WebRTC technology on MooC platforms could challenge the classic teaching paradigm still predominant even in advanced technological learning environments, and could open the way for assessment processes more suitable to learning in the digital age.

Research in this specific field is not yet available, and an array of research possibilities therefore lie ahead for genuine innovative language didactics in MooCs.

References

1. Siemens, G.: Connectivism: a learning theory for the digital age. Int. J. Instr. Technol. Distance Learn. **2**(1), 3–10 (2005)
2. Fournier, H., Kop, R., Durand, G.: Challenges to research in MOOCs. MERLOT J. Online Learn. Teach. **10**(1), 1–15 (2014)
3. Pappano, L.: The year of the MOOC. New York Times (2012). https://www.bgsu.edu/content/dam/BGSU/master-plan/documents/the-year-of-themooc.pdf
4. Perifanou, M.: Worldwide state of language MOOCs. In: Papadima-Sophocleus, S., Thouësny, S. (eds.) CALL Communities and Culture – Short Papers from EUROCALL 2016, pp. 386–390 (2016)
5. Kennedy, J.: Characteristics of massive open online courses (MOOCs): a research review, 2009-2012. J. Interact. Online Learn. **13**(1), 2–4 (2014)
6. Ebben, M., Murphy, J.S.: Unpacking MOOC scholarly discourse: a review of nascent MOOC scholarship. Learn. Media Technol. **39**(3), 328–345 (2014)
7. Waldrop, M.M.: Massive open online courses, aka MOOCs, transform higher education and science. Sci. Am. Nat. Mag. **495**, 160–163 (2013). https://www.nature.com/polopoly_fs/1.12590!/menu/main/topColumns/topLeftColumn/pdf/495160a.pdf
8. Konnikova, M.: Will MOOCs be Flukes? The New Yorker (2014). https://www.newyorker.com/science/maria-konnikova/moocs-failure-solutions
9. Liyanagunawardena, T.R., Adams, A.A., Williams, S.A.: MOOCs: a systematic study of the published literature 2008–2012. Int. Rev. Res. Open Distrib. Learn. **14**(3), 202–227 (2013)
10. Krokan, A.: Smart Læring. Hvordan IKT og sosiale medier endrer læring. Fagbokforlaget, Bergen (2012)
11. Bahadur Singh, A.: Learning through massive open online courses (MOOCs). A case of the first international MOOC offered by University of Oslo in 2015. Master thesis, Program in Higher Education, Faculty of Educational Sciences, University of Oslo, Norway (2016)

12. Siemens, G.: MOOCs are really a platform. Elearnspace blog, 25 July 2012. http://www.elearnspace.org/blog/2012/07/25/moocs-are-really-a-platform
13. Martin-Monje, E., Bárcena, E. (eds.): Language MOOCs: Providing Learning, Transcending Boundaries. De Gruyter Open, Berlin (2014)
14. Perifanou, M., Economides, A.: MOOCs for foreign language learning: an effort to explore and evaluate the first practices. In: Proceedings of INTED 2014 Conference, Valencia, Spain, 10th–12th March 2014, pp. 3561–3570 (2014)
15. Official Norwegian Reports NOU 2014: 5: MOOCs for Norway - New Digital Learning Methods in Higher Education. Ministry of Education and Research, Oslo (2014). https://www.regjeringen.no/contentassets/ff86edace9874505a3381b5daf6848e6/en-gb/pdfs/nou201420140005000en_pdfs.pdf
16. Kunnskapsdepartementet Strategidokument: Digitaliseringsstrategi for universitets- og høyskolesektoren. Ministry of Education and Research, Oslo (2017). https://www.regjeringen.no/contentassets/779c0783ffee461b88451b9ab71d5f51/no/pdfs/digitaliseringsstrategi-for-universitets--og-hoysk.pdf
17. Language Policy Programme, Education Policy Division, Education Department: Provisional edition September 2017: The Common European Framework of Reference for Languages: Learning, Teaching, Assessment. Companion Volume with new Descriptors. Council of Europe, Strasbourg (2017). https://rm.coe.int/common-european-framework-of-reference-for-languages-learning-teaching/168074a4e2
18. de Larreta-Azelain, D.C.: Chapter 5: Language teaching in MOOCs: the integral role of the instructor. In: Martin-Monje, E., Bárcena, E. (eds.) Language MOOCs: Providing Learning, Transcending Boundaries, pp. 67–90. De Gruyter Open, Berlin (2014)
19. Kop, R.: The challenges to connectivist learning on open online networks: learning experiences during a massive open online course. Int. Rev. Res. Open Distrib. Learn. **12**(3), 59–74 (2011)
20. Gibbons, P.: Scaffolding Language, Scaffolding Learning: Teaching English Language Learners in the Mainstream Classroom, 2nd edn, pp. 13–17. Heinemann, Portsmouth (2015)

An Investigation of the Impact of Haptics for Promoting Understanding of Difficult Concepts in Cell Biology

Mary Webb[1(✉)], Megan Tracey[1], William Harwin[2], Ozan Tokatli[2], Faustina Hwang[2], Natasha Barrett[2], Chris Jones[2], and Ros Johnson[3]

[1] School of Education, Communication and Society,
King's College London, London, UK
mary.webb@kcl.ac.uk
[2] School of Biological Sciences, University of Reading, Reading, UK
[3] The Abbey, Reading, UK

Abstract. This paper reports on a study which investigated whether the addition of haptics (virtual touch) to a three-dimensional (3D) virtual reality (VR) simulation promotes learning of key concepts in biology for students aged 12 to 13 years. We developed a virtual model of a section of the cell membrane and a haptic-enabled interface that allows students to interact with the model and to manipulate objects in the model. Students, in two schools in England, worked collaboratively on activities, in pairs, designed to support learning of key difficult concepts. These concepts included the dynamic nature of the cell membrane, passive diffusion and facilitated diffusion. Findings from observation of the activities and student interviews revealed that students were very positive about using the system and believed that being able to feel structures and movements within the model assisted their learning. Results of pre- and post-tests of conceptual knowledge showed significant knowledge gains but there were no significant differences between the haptic and non-haptic condition.

Keywords: Haptics · Virtual reality · Cell biology · Science learning

1 Introduction and Background

Haptics provides the additional sense of touch to a virtual reality (VR) environment, thus enabling people to feel the objects they are interacting with. Furthermore, a haptic-enabled interface can enable people to directly manipulate objects in a three-dimensional (3D) VR environment much more realistically than is possible through more standard interfaces such as mouse and tracker ball. Our research objectives were to: (1) design and develop a haptic-enabled VR environment that would enable students to explore difficult concepts through multisensory collaborative activities; (2) investigate whether or not the ability to feel the interactions through touch affected students' development of understanding of key concepts; and (3) examine students' perspectives on the interactive learning experience.

We focused on cell biology as an important area of science learning that poses significant challenges that may be addressed through the use of VR simulations.

Understanding cell biology is critical for understanding biology as a whole [1], but introductory courses tend to be limited in their scope, mainly owing to the difficulties of developing conceptual understanding of such complex systems that cannot be observed directly. Furthermore, there is evidence that persistent misconceptions are common in cell biology at school level [2, 3].

The model developed for this study was of a section of the plasma membrane, otherwise known as the cell membrane, which is the membrane surrounding all cells. The decision to focus the study on cell membrane structure and function was based on three main considerations: (1) the crucial importance of cell membranes for the overall understanding of biology; (2) the prevalence of conceptual difficulties and misconceptions in learning about membrane structure and function; and (3) the good opportunities for haptic exploration of the forces at work in membrane transport. The way in which the cell membrane controls movement of materials into and out of cells, through diffusion, active transport, facilitated diffusion, etc., is critical for the functioning of biochemical processes. Known problems in understanding these particular phenomena include: a persistent anthropomorphic view of processes and assignment of intentionality to cell functions [2]; issues in understanding magnification and scaling [4]; problems in understanding randomness in relation to diffusion [5]; and issues in visualisation of cell structures with different representations [6]. Specific misconceptions that have been identified previously include: molecules diffuse depending on the space available [7]; diffusion in a cell depends on the "living" processes of the cell and therefore stops following the death of the cell [8]; and a substance dissolved in a liquid spreads out by breaking into smaller particles.

Haptic interaction in a VR simulation can enable students to experience forces resulting from concentration gradients, suction effects of specific carrier proteins as well as to feel the virtual representations of microscopic structures whose shape is critical for their function. Thus, we have chosen to investigate a learning situation where haptic interaction may be particularly beneficial.

Previously, Webb et al. [9] argued that the potential benefits for learning science concepts, of the addition of haptics to a VR simulation, derive from: (1) the known general benefits of multisensory learning compared with uni-sensory; (2) engagement and motivational effects of a more realistic experience; and (3) the more specific possibility that haptic interaction will support the visualisation that is necessary for understanding many key processes in science [10]. A possible theoretical foundation for the suggested improved learning associated with haptic support for visualisation comes from Dual Coding Theory [11, 12] which proposes that distinct interconnected systems for different sensory modalities act synergistically.

In this paper, we first discuss the principles and design of the VR environment that we developed for this study, and the haptic-enabled interface designed to explore the VR environment. We then discuss the nature of the interactive learning environment and activities that we developed, based on findings from previous studies [9]. The methods for collecting data, preliminary results and discussion of findings then follow.

2 Design of the VR Environment

Designing the VR environment presented several challenges. First, cell membranes and the ways in which they control the movement of substances into and out of cells are very complex, so achieving a realistic model, for example by using real images, was impossible. Therefore, it was necessary to identify suitable iconic ways of representing structure and function. Understanding cell membrane function is crucial for understanding both the normal functioning of cell and organ systems as well as the opportunities for bio-engineering, and is an area of active research [see, for example, 13]. However, determining what level of understanding of such complex systems would be desirable and achievable for the target group of students presented a challenge. Furthermore, understanding of the functioning of cell membranes is an area of cell biology that leads to significant student comprehension problems and misconceptions, as explained earlier [2, 14]. It is likely that some of these problems and misconceptions result from poor models and representations currently used for teaching. Therefore, key considerations for the design of the model included:

1. Identifying a level of complexity that would be sufficiently accurate not to lead to misconceptions, while being feasible to be modelled in a virtual environment and not too complex for students aged 12 to 13 years to understand.
2. Deciding on the level of detail for representing molecular structures that would enable understanding of their function in membrane transport.
3. Representing the relative size and scale of structures within a confined space, given that manipulation of the haptic-enabled interface is restricted to a limited vertical and horizontal space.
4. Modelling the haptic forces in such a way that students would be able to feel forces and manipulate the structures.

The screenshot in Fig. 1 shows the cell membrane model near the start of the activity. The phospholipid bilayer of the membrane is depicted as a straw-coloured barrier with some hexagonal shapes representing the idea that the layer consists of many separate molecules and the bilayer is also indicated by the cross-sectional view. However, the details of the bilayer were not considered to be important for students aged 12 to 13 years to understand. The pale cream structures penetrating through the membrane represent the membrane proteins; several different types of membrane protein were modelled. Carbon dioxide and oxygen molecules, represented by their coloured atoms, following the CPK (Corey, Pauling, Koltun) colouring convention, can be seen in Fig. 1.

The user is able to interact with the system via two points of contact of the thumb and index finger on the same hand (either left or right) by means of a thimble device as shown in Fig. 2. In the model, the fingers are able to move freely through the cell membrane but when the user grabs hold of an object in the model, such as a glucose molecule, if the haptics is enabled, the user feels the object and any forces acting on that object, such as those resulting from concentration gradients. In the non-haptic condition, the user interacts using the same interface, but the haptics is turned off in the software, so the user must rely on visual cues to grab objects. When the user makes

Fig. 1. View of part of the cell membrane model

contact with one of the substances, the "Label" changes to show the name of the substance (carbon dioxide, oxygen, glucose, sodium and potassium). When haptics is enabled, users can feel forces on the substances, depending on their concentration, as they push a molecule or ion. During the simulation, users can add more molecules and ions, thus changing the concentration gradient. Some of the membrane proteins are modelled as glucose transporters, based on the GLUT1 transporter, as far as its structure and function is known [15]. When a user pushes a glucose molecule towards a glucose transporter, the user feels the force as the molecule is drawn into the transporter protein, and the model simulates the glucose transporter changing shape as it transports the glucose molecule through the membrane.

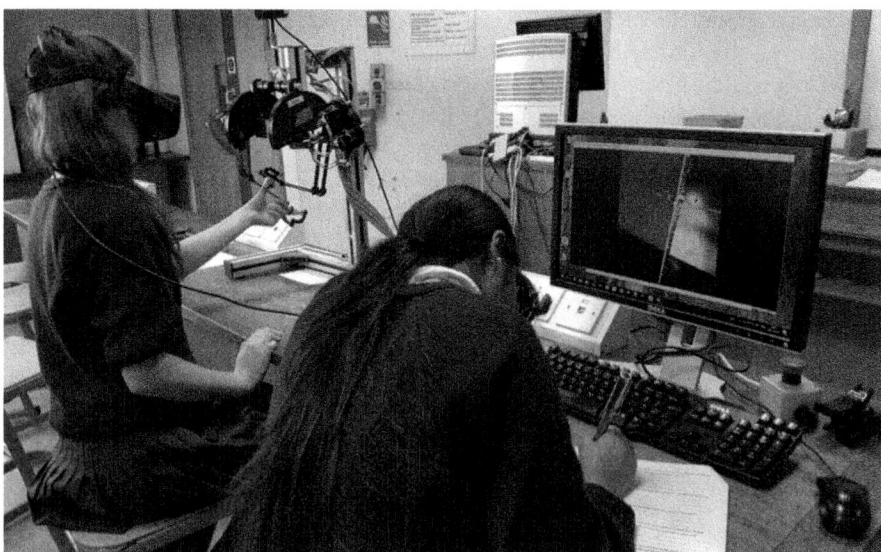

Fig. 2. Students using the system

3 The Interactive Learning Environment and Activities

As shown in Fig. 2, students worked in pairs, where one student (the pilot) was immersed in the VR environment using the interface and the head-mounted display, while the other student (co-pilot) had the same view of the 3D environment on a standard computer screen. The pilot controlled the interaction with the VR environment while the co-pilot directed the activity by: reading the instructions and questions on the worksheet; controlling some aspects of the model through the keyboard; and writing the answers onto the worksheet. The design of this learning environment was informed by a series of investigations with previous prototypes and discussions with teachers and students [9]. The following were the main design principles:

1. to focus students' attention on the haptic interaction and feel of the structures through the activities and questions;
2. to encourage students to learn collaboratively by discussing their ideas;
3. to encourage students to formulate their ideas precisely.

For the students, aged 12 to 13 years, who were the subjects in our study, their usual study of cell membranes included examination of cell preparations under the light microscope, where cell membranes appeared as a thin line stained with a dye, together with two-dimensional diagrammatic representations and teaching and discussion regarding how membranes function to control movement into and out of cells, specifically through diffusion, osmosis and active transport.

Based on considerations of the existing curriculum, activities were designed to develop understanding of the following key concepts:

1. The cell membrane is a barrier to the movement of some substances whereas others pass through freely.
2. Substances move in the cellular fluid by diffusion and some substances are able to continue moving by diffusion through the membrane.
3. The movement of substances that are able to freely diffuse depends on their individual diffusion gradients.
4. The cell membrane is a dynamic structure in which membrane proteins "float".
5. Carrier proteins enable the movement of some substances through the membrane by attracting a specific molecule and changing shape as the molecule passes through the channel of the transporter.

4 Research Methodology

The study was carried out in a boys' school and a girls' school with students who were in their first term of Year 8 (aged 12 to 13 years). Both schools were independent and selective, so the students were of relatively high academic ability. Opportunist sampling was used, based on which students could be freed from lessons at the time of the study. Pairs of students were assigned randomly to the haptic or non-haptic condition in equal numbers, and the students were not informed of this difference. In all, data were obtained from 32 pairs of students: 16 pairs in haptic-enabled condition, and 16 pairs in non-haptic condition.

In line with ethical considerations, the purpose of the study was explained carefully to the students, and theirs' as well as their parents' consent for the data collection was obtained. As some students were only exposed to the non-haptic condition, in a follow-up study later in the academic year, we ensured that all students had the opportunity to experience the haptic condition.

A test of biology knowledge, based on the key concepts listed above, and incorporating 14 true/false questions, was administered before and after the activity. While students were undertaking the activity (approximately 40 min in duration) they were video recorded. Students were observed by members of the research team who made notes on how students engaged with the activities and with each other. The research team later reviewed the notes and videos in order to identify advantages and limitations of the system and interaction. Students worked through the activity using the worksheet without teacher support; technicians were on hand to deal with technical issues with the hardware and software. Following the activity, students were interviewed in pairs using a semi-structured interview of about 20 min duration that elicited students' perspectives on: using the VR system; carrying out the activities; and collaborating while using the VR system as well as their thoughts on their learning during activities. The interviews were transcribed and subjected to inductive coding and thematic analysis. In this paper, we focus on the value of haptics for learning by examining both students' knowledge gains and their perspectives on their learning and how learning may be supported by the activities and the system.

5 Results

Observations of students during activities showed that both those in the haptic and non-haptic condition were engaged with the tasks and most pairs worked very well together to support each other in interacting with the system and answering the questions. The majority of the students had not previously used VR systems and therefore the experience was novel and exciting. Generally, students quickly became familiar with the system and were able to use it effectively. There were some technical problems, particularly with the thimble devices, so it was sometimes necessary to stop and restart the system in order to adjust the thimble devices. The technical problems were quickly resolved by technicians or the students themselves and generally did not interfere with the progress of activities.

Table 1 shows the scores for the 14 true/false questions on the knowledge tests. There was no significant difference in the pre-test scores for haptic ($M = 5.50$, $SD = 2.03$) and non-haptic ($M = 4.84$, $SD = 2.16$) conditions; $t(62) = 1.25$, $p = .22$. There was also no significant difference in the post-test scores for haptic ($M = 8.31$, $SD = 1.97$) and non-haptic ($M = 8.34$, $SD = 1.43$) conditions; $t(62) = -.07$, $p = .94$.

There was a significant difference ($p < 0.001$) between the pre-and post-test results suggesting that students had improved their understanding by undertaking the activities. However, whether the participants were in the haptic or non-haptic condition did not affect the change in score ($p = 0.23$). While the overall scores on the test improved, incorrect answers remained, including, particularly, answers related to Key Concepts 3 and 4 (see Sect. 3).

Table 1. Comparison of pre- and post-test results for the true/false questions

	Condition	Mean	Standard deviation	N
Pre-test score	Haptic	5.5000	2.03200	32
	Non-haptic	4.8438	2.15690	32
	Total	5.1719	2.10483	64
Post-test score	Haptic	8.3125	1.97464	32
	Non-haptic	8.3437	1.42805	32
	Total	8.3281	1.70949	64

All the pairs of students reported that they found the system generally easy to use. However, a significant minority of pairs, both in haptic and non-haptic conditions, said that they found difficulty in grasping the objects in the system. Nearly all the students reported that they enjoyed working in pairs in these activities and found learning collaboratively was well supported by the system.

All the students who experienced the haptic-enabled condition were positive about being able to feel the particles. They commented particularly that they believed they gained a better understanding through using the VR system and specifically through being able to feel, especially compared with more traditional methods of teaching and learning such as listening to the teacher or viewing static diagrams. For example, when asked what they liked about the system, one student commented: "*I liked the touch about it, so I'd know what it feels like*" and further when asked about the benefits for their learning: "*Well, because if you looking at it you can only imagine what it's like, so you don't actually know what's it's like for real*".

Students who worked in the "non-haptic" condition were also positive about the system and valued the visual experience but also commented on the value of being able to grasp and move the objects. The students were not told that the haptics had been disabled and were asked the same questions as the experimental group, including questions about the feel of the model, e.g. in the interview they were asked: "do you think being able to feel the membrane and the particles virtually can help you learn better, and why?" Some of these students were well aware of the lack of feel and commented on this as a limitation of the system, e.g. "*It was hard 'cause it kept asking the question how you feel, but I couldn't physically feel so I didn't actually understand what, like, the question...*" However, many of the students did not comment on this lack of feel. Some found the fact that they could grasp objects with their fingers but not feel them quite strange, e.g. "*We couldn't actually feel them in a way... It's really weird, it's like you can see you're moving something but you can't feel like actually sense that you're moving it.*" Others thought that they were somehow compensating by imagining the "feeling" of what they were seeing, e.g.:

"*I didn't feel too much, actually, with the haptic feedback... But, I think it really will improve kind of being able to feel the resistance, cos you can kind of feel it in what you're seeing. But there probably just needs to be a bit more actual vibrations, for example, coming out of the system*" (Student in non-haptic condition).

Overall, the students felt that being able to interact with a haptic-enabled VR system would support their learning.

6 Discussion and Conclusion

Findings from the interviews, together with observations of the activities and videos, showed that the students: were engaged with the system; they worked well together in pairs to complete the tasks; enjoyed the activities; found the experience fun and interesting; and believed that they were learning. Furthermore, findings from the pre- and post-tests revealed that students had better understanding of the subject matter after undertaking the activities with the system. Therefore, we can conclude that the design of the model and interface and the associated activities were: suitable for the students; enabled collaboration; were engaging and motivating; and supported students in learning most of the key concepts.

Observations of the students while they were undertaking the activities as well as students' own perspectives revealed that turning off the haptic feedback generally did not inhibit the students from interacting with the system and carrying out the activities. We can therefore conclude that students were able to compensate for the lack of feel through visual cues. As there was no significant difference in knowledge gains between the haptic and non-haptic condition in this study, turning off the haptics so that students could not actually feel the objects appears not to have affected their learning of concepts. This finding needs to be interpreted with caution. It is possible that just being able to grab the objects with their fingers enabled students to explore the environment and hence to learn. However, it is also noteworthy that on the post-test, students still found difficulty with some concepts that we had expected would be supported by their experiences of haptic feedback. Some observations during activities suggested that students were not experiencing the full effects of the haptic feedback that we had expected. This may have been because they had difficulties grasping objects, owing to problems with the thimble interface. Alternatively, or in addition, the forces may not have been sufficiently strong for students to notice. A possibility is that the students did not notice haptic stimuli because the visual stimuli, which were novel and exciting, directed their attention away from the haptic stimuli. "Visual dominance" is a well-known psychological phenomenon, which suggests that people are more likely to notice and respond to visual stimuli than those from their other senses. For example, even in experiments where participants were compelled to attend to a particular sensory stimulus, an irrelevant visual stimulus interfered much more with their response to an auditory stimulus than vice versa [16]. Lukas et al. explained these findings in relation to the theory of directed attention [17], which claims that visual stimuli are not as automatically attention-capturing stimuli as other modalities, so people have to actively focus their attention towards visual stimuli, which therefore occupy more of their attentional resources. A recent review [18] revealed that a majority of studies suggest that attentional resources are distinct for visual and auditory sensory modalities. However, findings vary, and may be dependent on the type of response being investigated and the context of the study. In this review, consistent with the majority of recent studies, the emphasis was on visual and auditory rather than haptic. Furthermore, the studies included in their review were focused in the real world whereas there is evidence that people's perceptions of touch vary between the real world and other representations. For example, Gaffary et al. [19] found, in an experimental study, that people's perceptions of a virtual piston differed between an augmented reality (AR) and VR environment. A recent review also shows that there are variations in multisensory perception with age and across different groups [20]. In summary, although we kept the other conditions of the investigation basically the same between the experimental and control groups, the interactions between students and the VR environment and between students in their pairs, provided many opportunities for variations that may have influenced learning. In further research, we will be conducting video analysis of the interactions and undertaking further experiments in order to examine these possibilities in depth.

Whether or not the haptic feedback is critical for students' learning, the addition of haptics to a VR system does provide a more complete and authentic experience. Furthermore, some students found the experience of being able to grasp objects without feeling them to be strange. Currently, the addition of haptics to VR systems presents significant technical challenges. Therefore, typically VR systems rely heavily on visual representation and haptics is generally lagging behind the visual in implementation, including in, for example, surgical applications, where there is evidence that incorporating haptic feedback would be valuable [21]. Currently, haptic interfaces are relatively expensive, whereas the costs of VR systems with 3D visual interfaces are reducing. If, as expected, it becomes possible to provide relatively inexpensive haptic interfaces to VR systems, then it will be important to identify the relative learning benefits and issues associated with haptic feedback in various situations.

While this investigation was of necessity conducted outside of their normal lessons and no elements of the usual interaction with a teacher were included in the activities, it is expected that similar activities could be incorporated into normal classroom lessons. For example, a haptic activity might be incorporated into a circus of investigations, in which students move around from one activity to the next during a lesson. Such activities might include various investigations using VR and haptics as well as the standard laboratory cell studies.

Acknowledgments. The authors are pleased to acknowledge support for this work from the Leverhulme Foundation project '3D Learning in a Rich, Cooperative Haptic Environment'. We are also pleased to thank our colleagues on this project, Jon Rashid, Carleen Houbart, Phil James, Richard Fisher, and Simon Bliss as well as all the students who participated.

References

1. Verhoeff, R.P., Waarlo, A.J., Boersma, K.T.: Systems modelling and the development of coherent understanding of cell biology. Int. J. Sci. Educ. **30**, 543–568 (2008)
2. Flores, F., Tovar, M.E., Gallegos, L.: Representation of the cell and its processes in high school students: an integrated view. Int. J. Sci. Educ. **25**, 269–286 (2003)
3. Tibell, L.A.E., Rundgren, C.-J.: Educational challenges of molecular life science: characteristics and implications for education and research. CBE-Life Sci. Educ. **9**, 25–33 (2010)

4. Marsh, G., Parkes, T., Boulter, C.: Children's understanding of scale-the use of microscopes. Sch. Sci. Rev. **82**, 27–31 (2001)
5. Garvin-Doxas, K., Klymkowsky, M.W.: Understanding randomness and its impact on student learning: lessons learned from building the biology concept inventory (BCI). CBE Life Sci. Educ. **7**, 227–233 (2008)
6. Rundgren, C.-J., Tibell, L.A.E.: Critical features of visualizations of transport through the cell membrane—an empirical study of upper secondary and tertiary students' meaning-making of a still image and an animation. Int. J. Sci. Math. Educ. **8**, 223–246 (2010)
7. Tekkaya, C.: Remediating high school students' misconceptions concerning diffusion and osmosis through concept mapping and conceptual change text. Res. Sci. Technol. Educ. **21**, 5–16 (2003)
8. Oztas, F.: How do high school students know diffusion and osmosis? High school students' difficulties in understanding diffusion & osmosis. Procedia – Soc. Behav. Sci. **116**, 3679–3682 (2014)
9. Webb, M., et al.: The potential for haptic-enabled interaction to support collaborative learning in school biology. In: Resta, P., Smith, S. (eds.) Society for Information Technology and Teacher Education International Conference 2017, pp. 927–935. Association for the Advancement of Computing in Education (AACE), Austin (2017)
10. Tuckey, H., Selvaratnam, M.: Studies involving three-dimensional visualisation skills in chemistry: a review. Stud. Sci. Educ. **21**, 99–121 (1993)
11. Paivio, A.: Mental imagery in associative learning and memory. Psychol. Rev. **76**, 241 (1969)
12. Paivio, A.: Intelligence, dual coding theory, and the brain. Intelligence **47**, 141–158 (2014)
13. Strzyz, P.: Connections, connections, connections. Nat. Rev. Mol. Cell Biol. **18**, 139 (2017)
14. Malińska, L., Rybska, E., Sobieszczuk-Nowicka, E., Adamiec, M.: Teaching about water relations in plant cells: an uneasy struggle. CBE-Life Sci. Educ. **15** (2016)
15. Deng, D., et al.: Crystal structure of the human glucose transporter GLUT1. Nature **510**, 121 (2014)
16. Lukas, S., Philipp, A.M., Koch, I.: Switching attention between modalities: further evidence for visual dominance. Psychol. Res. PRPF **74**, 255–267 (2010)
17. Posner, M.I., Nissen, M.J., Klein, R.M.: Visual dominance: an information-processing account of its origins and significance. Psychol. Rev. **83**, 157 (1976)
18. Wahn, B., König, P.: Is attentional resource allocation across sensory modalities task-dependent? Adv. Cogn. Psychol. **13**, 83–96 (2017)
19. Gaffary, Y., Gouis, B.L., Marchal, M., Argelaguet, F., Arnaldi, B., Lécuyer, A.: AR feels than VR: haptic perception of stiffness in augmented versus virtual reality. IEEE Trans. Visual Comput. Graph. **23**, 2372–2377 (2017)
20. Jonas, C., Spiller, M.J., Hibbard, P.B., Proulx, M.: Introduction to the special issue on individual differences in multisensory perception: an overview. Multisens. Res. **30**, 461–466 (2017)
21. Enayati, N., Momi, E.D., Ferrigno, G.: Haptics in robot-assisted surgery: challenges and benefits. IEEE Rev. Biomed. Eng. **9**, 49–65 (2016)

Personality-Based Group Formation

A Large-Scale Study on the Role of Skills and Personality in Software Engineering Education

Amir Mujkanovic[✉] and Andreas Bollin

Department of Informatics-Didactics, Alpen-Adria-Universität Klagenfurt,
Klagenfurt, Austria
amujkano@gmail.com, Andreas.Bollin@aau.at

Abstract. Extensive research confirms the benefits of group work in various educational and business domains. There has, however, been little consideration to rigorous formation of groups, especially project teams, in software engineering disciplines to improve the outcomes of these groups. Previous studies show that the outcome of groups will be affected by a number of different factors, such as the context in which these groups interact, the characteristics and the behaviour of each individual and the group composition. This research evaluates the extent to which it is possible to enhance the group outcomes by systematically reconstructing the groups of students and hence improve the performances and raise the overall outcome level of a software engineering lecture at two universities, the Alpen-Adria University of Klagenfurt and the Technical University of Košice. An empirical experiment has been carried out involving 69 groups and 140 individuals. The results of this experiment were then compared with historical data of 961 groups (approximately 2,400 students) on group outcomes over a period of 12 years. The findings show statistically significant improvements of the outcomes for those groups that were systematically constructed. These results could enable business leaders and educators to systematically form their groups for improving the outcomes of these groups.

Keywords: Software engineering · Systematic group formation · Improving group outcomes

1 Introduction

A winning team is required in almost any business and engineering discipline to achieve quality results such as, for example, the development of a product or the delivery of a service to clients. One can argue that every team within a company has to be successful in achieving their goals and many experts confirm that the composition of the team is the key to success. Examples of group types include business teams which might exist to generate financial profit, project teams which might exist to achieve certain project goals, club teams which might exist to have fun, families which might exist for reproduction purposes or educational groups which might exist to achieve certain learning outcomes. Panitz [1] points out a number of benefits that result from collaborative work in educational settings. These benefits include academic, social and psychological aspects which have been discussed in detail by Mujkanovic and Bollin [2] and by Mujkanovic et al. [3]. Groups generally exist for a particular reason and they typically target one or multiple outcomes [4].

A systematic and thorough construction of groups is a very demanding challenge, especially in composing the group members in a way that the intended group outcomes can be improved [5]. Many factors will have an impact on these outcomes, including the context in which the group activity takes place, the individual characteristics, the individual behaviour and the group composition. The meaning of these factors will be fully discussed in Sect. 2.

The composition of groups plays a significant role in achieving the outcomes, but we still do not know much about the strength of this influence. Therefore, this research assesses the extent to which a systematic formation of software engineering groups affects the outcomes of these groups. Specifically, we aim at assessing the extent to which group outcomes can be improved through systematic reformation of groups during an ongoing lecture. Additionally, we are interested in the extent to which the outcomes of a lecture can be improved through a systematic reformation of groups.

This paper presents the results of an examination of data that have been collected over more than 10 years, involving randomly formed and systematically formed groups. The systematic formation is based on personality types and skills of each participants. The results show an improvement in the group outcomes when groups were systematically formed.

We commence with reviewing and studying the existing literature in Sect. 2. Section 3 discusses the approach that has been taken to address the hypothesis and the subsequent research questions. Section 4 presents the findings of this research. Threats to validity will be discussed in Sect. 5, and conclusions and further work will be addressed in Sect. 6.

2 Background

There are important terms that will be used throughout this paper. It is therefore important to clarify the meaning of these terms. *Individual characteristics* are observable traits that can be used to differentiate between individuals. These traits exist independently of a human's behaviour and include cognitive and physical abilities, cultural values, personality traits, etc. Examples of individual characteristics include the age, the level of knowledge or the intelligence quotient of an individual. *Individual behaviours* are the actions of an individual within the context established by a particular task occurring within a particular environment. Examples include the level and diversity of chat dialogue that occurs between group members or potentially the number and nature of requests for assistance, etc. *Context* is the environment in which group activities take place. *Group outcomes* is the evaluation criterion that is defined to assess the group results. The *group composition* is a systematic arrangement of group members with certain personalities and skills which will contribute towards achieving the group outcomes.

In the following, we now briefly summarise related work in respect to group formation, project-based learning and the five-factor model, before presenting the research objectives that are covered by our study.

Many researchers [6–8] have studied the *group formation* problem. An overview is given by Magnisalis [9], in which the approaches to group formation have been summarised and clustered by the methods used to form these groups. Various approaches have used clustering techniques [8], fuzzy and genetic algorithms [7] and hidden Markov models, as well as approaches that used learning styles of students.

Graf and Bekele [10] point out the importance of collaborative learning and the group formation process. They address the formation of heterogeneous groups that is defined as the level of diversity of achievements within the groups. The heterogeneity is measured by the Euclidean distance between the attributes of group members. Ant colony optimisation is applied to improve the "goodness of the heterogeneity" of groups. Their research addresses the problem of the famous travelling salesman that is often discussed in literature on optimisation problems. Students are represented as nodes and the travelling salesman optimisation is applied to find the closest students and create groups. The evaluation of this approach has been made through a study that involved 512 students. The authors show also the scalability of their proposed method and the application to the real world. While their work uses sophisticated artificial intelligence methods to address an important problem and improve the group formation process, it does not consider the formation of homogeneous groups. The focus of their research seems to be the quality of the group formation process itself [10].

We are not aware of any existing research that has used personality types and skills for the systematic reformation of groups during an ongoing software project management course and a project-based learning scenario. Our approach uses a simple and scalable group formation model with focus on systematic group reformation within a well-established simulation environment called AMEISE. The reasons for using the AMEISE framework in our research include a high standard of the lecture's content that has not changed much over the past few years, as well as the nature of the lecture in which student groups perform two simulations. This provides a perfect context to test our hypothesis with random groups (1st simulation) and systematically formed groups (2nd simulation). Another reason that make the AMEISE a perfect environment for our research is the very stable assessment scheme of the entire lecture. More information on the AMEISE simulation framework and a justification for using this framework for this research can be found in a previous paper [2].

Concerning *project-based learning*, there are countless reasons for its importance for student careers. Krajcik and Blumenfeld [11] give an overview on the key elements that should be considered in project-based learning environments. These elements include: (1) a formulation of the key questions and hence a problem that has to be solved; (2) students tackle the problem by engaging in real problem-solving processes that are essential to expert work in the field; (3) teaching staff and fellow students including the community begin to engage in collaborative activities and support the project team; and (4) students develop a set of outcomes that represent the learning outcomes of the lecture. In project-based learning, students solve real-world problems and gain knowledge and skills and they also reflect on their skills and their personality [12]. To test our hypothesis, it is required to categorise individuals into different personalities. One way is using the Five-Factor Model.

Salleh et al. [13] and Yamada et al. [14] confirm that the personality has an impact on students' performances. They used the *Five Factor Model* (Extroversion, Agreeableness, Consciousness, Neuroticism, Openness) to assess the impact of personality on the outcomes. Salleh et al. found out that consciousness and openness had an impact on the performances of students. Yamada et al. suggest constructing the groups with members with different individual characteristics. Another study by Alfonseca et al. [6] found that certain learning styles impact on student performances and that collaborative learning might be improved through systematic formation of groups. Systematic group formation is exactly the core of this research, which aims at improving group outcomes.

In an initial study [2], we assessed the impact of the findings by other researchers [13, 14] in our context. As the results of our initial study provided promising results that supported our hypothesis, we felt strengthened to use these results for further studies. The learnings from existing work and our own examinations were applied to our group outcomes model. Initial studies [2] introduced the group outcome model where various factors that impact on these group outcomes had been discussed. This group outcome model had been further developed and includes now also the Five-Factor-Model (as represented in the top left in Fig. 1), using individual characteristics to obtain the personality types of each individual. These personality types are then used to compose the groups in a way that the desired group outcomes will be more likely.

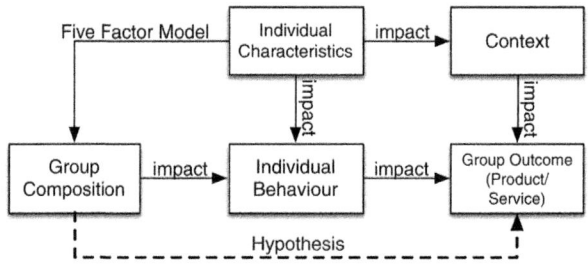

Fig. 1. Group outcome model: factors that have an impact on group outcomes [2]

To our knowledge, there has been no consideration of how groups might be reorganised during a lecture to improve learning outcomes. We have therefore formulated the following hypothesis and research questions that will address this research opportunity:

Hypothesis: By systematically reconstructing groups of students it is possible to enhance their outcomes and improve the individual performances and therefore raise the outcome level of the software engineering lecture.

Research question RQ1: To what extent is it possible to improve the group outcomes by systematically reorganising the student groups?

Research question RQ2: To what extent is it possible to improve the outcomes and raise the total outcomes of the lecture by reorganising the student groups?

3 Methodological Approach

The methodological approach was adapted from an initial pilot study in 2015 and was further developed through feedback of the pilot study [2]. Before we start discussing the details, it is useful to explain the structure of the experiment and the overall approach, which has been conducted in its two major phases. In the first phase, participants of the study performed an assignment during a software project management course using the AMEISE simulation framework that provided empirically validated and quantitative data for grading. In the second phase, participants of the study were systematically placed into groups of four different cohorts aiming at addressing our hypothesis and improving their outcomes through rigorous and systematic reformation of the project groups. After both phases, the atmosphere was observed through a pre-test (after phase 1 means prior to systematic group formation) and a post-test (after phase 2 means after systematic group formation) to capture any circumstances (e.g. conflicts between group members) which might have had an impact on the outcomes. The participants were split into four different student cohorts that were systematically constructed depending on their personality and results of the first simulation run. These cohorts included a random cohort (RG), a cohort (MC) that included at least one manager or coach per group as recommended by Sunaga et al. [15], a cohort of students that achieved best results in phase 1 (UC), and a cohort that included at least one analyst or renovator per group (AR). No roles were assigned to the students (so, only personality traits were used to form the groups). Results from both phases were then compared to examine whether the results could be improved through systematic formation of groups.

The students at both institutions were used to working together in different team constellations (even though they preferred to work with colleagues they knew), and then, from a student's perspective, they were randomly assigned, as explained before. All students were informed that they were taking part in an experiment, and surveys at the end of the course showed that they were satisfied with their group re-formation.

RQ1 was addressed by comparing the results of phase one (randomly formed groups) and phase 2 (systematically formed groups). These results are fully discussed in Sect. 4. RQ 2 was assessed by analysing the grades and historical data that was available for all the courses that used the AMEISE environment to teach software project management between 2006 and 2016. The group outcome (grade) is a weighted composite of a number of factors that were kept the same in both phases (for more details, see a previous paper [2]). Both research questions are addressed in the large-scale study reported here, designed and conducted at the University of Klagenfurt and the Technical University of Košice in 2016.

To address both research questions, two separate examinations were carried out. Research question one was addressed by analysing the results of the experiment as described above. During both phases, participants conducted a full AMEISE simulation which was assessed at the end of the course. A total number of 69 groups completed a software project management assignment and each group received grades on a scale between 1.0 and 5.0 (1 = excellent, 2 = good, 3 = passed, 4 = satisfactory, 5 = fail). The data collection process and determination of individual characteristics (skills and personality) remained the same as in our pilot study [2].

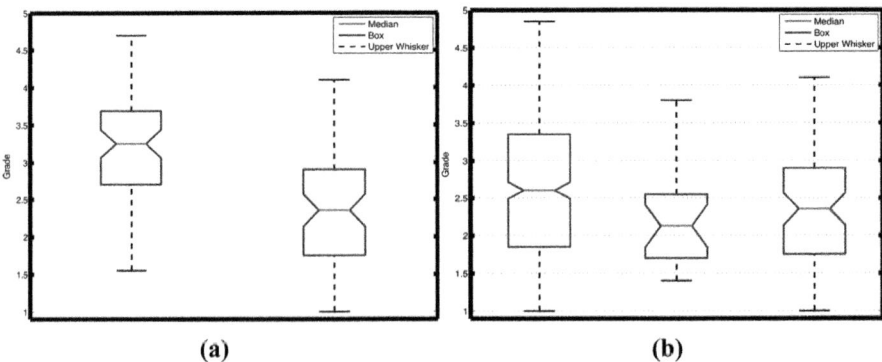

Fig. 2. (a) Box plot of the group outcomes of randomly formed groups in phase 1 (to the left, n = 69 groups) and systematically formed groups in phase 2 (to the right, n = 69 groups) and 140 individuals. (b) Box plot of grades achieved in software project management lectures at the University of Klagenfurt using AMEISE between 2006 and 2016 (left, n = 666) and 2015 (middle, n = 22) and in 2016 (right, n = 69).

RQ2 was addressed by examining historical data of 2,397 software engineering students (961 groups) enrolled in a software engineering course at the Alpen-Adria University of Klagenfurt (59 groups) and the Technical University of Košice in Slovakia (532 groups) over an observation period of 12 years. The remaining 370 groups were enrolled in the same course at other institutions. The students worked on their assignment mostly in *pairs* and *triads*, and in Klagenfurt some of the students had, due to their software engineering focus, a slightly higher previous knowledge in project management. During the experiments, when systematic group formation had been applied, students only knew that they were being part of a scientific experiment, but they did not know any details about the experiment.

4 Results

RQ1 examines the extent to which the groups' outcomes can be improved by systematically reorganising the student groups during a software project management course. Figure 2(a) depicts at the left the group grades in phase one, in which groups were randomly formed, as well as the grades of all groups in phase two (the right boxplot) that were systematically formed. The AMEISE framework determines several performance measures which are automatically transformed into grades. This scheme is a well-established assessment method that has been used for ten years. As a result of our large-scale study, the average group outcomes improved from 3.2 to 2.32, which is an improvement of approximately 27.5% on average. A comparison of the means through a t-test using the MATLAB function *ttest2* returns additional insight. The h and p values (representing the test for the null hypothesis) returns $h = 1$ and $p < 0.0001$ which tells that our null hypothesis can be rejected at a significance level of 0.0001.

The median of achieved grades in phase one is 3.25. The 75% percentile is 3.7 and the upper adjacent (lowest grade) is 4.7. The 25% quartile is 2.7. The best grade achieved is 1.6. Half of the data (inter-quartile range) lie between grades 2.7 and 3.25.

In phase two, where systematic formation of groups was applied, the grades were improved. Figure 2(a) shows at the right the grades achieved in phase two. The median lies at 2.35. The 75% quartile is at 2.9 and the maximum at 4.1, which is the lowest grade achieved by a group. The 25% quartile is at 1.75 and the lowest value (best grade) is exactly 1. Half of the data lie between 1.75 and 2.7. From these two box plots, it can be seen that in phase two, when the systematic formation of groups has been applied, the notches do not overlap with the notches of the results in phase 1. Krzywinski and Altman [16] confirm the medians differ significantly when notches do not overlap – supporting our hypothesis.

Figure 3 presents the distribution of the group grades in both. These grades were gathered from the AMEISE simulation framework with possible values between 1.0 and 5.0. Considering the histogram of random groups, it is obvious that this graph represents a unimodal (one peak) distribution with no outliers that is skewed left. We have a concentration of the grades among the lower grades, with a small number of good grades (2, meaning "good" on the Austrian grade scale) and no excellent grade. The centre of the distribution is around the average grade 3.2. The minimum value, which is the best grade achieved, is 1.6 and the highest value that represents the lowest grade is at 4.7. This represents a range of grades from 1.6 to 4.7 which is a range of 3.1.

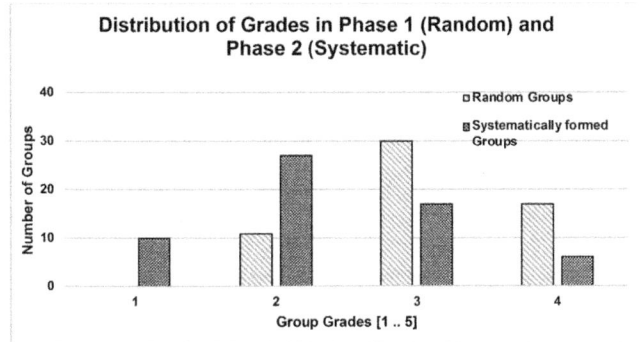

Fig. 3. Distribution of the outcomes of randomly formed groups from the different phases.

Now considering the distribution of the group grades when we applied our methodology of systematic formation of groups, we can report an improvement of the grades. The shape of the distribution is still a unimodal distribution that has changed the skew towards the right. The centre of the distribution is located around the average group grade 2.3. The minimum value is 1.00, which is the highest possible grade, and the maximum value is at 4.1. The range of grades remained the same (as in phase one where groups had been randomly formed); however, as the minimum and maximum values represent, we can report a shift of the mean to the right.

RQ2 examines the extent to which the results of the software project management course can be improved by systematically constructing the groups. To assess this issue, it is useful to consider historical data from the past years of the same course.

Figure 2(b) presents the achievements of groups between 2006 and 2016, when random group and self-assigned formation had been applied, as well as the results of studies when systematic group formation had been applied in 2015 [2] and 2016.

The lower adjacent of the results between 2006 and 2016, and therefore the best grade achieved, is a 1, which corresponds to an excellent grade. The upper adjacent, and therefore the lowest grade achieved, is a 5, which corresponds to a fail. The 75% percentile is at 3.65 and the median is at 2.75. The lower and upper limits of the notch are about 2.62 and 2.87. The 25% percentile is at 1.95. The inter-quartile range lies between the grades 1.9 and 3.65.

The lower adjacent of the results in 2015, and therefore the best grade achieved, is a 1.4, which corresponds to an excellent grade. The upper adjacent, and therefore the lowest grade achieved, is 3.8, which corresponds to a satisfactory grade. The 75% percentile is at 2.55 and the median is at 2.13. The lower and upper limits of the notch are about 1.84 and 2.4. The 25% percentile is at 1.7. The inter-quartile range lies between the grades 1.7 and 2.55.

The lower adjacent of the results in 2016, and therefore the best grade achieved, is 1, which corresponds to an excellent grade. The upper adjacent, and therefore the lowest grade achieved, is 4.1, which corresponds to a satisfactory grade. The 75% percentile is at 2.9 and the median is at 2.35. The lower and upper limits of the notch are about 2.13 and 2.56. The 25% percentile is at 1.75. The inter-quartile range lies between the grades 1.75 and 2.9. It is worthwhile mentioning that during the study in 2016 a new teaching staff (therefore with little experience) prepared the simulations in AMEISE, which might have had an impact on the overall results.

Comparing both results from our initial study in 2015 and the large-scale study in 2016 with the data of the past 10 years, there has been an improvement of the outcomes when systematic group formation has been applied. A comparison of the historical data of 12 years (the left box plot in Fig. 2(b)) and the results of the study in 2016 (the right box plot in Fig. 2(b)) through a t-test returns h = 1 and p = 0.0028, which is evidence that our results can be claimed as statistically significant.

5 Threats to Validity

Validity considers the entire scientific experiment and examines whether the findings meet the requirements of the scientific method. Before we discuss the details of validity issues, it is worthwhile mentioning that we kept everything the same between the pilot study in 2015 [2] and the study that examined research question one in this paper. The subject was taught by the same academic staff, with an additional teacher in 2016. Also, the course material including the assignments remained the same.

Internal validity focuses on the examination if each and every step of the experiment follows the scientific method and whether other factors that have not been considered could have an impact on the results. External validity focuses on the generalisation of the results to other settings and to other populations.

Internal validity might be affected by the nature of the experiment, as involving humans in research studies is a known challenge and we are aware that capturing individual characteristics through a survey may not accurately represent the skills and personality types of each participant, especially when the characteristics are self-perceived. An idea that might provide more accurate individual characteristics could be a system that collects data of how people perceive others when they interact with each other. Such a system would enable additional individual characteristics that are not self-perceived. However, as we have approximately 2,400 students that were included in our study, we are confident that most students respond carefully and honestly to the personality tests.

The experiment has been set up in two different phases; there is a possibility that the improvement of grades has been achieved through a learning effect. However, if the results have been biased by a learning effect, then this learning effect has influenced all participating groups on average. Therefore, a possible learning effect can be seen as irrelevant. An additional issue might be given by the diversity of students' previous knowledge. Even if they undergo the same curricula, their previous background and therefore their skills might have camouflaged impact on our findings.

External validity is certainly an issue of these finding as it cannot be assumed that these findings can be applied to other settings with a guarantee to achieve the same results. The settings that have been chosen for our work include two different cultural environments, one at the Alpen-Adria University of Klagenfurt in Austria and the second at the Technical University of Košice in Slovakia.

6 Conclusion and Further Work

The work presented in this paper intended to test our hypothesis and to assess the extent to which group outcomes can be improved by systematically re-organising the student groups during a software project management course. The hypothesis has been decomposed into two core research questions which have been addressed separately. The findings of both research questions provide results in favour of our hypothesis and therefore contribute to the body of knowledge.

Research question one considered the improvements of grades by systematically reorganising the student groups. The findings suggest that there is a statistically significant improvement of group outcomes by 27.5% when they are rigorously and systematically constructed. Research question two considered the improvements of the software project management course through a systematic formation of project groups. A comparison of data over ten years showed that the results were significantly improved on average by 14.6% when systematic formation of groups was applied. The performance increase is based on simple methods and two central questions in the Five Factor Model, rather than on complicated artificial intelligence methods.

These findings are promising, as they provide evidence that a systematic formation of groups might enable business leaders and educators to systematically form their teams, especially in highly technical environments, and therefore improve the key performance indicators of their business.

Teaching staff could systematically form groups of students across different school levels and therefore increase the learning outcomes of students. A transfer of these results and further studies in various schools, as well as in semiconductor industry, will be subject to further work.

References

1. Panitz, T.: The case for student centered instruction via collaborative learning paradigms. http://home.capecod.net/~tpanitz/tedsarticles/coopbenefits.htm (1999)
2. Mujkanovic, A., Bollin, A.: Improving learning outcomes through systematic group reformation: the role of skills and personality in software engineering education. In: Proceedings of the 9th International Workshop on Cooperative and Human Aspects of Software Engineering, pp. 97–103. ACM, Austin (2016)
3. Mujkanovic, A., Lowe, D., Willey, K.: Adaptive group formation to promote desired behaviours. In: Australasian Association for Engineering Education, Melbourne, VC, pp. 850–858 (2012)
4. Donelson, R.F.: Group Dynamics, 2nd edn. Brooks/Cole Publishing Company, Pacific Grove (1983)
5. Cole, G.A.: Organisational Behaviour. Continuum, London (2001)
6. Alfonseca, E., Carro, R.M., Martín, E., Ortigosa, A., Paredes, P.: The impact of learning styles on student grouping for collaborative learning: a case study. User Modell. User-Adapted Interact. **16**(3–4), 377–401 (2006)
7. Crespo, R.M., Pardo, A., Pérez, J.P.S., Kloos, C.D.: An algorithm for peer review matching using student profiles based on fuzzy classification and genetic algorithms. In: Ali, M., Esposito, F. (eds.) IEA/AIE 2005. LNCS (LNAI), vol. 3533, pp. 685–694. Springer, Heidelberg (2005). https://doi.org/10.1007/11504894_95
8. Zakrzewska, D.: Cluster analysis in personalized E-learning. In: Nguyen, N.T., Szczerbicki, E. (eds.) Intelligent Systems for Knowledge Management. SCI, vol. 252, pp. 229–250. Springer, Berlin (2009). https://doi.org/10.1007/978-3-642-04170-9_10
9. Magnisalis, I., Demetriadis, S., Karakostas, A.: Adaptive and Intelligent Systems for collaborative learning support: a review of the field. IEEE Trans. Learn. Technol. **4**(99), 5–20 (2011)
10. Graf, S., Bekele, R.: Forming heterogeneous groups for intelligent collaborative learning systems with ant colony optimization. In: Ikeda, M., Ashley, Kevin D., Chan, T.-W. (eds.) ITS 2006. LNCS, vol. 4053, pp. 217–226. Springer, Heidelberg (2006). https://doi.org/10.1007/11774303_22
11. Krajcik, J. S., Blumenfeld, P.C.: Project-based learning. In: The Cambridge Handbook of the Learning Sciences, pp. 317–333 (2006)
12. Graham, R.: UK Approaches to engineering project-based learning. Bernard M. Gordon-MIT Engineering Leadership Program, pp. 1–48 (2010)
13. Salleh, N., Mendes, E., Grundy, J., Burch, G.S.J.: An empirical study of the effects of personality in pair programming using the five-factor model. Presented in the 3rd International Symposium on Empirical Software Engineering and Measurement, pp. 214–225 (2009)

14. Yamada, Y., et al.: The impacts of personal characteristic on educational effectiveness in controlled-project based learning on software intensive systems development. Presented in the IEEE 27th Conference on Software Engineering Education and Training, pp. 119–128 (2014)
15. Sunaga, Y., Washizaki, H., Kakehi, K., Fukazawa, Y., Yamato, S., Okubo, M.: Relation between combinations of personal characteristic types and educational effectiveness for controlled project-based learning course. IEEE Trans. Emerg. Topics Comput. **99**, 1–9 (2016)
16. Krzywinski, M., Altman, N.: Points of significance: visualizing samples with box plots. Nat. Methods **11**(2), 119–120 (2014)

Learning in Social Networking Environments

Social Networks as Learning Delivery Platforms

Academic Achievement and Attitudes of Students

Yaacov J. Katz[✉]

Bar-Ilan University, Ramat Gan, Israel
yaacov.katz@biu.ac.il

Abstract. Social networks are technology-based applications that enable network members to communicate for mutual benefit. Research evidence has indicated that social networks can serve as learning delivery platforms that contribute to positive student learning. In the present study, three similar groups of students enrolled in an 'Introduction to Ethics' course, were exposed to either Facebook-based, WhatsApp-based or Twitter-based delivery of ethical concepts on their smartphones. At the end of the course, students were examined on ethical concepts. They also responded to a questionnaire that examined user-friendliness, learner motivation and learner satisfaction associated with the social networks they experienced. Results indicate that WhatsApp students attained a higher level of achievement than Facebook students who, in turn, attained higher grades than Twitter students. Additional results indicate that WhatsApp and Facebook students held more positive impressions of user-friendliness and learner motivation related to their delivery platforms than Twitter students. WhatsApp students also held more positive impressions of satisfaction with their delivery platform than Facebook students who maintained more positive feelings of satisfaction than Twitter students. Thus, WhatsApp, and to a lesser extent, Facebook, are associated with enhanced achievement and positive feelings toward their delivery platforms with Twitter students lower on academic achievement and affective variables.

Keywords: WhatsApp · Facebook · Twitter · Achievement · Affective variables

1 Social Networks and Learning

Mobile learning provides more flexibility, mobility, convenience and seamless integration of data access for students than other online distance learning environments [1, 2]. Social networks may be defined as applications that utilise mobile learning technology to enable users to communicate with each other by posting information, comments, messages, images, etc. [3]. Education and learning are perceived to be specific topics that can greatly benefit from social networks [4]. Recent studies have indicated the increasing effectiveness of the contribution of social networks to the learning process. Gilroy [5] intimated that social networks as educational tools in the academic landscape are catching on fast as universities, colleges and schools recognise the potential that social networks have for learning. Casey and Evans [6] reached the conclusion that learning via social networking is positively received by students and contributes to an enhancement of students' learning performance. According to Alvarez and Olivera-Smith [7] social networks offer ample and potentially effective opportunities to improve student learning at the university level. Sobaih et al. [8] confirmed that social networks used in the learning process increase motivation of students and stimulate study activities.

In summary, it may be said that research literature offers increasing evidence that supports the notion that social networks contribute to the fostering of student learning at the university, college and high school levels [9].

1.1 WhatsApp Learning Delivery Platform

One popular application of mobile technology is WhatsApp "instant messaging". Aburezeq and Ishtaiwa [10] found that the WhatsApp platform has the power to enhance students' learning and Shambare [11] confirmed that WhatsApp is user-friendly and contributes to the promotion of learning and student satisfaction with the learning process. Minimol and Angelina [12] intimated that the use of WhatsApp as a learning tool increases student curiosity and motivation in the learning process. Echenique et al. [13] contended that all social network tools, but most especially WhatsApp, are advantageous and facilitate motivation and curiosity in the learning process.

1.2 Facebook Learning Delivery Platform

Facebook, in addition to being the most popular social network for social groups, has also become a mobile learning-based learning resource. Isacsson and Gretzel [14] noted that students valued Facebook for providing an informal and motivating learning environment. Other research projects have indicated the positive potential of Facebook as a learning delivery platform at the university level [15]. De Villiers and Pretorius [16] found that when used as a learning delivery platform, Facebook enhances critical collaborative thinking and learning motivation. Facebook is also perceived to enhance student-centered as well as social learning [17]. Mitchell [18] indicated that Facebook-based learning facilitates language learning of foreign students as well as their cultural concept learning. Kassem [19] found that the use of Facebook in the Egyptian secondary educational system led to the narrowing of social gaps between students studying in general (more elite) and technical (less elite) high schools.

1.3 Twitter Learning Delivery Platform

Twitter is another social network application that has been used as a learning delivery platform. Junco et al. [20] postulated that the use of Twitter in university courses enhances students' learning potential. Other research results [21] indicated that the use of Twitter at the university level enhances learning collaboration among students, increases learning motivation, encourages students feel that learning could be "trendy" and fun and focuses the attention of students on the topic under study. West et al. [22] confirmed that use of Twitter for learning delivery leads to a positive effect on students' achievement as well as enhancing students' willingness and desire to engage in learning tasks.

2 Academic Achievement and Social Network Learning

Several research studies have indicated that students' academic achievement is positively related to the use of technology-based learning delivery platforms. Ituma [23] confirmed that university students who were enrolled in courses where learning was delivered by digital technology had positive perceptions of the learning delivery platform and were in favour of participating in additional courses where learning was delivered by technology-based social networks. Harris [15] indicated that learning via digital social network delivery platforms contributes significantly to improved student achievement and Chandra and Watters [24] confirmed that learning physics through the medium of technology-based social network learning delivery enhances students' learning outcomes. On the other hand, there are studies, such as research conducted by Gettman and Cortijo [25] as well as Kon Shing and Paredes [26] that cast doubt on the claim that technology-based social network learning delivery leads to significantly improved academic achievement. Thus, in the present study, the potential positive relationship between academic achievement and delivery of learning via WhatsApp, Facebook and Twitter applications will be examined.

3 Affective Attitudinal Variables and Social Network Learning

Research studies quoted by Katz [27] indicate that affective (non-cognitive) variables such as attribution, autonomy, control of the learning process, creativity, curiosity, flexibility, locus of control, motivation, satisfaction, self-confidence, self-efficacy, self-image, self-esteem and perception of user-friendliness are some of the major variables known to positively contribute to enhanced (improved and efficient) language and concept learning when delivered via social network-based delivery platforms. Furthermore, Katz [27] confirmed the positive relationship of some or all the above factors with effective social network-based delivery of language and concept learning. In this study, key affective (non-cognitive) variables, namely perception of user-friendliness, motivation and satisfaction of students will be examined vis-à-vis their relationship with different social network learning delivery platforms.

3.1 Perception of User-Friendliness and Social Network Delivery of Learning

Chapman and Henderson [28] showed that perception of user-friendliness by students is a vital indicator that assures the quality of a digital learning delivery platform and Katz [27] confirmed that user-friendliness is a significant attitude that contributes to the enhancement of positive attitudes toward learning in a technology-based environment. Llorente-Cejudo [29] presented expert evaluators' consensus that confirmed that perceived user-friendliness is a major variable vital for efficient use of different types of digital technology in the learning process. Thus, students' perceptions of user-friendliness of WhatsApp, Facebook and Twitter delivery of learning will be examined in this project.

3.2 Learner Motivation and Social Network Delivery of Learning

Motivation regarding the learning process is another major variable that leads to efficient and effective learning. Moon [30] contended that information is retained longer if it is presented in an interesting way and evokes motivation and curiosity. Rosen and Beck-Hill [31] confirmed that learning delivery that arouses student motivation enhances the quality of learning and is necessary for learners to successfully utilise technology-based social network learning delivery platforms. Considering the above evidence, the contribution of learner motivation towards the use of WhatsApp, Facebook and Twitter learning delivery platforms will be investigated in this study.

3.3 Learner Satisfaction and Social Network Delivery of Learning

With reference to learners' satisfaction, Katz [27] found in a comprehensive research study that one of the key constructs that positively affects student performance is the satisfaction derived from studying through social network delivery platforms. When students utilise social networks for their learning, the level of their satisfaction with the educational process increases as does their performance. Minimol and Angelina [12] confirmed how student satisfaction with the use of social networks, such as WhatsApp, Facebook and Twitter in the learning process, leads to higher levels of student engagement, learning, and success. The above evidence highlights the key relationship between satisfaction of students resulting from the use of social networks in the learning process. Thus, in the present study, the comparative learner satisfaction with the three social network delivery platforms will be examined.

4 Aims of the Present Study

In summary, the aims of the present study are twofold: (a) to examine the contribution of WhatsApp, Facebook and Twitter learning delivery platforms to students' achievement; and (b) to investigate students' affective perceptions of user-friendliness, learner motivation and learner satisfaction derived from studying via WhatsApp, Facebook and Twitter delivery platforms. These aims are based on significantly positive empirical evidence presented by Casey and Evans [6] who described the positive use of social networks such as WhatsApp, Facebook and Twitter for learning in communities, and by Shambare [11], who indicated the feasibility of using social networks such as WhatsApp, Facebook and Twitter as effective learning delivery platforms.

5 Method

5.1 Participants

The research sample consisted of 363 first year university social science students enrolled in a 14-week semester-long mandatory "Introduction to Ethics" foundation course offered at one of the seven chartered universities in Israel. The sample included students who came from similar socio-economic backgrounds, and studied in various departments attached to the Faculty of Social Sciences at the university. All students complied with university acceptance criteria (national psychometric university entrance examination and a school-leaving matriculation certificate). All participating students owned smartphones equipped with WhatsApp, Facebook and Twitter access. The students were randomly assigned to three comparison groups ensuring similarity of the groups. The first group of 131 students received their concept definitions via WhatsApp delivery; the second group of 107 students were sent concept definitions by way of Facebook delivery; the third group of 125 students obtained their definitions of concepts through Twitter delivery.

5.2 Research Instruments

Two research instruments were administered to the students in this research study:
a. The first instrument was a standardised ethical concept achievement test which was specially compiled to assess students' mastery of the 140 ethical concept definitions studied in the semester-long course (10 concepts sent to students weekly during the 14-week long course) The test scale ranged from 0–100, the higher grades indicating higher levels of achievement on the test.
b. The second instrument administered to the participants was a 23-item Likert-type scale response questionnaire (students responded to a five-point scale with 1 = totally disagree to 5 = totally agree) designed to examine the attitudes of participants towards their particular learning delivery platform (WhatsApp, Facebook, Twitter) regarding their perceptions of user-friendliness (8 items; Cronbach $\alpha = .87$); learner motivation (8 items; Cronbach $\alpha = .85$); and learner satisfaction (7 items; Cronbach $\alpha = .89$).

5.3 Procedure

Following the establishment of the three comparison groups to which the participants were randomly assigned, students in the first group received ethical concept definitions by way of WhatsApp delivery to their smartphones; students in the Facebook group received identical ethical concept definitions relayed to their smartphones; and students in the Twitter delivery group received their ethical concept definitions on their smartphones. The students in the three groups were sent concise definitions of ethical concepts studied in the course with each weekly list containing 10 identical definitions delivered via the three respective learning delivery platforms. Thus, each of the students received the same 140 academic ethical concept definitions during the 14-week long course. On completion of the course, the students in the three comparison groups were administered a standardised ethical concept achievement test to assess their level of knowledge and understanding of the 140 definitions sent to them during the course. In addition, they were administered the 23-item attitudinal questionnaire which examined their scores on the three attitudinal research factors, namely perception of user-friendliness, learner motivation and learner satisfaction regarding the learning delivery platform that they personally experienced during the course (Fig. 1).

Fig. 1. Example of Identical Philosophical Concept presented on the 3 Platforms

The research project adhered to the university research ethics criteria and was approved by the Ethics Committee of the university School of Education.

6 Results

The main aim of this study was to examine the contribution of WhatsApp, Facebook and Twitter learning delivery platforms to students' achievement as well as to investigate students' affective perceptions of user-friendliness, learner motivation and learner satisfaction derived from studying via WhatsApp, Facebook and Twitter delivery platforms. Descriptive statistics as well as results of analyses of variance were conducted to ascertain possible intergroup differences on the four research variables, as related to the three social network learning delivery platforms, are presented in Table 1.

One-way analyses of variance (ANOVA) were conducted to investigate intergroup differences on the four research variables. This statistical procedure was chosen as best suited to assess the differences between the three research groups regarding the relationships between the different delivery platforms and the research variables. Results indicate significant differences on achievement scores between students in the WhatsApp, Facebook and Twitter delivery groups. Results of post-hoc Scheffe tests confirmed that students in both WhatsApp and Facebook delivery groups attained significantly higher grades than students in the Twitter group on the ethical concept definitions achievement test. There were no significant differences between grades of students in WhatsApp and Facebook learning delivery groups on the concept definitions test.

Table 1. One-way ANOVA results for achievement, perception of user-friendliness, learner motivation and learner satisfaction in WhatsApp, Facebook and Twitter learning delivery groups

Variable	Group				
	WhatsApp	Facebook	Twitter	F (2,360)	P
Concept achievement	M = 88.40 S.D. = 3.31	M = 87.30 S.D. = 3.58	M = 81.90 S.D. = 1.79	170.46	0.000
User friendliness	M = 3.69 S.D. = 0.45	M = 3.61 S.D. = 0.53	M = 3.26 S.D. = 0.62	6.41	0.002
Learner motivation	M = 3.97 S.D. = 0.59	M = 3.77 S.D. = 0.61	M = 3.23 S.D. = 0.71	7.00	0.001
Learner satisfaction	M = 4.25 S.D. = 1.24	M = 3.82 S.D. = 1.32	M = 3.28 S.D. = 1.23	8.80	0.000

Similar significant results were evident from the one-way ANOVAs conducted to examine intergroup differences on the perception of user-friendliness, learner motivation and learner satisfaction variables. Post-hoc Scheffe tests indicated that students in WhatsApp and Facebook delivery groups were characterised by significantly higher levels of perception of user-friendliness and learner motivation than students in the Twitter group. No significant differences were indicated in the post-hoc test between students in the WhatsApp and Facebook groups on these two variables. Regarding the learner satisfaction variable, post-hoc Scheffe tests confirmed that students in the WhatsApp group were typified by a significantly higher level of satisfaction than students in either Facebook or Twitter groups. Results of a post-hoc Scheffe test confirmed that students in the Facebook group were characterised by a higher level of learner satisfaction than students in the Twitter delivery group.

7 Discussion

The present study examined the comparative contributions of three social network learning delivery platforms (WhatsApp, Facebook and Twitter) to first-year university social science students' knowledge and understanding of definitions of ethical concepts studied in a semester-long "Introduction to Ethics" foundations course. In addition, the study examined the perceptions of the students regarding the user-friendliness of the three delivery platforms as well as the students' levels of learning motivation and learning satisfaction derived from the learning that they experienced in their studies via the different learning delivery platforms.

Results of statistical analyses of the data collected in this study regarding achievement indicate that students in the WhatsApp and Facebook delivery groups attained similarly high grades on the standardised ethical concept definitions knowledge and understanding assessment with students in the Twitter group achieving significantly lower grades on the same standardised measure. These results confirm results of previous research that indicated that both WhatsApp [10] and Facebook [16] learning delivery contribute to enhanced student learning and achievement. The results are congruent with previous results [32] regarding the disadvantages of Twitter delivery vis-a-vis students' learning and achievement when compared to the contribution of other social networks, such as WhatsApp and Facebook, to students' performance.

Additional results of the statistical analyses regarding the affective attitudinal variables confirm that students who received their learning content through WhatsApp and Facebook delivery were characterised by similar levels of perceptions of user-friendliness and learner motivation that were significantly more positive than the levels of perception of user-friendliness and learner motivation of students who experienced their learning delivery via Twitter delivery. These results confirm research findings about perceptions of user-friendliness and learner motivation especially associated with WhatsApp [11] and Facebook [14] learning delivery as reported by students who experienced learning via social networks. A last finding of the present study showed that students in the WhatsApp delivery group were significantly more positive about learning satisfaction than students in both Facebook and Twitter delivery groups, with students in the Facebook group indicating a significantly higher level of learner satisfaction than students in the Twitter group. This result is congruent with research results reported by Echenique et al. [13] regarding the relative advantage of WhatsApp learning delivery over delivery by either Facebook or Twitter.

8 Conclusions

It may be speculated that the use of WhatsApp and, to a lesser extent, of Facebook platforms, can enhance students' learning achievement significantly more than the use of the Twitter platform. Moreover, the use of these platforms seems to promote more positive feelings of user-friendliness, learner motivation and learner satisfaction. This result can be ascribed to the comprehensiveness of WhatsApp and Facebook styles of communication which are virtually unlimited when compared to a short communication style that characterises Twitter. In addition, WhatsApp, more than Facebook and Twitter, is more hermetically sealed against infiltration of unwanted members who could disrupt the learning process, with Twitter especially open to infiltration of members not interested in the learning process.

It also appears that, despite the vast popularity of Twitter as a means of communication within social communities, students do not rate Twitter as an efficient learning delivery platform that positively contributes to achievement or positive affective attitudes when compared to WhatsApp or, to a lesser extent, to Facebook as learning delivery platforms. Thus, it may be concluded from the results of the present study that students are positive about WhatsApp, and to a lesser extent, about Facebook delivery of learning regarding key variables such as student achievement, as well as learner perception of user-friendliness, learner motivation and learner satisfaction. The results also indicate that Twitter is not considered by students to be as effective as WhatsApp and Facebook as a medium of learning delivery. On the whole, results of the present study confirm and emphasise earlier research findings [1, 2] that clearly indicated that social networks, and especially WhatsApp and Facebook applications, can serve as viable platforms for the delivery of learning content via mobile learning technology.

References

1. Ducate, L., Lomicka, L.: Going mobile: language learning with an iPod touch in intermediate French and German classes. Foreign Lang. Ann. **46**(3), 445–468 (2013)
2. Premadasa, H.K.S., Meegama, R.G.N.: Mobile learning environment with short messaging service. Campus-Wide Inf. Syst. **30**(2), 106–123 (2013)
3. Wallace, S.: A Dictionary in Education, 2nd edn. Oxford University Press, Oxford (2014)
4. Kapuler, D.: Top 20 social networks for education. Tech Learn. **32**(2), 16 (2011)
5. Gilroy, M.: Higher education migrates to YouTube and social networks. Educ. Digest **75**(7), 18–22 (2010)
6. Casey, G., Evans, T.: Designing for learning: online social networks as a classroom environment. Int. Rev. Res. Open Dist. Learn. **12**(7), 1–26 (2011)
7. Alvarez, I.M., Olivera-Smith, M.: Learning in social networks: rationale and ideas for its implementation in higher education. Educ. Sci. **3**(3), 314–325 (2013)
8. Sobaih, A.E.E., Moustafa, M.A., Ghandforoush, P., Khan, M.: To use or not to use? Social media in higher education in developing countries. Comput. Hum. Behav. **58**, 296–305 (2016)
9. Derakhshan, A., Hasanabbasi, S.: Social networks for language learning. Theory Pract. Lang. Stud. **5**(5), 1090–1095 (2015)
10. Aburezeq, I.M., Ishtaiwa, F.F.: The impact of WhatsApp on interaction in an Arabic language teaching course. Int. J. Arts Sci. **6**(3), 165–180 (2013)
11. Shambare, R.: The adoption of WhatsApp: breaking the vicious cycle of technological poverty in South Africa. J. Econ. Behav. Stud. **6**(7), 542–550 (2014)
12. Minimol, K.T., Angelina, J.M.: Teenagers' perception of social network sites in relation to academic motivation and interpersonal relationships: a focus group approach. Indian J. Posit. Psychol. **6**(1), 93–97 (2015)
13. Echenique, E.G., Molías, L.M., Bullen, M.: Students in higher education: social and academic uses of digital technology. RUSC **12**(1), 25–37 (2015)
14. Isacsson, A., Gretzel, U.: Facebook as an edutainment medium to engage students in sustainability and tourism. J. Hosp. Tour. Technol. **2**(1), 81–90 (2011)
15. Harris, C.W.: The uses of Facebook technologies in hospitality curriculum on an experiential learning platform for a new generation of students. Asia Pac. J. Mark. Logist. **24**(5), 805–825 (2012)
16. De Villiers, M.R., Pretorius, M.C.: Evaluation of a collaborative learning environment on a Facebook forum. Electron. J. Inf. Syst. Eval. **16**(1), 56–70 (2013)
17. Duncan, D.G., Barczyk, C.C.: Facebook in the university classroom: do students perceive that it enhances community of practice and sense of community? Int. J. Bus. Soc. Sci. **4**(3), 1–14 (2013)
18. Mitchell, K.: A social tool: why and how ESOL students use Facebook. CALICO J. **29**(3), 472–493 (2012)
19. Kassem, M.M.: Facebook as a nation-wide civic education classroom listening to the voices of Egyptian secondary school students. J. Emerg. Trends Educ. Res. Policy Stud. **4**(5), 771–785 (2013)
20. Junco, R., Heiberger, E., Loken, E.: The effect of Twitter on college student engagement and grades. J. Comput. Assist. Learn. **27**(2), 119–132 (2011)
21. Prince, H.B., Adams, S.: Learning technologies: tweeting in a high school social studies class. I-Manager's J. Educ. Technol. **8**(4), 26–33 (2012)
22. West, B., Moore, H., Barry, B.: Beyond the tweet: using Twitter to enhance engagement, learning, and success among first-year students. J. Mark. Educ. **37**(3), 160–170 (2015)

23. Ituma, A.: An evaluation of students' perceptions and engagement with e-learning components in a campus based university. Act. Learn. High Educ. **12**(1), 57–68 (2011)
24. Chandra, V., Watters, J.J.: Re-thinking physics teaching with web-based learning. Comput. Educ. **58**(1), 631–640 (2012)
25. Gettman, H.J., Cortijo, V.: Leave me and my Facebook alone! Understanding college students' relationship with Facebook and its use for academic purposes. Int. J. Scholarsh. Teach. Learn. **9**(1), 1–16 (2015)
26. Kon Shing, K.C., Paredes, W.C.: Towards a social networks model for online learning & performance. J. Educ. Technol. Soc. **18**(3), 240–253 (2015)
27. Katz, Y.J.: Mobile learning delivery via social networks: what platforms do first-year university students prefer? In: Teixeira, A.M., Szucs, A. (eds.) Challenges for research into open & distance learning: doing things better - doing better things - Proceedings of EDEN 2014. European Distance Education Network, Budapest, pp. 249–256 (2014)
28. Chapman, B.F., Henderson, R.G.: E-learning quality assurance: a perspective of business teacher educators and distance learning coordinators. Delta Pi Epsil. J. **52**(1), 16–31 (2010)
29. Llorente-Cejudo, M.C.: Assessing personal learning environments (PLEs): an expert evaluation. New Approaches Educ. Res. **2**(1), 39–44 (2013)
30. Moon, J.A.: Using Story: In Higher Education and Professional Development. Routledge, New York (2010)
31. Rosen, Y., Beck-Hill, D.: Intertwining digital content and a one-to-one laptop environment in teaching and learning: lessons from the time to know program. J. Res. Technol. Educ. **44**(3), 225–241 (2012)
32. Yakin, I., Tinmaz, H.: Using Twitter as an instructional tool: a case study in higher education. TOJET: Turk. Online J. Educ. Technol. **12**(4), 209–218 (2013)

Learning to Share by Reflection-on-Action on an Enterprise Social Media Platform

Halvdan Haugsbakken[✉]

Department of Sociology and Political Science, Norwegian University of Science and Technology, Trondheim, Norway
Halvdan.Haugsbakken@ntnu.no

Abstract. Enterprise Social Media Platforms are now commonplace in organisations. They are argued to bring benefits, like simplifying work processes, enhance internal communications and reduce internal organisational barriers. Such benefits can be obtained on the assumption that employees naturally engage on a platform and share knowledge. But how to and what to share on an enterprise platform is not always a straightforward task and is a practice that must be learned through sense-making of sharing. Therefore, this challenges the assumption that sharing on Social Media Enterprise Platforms can bring benefits. Consequently, the paper examines the challenges in making sense of the meaning of the practice of sharing. The paper explores a case study on how a County Authority in a Nordic country implemented an Enterprise Social Media Platform and how a group of employees tried to make sense of the practice of sharing by reflection-on-action. The results show that the employees interpreted sharing as an informing practice, resulting in information-overload and disengaged users.

Keywords: Sharing · Enterprise social media platforms · Organisation · Norway

1 Introduction

Over the years, Nordic public organisations have implemented Enterprise Social Media Platforms (ESMPs). In 2010, the top management in a County Authority (CA) in a Nordic Country decided to implement one. The main objective was to improve internal communication and simplify work surfaces. Also, the goal was to motivate the CA's employees to replace work practices by transferring work interaction from e-mail to shared work on the ESMP. The platform was embedded with features facilitated for sharing of digital items, user profiles, a news feed, groups, possibilities to follow colleagues, etc. Although the implementation went well, one later experienced a conundrum. The top management saw an increased volume of shared information, but the employees did not adopt the practice of sharing as expected, as there were few traces of collaborative work practices and awareness of an online community.

This paper uses a *qualitative research perspective*, and asks how a small group of employees interpret the meaning of sharing and how they use reflection-on-action to make sense of sharing in an ESMP intended to be the new work surface for roughly about 2,800 employees. To answer the research question, this is analysed over the paper's five parts. The next section addresses a relevant research horizon, the subsequent part outlines methods. Thereafter, the research findings are presented, and the final part concludes the analysis.

2 Relevant Research Horizon

In short, sharing on social media can be defined as the act to post information. Over the last decade, researchers have tried to conceptualise the meaning of sharing in organisations without having a clear understanding of what is actually shared [1]. In early studies, for example, sharing on Knowledge Sharing Platforms was understood as information that could be coded, stored, and be retrieved by employees. Also, studies focused on making assumptions on knowledge sharing and establishing technological definitions of communities [2]. Scholars explored the conditions and requirements essential to making online communities thrive [3], what characterises "knowledge" [4], distinguishing what motivates users to share knowledge [5], and what role cultural values [6] and social capital play in knowledge sharing processes [7]. This led to an understanding of sharing as a controlled process, omitting that a knowledge-sharing process is an active and relational communication process between two parties [8]. With the arrival of ESMPs, researchers mapped the impact of these technologies, raising new questions about what is to be shared and how to perform sharing. A growing ESMPs research stream shows different experiences. For example, studies find that employees use ESMPs to connect and expand professional networks [9] and researchers chart basic user patterns [10, 11]. Also, researchers examine the challenges of adopting ESMPs. Studies demonstrate how employees still prefer to communicate via e-mail and chat and silently monitor news streams [12]. Experimental papers have used the affordance concept to theorise what benefits ESMPs can provide to understand organisational processes like socialisation and the organisation of work processes [13].

Lacking within the above research stream is an updated *learning perspective* on how knowledge workers learn the practice of sharing, to organise knowledge work. This analytical perspective can be developed by combining the concepts of reflection-on-action, [14] and situated learning [15], viewing them in the light of the learning theory for the digital age, connectivism [16]. Connectivism draws up a number of new principles for learning but assumes that knowledge resides outside us in forms of social structures like databases and in nodes of complex social networks. This means there is a need to focus more on pattern recognition; and the way in which knowledge workers interact on ESMPs can be understood using network learning approaches. This argument is indeed relevant, as knowledge workers interact in a social context characterised by complexity and chaos, which can easily lead to information overload. Confronted with a new disrupted work context, the attention is redirected to how workers can apply a skill set that forces them to reflect on their action in interactive situations on ESMPSs. This perspective does not appear to be developed in the current research literature on ESMPs.

3 Methods

The study used a qualitative research strategy, following an explorative research design. The motivation for using it was to gain in-depth knowledge on how the practice of sharing is interpreted and performed on an ESMP by users. The study's main method was the use of qualitative research interviews following the principles outlined by Brinkmann and Kvale [17]. Brinkmann and Kvale argue that qualitative research interviews can be used as a means to learn more about a particular phenomenon. Eight singular in-depth and open qualitative research interviews were conducted with eight different people working in the CA. The interviews were one-to-one, meaning that only the researcher and the informant were present in the interview setting. The interviews were semi-structured with the use of a guide and lasted an hour. Each interview was recorded on a digital audio recorder and covered topics that focused on sharing. After completion, the research interviews were transcribed. The data analysis was inspired by an open coding strategy of the interview data, where the main focus was on finding emerging patterns. The participants' perceptions, user patterns and experiences were compared and grouped, with reference to how they used the ESMP. In order to offer the participants a voice, direct quotations are used in the data presented. Data were collected in May 2013 and April 2014.

4 Research Results

The results from the data analysis consists of four themes. The themes are based on an interpretive analysis of the participants' use of the ESMP and shows how they use a reflection-on-action approach to frame the organisation of knowledge work.

4.1 Theme 1: Sharing as an Enabler for Organisational Change

The first theme relates to how sharing is interpreted as an enabler for *organisational change*, which is framed from a top management perspective. Here, sharing was used to solve a problem in CA. The motivation for the implementation was to cope with a challenge seen in organisations - e-mail overload and use of various ICTs.

The top-management aimed at simplifying the work surface, as employees worked across several information and communication technologies (ICTs) and stored information in various places. This made it difficult to get an overview. A single site was needed, which could work as the central access point connecting the employees. Introducing an ESMP could resolve the matter, but a new interface would break a work pattern. While the intranet was run as an internal web site, the new design suggested that the ESMP should be the site an employee opened each day with embedded sharing features and URL-links to various information technology (IT)-systems. Afterwards, a discourse emphasising the importance of a sharing culture emerged:

> "It was acknowledged that we needed something that could enable us to work with the culture across [the organization], knowledge of each other's work. My responsibility has been to legitimize sharing in the management structure. Parallel to that, we made attempts to raise discussion about organizational culture and work processes internally. Should we establish a

greater sharing culture, in the sense that people can easily participate in and reinforce each other's work, or take part in reports, or take part in other kinds of things, take part in the knowledge we have, this requires a culture where [people] actively share".

Translating sharing into a practice proved difficult, as it surfaced as ambiguous:

"It sounds very good. It has a positivity to it, when it's presented, but not so great when you try it out in practice. You didn't know exactly what it was. There was this belief that we should change the work culture".

Later, this awareness amplified. The ESMP initiators realised that the employees seldom started a work process by beginning from scratch—by creating a document that everyone can engage in, for example—but viewed sharing as an *informing practice* of circulating ready-made documents. Sharing was linked to previous publishing habits. The employees were accustomed to an "article format", meaning that postings on the ESMP had a "news story" label attached to them. User interaction was characterised by seeing the ESMP as a channel where information was "pushed out", not a platform where one engaged in a two-way dialogue. The employees fulfilled activities that required little commitment, like posting a profile picture, writing status updates, etc. Beyond that, there was little evidence that users participated to share:

"Ninety percent of the information posted on the ESMP is not something that we've published. It's made by the organization. People share when documents are finished. You don't see many examples where people collaborate on a document, which is part of a work process. That's where we struggle".

4.2 Theme 2: Sharing Viewed as Self-censorship and Risk-Taking

The second theme shows that sharing is associated with *self-censorship*, as the employees used private and previous experiences from engaging on social media to establish views on sharing. For example, the participants viewed Facebook as a site for "scrolling after fun stuff and setting likes" and Twitter as a place where "you only send URL-links to news you have already read". Not surprisingly, monitoring online grooming and gossiping for years on social media generated scepticism, producing a belief that sharing is seldom seen as a public two-way communicative practice, but as a means to monitor what others do, although the participants acknowledged the benefits of sharing. Hence, sharing is practiced on the basis of *being informed* and t*o inform rather than to engage*, meaning that personal branding and information about oneself disregards participation on the ESMP. Instead, one should share "interesting" and "relevant" items, implying that the value of what can be shared has to be informative and of high quality.

So, the experiences mentioned above create certain boundaries for how one should engage. For example, the participants remarked that appropriate items need to be "work-related", setting standards for what internal communication should be like. Sharing on the ESMP should be a safe matter as no external audience has access. Findings show otherwise. In fact, sharing is *risk-taking*, which was expressed in the participants' views on how they are willing to make a work process transparent to others:

"I don't have a problem with posting something that is not one hundred percent complete. I would have made it clear that this is "work-in-progress" and I want feedback".

We find examples that sharing can have greater risks, as participants can be criticised. Publishing unfinished work can create misunderstandings:

"One thing is that some of us find it a bit uncomfortable to share things that are not finished, because then we get criticized. If things are just published and not finished, it can cause harm because it creates sanctions on something that it was not intended to be. We have specific discussions within our work areas, documents concerning the management side and on the political aspects, which we publish. When things are at a certain stage, a working document, it is not intended that everybody should see it".

Data show that participants seek "approval" from their managers to publish content and do not want to be held accountable for what they share. Rather than deciding independently, as the basis for sharing a document, the participants enforce a quality-safety practice where they "ask permission" from someone in the management structure:

"Things that are unfinished and not approved can create panic, when it is a different figure from what you think is going to be on paper. If we begin to rewrite the CA's economy and everyone can read it, there will be something new to most people. People absorb it, even when it is wrong. It creates a lot of "storm" in your organization, if it is not correct".

4.3 Theme 3: Sharing in Separate Digital Eco-Systems

The third theme illustrates how sharing is accepted when using social media as part of a work practice, showing sharing of work beyond the ESMP. This shows how employees create *"separate digital eco-systems"*, which are used when they perceive that the ordinary ICTs the CA provide are not sufficient to perform their work, a technology adoption taking place "under the radar" of the IT department.

Looking at practice, an informant explained how they combined Dropbox and Google Drive to complete a public procurement. In several cases, the CA works together with the neighbouring municipalities. Here, the CA takes on the role of the leading organiser and acts on behalf of many municipalities to achieve greater benefits. This requires collaboration with colleagues in other municipalities. In this regard, colleagues in municipalities can have different needs and competences, which can lead to long e-mail exchanges and many attached documents. And one can lose the overview. Instead of sending e-mails with attached documents back and forth, they combined various applications to make the work simpler:

"We created a Dropbox account because we don't have the same e-mail system or share the same case management system. You don't get Dropbox solutions on the PCs here. The IT department thinks it's unsecure, [lacking] information security. We need tools to do our job, so we ended up defying that a bit and we downloaded the software to our PCs. I used Google Drive to share documents more efficiently than by e-mail".

Another example is how Facebook groups are used as information repositories or as a mean to reach particular groups who use the welfare services of the CA. Here, one does not find examples of practice showing sharing between several parties, but how Facebook groups are used as public bulletin boards. Again, sharing is an informing practice. One employee was a representative in a worker union and interacted with representatives from other CAs. As part of it, they created a Facebook group which enabled them to stay in contact and inform each other:

> "I had contact with others with the same role in other CAs. We used the Facebook group to share information that was more or less of the same nature. It was a way to share knowledge on issues of health and safety at work".

An employee explained how they created a Facebook group to communicate with high school students. As students are in the social media landscape, one concluded that they also needed to be present there in a similar way. After some years of use, the Facebook group is used as a public bulletin board:

> "It runs every day. We don't get many requests. We publish when we have specific information. We were unsure whether it would be an active user channel. I think it's going to become that in the long run".

4.4 Theme 4: Sharing Performed as an Individual Informing Strategy

The fourth theme shows how sharing is practiced as an *individual informing strategy* where it is enacted as a "push-of-information", which discourages internal communication on the ESMP. Sharing is rarely practiced as part of a two-way communication process but turns into an informing practice where users publish information that is already stored elsewhere. This creates situations where participants share information, but experience that nobody responds to their sharing. Thus, sharing has little benefit.

This is exemplified by analysing a feature created for sharing on the ESMP, the so-called "rooms". The room feature is a space for collaboration. Generally, the data show that all participants adopted the rooms to perform simple assignments, but afterwards they experienced challenges. Firstly, the participants created rooms and registered members who worked in the same department or who worked in the same field as themselves. Secondly, findings indicated that uploaded documents were republished information which was already stored in other sites. Also, employees seldom created new documents and started to co-write them in real-time, but they instead uploaded approved documents that were only read for notification purposes. Thirdly, the participants reported little interactivity, like participating and reading discussions. In sum, the participants saw the rooms as *information repositories* rather than sites for *collaboration*.

Later, employees with super-user status—users with administrative roles in the rooms—tried to stimulate interactivity and adopted individual strategies to promote engagement. Looking at practices, a super-user adopted an "online gardener" strategy. She tried to encourage co-workers to engage in the two rooms she administrated. This role-performance is not dissimilar to an automated e-mail notification feature, which is generated when there has been interactivity in a knowledge repository. The user extended this strategy and took on the role of a "sharer-and-pusher of information", which consisted of sending friendly e-mail reminders when she uploaded something:

> "I send an e-mail to everyone who has an interest. Then, I share information with them that it's posted on the ESMP. I invite them to follow the room. I think I've been sending reminders for a year".

She informed across multiple channels too, but afterwards questioned the value of sharing. She did not know if what she shared was used, a thought shared by another informant:

> "*I note that there are not many who follow the rooms, after many invitations to others who I think might have an interest in it. Then, do we spend unnecessary time on posting information that people do not read?*"

This raised a question of whether the rooms are used in the intended way. For example, after uploading, this informant received telephone calls from co-workers:

> "*I often get the question, if I also can send them an e-mail, when there is new information in the rooms. We have decided on that, no, we don't send an extra e-mail. We put it out there and then people must seek it out themselves. I feel that people don't pay attention to all that is posted in the rooms*".

This user-experience shows a gradual disengagement from sharing, as it vanishes and is overtaken by other assignments seen as more important to complete:

> "*We have two rooms. I post a lot of information in them. But I do not use the opportunity to follow other rooms, as I had hoped and thought I would. It disappears into my daily work life. When I need information, I don't find it with the search mechanisms that we have today as we had with the old intranet, although there is more information out there now*".

Informing over a long period of time creates an awareness that sharing has an embedded information overload problem attached to it. This is illustrated by repeatedly performing an informing practice wherein users redirect information that is stored elsewhere, for example on servers or local folders; but they observe that the information is redistributed many times in the rooms. Making information available to create transparency thus leads to other results:

> "*The intention with the ESMP was that we should move away from local storage of information in our own local folder structures. Everything was to be stored on the ESMP. I'm skeptical of it, because it is such a vast amount of information that it makes it difficult to identify what is relevant. We end up with huge hits when we search, and we spend a lot of time on finding out what is relevant. The most concerning thing, however, is that it has become such a huge volume of information*".

Exposure to too much information leads to users enforcing a personal filter and returning to established work principles like using email to communicate, leading to disengagement and a disapproved view on sharing:

> "*In the start, when it was brand new, I tried to make use of any opportunity. We had the possibility to create rooms. But afterwards, I failed to follow up all that. In neither the rooms I administer, did I manage to develop anything. I'm rarely there and don't check the rooms I am a member of*".

This user saw the rooms as an opportunity to create better conditions for interaction with the high schools with which she has frequent contact as part of her work. Much of the daily contact with them consisted of sending general information. Instead of sending all of that via e-mail, it could be transferred to the rooms, but later the good intentions faded out:

"I haven't had time to prioritize the rooms. My workday is packed with "to-do tasks". To sit down to try to use the possibilities and communicate in the rooms, has instead led me not doing that. Now, I don't bother checking notifications from the rooms I administer or follow or what my colleagues have written in their status updates. I skip that very fast and I go directly to check my e-mails".

The pattern of disengagement was found in another experience. This user explained that the challenges of generating engagement were related to the ESMP's user interface itself. For example, it was difficult to ascertain whether the rooms were used by others as there was no panel to show the numbers of visitors. The user also argued that the information shared in the rooms was already available and ready-made in other spaces, which meant that co-workers had it stored in their e-mail inbox:

"The challenge is that there are too many rooms. It's almost like we have a room for each employee. Then you have to click around a great deal before you find [what] you're looking for".

As the participants were uncertain to what extent sharing in the rooms had benefits, other experience indicated otherwise. A user working with accounting explained that the rooms are a "manual". She was an active user and saw the benefit of retrieving and finding information that had been shared by others:

"For example, I'm working in the accounting system and I find out that I need to get hold of a manual or retrieve information on an account. I go on the ESMP. There, I locate documents or things that are written about the case I'm working on. I'm a member of all the rooms that have something to do with accounting, a factor allowing me to know what we've posted and what others ask about".

The rooms were beneficial in different ways. For example, they were information depositories, where one could find quick answers, as they narrowed down the need for searching. Alternatively, this employee would have to search for the same information in larger web-based databases:

"They are part of a knowledge you can easily use. In accounting, there are clear definitions, clear rules for use. Things that are not so relevant one day, I often get information about in advance. But then I get questions from colleagues working in other departments, who ask about a deadline. What date is set as a deadline for the final reporting? Now, I know where I can quickly get and give an answer back on that. It's not necessarily that I have that knowledge in my head, but now I have good knowledge of where the answer is located".

5 Conclusion

In short, research on ESMPs is still in its infancy, but it shows that employees in organisations use ESMPs for online social interaction like connecting and expanding professional networks [9]. Also, researchers have charted basic user patterns [10, 11, 18] and examined the challenges of adopting ESMPs. A number of studies have tried to theorise the material understanding of ESMPs, like expanding our understanding of the concept of affordance. This has been used to hypothesise what potential benefits ESMPs can provide to grasp organisational processes like socialisation and the organising of work processes [13, 19]. Missing from the ESMP research stream is a *learning perspective* on how users learn to share knowledge. This can be established by looking at the main finding from the study, which suggests filling a gap in the research on ESMPs.

Throughout the analysis, we can establish a contradiction, which is often on display in unsuccessful implementations of new technologies in organisations – end-users do not use the technology as intended. This study finds that an ESMP, intended to simplify the work surface among employees in a public organisation in a Nordic country, gives opposite outcomes among the end-users. Sharing, introduced as a new workplace principle, expected to create transparency and enhance internal communication, creates disengaged users. Instead, sharing is learned to be a practice that is difficult to master, an aspect that is learned by the participants when they attempt to engage on the ESMP and use features facilitated for sharing. In fact, they learn by reflecting on their actions that they seldom engage in a two-way communication process where knowledge is created by collaboration. Rather, they perform *an informing practice* to fulfil the goal of sharing. This informing practice, which is an essential ingredient in creating a knowledge-sharing process, is performed on the premise of informing an audience and to be informed. Moreover, the informing practice is seldom the start of a knowledge process where two users exchange information to create knowledge, for example. Instead, the practice of sharing is a republishing of ready-made and approved official documents found elsewhere in the CA, creating an information overload problem. Furthermore, this gives clues to what is shared, which in this explorative case study relates to information that is already known to an organisation. Sharing proves to be challenging and is associated with great risk-taking for those carrying it out, leading to the enforcement of self-censorship and the construction of separate and private workplaces that the participants deem beneficial to complete their work. In contrast, the users institute personal filters and return to work surfaces which they believe "works", which in most cases is e-mail. In other words, the meaning of the practice of sharing on the ESMP found in this case study is performed as an informing strategy and used to be informed.

References

1. Ardichvili, A., Page, V., Wentling, T.: Motivation and barriers to participation in virtual knowledge-sharing communities of practice. J. Knowl. Manag. **7**(1), 64–77 (2003)
2. Chen, C.J., Hung, S.W.: To give or to receive? Factors influencing members' knowledge sharing and community promotion in professional virtual communities. Inf. Manag. **47**(4), 226–236 (2010)
3. Yoo, W., Suh, K., Lee, M.B.: Exploring the factors enhancing member participation in virtual communities. J. Glob. Inform. Manag. **10**(3), 55–71 (2002)
4. Usoro, A., Sharratt, M.W., Tsui, E., Shekhar, S.: Trust as an antecedent to knowledge sharing in virtual communities of practice. Knowl. Manag. Res. Pract. **5**(3), 199–212 (2007)
5. Ardichvili, A.: Learning and knowledge sharing in virtual communities of practice: motivators, barriers, and enablers. Adv. Dev. Hum. Resour. **10**(4), 541–554 (2008)
6. Ardichvili, A., Stuedemann, R., Maurer, M., Wentling, T., Li, W.: Cultural influences on knowledge sharing through online communities of practice. J. Knowl. Manag. **10**(1), 94–107 (2006)

7. Chang, H.H., Chuang, S.S.: Social capital and individual motivations on knowledge sharing: participant involvement as a moderator. Inf. Manag. **48**(1), 9–18 (2011)
8. Kosonen, M.: Knowledge sharing in virtual communities - a review of the empirical research. Int. J. Web Based Commun. **5**(2), 144–163 (2009)
9. Steinfield, C., DiMicco, J.M., Ellison, N.B., Lampe, C.: Bowling online: social networking and social capital within the organization. In: Proceedings of the Fourth International Conference on Communities and Technologies, New York, NY, pp. 245–254 (2009)
10. Zhao, D., Rosson, R.: How and why people Twitter: the role that micro-blogging plays in informal communication at work. In: The International Conference on Supporting Group Work, Sanibel Island, FL, pp. 243–252 (2009)
11. Zhang, J., Qu, Y., Cody, J., Wu, Y.: A case study of micro-blogging in the enterprise: use, value, and related issues. In: Proceedings of the SIGCHI Conference on Human Factors in Computing Systems, Atlanta, GA, pp. 123–132 (2010)
12. Lüders, M.: Networking and notworking in social intranets: user archetypes and participatory divides. First Monday **18**(8) (2013)
13. Leonardi, P.M.: Ambient awareness and knowledge acquisition: using social media to learn "who knows what" and "who knows whom". MIS Q. Exec. **39**(4), 747–762 (2015)
14. Schön, D.A.: The Reflective Practitioner: How Professionals Think in Action. Basic Books, New York (1983)
15. Lave, J., Wenger, E.: Situated Learning: Legitimate Peripheral Participation. Cambridge University Press, Cambridge (1991)
16. Siemens, G.: Connectivism: a learning theory for the digital age. Int. J. Instr. Technol. Dist. Learn. **2**(1) (2005)
17. Brinkmann, S., Kvale, S.: InterViews: Learning the Craft of Qualitative research Interviewing. Sage, Thousand Oaks (2015)
18. Ehrlich, K., Shami, N.S.: Microblogging inside and outside the workplace. In: Proceedings of The Fourth International Conference on Weblogs and Social Media, Washington, DC, pp. 42–49 (2010)
19. Oostervink, N., Agterberg, M., Huysman, M.: Knowledge sharing on enterprise social media: practices to cope with institutional complexity. J. Comput.-Mediat. Commun. **21**(2), 156–176 (2016)

Self-Assessment, e-Assessment and e-Examinations

The Application of Anchoring Vignettes in the Analysis of Self-assessment of ICT Skills

A Pilot Study Among Czech Secondary School Students

Hana Voňková, Miroslava Černochová[(✉)], Hasan Selcuk,
Jan Hrabák, and Kateřina Králová

Faculty of Education, Charles University, Prague, Czech Republic
{hana.vonkova,miroslava.cernochova,hasan.selcuk,
katerina.kralova}@pedf.cuni.cz, kabarh.naj@seznam.cz

Abstract. This paper presents pilot study findings of a research project about the application of anchoring vignettes in the analysis of Czech upper secondary school students' self-assessment of ICT skills. The pilot study was conducted in December 2017 with 166 respondents from four different types of upper secondary schools. Anchoring vignettes, which are brief texts describing hypothetical people who illustrate a certain level of the trait of interest (e.g. information and communication technology (ICT) skills), is a method implemented to identify response scale differences in survey questions and to adjust self-assessments caused by response scale differences. Methodologically, as there are only a few examples of the application of this method in the self-assessment of ICT skills and also in educational research, this pilot study has enabled the researchers to test how comprehensible a questionnaire with a set of vignettes was for the upper secondary school students. This enhanced research method based on anchoring vignettes will be used for the main study in spring 2018. The pilot study findings confirmed the high variability of the use of scale for respondents' self-assessments and vignettes.

Keywords: Information and communication technology · Self-assessment · Anchoring vignette · Upper secondary schools

1 Introduction

This paper presents pilot study findings of a research project about the application of anchoring vignettes in the analysis of Czech secondary school students' self-assessment of ICT skills. As explained by King et al. [1], anchoring vignettes is a method to identify response scale differences in survey questions and to adjust the self-assessments caused by response scale differences. For example, when students are asked to self-assess their ICT skills in a survey question on a scale of 1 to 7 (1 being the lowest and 7 the highest), students might either overvalue or undervalue their ability in the self-assessment. Hence, anchoring vignettes, which are brief texts describing hypothetical people who illustrate a certain level of the trait of interest (e.g. ICT skills), enable researchers to identify response scale differences in self-assessments and thus, to adjust them.

Since the early 2000s, the anchoring vignette method has been implemented in a variety of areas of research, such as political efficacy [1], work disability [2], job satisfaction [3], health [4–6], health system performance [7], life satisfaction [8], and satisfaction with social contacts [9]. However, there are only a few examples of the application of this method for educational research. Regarding one of these, Buckley and Scheider [10] implemented anchoring vignettes when investigating charter schools in the United States of America (USA) and parents' satisfaction with different types of schools. Vonkova and Hrabak's study [11] focused on Czech upper secondary school students' self-assessment of ICT knowledge and skills through the anchoring vignette method. Moreover, Vonkova et al. [12] investigated Czech lower-level secondary school students' self-assessment of dishonest behaviour in school by using the anchoring vignette method. Von Davier et al. [13] examined the effects of vignette scoring on reliability and validity of student self-assessment, according to the Programme for International Student Assessment (PISA) 2012 dataset. He et al. [14] conducted a study on effects of this method on comparability and the predictive validity of student self-assessment in 64 countries based on data from PISA 2012. Vonkova et al. [15, p. 3] looked into cross-country heterogeneity in students' self-assessment of their teacher's classroom management also based on the PISA 2012 dataset and they found that the anchoring vignette method was potentially a useful tool to enhance the comparability of the self-reported measures in education. To contribute to research in the field of education, we have conducted a study aimed at designing an enhanced data collection method based on anchoring vignettes to explore different realms in educational research, such as digital literacy.

2 Literature Review: The Application of Anchoring Vignettes in the Self-assessment of ICT Skills

This section presents a review of existing studies that are pertinent to the application of anchoring vignettes in the self-assessment of ICT skills in the context of education. Before moving to reviewing the existing studies, it is worthwhile mentioning the European Computer Driving Licence (ECDL) foundation study [16], which highlighted how people's self-assessment of their ICT skills can be different from their actual ability. The ECDL foundation's study was conducted in five European countries, namely Austria, Denmark, Finland, Germany and Switzerland, to identify people's ICT skills. Respondents (aged 15–64 years) were given a questionnaire in two parts, with the first focusing on self-assessment of ICT skills, and the second testing their real level. The findings of the study showed that in all the countries surveyed, respondents overestimated their ICT skills. Taking into account the study of the ECDL foundation [16], we suggest that anchoring vignettes could provide dependable findings from respondents' answers with respect to self-assessment in surveys.

Regarding studies that have applied anchoring vignettes in self-assessments, Vonkova and Hrabak [11] compared the ICT knowledge and skills of two distinct groups of upper secondary school students by examining their self-assessed perspective on these, both before and after the anchoring vignette adjustment for the different usage of scale. The study findings revealed that the anchoring vignette method enabled the researchers to distinguish between the two groups of students' differences in terms of scale usage and showed how adjusted self-assessments corresponded to the assumed level of students' ICT knowledge and skills. Cerna [17] investigated the self-assessment of undergraduate university students' ICT knowledge by applying the anchoring vignette method. Respondents were students from the Faculty of Education at Charles University and specialised in three different study programmes (information technology (IT), social science, and mathematics). The findings of Cerna's study showed significant differences between respondents' self-assessment and their assumed actual ICT knowledge. Moreover, the author found that those who study IT as their specialisation in education have a greater tendency to exaggerate the level of their ICT knowledge compared to other respondents studying different subject areas.

3 Pilot Study Methodology

3.1 Aims of the Pilot Study

Generally, a pilot study refers to "a small-scale version or trial run, done in preparation for the major study" [18, p. 467]. As described by Vogt [19], it can be considered as a 'dress rehearsal' to identify any possible problems before undertaking the major study. The main aim of our pilot study was to inform and design the main study methodology, specifically to test the feasibility of the data collection method, which consists of a questionnaire with a set of vignettes focused on self-assessment of the ICT knowledge and skills of young people.

In the pilot study, we aimed to test how comprehensible our questionnaire was for upper secondary school students, who are at Year 1 (age 15 years) and 4 (age 19 years). The pilot was conducted in December 2017 among (N = 166) students from four upper secondary schools in the Czech Republic. Experiences gained from the pilot study were then used in the main study, conducted in spring 2018 with a representative sample of 2,600 students from 56 secondary schools in the Czech Republic.

3.2 Procedures of Developing the Data Collection Method

"The aim of the anchoring vignette method is to clear/correct the self-assessment of respondents so that they can be comparable" [20, p. 14]. Respondents in the area (in our case ICT skills and knowledge) use a self-assessment question, as well as evaluating hypothetical people described in a short story (anchor). The presented verbal characteristics of hypothetical people in vignettes in the case of categorical assessment scales can be evaluated by different respondents in different ways. Respondents' answers to self-assessment can be affected by the different use of scale categories. For example, respondents with a lot of ICT experience and a deep interest in ICT can use different scale categories for evaluating a given level of ICT knowledge than beginners and ordinary ICT users. Our main data collection method was a questionnaire, which consisted of a set of anchoring vignettes and fixed-choice questions to obtain background information about each respondent (age, sex, school, grade in ICT subjects, field of study, interest about ICT, participation in programming or informatics competitions, number of hours spent on a computer at school or at home, respondents' use of ICT within different types of activities, parents' education and parents' use of ICT in their job or free time). Briefly, in our pilot study, we used one self-assessment question (S) and three vignettes (V1, V2, V3), with a scale of 1 to 7 (1 – the lowest level and 7 – the highest level).

In the vignettes designed for our pilot study (see Table 1), we focused on five domains of computer literacy (information and data literacy, communication and collaboration, digital content creation, safety, and problem-solving) in accordance with the concept of digital literacy, as defined in DigComp (see [21, pp. 8–9]).

Table 1. Overview of the self-assessment question and three vignettes

General self-assessment question (S)	How do you evaluate your knowledge and skills in ICT? Note: the following was applied to each of the vignettes below: *Use a scale of 1 to 7 ('1' being the lowest and '7' the highest)*
Vignette 1 (V1)	Filip can work with texts and charts with the use of basic functions available from the ribbon. He saves his files on a desktop, he doesn't use sharing or cloud saving, but instead, sends the files via email. He uses the same password for the social network, email, etc. accounts. If he encounters any problem while working on a computer, he usually asks his friend for help
Vignette 2 (V2)	Kristin can process texts and charts with the use of advanced functions (e.g. created personal styles, automatic table of content). She goes in for creating graphics (designing business cards) and short original footage, which she shares on YouTube. She doesn't post any sensitive information on social networks. If she encounters any problem while solving a task, she searches for an instruction on the internet and determines the solution procedure with its help
Vignette 3 (V3)	Adam can process texts and charts with the use of advanced functions. He is able to program his own functions for more difficult tasks. He goes in for computer graphics (designing posters), creating footage and programming websites. He manages two Facebook groups and verifies the credibility of the shared posts. He uses multi-layered security (SMS verification) for his accounts on the internet

In formulating the vignettes, we presented stories that would be comprehensible to students in the social sciences areas as well as the students of technical fields, including IT specialisation, in addition to being accessible to the two chosen age groups (Year 1 aged 15–16, and Year 4 aged 18–19 years). The vignettes should be understandable to all respondents also from a curricular point of view (note that in the Czech Republic, the current curriculum for ICT subjects does not cover all domains of DigComp).

The level of ICT skills and knowledge presented in vignettes is as follows: V1 describes a basic level (Filip's knowledge and skills in ICT correspond to the knowledge of a basic school graduate in the Czech Republic). V2 describes a more advanced level (Kristin uses ICT for creative activities and some problem-solving; she behaves safely on social networks); the majority of respondents from all secondary schools should achieve this level. V3 describes highly advanced ICT skills and knowledge beyond curriculum requirements (programming additional functions for more difficult tasks, programming a website, using multi-layered security, etc., which are not included in the curriculum for general education). This vignette should mainly distinguish students with ICT specialisation. By providing a score on the self-assessment question and for all three vignettes in Table 1, students provided a personal rating and calibration points for inter-participant comparison.

3.3 Procedures of Data Collection

We gathered data in December 2017 through an on-line questionnaire from 166 students of Year 1 and 4, attending four different public upper secondary schools (see Table 2): School 1 focuses on general education (a gymnasium) and is located in Prague. School 2 focuses on humanities and is located in Beroun, whilst School 3 is a technical school specialising in IT and located in Prague, and lastly, School 4 is a technical school specialising in transport and mechanisation in Mladá Boleslav. These schools were not selected at random, so respondents do not represent a representative sample of the secondary school population. However, these schools represent different specialisations among Czech upper secondary schools. Respondents filled out the on-line questionnaire at their schools with the participation of the researcher.

Table 2. Characteristics of the pilot schools

	Number of respondents	Male (%)	Female (%)	Male Age	Female Age	Respondents Year 1 (%)	Year 4 (%)
School 1	47	17.0	83.0	17.3	16.5	59.6	40.4
School 2	56	12.5	87.5	17.0	17.6	53.6	46.4
School 3	38	84.2	15.8	17.6	16.6	71.1	28.9
School 4	25	84.0	16.0	17.5	16.7	60.0	40.0
Total	166	41.0	59.0	17.4	16.9	60.2	39.8

3.4 Procedures of Data Analysis

For data analysis, we used Microsoft Office Excel 2011 and the statistical software called GRETL [http://gretl.sourceforge.net]. Table 3 shows how all respondents (N = 166) assessed the self-assessment question and three vignettes from across scale 1 to 7 ('1' was the lowest and '7' was the highest). The variability of the use of scale for both self-assessments and vignettes is high; respondents use (almost) the whole range of the scale categories. Concerning vignettes, it shows a high heterogeneity in reporting behaviour of respondents – the same level of ICT skills described in the vignettes is evaluated differently by different respondents. We expected the respondents would assess vignettes in the natural order V1 < V2 < V3 (the order given by a researcher). It means the expected value for V1 would be lower than the value for V2 and the value for V2 would be lower than that for V3. However, 5.4% of respondents assessed the vignettes in another way; they typically tied their assessment to two subsequent vignettes (see Table 3).

Table 3. Variability of the use of scale for self-assessment

Scale	1 (%)	2 (%)	3 (%)	4 (%)	5 (%)	6 (%)	7 (%)
Self-assessment (S)	4,22	18,07	27,71	25,90	19,28	4,82	0,00
Vignette 1 (V1)	7,23	26,51	35,54	26,51	3,61	0,60	0,00
Vignette 2 (V2)	0,00	1,20	3,61	15,66	34,34	35,54	9,64
Vignette 3 (V3)	0,60	0,60	1,20	5,42	10,24	31, 93	50,00

4 Findings from the Pilot Study

For further data analysis, we analysed each school separately and tried to distinguish the differences in scale usage among different schools. Using the correction based on the non-parametric approach, which consists of how the self-assessment S of a respondent relates to his/her vignette evaluations V1, V2 and V3 "assuming that the vignettes are naturally ordered (for example, from the lowest skills level of a hypothetical vignette person to the highest)" (see [11, p. 192]), we corrected the values for each respondent for each school (see Table 4).

Table 4. Average self-assessments of respondents in all schools before and after correction

	Number of respondents	Average value of self-assessment S		Ranking of schools		Comment
		Before correction	After correction	Before correction	After correction	
School 1	47	3.02	2.22	4	4	The position is the same
School 2	56	3.34	2.44	3	2	The position improved, high standards
School 3	38	4.29	3.27	1	1	The position is the same
School 4	25	3.72	2.43	2	3	The position decreased, low standards

The findings in Table 4 show that the ranking of two schools has changed after the correction, with the most considerable change being in the ranking for School 4 – its position has decreased more, indicating its low standards for evaluating ICT skills. Table 5, and Figs. 1 and 2 show comparisons of self-assessments before and after correction for School 4 and the best performing School 3. We showed there were statistically significant differences between Schools 3 and 4, not only before the self-assessment correction, but also after the correction.

Table 5. Comparison of self-assessment of respondents from School 3 and School 4 before and after correction

Scale	Uncorrected self-assessment (before correction)				Corrected self-assessment (after correction)			
	School 3		School 4		School 3		School 4	
	Absolute value	Relative value (%)	Absolute value	Relative value (%)	Absolute value	Relative value (%)	Absolute value	Relative value (%)
1	0	0.0	0	0.0	5	13.51	4	19.0
2	2	5.3	2	8.0	3	8.1	7	33.3
3	5	13.2	10	40.0	14	37.8	7	33.3
4	14	36.8	7	28.0	11	29.7	3	14.3
5	14	36.8	5	20.0	1	2.0	0	0.0
6	3	7.9	1	4.0	2	5.4	0	0.0
7	0	0.0	0	0.0	1	2.7	0	0.0
Number of respondents	38		25		37		21	
Average	4.29		3.72		3.27		2.43	
Standard deviation	0.97		1.00		1.36		0.95	
T-test: p value	0.03414				0.01730			

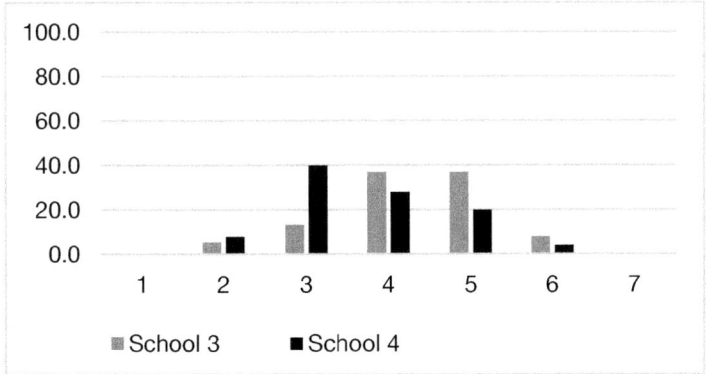

Fig. 1. Comparison of self-assessment of respondents from School 3 and School 4 before correction

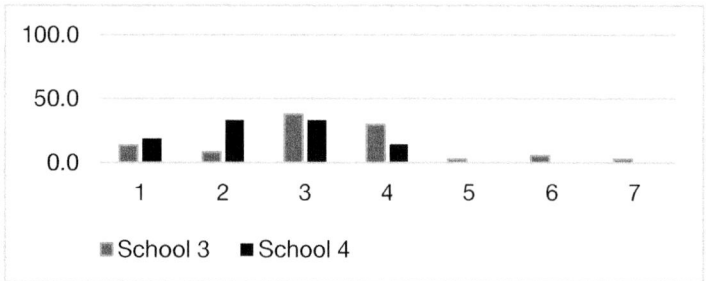

Fig. 2. Comparison of self-assessment of respondents from School 3 and School 4 after correction

To understand better how respondents evaluated their skills, we compared schools using the background variables of respondents. Analyses of questions focused on respondents' interests and ways of using ICT in their free time, which showed respondents do not differ too much. Generally speaking, ICT knowledge, skills and interests of respondents correspond to topics they have learned mainly at school. Regarding respondents' grades, 69.9% of all the respondents from Schools 1–4 have obtained an average grade between 1 to 2 in ICT school subjects (1 is the best grade and 5 is the worst grade in Czech schools); only respondents from School 4 got worse grades (the average is 2.45). This corresponds to our ranking of schools based on adjusted self-assessments. Nonetheless, 14.5% of respondents reported that they had never studied such a subject before.

As already mentioned, School 3 is a technical upper secondary school specialising in ICT located in Prague and School 4 is a secondary school without any specialisation in ICT located in an industrial city. In both schools, practically the same number of respondents (about 65%) agreed with a statement "I am doing my best to have good results in ICT because I am expected to do so". Respondents from School 3 differed in some characteristics from respondents in School 4. The ratio between university-educated mothers and fathers of respondents from School 3 was 2.2 and for School 4 was 0.7. Respondents of School 3 spent 1.8-times more time on computers at weekends compared to working days, while at School 4 only 1.3-times more. On weekends, respondents in School 3 spent an average 4.2 h/day on computers, while respondents in School 4 only 3.4 h/day. Seventy-four per cent of respondents in Schools 3 and 4 spent practically every day surfing on the Internet for fun. Comparing respondents in School 4 with those in School 3, more enjoyed creating digital music, were active on social networks and enjoyed playing computer games. Respondents in School 3 dedicated more time to web design activities, work with graphics software, publishing on YouTube or creating digital animations than respondents in School 4. Respondents in School 3 were more interested (53%) in the latest ICT news, new technologies, computer graphics, etc., than respondents in School 4 (24%). Respondents in School 3 liked learning new things in ICT (87%) much more than respondents in School 4 (48%). Respondents in School 3 (68%) were fond of creative activities using ICT much more than respondents in School 4 (36%). Ninety-two per cent of the respondents in

School 3 agreed with the statement: "To do my best in the ICT lessons pays off because it can help me to get a job I want to do in the future", while in School 4 this was only 60% of respondents. To summarise, the background characteristics of respondents are in line with our adjusted self-assessments using anchoring vignettes.

5 Conclusion

The main aim of our pilot study was to inform and design the main study methodology, specifically to test the feasibility of the data collection method, consisting of a questionnaire with a set of vignettes focused on self-assessment of ICT knowledge and skills of young people. From this pilot study, we identified some problems that shed light on the main research, conducted in spring 2018 in the Czech Republic.

The pilot study showed us that in terms of data interpretation, it was very important that researchers could visit all schools to instruct respondents what to do and how to fill out the on-line questionnaire. The researchers could understand better some contexts related to students' ICT knowledge, skills, motivation, and approaches to ICT.

Some questions need to be adapted for the main research (questions about type of school, number of inhabitants living in a respondent's town/village, grades from ICT subjects, arrangement and ordering vignettes on a page, questions about the family). The pilot also highlighted questions about how to organise data collection through an on-line questionnaire in school computer laboratories, how to support teacher co-operation to motivate students to answer the questionnaire responsibly and maintain classroom discipline, etc. It is necessary in the classes to ensure peace and discipline in order for the respondents to read attentively all questions, especially vignettes.

Limitations of this study are as follows. Findings obtained in the pilot cannot be generalised; sampling does not allow this. However, findings are definitely of interest since they indicate huge differences in scale usage between different types of schools – students from some schools have high/low standards when evaluating their ICT skills. However, all three vignettes V1, V2 and V3 were presented to respondents on one page of the questionnaire - this might have affected respondents' assessment of vignettes.

Acknowledgments. This study is a result of the research funded by the Czech Science Foundation, project GA ČR 17-02993S "Factors influencing the ICT skill self-assessments of upper-secondary school students".

References

1. King, G., Murray, C.J.L., Salomon, J.A., Tandon, A.: Enhancing the validity and cross-cultural comparability of measurement in survey research. Am. Polit. Sci. Rev. **98**(1), 567–583 (2004)
2. Kapteyn, A., Smith, J.P., van Soest, A.: Vignettes and self-reports of work disability in the US and the Netherlands. Am. Econ. Rev. **97**(1), 461–473 (2007)
3. Kristensen, N., Johansson, E.: New evidence on cross-country differences in job satisfaction using anchoring vignettes. Labour Econ. **15**, 96–117 (2008)

4. Bago d'Uva, T., van Doorslaer, E., Lindeboom, M., O'Donnell, O.: Does reporting heterogeneity bias the measurement of health disparities? Health Econ. **17**(3), 351–375 (2008)
5. Peracchi, F., Rossetti, C.: Heterogenity in health responses and anchoring vignettes. Empir. Econ. **42**(2), 513–538 (2012)
6. Vonkova, H., Hullegie, P.: Is the anchoring vignettes method sensitive to the domain and choice of the vignette? J. Roy. Stat. Soc.: Ser. A **174**(3), 597–620 (2011)
7. Sirven, N., Santos-Eggimann, B., Spagnoli, J.: Comparability of health care responsiveness in Europe. Soc. Indic. Res. **105**(2), 255–271 (2012)
8. Angelini, V., Cavapozzi, D., Corazzini, L., Paccagnella, O.: Age, health and life satisfaction among older Europeans. Soc. Indic. Res. **105**(2), 293–308 (2012)
9. Bonsang, E., van Soest, A.: Satisfaction with social contacts of older Europeans. Soc. Indic. Res. **105**(2), 273–292 (2012)
10. Buckley, J., Schneider, M.: Charter Schools: Hope or Hype? Princeton University Press, Princeton (2007)
11. Vonkova, H., Hrabak, J.: The (in) comparability of ICT knowledge and skill self-assessments among upper secondary school students: the use of the anchoring vignette method. Comput. Educ. **85**, 191–202 (2015)
12. Vonkova, H., Bendl, S., Papajoanu, O.: How students report dishonest behavior in school: self-assessment and anchoring vignettes. J. Exp. Educ. **85**(1), 36–53 (2017)
13. von Davier, M., Shin, H.J., Khorramdel, L., Stankov, L.: The effects of vignette scoring on reliability and validity. Appl. Psychol. Measure. **42**(4), 291–306 (2017)
14. He, J., Buchholz, J., Klieme, E.: Effects of anchoring vignettes on comparability and predictive validity of student self-reports in 64 cultures. J. Cross Cult. Psychol. **48**(3), 319–334 (2017)
15. Vonkova, H., Zamarro, G., Hitt, G.: Cross-country heterogeneity in students' reporting behavior: the use of the anchoring vignette method. J. Educ. Meas. **55**(1), 3–31 (2018)
16. ECDL: Perception and Reality. Measuring Digital Skills in Europe (2016). http://ecdl.org/media/perception_and_reality_-_annex_1.pdf
17. Černá, P.: Self-assessment of teacher students' knowledge in the field of information and communication technologies [Master's thesis]. Charles University, Prague (2017)
18. Polit, D.F., Beck, C.T.: Essentials of Nursing Research: Methods, Appraisal and Utilization, 6th edn. Lippincott Williams & Wilkins, Philadelphia (2006)
19. Vogt, W.P.: Dictionary of Statistics and Methodology: A Nontechnical Guide for the Social Sciences. Sage, Newbury Park (1993)
20. Vonkova, H.: Metoda ukotvujících vinět a její využití v pedagogickém výzkumu. Pedagogická fakulta, Univerzita Karlova, Praha (2017)
21. Vuorikari, R., Punki, Y., Carreto Gomes, S., Van den Brande, G.: DigComp 2.0: The digital competence framework for citizens. Update phase 1: the conceptual reference model. Publication Office of the European Union, Luxembourg (2016)

Student Experiences with a Bring Your Own Laptop e-Exam System in Pre-university College

Mathew Hillier[1(✉)] and Nathaniel Lyon[2]

[1] Monash University, Melbourne, Australia
Mathew.Hillier@monash.edu
[2] Monash College, Melbourne, Australia
Nathaniel.Lyon@monashcollege.edu.au

Abstract. This study investigated students' perceptions of a bring-your-own (BYO) laptop based e-Examination system used in trials conducted at an Australian pre-university college in 2016 and 2017. The trials were conducted in two different subjects, in geography and globalisation. Data were gathered using pre-post surveys (n = 128) that comprised qualitative comments and Likert items. Students' perceptions were gathered relating to the ease of use of the e-Examination system, technical reliability, suitability of the assessment task to computerisation and the logistical aspects of the examination process. Many of the typists were taking a computerised supervised test for the first time. A divergence of opinions between those that typed and those that hand-wrote regarding students' future use intentions became more prominent following the examination event.

Keywords: e-Exam system · Assessment · Student perceptions · Acceptance

1 Introduction and Background

In this study, we characterise an e-Examination (e-Exam or e-exam) as a "timed, supervised, summative assessment conducted using each candidate's own computer running a standardised operating system" [1]. We would add that the use of authentic software applications as part of the examination environment is an important element of our approach. As such, we distinguish our approach to computerised examinations from 'online assessments' that are limited to the test or quiz functionality of a learning content management system (Moodle, Blackboard) or specialised testing software (TCExam, QuestionMark Perception, ExamSoft) that may or may not be directly supervised by human invigilators.

This study is part of a wider project [2–4] investigating authentic approaches to supervised high stakes assessment typically carried out in examination halls and classrooms suited to the Australian higher education context. In this respect, our paper takes a departure from other trials we have conducted in that we focus here on e-exam use in a pre-tertiary pathway college context.

In this paper, we explore the literature related to e-exams, including matters relating to student choice and acceptance of the e-exam approach. Data were collected on the students' impressions of the process as expressed through written comments and selected response items in a pre- and post-assessment surveys.

2 Literature

Computerised examinations have been increasingly gaining attention in the last decade. Whilst one of the first reported uses of computers for assessment was in 1965 [5], little movement away from pen-on-paper examinations has occurred in the higher education or school systems around the world. Only recently has attention shifted to modernising the examination room. Examples of efforts underway in higher education and other sectors were reviewed [1, 6]. The 'Dublin Declaration' developed by the International Federation of Information Processing Technical Committee Three for Education conference sets a future direction for computers in assessment [7] (pp. xvii–xviii):

> "To see computers used effectively in education, it is necessary to develop fair, reliable and resilient computer-based assessment methods. Assessment methods must go far beyond imitating paper-based assessment, and prioritise the pedagogical affordances of computers over administrative convenience. The use of computers in timed, supervised assessments offers the chance to transform curricula in the light of computational thinking".

In particular, the Declaration recommends that e-Exams must be:

> "authentic assessment that matches modern workplace practices and many student learning experiences" ([7], p. xviii).

We particularly find resonance with the idea of promoting authentic assessment [8] in high stakes examinations. One way to enable such assessment is to provide a rich array of software tools of the trade to candidates in the examination room. Doing so opens up the possibility of designing complex constructed assessment tasks to be done under supervised conditions. This enables assessment designers to push into the Modification and Redefinition stages of the Substitution, Augmentation, Modification and Redefinition (SAMR) model [9, 10] or to target 'higher order thinking' of Bloom's taxonomy [11] with respect to pedagogical efficacy. Systems such as 'Secure Exam Environment' and the work described in [4] place authentic assessment at the heart of the project. The e-Exam platform [4] used for this study uses a bring-your-own laptop approach and provides the same full operating system and application suite that includes an office suite, multimedia tools and optional discipline-specific applications (e.g. mathematics, computer aided design (CAD), chemistry, accounting). In this instance, we used the fully functional word processor as the question presentation and response environment, thus providing an authentic tool typically used to produce essays and reports.

The perceptions and attitudes of users with respect to ease of use and usefulness (being fit for purpose) have been found to be important factors in people accepting new computer technology [12, 13], but not the only factors at play [14]. This particularly applies to the students as the people most directly impacted by e-exam systems, although they often do not have a strong voice when it comes to selecting software deployed in education institutions. Therefore, it is important to ensure their views are heard if we desire smooth acceptance and operation of a high-stakes e-exam system. A survey of students [15] at the University of Bradford in the United Kingdom (UK), following their use of QuestionMark Perception, included a range of topics. Other studies include the use of Examsoft in pharmacy courses in Canada [16] and an institution-wide survey [17] capturing students' hopes and fears prior to the trialling of e-Exams at The University of Queensland in Australia. e-Exam trials followed the latter study, exploring the students' experiences of the process [18]. These studies on student perceptions of the e-exam process informed construction of survey tools in this study.

Another characteristic is how each system architect treats the idea of technology reliability. Where an e-Exam solution has a heavy reliance on a network during the examination, the risk of a 'single-point of failure' impacting on a whole cohort of students is increased and so the need to ensure extra redundancy measures is heightened. One study [17] reported that the fear of technology failure is a major barrier to the adoption and intention to use e-Exams by students. A recently publicised case of failure during a national high stakes Medical board e-exam event in Australia [19, 20] highlights the critical need to ensure a robust system and to avoid 'single point of failure' designs. Earlier online assessment systems tended to stop working the moment the network dropped out. Advances in web technologies mean that some systems may handle or mitigate network outages of a short duration (e.g. auto-save for Moodle quiz) but extended outages will result in an unscheduled end to the session. Only a small number of e-exam systems are able to continue to operate and successfully complete the e-exam session without a network connection. This includes the commercial product 'Examsoft' [21] and the e-Exam platform [2, 4] used in this study. Avoiding system-wide failures means that any technical issues that do occur are likely to be isolated to a single student. Therefore, an issue can be managed according to existing examination protocols with respect to individual interruptions, breaks and extra time.

This review of prior work has outlined several areas of concern that will serve as a focus for our evaluation in this study. These are summarised in Table 1.

Table 1. Areas for investigation

Area	Example research questions
Intention and attitude	Were candidates in favour of the e-Exam system? Would they recommend it to others or use it again? Did they have any concerns about undertaking an e-exam? If they typed their examination, was their attitude changed or any concerns lessened following the event?
Ease of use	Were the students able to use the system with relative ease? Did they have any issues related to the e-exam processes?
Technical reliability	Did any technical issues or interruptions arise? If so, did such issues interfere with the examination or result in lost work?

3 Study Context

In Australia, the lead author is conducting a nationwide project investigating the scalable provision of authentic assessment in the examination room using BYO laptops [2, 4]. The study reported in this paper investigates if prior work carried out in the higher education sector would work successfully in the pre-university context. The study was undertaken at Monash College, Australia within the 'Foundation Year' [22] programme. This programme is at the equivalent level as an Australian year 12 high school leaving certificate or the International Baccalaureate. The study was run in conjunction with the second author who is a unit coordinator and teacher in the two units in which trials were conducted. The trials were carried out using in-class supervised written assessments. These took the form of a couple of mini-cases that included photographs, charts and data tables, each with one or several questions requiring a short text or essay-style response.

4 Method and Approach

This study examined two live trials of the e-Exam system and approach in two separate units at the College, involving 128 students. The units selected were geography (Geo) in semester 1, 2016 and globalisation (Glo) in semester 2, 2017. The process used to run each trial is represented in Table 2.

The formative ungraded practice session was run in-class time with all students participating. Students were free to choose typing or handwriting for the real examination.

Table 2. e-Exam trial process

Stage	Activities
1. Call for interest	Students indicate interest in either typing or handwriting their examination and complete research study consent forms
2. Practice session done two weeks prior to examination	Preview the examination process and practice following provided instructions for starting up their laptop from an e-Exam universal serial bus (USB) stick. Students complete the practice questions. Data collected about hardware compatibility via hardware logging, observation of use and student impressions via pre-examination survey. Following the session, data analysis of the surveys was carried out to detect any concerns

(*continued*)

Table 2. (*continued*)

Stage	Activities
3. Real examination for both typists and hand-writers	Individual desks were set up with a paper copy of the 'e-Exam quick start guide' and post-examination survey. A power socket was provided for each typist. Hand-writers were given a paper copy of the examination questions and response booklets. These were available to typists upon request. Both typists and hand-writers sat in the same room 1. Students entered the room and were seated at a suitable desk 2. Typists were given an e-Exam USB stick containing the questions 3. Students started their computer with a USB stick progressing to the e-Exam desktop. A desktop background image provided a visual check that all had booted from the correct USB 4. Invigilator announced the start of the examination. Students entered their student ID and name into the starter screen. The system then opened the examination document. Auto-save occurred every two minutes 5. Examination ended: saved work one last time and shut down the computer 6. Students returned the USB sticks containing their response 7. Students completed the post-examination survey before leaving the room
4. Grading	In the following week, the teacher did the grading. Students were given grades and feedback comments. Surveys results were analysed

Selected response survey questions as shown in Tables 3, 4 and 5 were analysed using SPSS v24 using an alpha level of .05. Likert data pertaining to students' opinions were treated as non-parametric [23]. Another study [15] did the same when analysing students' perceptions of their experience with an e-Assessment system. Mann and Whitney's U test [24] was used to test the variance between groups (typists versus hand-writers) on Likert items. When comparing paired pre-post Likert items, a Wilcoxon Signed Ranks Test [25] was used with the requirement of a normal distribution of differences met. Chi-squared was also used to test if experiencing a technical issue impacted in the decision to type the examination.

It is important to note that participants were not randomly assigned to the typing or hand-writing groups so results are only descriptive of this group. As per [15], we take the stance that statistical tests serve as a tool to summarise the body of students' opinions rather than to be representative of an objective truth.

Table 3. Pre-examination survey responses by text production mode

Question	Type			Hand write			MW	
Pre survey (practice run)	n	M	SD	n	M	SD	diff	U	p
Written instructions were easy to follow	55	4.1	0.7	55	4.0	1.0	0.2	1466	0.759
It was easy to learn the necessary technical steps	55	4.2	0.7	56	3.9	1.1	0.3	1307	0.128
It was easy to start my computer using the e-Exam USB stick	55	4.0	1.0	56	3.7	1.2	0.3	1333	0.194
I feel confident I will be able to do these steps in a real examination	55	3.9	1.0	56	3.3	1.2	0.6	1093	**0.006**
The software within the e-Exam System was easy to use	54	4.0	0.8	56	3.8	1.0	0.2	1439.5	0.642
I now feel relaxed about using the e-Exam system for my examination	54	3.8	1.0	56	3.3	1.1	0.5	1171.5	**0.034**
I would like to use a computer for examinations in the future	55	4.0	1.0	56	3.0	1.2	1.0	842.5	**<.001**

5 Findings

The trials involved 128 pre-tertiary students; 65% were female and 35% were male. We examined the students' opinions regarding their first encounter with the e-Exam system in terms of differences between those that went on to type the examination and those that handwrote the examination using a Mann-Whitney U test. Table 3 displays the results from Likert items (strongly agree = 5, neutral = 3 and strongly disagree = 1) collected on the pre-examination survey (done at the practice session). The strongest difference was for "I would like to use a computer for exams in the future" (U = 842.5, p = <.001). Means and standard deviations are provided in the tables for clarity.

Following the examination, typists (52%) were asked to reflect on the e-Exam system itself with regard to suitability, usability and reliability (see Table 4 and Fig. 1). The majority of items received positive agreement, most with mean agreement ratings of 4 or above out of 5. The sentiment within the group was relatively uniform, as evidenced by the small standard deviations (Table 4) and boxplots in Fig. 1.

Table 4. Post-examination survey responses regarding the e-exam system

Question	n	M	SD
I felt this particular examination suited the use of computers	63	4.2	0.7
I liked the fact I could use my own computer	57	4.5	0.7
I felt the e-exam system was easy to use	63	4.2	0.8
I felt the e-exam system was reliable against technical failures	62	4.0	0.8
I felt the e-exam system was secure against cheating	63	4.2	0.9
I would recommend the e-exam system to others	63	4.0	0.9

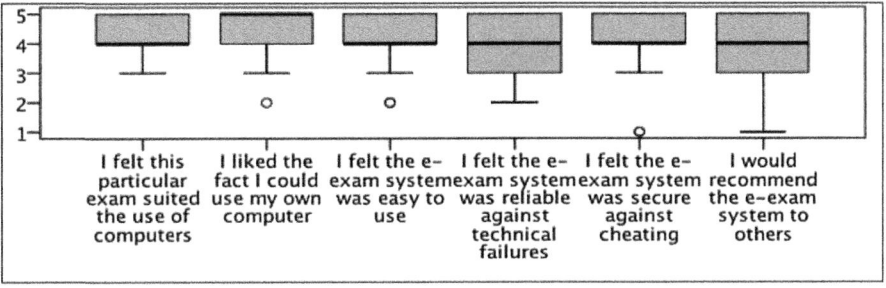

Fig. 1. Opinions of the e-exam system

Typists were asked "Did you experience any technical difficulties during this exam?" Responses yes (n = 17, 24%) and no (n = 53, 76%) were gathered via a comment box and a list covering usability, technology and logistics. It should be noted that all those who typed successfully completed and submitted their work. A comparison of problems encountered in the pre- and post-sessions is shown in Fig. 2. A Chi-squared test indicated that there was no statistically significant relationship between encountering a problem in the practice session and electing to type or handwrite the examination ($\chi^2(1) = 0.003$, $p = 0.956$). This could indicate that the practice session did its job in preventing serious problems from reaching the examination room, or that problems were considered to be minor by those that encountered them.

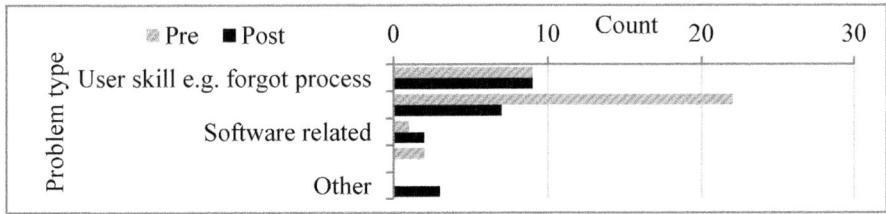

Fig. 2. Reported issues

Table 5. Post-examination survey future intention to use

Question	Type			Hand write				MW	
Post survey	n	M	SD	n	M	SD	diff	U	p
I would like to use a computer for examinations in the future	61	4.2	0.7	53	2.1	1.0	2.1	160.5	**<.001**

A comparison between typists' and hand-writers' intentions to use a computer for future examinations following the examination event (see Table 5) showed a significant Mann-Whitney U test result (U = 160.5, p = <.001).

Finally, we examined if students' declared future use intentions may have changed between pre- and post-examination surveys for typists and hand-writers using the question "I would like to use a computer for examinations in the future". Those that typed the examination were in slightly stronger agreement following the examination (n = 61, M = 4.2 SD = 0.7) than prior (n = 55, M = 4.0, SD = 1.0). However, the difference was not significant when tested with a Wilcoxon Signed-Ranks test, Z = −1.763, p = 0.078. Both pre- and post-median agreement was 4. Those that handwrote the examination became more negative following the examination to a significant extent (Z = −3.757, p = >.001), with the median agreement 3 prior and 2 following the examination. For clarity, mean agreement for hand-writers pre-examination was M = 3.0 (SD = 1.2, n = 56) and post-examination M = 2.1 (SD = 1.0, n = 53).

6 Discussion

In the practice session, most students were able to successfully undertake the steps required for doing the e-exam using their laptop, although some did require assistance. This included starting up their laptop from the USB stick and using the software (see Table 3). The Chi-squared result shows that encountering a problem in the practice session did not impact the decision to type or handwrite. The practice session appeared to resolve most serious problems (see Fig. 2) before they reached the examination itself as seen by the reduced number of issues reported between the pre- and post-sessions. Most problems that remained related to user familiarity with the software or process (i.e. forgetting the boot key, not realising that short-cut keys behaved like 'Windows' rather than Apple OSX) or minor hardware incompatibility (i.e. their laptop touchpad being too sensitive; although a wired mouse would have solved the issue). However, the persistence of these issues indicates that further opportunities for practice and increased awareness of the option to bring a wired mouse were needed.

Those that went on to type the examination, not surprisingly, expressed stronger agreement in being able to undertake the practical steps of the e-exam process but the differences in opinions with hand-writers were not statistically significant. However, the items reflective of confidence "I feel confident I will be able to do these steps in a real examination", "I now feel relaxed about using the e-Exam system for my examination" and future intentions "I would like to use a computer for examinations in the future" did show a significant difference between the groups. This gap between their perceptions of process and their expressed levels of confidence or intentions could be indicative that other matters beyond those surveyed played a role in students' decision making. Additional findings related to students' preferences with respect to writing styles, behaviours and proficiency, where a link to their selected text production mode was found to be stronger, are reported separately [26].

Following the examination event, the results in Table 4 and Fig. 1 showed that a large majority of students who typed the examination were satisfied that the assessment task was suited to computerisation, they appreciated being able to use their own computer, and that the system was easy to use, reliable and secure against cheating. Most also agreed that they would recommend the e-exam system to others. This was consistent with prior work in the university sector [18].

A moderate, but not statistically significant, divergence of opinion between handwriters and typists emerged across most items in the pre-examination survey. Overall, it would appear that people tended to reaffirm their choice to type or handwrite in terms of their future intentions following the examination. This divergence can be seen when looking at future intentions stated prior to the examination with difference in agreement of 1 widening to 2.1 in the post-examination survey. It would appear that students' opinions 'hardened' once the real examination was over, in that typists became more positive about their future intentions to type an examination and hand-writers more negative.

Finally, the decision to allow students to self-select typing or handwriting served to lessen the stress for students, but it also limited the degree of task sophistication that was possible (i.e. keeping to the lower levels of SAMR). However, this can only ever be a temporary state of affairs if we want to progress up the SAMR ladder to include re-designed, higher order assessment tasks that assume sophisticated tools will be available. To take advantage of the affordances of modern software, means all students must ultimately use a computer in the examination. Our work on e-Exams is also about providing a strategy [4] for moving from paper-equivalent e-exams to sophisticated post-paper e-exams where all must type. This phased strategy, along with associated support, will be important in helping staff and students to make this transition.

7 Conclusion

We have successfully completed two trials of e-exams centred on the use of a fully featured word processor in two different units within a pre-university context. From this point of view, we broadly achieved what we set out to do in that the e-Exam technology and BYO laptop centric processes were shown to have worked in this context. We have also seen that most students were satisfied with the approach to doing e-Exams within a classroom setting. The strength of opinions regarding the process and technology between those that typed the examination and those that elected to hand-write were not significantly different, although there was a general trend towards typists holding more positive opinions. Their levels of confidence did differ significantly and this likely played a role in their choices. The results are not at all surprising given the self-selecting nature of the groups who went on to type the examination. However, it does reinforce the need to ensure adequate support is available to students who are not all equally prepared for the computerisation of high-stakes examinations.

Future work will involve comparisons with similarly run examinations in the university system and within different discipline contexts. The next phase will be to trial e-Exams using post-paper, higher-order tasks where all members of the class will type. Further technical work on the e-Exam system is progressing that will see integration with the Moodle quiz tool alongside the ability to use authentic software tools in a manner that is robust against network outages [27].

Acknowledgments. The authors would like to thank the Australian Government Department of Education and Training for financial support and the students at Monash College for being willing to 'give it a go'.

References

1. Fluck, A., Hillier, M.: eExams: strength in diversity. In: Tatnall, A., Webb, M. (eds.) Tomorrow's Learning: Involving Everyone. Learning with and about Technologies and Computing, vol. 515, pp. 409–417. Springer, Cham (2017). https://doi.org/10.1007/978-3-319-74310-3_42
2. TEAA: Transforming exams across Australia. Australian Government Department of Education and Training, Grant ID15-4747 (2015). http://transformingexams.com
3. Fluck, A., Hillier, M.: Innovative assessment with eExams. Presented at the Australian Council for Computers in Education Conference, Brisbane, Australia (2016). http://conference.acce.edu.au/index.php/acce/acce2016/paper/view/34/27
4. Hillier, M., Fluck, A.: Transforming exams - how IT works for BYOD e-Exams. Presented at the Australasian Society for Computers in Learning in Tertiary Education Conference, 100–105. Toowoomba, Australia (2017). http://2017conference.ascilite.org/wp-content/uploads/2017/11/Concise-HILLIER.pdf
5. Swets, J.A., Feurzeig, W.: Computer-aided instruction. Science **150**(3696), 572–576 (1965)
6. Fluck, A., et al.: eExam symposium: design decisions and implementation experience. Presented at the IFIP World Conference on Computers in Education, 3–6 July, Dublin, Ireland (2017). http://transformingexams.com/files/Fluck_etal_2017.pdf
7. Tatnall, A., Webb, M. (eds.): Tomorrow's Learning: Involving Everyone. Learning with and about Technologies and Computing. Springer, Heidelberg (2017). https://doi.org/10.1007/978-3-319-74310-3
8. Crisp, G.: Towards authentic e-assessment tasks. Presented at the EdMedia: World Conference on Educational Media and Technology, Honolulu, HI, pp. 1585–1590 (2009). http://www.editlib.org/p/31689/
9. Puentedura, R.R.: A matrix model for designing and assessing network-enhanced courses (2003). http://hippasus.com/resources/matrixmodel/index.html
10. Puentedura, R.R.: Transformation, technology, and education (2006). http://hippasus.com/resources/tte/
11. Krathwohl, D.R.: A revision of Bloom's taxonomy: an overview. Theory Pract. **41**(4), 212–218 (2002)

12. Davis, F.D.: Perceived usefulness, perceived ease of use, and user acceptance of information technology. MIS Q. **13**(3), 319–340 (1989)
13. Farzin, S.: Attitude of students towards e-examination system: an application of e-learning. Sci. J. Educ. **4**(6), 222–227 (2017)
14. Lunceford, B.: Reconsidering technology adoption and resistance: observations of a semi-luddite. Explor. Media Ecol. **8**(1), 29–47 (2009)
15. Dermo, J.: E-assessment and the student learning experience: a survey of student perceptions of e-assessment. Br. J. Edu. Technol. **40**, 203–214 (2009)
16. Bussières, J., Métras, M., Leclerc, G.: Use of moodle, ExamSoft, and Twitter in a first-year pharmacy course. Am. J. Pharm. Educ. **76**(5), 1–3 (2012)
17. Hillier, M.: The very idea of e-exams: student (pre)conceptions. Presented at the 31st Australasian Society for Computers in Learning in Tertiary Education Conference, 24–26 November, Dunedin (2014). http://ascilite.org/conferences/dunedin2014/files/fullpapers/91-Hillier.pdf
18. Hillier, M.: e-Exams with student owned devices: student voices. In: Proceedings of the International Mobile Learning Festival: Mobile Learning, MOOCs and 21st Century learning, 22–23 May, Hong Kong SAR China, pp. 582–608 (2015). http://transformingexams.com/files/Hillier_IMLF2015_full_paper_formatting_fixed.pdf
19. Aubusson, K., Noyes, J.: Burnt-out doctors deeply distressed by botched high-stakes exam. The Sydney Morning Herald, 20 February 2018. https://www.smh.com.au/national/nsw/burnt-out-doctors-deeply-distressed-by-botched-high-stakes-exam-20180220-p4z117.html
20. Aubusson, J., Noyes, K.: Company behind botched medical exam has track record of failure. The Sydney Morning Herald 21 February 2018. https://www.smh.com.au/national/company-behind-botched-medical-exam-has-track-record-of-failure-20180221-p4z15a.html
21. ExamSoft: Examsoft Worldwide Inc. (2019). http://www.examsoft.com
22. Foundation Year: Monash College, Australia (2016). https://web.archive.org/web/20160402024339/. http://www.monashcollege.edu.au:80/courses/foundation-year
23. Jamieson, S.: Likert scales: how to (ab)use them. Med. Educ. **38**(12), 1217–1218 (2004)
24. Mann, H.B., Whitney, D.R.: On a test of whether one of two random variables is stochastically larger than the other. Ann. Math. Stat. **18**(1), 50–60 (1947)
25. Wilcoxon, F.: Individual comparisons by ranking methods. Biometrics Bull. **1**(6), 80–83 (1945)
26. Hillier, M., Lyon, N.: Writing e-Exams in pre-university college. In: Passey, D., et al. (eds.) OCCE 2018. IFIP AICT, vol. 524, pp. 264–274. Springer, Heidelberg (2019)
27. Hillier, M., Fluck, A.: Robust networked e-Exams with moodle. System Showcase Session Presented at the Open Conference on Computers in Education (IFIP TC3), Linz, Austria, 25–28 June 2018. http://transformingexams.com/files/Hillier_Fluck_OCCE2018_Robust_networked_e-exams_abstract.pdf

Writing e-Exams in Pre-University College

Mathew Hillier[1(✉)] and Nathaniel Lyon[2]

[1] Monash University, Melbourne, Australia
Mathew.Hillier@monash.edu
[2] Monash College, Melbourne, Australia
nathaniel.lyon@monashcollege.edu.au

Abstract. This study examined students' expressed strategies, habits and preferences with respect to responding to supervised text-based assessments. Two trials of a computerised examination system took place in an Australian pre-university college in 2016 and 2017. Students in several classes studying geography and globalisation completed a sequence of practice and assessed work. Data were collected using pre- and post-surveys about their preferred writing styles, habits and strategies in light of their choice to type or handwrite essay and short answer examinations. Comparisons were made between those that elected to handwrite and those who chose to type the examination, with several areas being significant. The performance (grades), production (word count) of the typists and hand-writers were also correlated and compared.

Keywords: e-Exams · Writing strategies · Student perceptions · Affordances

1 Introduction and Background

This study is part of a nationally funded project [1–3] looking at modernising supervised high stakes assessment within the Australian higher education context. This paper builds on previous e-examination (e-Exam or e-exam) trials held in Australian universities, investigating how students in a pre-tertiary pathway college context perceive the task of writing e-Exams.

We use the term e-Exam to specifically refer to a "timed, supervised, summative assessment conducted using each candidate's own computer running a standardised operating system" [4]. This differentiates our work from those employing 'online' testing tools that take the format of a data collection instrument (e.g. Moodle quiz, Blackboard test, TCExam, QuestionMark Perception, ExamSoft). In our case, we include the use of 'authentic' software applications fit for the purpose of the assessment task, e.g. a full office suite is provided to write reports or essays.

We will explore the literature related to the writing of high stakes assessment tasks and in particular computerised examinations before moving on to explain the process used in the study. This is followed by survey results and a discussion of the findings that draws out implications for future research and practice.

2 Literature

The idea of using computers for assessment has been around for 60 years [5], yet pen-on-paper still dominates most higher education and school examinations around the world. However, attention has recently shifted to modernising the examination room. The 'Dublin Declaration' [6] features the idea of 'authentic assessment' [7] as one of its core recommendations when considering the use of computers for assessment. The Declaration specifically recommends that an e-Exam must be an:

> "authentic assessment that matches modern workplace practices and many student learning experiences". (p. xviii)

If we consider the modern classroom, or the majority of work places, we find that computer and software technology is near ubiquitous. From accountancy to zoology, computers are now key tools of the trade. From keeping track of laboratory experiments to report writing and bookkeeping, we could be confident that a computer was involved. Similarly, in higher education, reports, essays and communications are conducted via the typed medium. The vast majority of students in the developed world today use software tools as part of their course work and in addressing unsupervised assessment tasks. University students could hardly remember or even know what it would be like to hand-write their class work, yet we ask them to write examinations that can take up to three or more hours. The keyboard is now so commonly used that the very skill of handwriting is in decline [8], with a subsequent loss of the motor skills required to write proficiently. A previous study [9] found that hand-writers in examinations beyond about 70 min felt physical discomfort while typists were unaffected. Fortunately, there are a number of examples where the transition to e-exams is well underway or at least beginning. Prior work [4, 10] described and reviewed several e-Exam projects, with a longer list available [11].

As part of the conversion effort, teachers and students may have an adjustment period when transitioning from hand-writing under examination conditions to typing. A survey [12] of students at the University of Bradford in the United Kingdom (UK) on their experience of using QuestionMark Perception covered a range of topics. Differences between handwriting and typing an essay-style examination were explored [13], and the authors looked at self-reported typing prowess, confidence, stress, use of time, writing strategies, pre-planning, structuring, editing and reviewing prior to submission. Similarly work by other authors [14] looked at the preferences of students with regard to typing or handwriting essay examinations when they were given the choice. They noted a 10% uptake by students of the typing option. Another researcher [15] reported on students' preconceptions of what an e-exam may involve prior to the start of several e-Exam trials at an Australian university, with interest by students varying significantly between discipline areas. A follow up study of e-exam trials in six courses at the same institution [9] showed the typing option was selected by 5% to 34% of students. The top three comments from typists were that they could type faster, it was neater than handwriting, and that they were easily able to edit their work leading to more polished responses.

Finally, we turn to the matter of performance. Stakeholders are concerned that computerising the examination room may have an uneven impact on student performance by advantaging some and disadvantaging others [16]. Concerns over typing prowess, speed, and computer access have been raised. However, similar concerns could be raised with respect to the uneven abilities of students in terms of speed, neatness and physical strength for handwriting long examinations (ibid). Performance in an e-exam in a dentistry unit found that there was a moderate increase in marks for those that typed the examination compared to those handwriting. There could be no causal link established, due to the self-selecting sample groups [2]. Hand-writers that produced more words generally did better while more typed words did not see marks increase by as much. Another study [17] compared typists and hand-writers and found that the typists produced around 20% more words in an e-exam. Similarly, a further study [16] found that typists produced more words than hand-writers but there was no statistically significant difference in grades. In terms of presentation effects, one researcher [18] found no significant difference in scores due to presentation mode (typed or transcribed handwritten) on a large-scale writing assessment. Prior studies have also looked at demographics such as gender [19] and how this may impact a student's performance when faced with a typed examination.

The review of prior work has outlined several areas of focus that informed questions to be investigated (see Table 1), and provided an up-front frame for analysis.

Table 1. Areas for investigation

Area	Example research questions
Rationale of students	What proportion of candidates were in favour of typing their examination? What rationale was provided for their choice? Did the e-Exam environment support their writing?
Writing strategies	Were there differences in the writing preferences and strategies used by those that typed and those that handwrote?
Student performance	Were there differences in words produced and grades achieved by those that typed and those that handwrote?

3 Study Context

In Australia, the first author is leading an Australian federal government funded grant project [1] investigating how authentic e-assessment can be introduced into the examination rooms of universities using bring-your-own-devices (BYOD). This study was undertaken within two units offered in the Foundation Year [20] programme at Monash College, Australia. The programme is the equivalent of an Australian year 12 high school certificate or the International Baccalaureate. The second author is a unit coordinator and teacher of the units in which the e-exam trials were conducted. The trials were carried out using in-class supervised written assessments requiring short text and essay-style responses.

4 Method and Approach

Students in several classes undertaking geography (Geo) in semester 1, 2016 and globalisation (Glo) in semester 2, 2017 at Monash College took part in a two phase trial of the e-Exam system. Ethics protocol approval was gained via Monash University prior to the trials. In this study a fully functional word processor was used that was part of the e-Exam platform as previously described [3]. Students used a custom Live Linux universal serial bus (USB) environment on their own laptops that provided a full office suite. They could use editing tools such as spelling, grammar and highlighting to help with their writing tasks. Being able to copy, delete or move text around with ease meant that there were functional differences to undertaking the same task using pen-on-paper.

In phase one, students participated in an in-class, ungraded preview session. They were provided with instructions on how to use the e-Exam system with laptops and opportunity to practice e-exam processes, use the software, and try the question response format. Students completed a pre-examination survey requesting technical information about their laptop and first impressions of the e-Exam process and software. Attitudes and responses to e-Exam software use are reported separately [21].

Phase two occurred two weeks later in the form of an in-class, graded, supervised assessment task; students could choose to type or handwrite. Materials were provided on paper or as a word processor document and included photographs, diagrams, charts and data tables. In Geo, the assessment task was a single case study with an extended essay response. In Glo, two short answer sections and a mini-case essay response were required. Students then completed a post-examination survey before leaving the room. An extended account of the trial process is provided elsewhere [21].

Qualitative survey data relating to students' opinions on writing in examinations was analysed using SPSS v24. Likert items were treated as non-parametric as per advice [22]. This stance is supported by other authors [12] when analysing students' perceptions of e-Assessment. The Mann-Whitney U test [23] was used to test the variance between groups (males versus females and typists versus hand-writers) of Likert responses. Chi-squared was also used to test if gender played a role in the decision to type the examination. A Fisher's exact test [24] was used when comparing categorical variables. When it came to performance data (grades) a T-test was used to compare between groups while a Spearman test [25] was used to test for correlation between word count and grades. We used an alpha level of .05 for all statistical tests, unless otherwise noted. However, the participants were not randomly assigned to the typing or hand-writing groups, which makes the results only descriptive of this study. In terms of items reflecting students' opinions, we used statistical tests as a tool to summarise rather than to be representative of an objective truth [see 12].

5 Findings

The trials involved 128 pre-tertiary students; 65% female and 35% male. In the examination, 52% of students elected to type. Table 2 shows participation at each stage.

Table 2. Intention to type the examination at each stage of the study (counts)

Participation	Initial interest	After practice	At the examination
Type	73	72	64
Handwrite	26	30	59
Missing	29	26	5

A Chi-squared test revealed a statistically significant difference in relation to gender and choice to type the examination ($\chi^2(1) = 5.299$, $p = 0.021$) with 68% of males choosing to type compared to 46% of females. However, the differences due to gender were not significant in the earlier stages of the trial. This may be due to the larger number of undecided ('missing') cases in the earlier stages.

Opinions

We examined the differences in opinions on five-point Likert items (where strongly agree = 5, neutral = 3, and strongly disagree = 1) between those that typed the examination and those that handwrote it using a Mann-Whitney U test. Table 3 displays the extent of agreement, with means and standard deviations provided for clarity, along with the results of significance tests with the difference between the means shown.

Table 3. Post-examination survey responses by text production mode

Question	Typed			Handwrote				MW	
Post-examination survey	n	M	SD	N	M	SD	diff	U	p
I type faster than I handwrite	64	4.1	1.1	55	1.8	1.2	2.2	412	>.001
I type accurately	63	4.1	0.8	52	2.5	1.1	1.7	379	>.001
When I make errors, I am able to quickly correct them when typing	64	4.3	0.8	53	2.9	1.3	1.4	634	>.001
I often rely on spell check to detect errors	62	3.8	1.3	54	2.9	1.3	0.9	1060.5	>.001
I work more efficiently when I type on a familiar keyboard	64	4.2	0.9	53	3.0	1.3	1.2	721.5	>.001
My hand-writing is normally neat and legible	63	3.6	1.3	52	3.1	1.1	0.5	1183.5	0.008
I go back to re-read and revise my writing quite a lot	63	3.8	1.0	53	2.9	1.2	0.9	969.5	>.001
I prepare most of my assignments/reports using a computer	64	4.0	0.9	53	3.0	1.4	1.0	1012.5	>.001

Those that chose to hand-write the examination were asked about the neatness of their writing and comfort levels experienced during the examination (see Table 4). The examination duration was 70 min in both cases.

Table 4. Post-examination survey responses on hand-writing

Question	n	M	SD
I think my hand writing was neat and legible	53	3.6	0.9
I experienced discomfort (sore/tired/cramp) in my writing hand	53	2.9	1.2

Typists in the geography unit were also asked to reflect specifically on using a computer for the examination, given the nature of the task (see Table 5).

Table 5. Post-examination survey responses on using a computer for the assessment

Question	n	M	SD
I was able to produce a better final version of this assessment	24	4.3	0.6
I was able to quickly complete the assessment	24	4.3	0.7
I was able to easily edit and make changes	24	4.6	0.6
I was able to easily refer to reference materials and resources	24	3.7	1.0
I was able to easily think and compose my answer using a computer	24	4.3	0.6
I would like to use a computer for similar assessments in the future	23	4.2	0.7

Students were asked about their preferences for production method ('computer' (C), 'same' (S) or 'pen and paper' (P)) for a range of writing activities, style and features. A Fisher exact test for categorical variables was used to see if their preferences may have influenced their choice to type or handwrite the examination (see Table 6). Counts and percentages in brackets are shown for each production method (C, S or P) for the two groups (typists and hand-writers). Significant differences were noted across many of the items with preferences in alignment with their actual choice of examination mode.

Performance

Performance was expressed as a percentage grade. There was a statistically significant performance difference between the two units (Geo, n = 38, Mdn 73.75 and Glo, n = 85, Mdn 57.14) using a Mann-Whitney U test ($U = 1100$, $p = .005$).

When the grade data were grouped by gender (shown in Table 7) it was not found to be statistically significant, although the result was borderline at $p = .050$. In the geography unit, a significant difference in grades between genders was found ($p = .006$); however, this was not so in globalisation. Normal distributions were confirmed for each gender pair using standardised skewness and the Shapiro-Wilks test with Levene's test (shown in Table 7) demonstrating equivalence of variance. Means and standard deviations are also provided for clarity.

Table 6. Post-examination survey responses on examination writing strategies

Question C = computer, S = same, P = pen	Typed				Handwrote				Fisher
	C	S	P	n	C	S	P	n	p
I write more words in an examination when…	35 (56)	23 (37)	5 (8)	63 (53)	1 (2)	18 (32)	37 (66)	56 (47)	>.001
I write faster in an examination when…	42 (66)	17 (27)	5 (8)	64 (53)	3 (5)	9 (16)	44 (79)	56 (47)	>.001
I think more carefully before I start writing in an examination when…	32 (50)	13 (20)	19 (30)	64 (54)	3 (5)	17 (31)	35 (64)	55 (46)	>.001
I pause to think most in an examination when…	21 (33)	19 (30)	24 (38)	64 (53)	11 (20)	26 (46)	19 (34)	56 (47)	0.123
I write in a style that feels more normal in an examination when…	29 (46)	24 (38)	10 (16)	63 (53)	1 (2)	17 (30)	38 (68)	56 (47)	>.001
I try not to make changes unless they are really important when…	18 (28)	18 (28)	28 (44)	64 (53)	3 (5)	25 (45)	28 (50)	56 (47)	0.003
I change, move or correct words or phrases most when…	42 (67)	13 (21)	8 (13)	63 (53)	11 (20)	21 (38)	24 (43)	56 (47)	>.001
I think the overall structure/argument of my response is better when…	38 (59)	15 (23)	11 (17)	64 (53)	3 (5)	21 (38)	32 (57)	56 (47)	>.001
I make more effective use of the time available in an examination when…	43 (67)	16 (25)	5 (8)	64 (53)	2 (4)	15 (27)	39 (70)	56 (47)	>.001
I go back and read over my response most in an examination when…	28 (44)	28 (44)	8 (13)	64 (53)	3 (5)	23 (41)	30 (54)	56 (47)	>.001
I feel more stressed in an examination when…	15 (23)	28 (44)	21 (33)	64 (53)	18 (32)	22 (39)	16 (29)	56 (47)	0.589
I am more likely to run out of time in an examination when…	13 (20)	28 (44)	23 (36)	64 (53)	16 (29)	22 (39)	18 (32)	56 (47)	0.601
Overall, I feel I perform better in an examination when…	37 (59)	22 (35)	4 (6)	63 (53)	1 (2)	14 (25)	41 (73)	56 (47)	>.001

When comparing the grades of typists and hand-writers (shown in Table 8) across both units, no statistically significant difference was found. However, within the globalisation unit there was a small statistically significant difference in grades between typists and hand-writers ($p = .033$). The distribution of each pair was found to be

Table 7. Grades out of 100 by gender

Unit	Female			Male				T-test		Levene's test	
	n	M	SD	n	M	SD	Df	T	P	F	p
Geo	24	76.2	17	12	56.4	23	(1,34)	2.912	**0.006**	1.422	0.241
Glo	53	58.3	18.5	29	56	20.7	(1,80)	0.519	0.605	0.002	0.961
Both	77	63.9	19.8	41	56.1	21.1	(1,116)	1.98	0.050	0.005	0.943

normal using standardised skewness and the Shapiro-Wilks tests, with Levene's test (shown in Table 8) establishing equivalence of variance. Means and standard deviations are provided for clarity.

Table 8. Grades out of 100 for typists and hand-writers

Unit	Typed			Handwrote				T-test		Levene's test	
	n	M	SD	n	M	SD	Df	T	p	F	p
Geo	25	64.3	21.5	13	76.7	18.8	(1,36)	−1.754	0.088	0.212	0.648
Glo	39	62.9	21.0	44	53.7	17.4	(1,81)	2.174	**0.033**	1.636	0.205
Both	64	63.4	21.0	57	59.0	20.1	(1,119)	1.190	0.236	0.333	0.565

Within each of the geography group ($n = 38$) and the globalisation group ($n = 32$) positive, statistically significant correlations were found between the number of words written and the grade achieved from Spearman tests (Geo: $r_s = .628$, p = >.001 and Glo: $r_s = .865$, p = >.001). See Fig. 1.

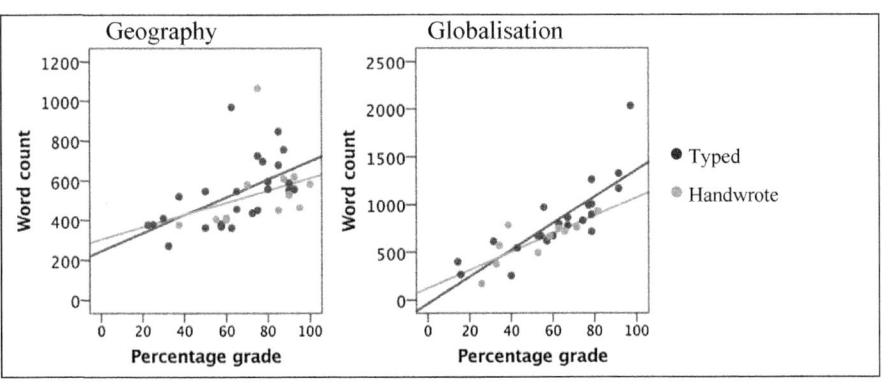

Fig. 1. Correlation between number of words and grade

Mann-Whitney U tests found no statistically significant difference in the number of words produced by typists and hand-writers (see Table 9). It is worth noting that word count data were only available for half the globalisation group and that assessment tasks were different between Glo and Geo, so the two groups are not comparable.

Table 9. Words produced by typists and hand-writers

Unit	Typed			Handwrote				MW	
	n	M	SD	n	M	SD	diff	U	p
Geography	25	536	170	13	541	178	5	157.5	0.878
Globalisation	22	833	83	10	620	71	213	71	0.113

6 Discussion

The choice to type or handwrite appears to be multifaceted, but with the strongest differences declared around being able to type more quickly than handwrite and typing accuracy. Overall, the results showed an alignment between writing strategies and choice of text production mode in the examination (see Tables 3 and 6). The result of 52% of students electing to type is much higher than reported in previous studies involving free choice [9, 14]. The use of in-class practice sessions compared to optional out-of-class practice sessions used [9] may have contributed to the increased uptake of the typing option in our study.

In both 70-min assessment tasks, only a minority of hand-writers experienced discomfort (i.e. agreement of 2.9 out of a maximum 5 with standard deviation 1.2 indicating that only some were impacted). This was consistent with previous work [9] where a 70-min duration was the cross-over point where discomfort started to become a problem.

Typists generally agreed that the computer allowed them to produce better responses on the assessment task (i.e. most Likert items in Table 5 were rated above 4 on the 5-point scale), including that they would like to be able to use a computer for similar assessments in the future. The weakest agreement related to their ability to easily refer to reference materials. In this study, students had to scroll up and down between the materials and their written response. Providing reference materials in a separate file (that would allow side-by-side window arrangement or 'Alt-Tab' between windows), in a split screen format within the document [26] or on paper, may help in this regard.

In terms of performance, there were mixed results. The number of words produced by typists was greater in Glo, as shown elsewhere [16, 17], but less in Geo. The classes were relatively small and assessment tasks were different, so this may have played a role. In Geo, hand-writers achieved slightly better grades (but not significantly so) and in Glo, typists did better with a borderline statistically significant difference in grades. When comparing by gender, in Geo, females did significantly better. In Glo, they also did slightly better, but not significantly so. Overall, a weak link between gender and performance could be claimed within these groups. In both classes, we found a statically significant correlation between words produced and marks. The scatter plot in Fig. 1 shows that the correlation occurred over a narrow band in Geo, with a minimum of 300 words required before a pass was possible. Yet an adequate word count certainly does not guarantee a pass. Similarly, a larger number of words above 600 did not see the highest grades; indeed, those with the highest grades wrote about the same as the group mean of 538 words. The scatter plot for Glo shows a more tightly monotonic relationship between words and grades. Again, correlation is certainly not causation in terms of word count – quality still matters!

7 Conclusion

Overall, we observed a significant alignment between preferred writing strategies and choice of text production method in the two trials. Further, the grades achieved between typists and hand-writers did not differ significantly. These two facts are not surprising when dealing with thinking, purposeful humans who aim to maximise outcomes. However, this does raise the concern that should a shift occur towards fully-typed assessment, then a period of transition with assistance for those who preferred hand-writing should occur to ensure they are able to adapt successfully.

Acknowledgments. The authors would like to thank the Australian Government Department of Education and Training for financial support and the students at Monash College for being willing to 'give it a go'.

References

1. TEAA: Transforming exams across Australia. Australian Government Department of Education and Training, Grant ID15-4747 (2015). http://transformingexams.com
2. Fluck, A., Hillier, M.: Innovative assessment with eExams. Presented at the Australian Council for Computers in Education Conference, Brisbane, 29 September to 2 October (2016). http://conference.acce.edu.au/index.php/acce/acce2016/paper/view/34/27
3. Hillier, M., Fluck, A.: Transforming exams - how it works for BYOD e-Exams. Presented at the Australasian Society for Computers in Learning in Tertiary Education Conference, pp. 100–105. Toowoomba, Australia (2017). http://2017conference.ascilite.org/wp-content/uploads/2017/11/Concise-HILLIER.pdf
4. Fluck, A., Hillier, M.: eExams: strength in diversity. In: Tatnall, A., Webb, M. (eds.) WCCE 2017. IAICT, vol. 515, pp. 409–417. Springer, Cham (2017). https://doi.org/10.1007/978-3-319-74310-3_42
5. Swets, J.A., Feurzeig, W.: Computer-aided instruction. Science **150**(3696), 572–576 (1965)
6. Tatnall, A., Webb, M. (eds.): Tomorrow's Learning: Involving Everyone. Learning with and about Technologies and Computing. Springer, Heidelberg (2017). https://doi.org/10.1007/978-3-319-74310-3
7. Crisp, G.: Towards authentic e-assessment tasks. Presented at the EdMedia: World Conference on Educational Media and Technology, Honolulu, HI, pp. 1585–1590 (2009). http://www.editlib.org/p/31689/

8. Sülzenbrück, S., Hegele, M., Rinkenauer, G., Heuer, H.: The death of handwriting: secondary effects of frequent computer use on basic motor skills. J. Motiv. Behav. **43**(3), 247–251 (2011)
9. Hillier, M.: To type or handwrite: student's experience across six e-Exam trials. In: Reiners, T., von Konsky, B.R., Gibson, D., Chang, V., Irving, L., Clarke, K. (eds.) Proceedings of the ASCILITE Conference, Perth, Australia, pp. 143–154 (2015). http://transformingexams.com/files/Hillier_2015_ascilite_fp.pdf
10. Fluck, A., et al.: eExam symposium: design decisions and implementation experience. Presented at the IFIP World Conference on Computers in Education, 3–6 July, Dublin, Ireland (2017). http://transformingexams.com/files/Fluck_etal_2017.pdf
11. Hörnblad, P., Brenner, M.: Digital Exam. SUNET Incubator project, NORDUnet (2016). https://portal.nordu.net/display/Inkubator/Digital+Tentamen
12. Dermo, J.: E-assessment and the student learning experience: a survey of student perceptions of e-assessment. Br. J. Edu. Technol. **40**, 203–214 (2009)
13. Mogey, N., Fluck, A.: Factors influencing student preference when comparing handwriting and typing for essay style examinations: essay exams on computer. Br. J. Educ. Technol. **46**, 793–802 (2014)
14. Purcell, M., Paterson, J., Mogey, N.: Exams: comparing handwritten essays with those composed on keyboards (Final Report). Heslington: The HEA (2012)
15. Hillier, M.: The very idea of e-exams: student (Pre) conceptions. In: Proceedings of the ASCILITE Conference, Dunedin, New Zealand, pp. 77–88 (2014). http://ascilite.org/conferences/dunedin2014/files/fullpapers/91-Hillier.pdf
16. Mogey, N., Paterson, J., Burk, J., Purcell, M.: Typing compared with handwriting for essay examinations at university: letting the students choose. Res. Learn. Technol. **18**(1), 29–47 (2010)
17. Fluck, A.: eExaminations Strategic Project Final Report for Academic Senate (unpublished report). University of Tasmania, Australia (2011)
18. Rankin, A.: A comparability study on differences between scores of handwritten and typed responses on a large-scale writing assessment (unpublished Ph.D. dissertation). University of Iowa, IA (2015)
19. Terzis, V., Economides, A.A.: Computer based assessment: gender differences in perceptions and acceptance. Comput. Hum. Behav. **27**(6), 2108–2122 (2011)
20. Monash College Australia, Foundation Year (2016). https://web.archive.org/web/20160402024339/http://www.monashcollege.edu.au:80/courses/foundation-year
21. Hillier, M., Lyon, N.: Student experiences with bring your own laptop e-Exams in pre-university college. In: Passey, D. et al. (eds.) OCCE 2018, IFIP AICT, vol. 524, pp. 253–263. Springer, Heidelberg (2019)
22. Jamieson, S.: Likert scales: how to (ab)use them. Med. Educ. **38**(12), 1217–1218 (2004)
23. Mann, H.B., Whitney, D.R.: On a test of whether one of two random variables is stochastically larger than the other. Ann. Math. Stat. **18**(1), 50–60 (1947)
24. Freeman, G.H., Halton, J.H.: Note on an exact treatment of contingency tables, goodness of fit and other problems of significance. Biometrika **38**, 141–149 (1951)
25. Spearman, C.: The proof and measurement of association between two things. Am. J. Psychol. **15**, 72–101 (1904)
26. Al Nadabi, Z.: Features of an online English language testing interface. In: Proceedings of the ASCILITE Conference, 30 November–3 December, Perth, Australia, pp. 369–373 (2015)

Students' Perceptions of e-Assessment

A Case Study from Germany

Bastian Küppers[1(✉)] and Ulrik Schroeder[2]

[1] IT Center, RWTH Aachen University, Aachen, Germany
kueppers@itc.rwth-aachen.de
[2] Learning Technologies Research Group, RWTH Aachen University,
Aachen, Germany
schroeder@cs.rwth-aachen.de

Abstract. In order to verify common findings in the literature regarding the conception of e-assessment among students, we carried out a survey based on common findings. Our survey, which has been carried out over several higher education institutes, enhances the already existing findings by adding new facets. The achieved results are promising in that students seem to be open-minded regarding e-assessment, which is in line with the findings in the already existing literature. However, there are some open points that have to be resolved in a reliable way in order to completely convince the students of the opportunities offered by e-assessment.

Keywords: Computer-based assessment · e-Assessment · BYOD · Cheating

1 Introduction

If e-assessment is to be introduced into the examination system of an institute of higher education (IHE), it is not only the staff of the latter that have to accept this type of assessment, but also the students [1], especially when it comes to e-assessment on students' devices (BYOD) [2]. Therefore, it is of interest for IHEs that are willing to introduce e-assessment, to be aware of the possible limiting factors from the students' points of view, to tailor the e-assessment system and the process of integration to the students' needs.

To verify that the findings regarding the students' points of view in the literature are valid for our institution, we carried out our own survey about e-assessment, BYOD scenarios and cheating in examinations.

The paper is structured as follows: in the second section, we give a brief overview of the findings already presented in the literature. In the third section, we discuss the setup of our survey, followed by a discussion of the achieved results in the fourth section. The paper closes with a summary and an outlook.

2 Related Research

There is a lot of literature about students' perceptions of e-assessment, which has been written over the last years. Most of these papers focus on a particular IHE, e.g. Saudi Electronic University, Saudi Arabia [3] and Dow University of Health, Pakistan [4]. Some papers focus even on a single study course, e.g. Polytechnic Institute of Porto, Portugal, Marketing Degree [5], University College London, UK, Chemical Engineering [6], Hong Kong Polytechnic University, Hong Kong, Rehabilitation Sciences) [7] and Kocaeli University, Turkey, Desktop Publishing [8]. The findings reported in these papers testified generally positive students' attitudes regarding e-assessment.

For the course of this paper, the most important publication is "e-Exams with student owned devices: Student voices" by Hillier [2], since his paper focuses on a BYOD scenario. There are many interesting findings about students' perceptions not only regarding e-assessment, but especially about their perceptions regarding e-assessment on their own devices. However, even Hillier's research was conducted only in one IHE.

3 Design of the Survey

We constructed our survey based on the findings in a previous paper [2], to answer our research question: **Which factors influence students' perceptions of e-assessment?**

We anticipated that the perception of e-assessment is influenced by:

- gender
- age
- the study programme (science, technology, engineering and mathematics (STEM) versus humanities, for example)
- technology affinity
- the stage of study (Bachelor versus Master level)

Since we expected the results to be additionally influenced by the general technology affinity of the students, we incorporated another questionnaire as part of our survey to be able to distinguish technology accepting students and technology reluctant students. This questionnaire is the TA-EG questionnaire by Karrer et al. [9], which is designed to measure technology affinity. The items of the TA-EG questionnaire have been reordered to eliminate effects that could originate from the clustered answers of the original questionnaire. Additionally, unlike existing surveys, we wanted to carry out the survey at multiple IHEs and for different study courses.

Altogether, this resulted in the, originally German, survey as shown in Table 1. The survey was carried out mainly with students of RWTH Aachen University and FH Aachen University of Applied Sciences, but also students at Maastricht University, Alpen-Adria-University Klagenfurt, TU Berlin, FOM Hochschule für Oekonomie und Management (Study Centre Aachen) and Albstadt-Sigmaringen University were invited to participate. The study programmes mentioned explicitly in the survey are the main study programmes, which are related computer science courses at those universities.

Table 1. The survey (translated to English).

Part	Item	Scale
General	Age	3 Options[a]
	Study programme	9 Options[b]
	Gender	2 Options
TA-EG	I like to have new electronic devices	Five-level Likert Scale (5LLS)
	Electronic devices cause illness	
	I like to go to stores for electronic devices	
	I (would) have problems understanding electronic and computer magazines	
	Electronic devices provide a high standard of living	
	Electronic devices lead to intellectual impoverishment	
	Electronic devices make many things more complicated	
	I inform myself about electronic devices, even if I have no intention to buy them	
	Electronic devices make you independent	
	I enjoy trying out electronic devices	
	Electronic devices make everyday life easier for me	
	Electronic devices increase security	
	Electronic devices reduce personal contact between people	
	I know most of the functions of the electronic devices I own	
	I am thrilled when a new electronic device comes onto the market	
	Electronic devices cause stress	
	I know about electronic devices	
	It is easy for me to learn how to operate an electronic device	
	Electronic devices help to obtain information	
e-Assessment	E1: I think it is very good to have electronic examinations in my studies	5LLS
	E2: I think that electronic examinations are a good complement to paper-based examinations	
	E3: I think that electronic examinations are a good substitute to paper-based examinations	
	E4: I see advantages of electronic examinations, namely	4 Options[c]
	E5: I see disadvantages of electronic examinations, namely	4 Options[d]
BYOD	B1: I find it very advantageous if electronic examinations are carried out on my own electronic device (laptop)	5LLS
	B2: I see the following advantages in using my own electronic device (laptop) for an examination, namely	3 Options[e]

(*continued*)

Table 1. (*continued*)

Part	Item	Scale
	B3: I see the following disadvantages in using my own electronic device (laptop) for an examination, namely	3 Options[f]
Fraud	C1: I think that cheating in paper-based examinations can be done very easily	5LLS
	C2: I think that cheating in electronic examinations can be done very easily	

The options for the items noted in Table 1 are:
[a]<18; 18–25; >25
[b]Bachelor of Computer Science, Master of Computer Science, Scientific Programming, Technomathematics, Bachelor of Technical Communication, Master of Technical Communication, Bachelor of Computer Science (Teacher), Master of Computer Science (Teacher), Other (free text)
[c]Faster Correction, More Realistic Examinations, More Diverse Examination Tasks, Other (free text)
[d]Security, Usability, Fairness, Other (free text)
[e]Familiar Device, Location-independent Examinations, Other (free text)
[f]Security, Differences Between Devices, Other (free text)

4 Analysis of the Results

In total, 408 students responded to the survey with demographics as shown in Table 2.

Table 2. Demographics of the participating students.

	Male	Female	Not answered	$\sum$
<18	1.2%	0.25%	0%	**1.5%**
18–25	60.3%	16.67%	0.5%	**77.5%**
>25	14%	6.4%	0%	**20.3%**
Not answered	0.46%	0	0.25%	**0.7%**
$\sum$	**75.96%**	**23.3%**	**0.74%**	**100%**

About three quarters of the participating students were male and one quarter were female. A similar distribution can be seen for the age, where about three quarters were aged between 18 and 25 years and nearly a fifth of the students were aged above 25 years.

The students came from a variety of study programmes, as can be seen from Fig. 1. Other programmes of study included artificial intelligence, engineering and physics. So, despite individual students studying in programmes like economics and literature, the vast majority of the study programmes were related to a STEM topic. Therefore, it is not surprising that the results of the TA-EG questionnaire did not allow for identifying subgroups with different affinities regarding technology.

The plots in Fig. 2 refer to the original grouping of the TA-EG questionnaire, which has four groups: Enthusiasm, Competency, Positive Attitude, and Negative

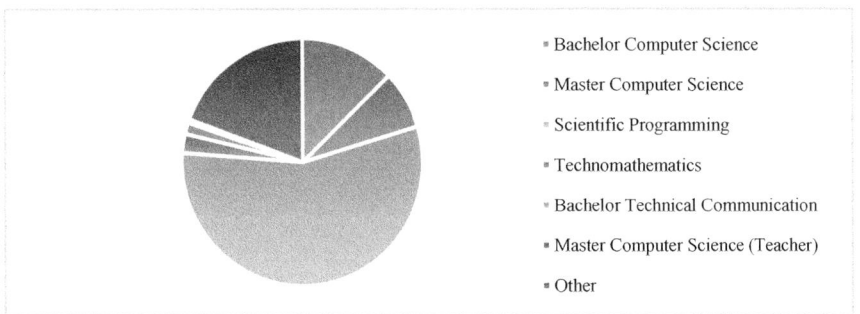

Fig. 1. Distribution of study programmes.

Attitude. The five subplots in each of these plots refers to a question in the corresponding group of questions of the TA-EG questionnaire. Please note that every item in the TA-EG questionnaire in our survey used a five-level Likert scale ranging from 1 ("Strongly agree") to 5 ("Strongly disagree"). The overall variance of these items was 0.76, which accounts for the indistinguishability of different subgroups.

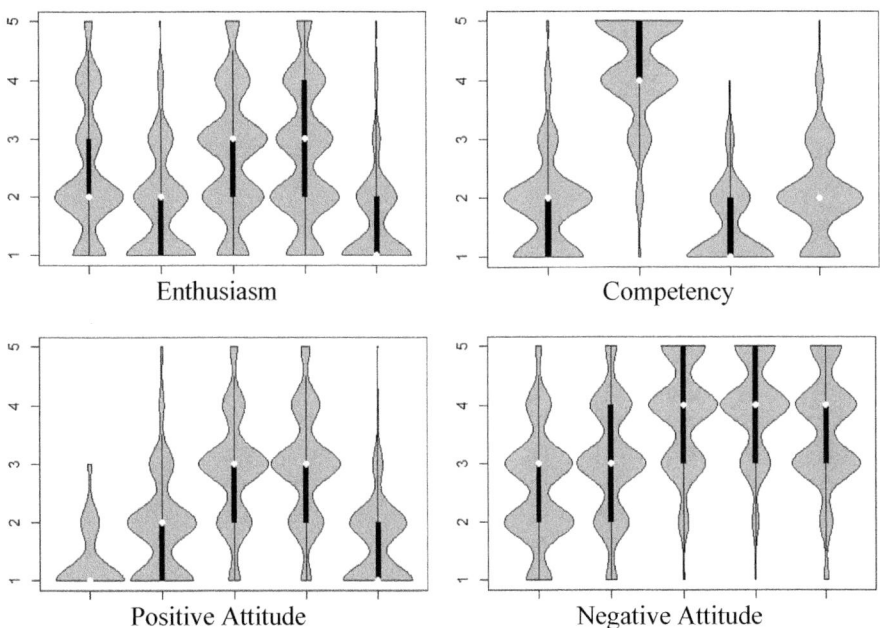

Fig. 2. Violin plots [10] of the TA-EG sub-questionnaire.

Since there were too few students enrolled in a study course that were not from the STEM field, the collected data were not suitable to answer whether the study course influenced the students' perceptions of e-assessment. The absence of those students may be caused by the decision to carry out the survey via an online portal, which may have biased the results so that only students participated who had an affinity for technology. However, that cannot be concluded from the data.

4.1 Influences of Gender and Age

To examine the influence of gender, age, and study level (bachelor or master) the data set was split into subsets accordingly. These subsets were then tested for significant differences with a Fisher test [11]. The results for the Likert-scaled questions can be found in Table 3.

Table 3. p-values for the Fisher test.

	p-Value		
	Gender	Age	Study level
E1	0.04536 < 0.05	0.0951 < 0.1	0.1661
E2	0.4115	0.002503 < 0.01	0.0534 < 0.1
E3	0.6161	0.14	0.7155
B1	0.2079	0.211	0.1844
C1	0.5356	0.6287	0.3458
C2	0.5694	0.5445	0.185

Given these p-values, conclusions about the influence of gender, age and study level are possible to a certain extent. Regarding question E1, it seems that women are more hesitant to accept e-assessment as part of the examination system. In addition, students between 18 and 25 years seem to be more positive about e-assessment than students of other ages. For question E2, the age again makes a difference, as students older than 25 years seem to be less convinced that e-assessment is a good complement to paper-based examinations compared to younger students. The same tendency is revealed when considering the question about whether the study level influences the perception of e-assessment. Students that are enrolled in a master's programme seem to be more reluctant regarding e-assessment than students in a bachelor's programme. If this tendency is caused by the progress in the studies or by age, again, is a crucial factor that cannot be concluded from the data, which is shown in Fig. 3.

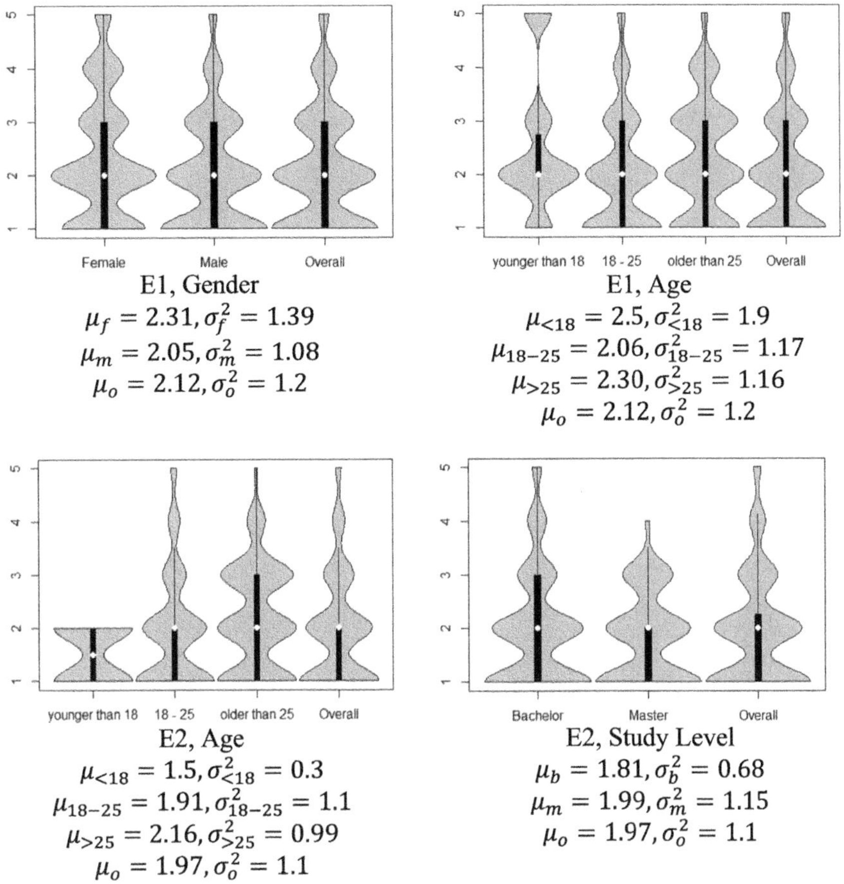

Female
Male
Overall
E1, Gender
$\mu_f = 2.31, \sigma_f^2 = 1.39$
$\mu_m = 2.05, \sigma_m^2 = 1.08$
$\mu_o = 2.12, \sigma_o^2 = 1.2$
younger than 18
18 - 25
older than 25
Overall
E1, Age
$\mu_{<18} = 2.5, \sigma_{<18}^2 = 1.9$
$\mu_{18-25} = 2.06, \sigma_{18-25}^2 = 1.17$
$\mu_{>25} = 2.30, \sigma_{>25}^2 = 1.16$
$\mu_o = 2.12, \sigma_o^2 = 1.2$
younger than 18
18 - 25
older than 25
Overall
E2, Age
$\mu_{<18} = 1.5, \sigma_{<18}^2 = 0.3$
$\mu_{18-25} = 1.91, \sigma_{18-25}^2 = 1.1$
$\mu_{>25} = 2.16, \sigma_{>25}^2 = 0.99$
$\mu_o = 1.97, \sigma_o^2 = 1.1$
Bachelor
Master
Overall
E2, Study Level
$\mu_b = 1.81, \sigma_b^2 = 0.68$
$\mu_m = 1.99, \sigma_m^2 = 1.15$
$\mu_o = 1.97, \sigma_o^2 = 1.1$

Fig. 3. Violin plots for questions E1 and E2.

1
2
3
4
5
E3
B1
C1
C2

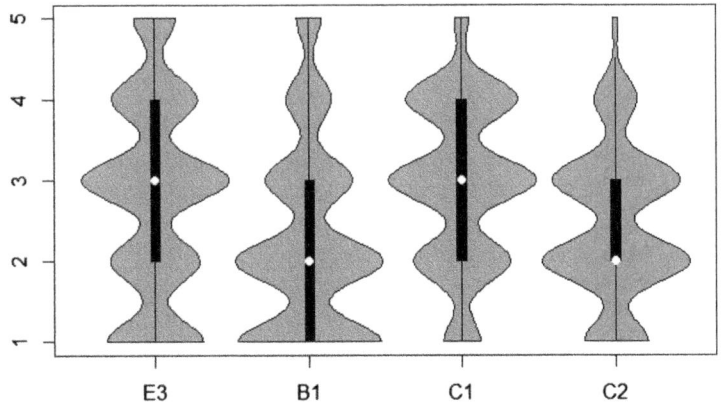

Fig. 4. Violin plots of questions E3, B1, C1, and C2.

5 Discussion

The achieved results from the survey show a rather clear picture. The students would like to have electronic examinations in their studies, but not necessarily as a replacement for paper-based examination, but rather as a complementary approach, as the answers of questions E2 and E3 (see Fig. 4) suggest. This perception of e-assessment is understood through advantages, which cover topics like faster correction (75.98%, E4), more realistic assignments (62.74%, E4), more diverse examination tasks (45.34%, E4), and readability (which was stated in free text comments). However, students are also concerned about disadvantages, like security (41.67%, E5), usability (42.64%, E5), and fairness (34.56%, E5). Additionally, technical difficulties and the subsequent loss of already solved assignments are mentioned very often in the comments. Overall, less than half of the students sees disadvantages in e-assessment; however, especially when it comes to a BYOD approach, the students are afraid that technical difficulties may lead to a handicap for them or that they have to have a capable device on their own. Still, the tendency seems to be positive regarding a BYOD approach (see B1 in Fig. 4), as students see the advantage of a familiar device (89.7%, B2). However, due to the reported concerns, it is very important to have a reasonable backup strategy for these situations. As we have discussed elsewhere [12], it is important to regularly have backups during an e-assessment, so that a student can simply switch to an emergency device provided by the IHE in case her own device breaks down. These emergency devices could also be used for students that cannot afford a device on their own in order to enable these students to participate in electronic examinations. Additionally, the topic of fairness is important to the students, as they state differences between the students' devices as the main concern when utilising BYOD (82.84%, B3). Furthermore, topics like security or cheating are of importance for the students. The students are rather split about the risk of cheating in paper-based examinations; however, there is a tendency that students think that it is easier to cheat in electronic examinations (see C1 and C2 in Fig. 4). Therefore, new ways of reducing the risk of cheating in electronic examinations have to be found, as we have discussed elsewhere [13] and presented an approach to security [14].

Age is seemingly a factor; it does influence the perception of e-assessment in line with the concept of *Digital Natives* introduced by Prensky [15]. He claims that "[t]oday's students have not just changed incrementally from those of the past", but underwent a drastic change of attitude, because "the arrival and rapid dissemination of digital technology in the last decades of the 20th century [was] an event which changes things so fundamentally that there is absolutely no going back". The evidence gained from the survey suggests a similar conclusion, because there is a statistically significant difference between students over the age of 25 years in comparison to younger students. Shelley White states in her article "The Generation Z effect" [16] that "Gen Z is loosely accepted as people born in the mid - to late-1990s and later. (According to the Pew Research Center in the United States, the last Gen Y was born in 1997, while Statistics Canada says Gen Z starts with people born in 1993)". The timespan mentioned in her article is exactly in line with our findings of the age that has an influence on the perception of e-assessment.

Gender having an influence on the perception of e-assessment is actually not surprising, as many studies show that women seem to have a lower confidence in using technology in general than men, for example Kadijevich [17], Kahveci [18], and Yau and Cheng [19], whether this is justified or not. Therefore, it is reasonable to assume that the same tendency can be observed when examining the perception of e-assessment.

6 Summary and Outlook

In order to identify factors that influence students' perceptions of e-assessment, we carried out our own survey based on the findings in a previous paper [2]. However, we extended our survey over multiple IHEs to gain a broader view. The results are promising, in that students seem to be open-minded regarding e-assessment, which is in line with the findings in the already existing literature. However, there are open points that have to be reliably resolved in order to convince the students completely of e-assessment. Therefore, more research is needed to uncover all the open questions that exist among the students as well as to find solutions to these open questions. Further research could also tackle the question as to whether affinity to technology and the field of study have a direct influence on the perception of e-assessment. In addition, it could be further investigated if the influence of the study level is indeed significant, due either to further progress in studying or if there is a hidden correlation between age and level of study.

References

1. Terzis, V., Economides, A.A.: The acceptance and use of computer based assessment. Comput. Educ. **4**(56), 1032–1044 (2011)
2. Hillier, M.: e-Exams with student owned devices: student voices. In: Proceedings of the International Mobile Learning Festival 2015: Mobile Learning, MOOCs and 21stCentury learning, Hong Kong SAR, China, pp. 582–608 (2015)
3. Alsadoon, H.: Students' perceptions of e-assessment at saudi electronic university. Turkish Online J. Educ. Technol. **16**(1), 147–153 (2017)
4. Jawaid, M., Moosa, F.A., Jaleel, F., Ashraf, J.: Computer based assessment (CBA): perception of residents at Dow University of Health Sciences. Pakistan J. Med. Sci. **30**(4), 688–691 (2014)
5. Babo, R., Azevedo, A., Suhonen, J.: Students' perceptions about assessment using an e-learning platform. In: Sampson, D.G., Huang, R., Hwang, G.-J., Liu, T.-C., Chen, N.-S., Kinshuk, C.-C.T. (eds.) Proceedings of the IEEE 15th International Conference on Advanced Learning Technologies, Hualien, Taiwan, pp. 244–246 (2015)
6. Sorensen, E.: Implementation and student perceptions of e-assessment in a chemical engineering module. Eur. J. Eng. Educ. **38**(2), 172–185 (2013)
7. Hodgson, P., Pang, M.Y.C.: Effective formative e-assessment of student learning: a study on a statistics course. Assess. Eval. High. Educ. **37**(2), 215–225 (2012)
8. Özden, M.Y., Ertürk, I., Sanli, R.: Students' perceptions of online assessment: a case study. J. Distance Educ. **19**(2), 77–92 (2004)

9. Karrer, K., Glaser, C., Clemens, C., Bruder, C.: Technikaffinität erfassen – der Fragebogen TA-EG. Der Mensch im Mittelpunkt technischer Systeme. 8. Berliner Werkstatt Mensch-Maschine-Systeme, pp. 196–201 (2009)
10. Hintze, J.L., Nelson, R.D.: Violin plots: a box plot-density trace synergism. Am. Stat. **52**(2), 181–184 (1998)
11. Upton, G.J.G.: Fisher's exact test. J. Roy. Stat. Soc. **155**(3), 395–402 (1992)
12. Küppers, B., Politze, M., Schroeder, U.: Reliable e-assessment with GIT - practical considerations and implementation. In: EUNIS 2017 Book of Proceedings, Münster, Germany, pp. 253–262 (2017)
13. Küppers, B., Kerber, F., Meyer, U., Schroeder, U.: Beyond lockdown: towards reliable e-assessment. In: GI-Edition - Lecture Notes in Informatics, vol. P273, pp. 191–196 (2017)
14. Küppers, B., Politze, M., Zameitat, R., Kerber, F., Schroeder, U.: Practical security for electronic examinations on students' devices. In: Arai, K., Kapoor, S., Bhatia, R. (eds.) SAI 2018. AISC, vol. 857, pp. 290–306. Springer, Cham (2019). https://doi.org/10.1007/978-3-030-01177-2_21
15. Prensky, M.: Digital natives, digital immigrants. On the Horizon **9**(5), 1–6 (2001)
16. White, S.: The generation Z effect (2018). https://www.theglobeandmail.com/news/national/education/canadian-university-report/the-genz-effect/article26898388/. Accessed 15 Jan 2019
17. Kadijevich, D.: Gender differences in computer attitude among ninth-grade students. J. Educ. Comput. Res. **22**(2), 145–154 (2000)
18. Kahveci, M.: Students' perceptions to use technology for learning: measurement integrity of the modified Fennema-Sherman attitudes scales. Turkish Online J. Educ. Technol. **9**(1), 185–201 (2010)
19. Yau, H.K., Cheng, A.L.F.: Gender difference of confidence in using technology for learning. J. Technol. Stud. **38**(2), 74–79 (2012)

Author Index

AlOkaily, Rasha 175

Banzato, Monica 101
Barrett, Natasha 197
Bollin, Andreas 3, 77, 128, 207
Bonvin, Guillaume 161
Brinda, Torsten 47

Carabott, Kelly 91
Casado, Rémi 161
Černochová, Miroslava 243
Champin, Pierre-Antoine 161
Chin, C. K. H. 34

De Caro-Barek, Veruska 187
Djelil, Fahima 67

Ehlenz, Matthias 167
Eickelmann, Birgit 14

Fluck, Andrew E. 34

Guin, Nathalie 161

Hadzilacos, T. 112
Harwin, William 197
Haugsbakken, Halvdan 122, 231
Hillier, Mathew 253, 264
Holvikivi, Jaana 141
Hrabák, Jan 243
Hwang, Faustina 197

Johnson, Ros 197
Jones, Chris 197
Juurola, Leenu 141

Kadijevich, Djordje M. 24
Katz, Yaacov J. 221
Kelter, Riko 47
Kesselbacher, Max 77
Králová, Kateřina 243
Kramar, Nicolas 151
Kramer, Matthias 47
Küppers, Bastian 275

Labusch, Amelie 14
Langseth, Inger 122
Lefevre, Marie 161
Leonhardt, Thiemo 167
Lyon, Nathaniel 253, 264

Matsuzawa, Yoshiaki 56
McLeod, Amber 91
Micheuz, Peter 3
Miltiadous, M. 112
Mujkanovic, Amir 207
Muller, Pierre-Alain 67
Müller, Sylvia 151
Müller, W. 112
Murata, Kazuyoshi 56

Neofytou, C. 112
Nuorteva, Maija 141

Otero, N. 112

Pasterk, Stefan 77
Paukovics, Elsa 151

Ranmuthugala, Dev 34
Reçi, Elisa 128

Sanchez, Eric 67, 151, 161
Schroeder, Ulrik 167, 275
Selcuk, Hasan 243

Tani, Seiichi 56
Tokatli, Ozan 197
Tosato, Paolo 101
Tracey, Megan 197

Vennemann, Mario 14
Voňková, Hana 243

Webb, Mary 197
Widmer, Antoine 151

Yiannoutsou, N. 112

Printed by Printforce, the Netherlands